THE CENTRAL DAKOTA GERMANS

Their History, Language, and Culture

Shirley Fischer Arends Ph.D.

Originally published by the Georgetown University Press, 1989
Washington, D.C.
Revision of copyright given to Author

SFA Publishing
© Copyright February 2016

All Rights Reserved
Printed in the United States of America

ISBN-13: 978-06157203236
ISBN-10: 0615720323

TO EMMA AND CHRISTOPH FISCHER
WHO SUPPORTED MY EFFORTS
AND TAUGHT ME A LOVE
OF THESE PIONEERS
WHO CONTRIBUTED
TO OUR AMERICAN
HERITAGE

Preface

Growing up as a young girl in North Dakota, I was surrounded by the language and the culture of the Germans from Russia. But it was not until I began work on my Masters Thesis in 1961 that I became aware of what a unique background I had. My adviser told me to write about my people. My people, I asked? Yes, he said, you have a story to tell, you have research to do, it will be difficult, but it will be a contribution to scholarship. What I bring you has not only been accepted as a distinguished contribution to scholarship, but I bring you the story of a treasure I discovered in my research.

Think of the ancient tombs of the Pharaohs. Research and study brought the knowledge to unlock those tombs and to discover the incredible treasures stored there. Thirty years of research on the Germans from Russia who live in the Dakotas brought me the knowledge to unlock and discover the beautiful treasure stored here on this Great American Plain, on the prairies of North and South Dakota. In bringing together the many materials that give a full and complete picture of a people, I found that we have here a treasure, a rare archeological find. Our society, our culture, is a beautiful relic that has been preserved for us, and gives us a view into another time. The key that opens the door to the treasures of our culture is our beautiful and very old German dialect.

We speak a language spoken during the 18th century in Southwest Germany. This dialect, which I have termed Central Dakota German is the language of Swabia. The Swabians go back to the early Germanic tribe of the Alemannen.

We speak the Swabian dialect using those ancient rhythms of sound with words that are not only lovely, but are relics from a time when German had not yet been formed into the language which is today known as Standard High German. Because these people left Germany and moved to isolated communities, first in the Odessa Territory and Bessarabia in Russia, then to the prairies of Dakota Territory, the language did not undergo speech changes. We lived in speech communities called "linguistic islands". The language stayed as it had been due to isolation from the currents of change, and stored within our dialect is the language of our culture. The way we express ourselves and the way we think is often different than that of others. It is because we are very influenced by an old culture and values that could live on for many generations inside of the language. The dialect that you speak is like a vessel, and inside that vessel is the culture. The language and the culture go together.

The fact that we retained our language for so many years, was aided by an important ingredient. The Black Sea Germans were 80% Lutheran and the Bessarabians were practically all Lutherans. This does not mean that our Catholic brothers or our fellow Protestants are not included here. What I am talking about is language. Dr. Martin Luther is one of the pivotal figures in German history not only because of the Reformation in the 16th centuury, but because he was the person who gave form to the German language. Dr. Martin Luther's translation of the Bible into German (completed and published in 1532) gave the German language its first standard which we today call Standard High German. Before his translation you found only the dialects spoken by the different groups of Germans like the Swabians, the Bavarians, the Hessians, the Saxons, and others. Germany was not even one nation until Otto von Bismarck, a Prussian, united the Germans in 1871. Thus your group identity was very closely tied with your dialect.

In his translation of the Bible, Luther strove to make the language not only beautiful in its expression, but meaningful to what he termed the man in the market place, the mother and child in the home. He thus brought the language of the people into the church. Each child in Russia attended a church school and learned German. In America they attended English speaking public schools, but they still had to learn to read and write Standard High German in order to be Confirmed in the Lutheran church.

Not all Central Dakota Germans are Lutherans, but this hard core of Lutherans predominated throughout the region and kept German a viable language for a very long time. The Lutheran Church and the

Luther Bible, the Standard High German language of the church, and the German dialect found in the home, all supported and sustained each other.

Luther also brought folksongs into the church. His acceptance of the language of the home and the market place and of the folksongs and folkways was in my view, important in the incredible cultural retention found in the Dakotas. We have facets of our culture that can be traced back through the ages. Luther accepted traditions like *brauche*, the 'healers' or medical people of the communities before the age of scientific medicine. Luther allowed old German customs and practices to continue.

Many may not have read much German literature, especially the legends and great stories that flowered in the 12th century. If you read them, you will see our own Dakota culture is a modern day reflection of traditions that existed even then. We celebrated our *hohezeiten* 'high occasions' with a drama, ritual, and festivity analogous to those found in the great and ancient legends of the German people. Our weddings which used to last for three days and the rituals they contained, such as the ribbons worn by everyone, the decorations on the horses, the paper flowers, can be read about in the wedding of Kriemhild in the Niebelungenlied, the oldest German legend which in oral history, dates back even further.

The funerals, the night watch with the caskets remaining in the home, the processions through the streets, the music which we so love that we sing those melancholy songs when we get together for an evening of fellowship, the way we depart from our dead, are again reflections of our cultural history, and of the time when Catholic and Protestant belonged to one union, one church. This relic, this treasure, this culture we have nurtured for so long is preserved for us and is our heritage.

I would like to ask you today to focus on your culture and to record your own family traditions and stories just as you search out and record the genealogy of your family. If you study your genealogy you know who your grandmother was, who your grandfather was, but do you know: What were their favorite Bible verses? What were the hymns that they loved to sing? What was it that was meaningful to them at Christmas, how did they celebrate Easter, and what foods did they cook on special occasions?

Many of you must know proverbs that your mother or grandmother said to you. Proverbs teach lessons, they show a view of the world and a way of life is preserved. Proverbs can bring a smile and a laugh as we share the humor of our ancestors.

Then there are superstitions that you know. There are admonitions like the advice to place a broom across the door when you leave your house for a witch will never cross it. Record home remedies. What did your mother or your grandmother tell you to do for an ailment?

Write down the family recipes that have been handed down for generations. They too will be lost if you do not record them. The Dakota Germans have food traditions from Southwest Germany, Switzerland, the Alsace Region (today France), and the foods they learned while living in the Czars' Russian Empire. They enjoyed American foodways, and particularly liked pies and cookies. What an interesting people, what a marvelous cuisine.

The German pioneers loved music. They loved to sing both their folksongs and the hymns of their church. What were the favorite songs of your family? What songs were sung on which special occasions? Are there verses or poems that were family favorites?

Song, legend, story, have always been a part of culture. There is so much in your heritage, write it down.

Whether your interest is family genealogy, or your ethnic and language community, I ask you to work to retain that which made your parents and grandparents such a unique presence upon this earth. Try to capture and retain the spirit and essence of your forefathers. It is a worthwhile endeavor that captures you as everyone is so grateful to participate and to be included. Do not lose for your children and their children, the beautiful heritage that was given to you.

CONTENTS

PREFACE/V

CHAPTER 1: INTRODUCTION/1

  1.0 INTRODUCTION/1
    1.1 The Black Sea and Volga Germans/2
    1.2 Divisions of this study/3
    1.3 Ethnographic problems/4
    1.4 Genesis of this research/5
    1.5 Persons to whom this research is especially indebted/5

CHAPTER 2: THE HISTORICAL BACKGROUND/7

  2.0 INTRODUCTION/7
    2.1 Germany: The political and philosophical situation/9
    2.2 Russia: The need for immigrants from the West/15
        2.2.1 The Black Sea Colonies/20
        2.2.2 Bessarabia/30
        2.2.3 Forces behind a new migration to the Dakotas/35
        2.2.4 The Germans who stayed in Russia/37
    2.3 America: Dakota Territory, the call of the empty lands/40
        2.3.1 The immigration of the Germans to the Dakotas from Russia and their general pattern of settlement/41
        2.3.2 The remembered past/50
            2.3.2.1 The remembered past of the years in Russia and the immigration to the United States/52
            2.3.2.2 The remembered past as reflected in the oral history of "one who stayed behind in Russia"/60
            2.3.2.3 The remembered past of the early years in Dakota/62

CHAPTER 3: THE CENTRAL DAKOTA GERMAN DIALECT/75

  3.0 INTRODUCTION/75
    3.1. The Central Dakota German dialect (CDGer.)/77
        3.1.0 Introduction/77
        3.1.1 The segmental phonemes of Central Dakota German (CDGer.) contrasted with the inventory of the segmental phonemes of Standard High German (SHGer.)/78
        3.1.2. The lexicon of Central Dakota German contrasted with the lexicon of Standard High German/80

      3.1.2.1 The Swadesh lexicostatistical word lists/80
         3.1.2.1.1 The Swadesh 100-word list/81
         3.1.2.1.2   The Swadesh 200-word list/84
      3.1.2.2 The Mitzka 200-word list/89
      3.1.2.3   List based on the Wenker set of 40 sentences/97
      3.1.2.4 Representative sample of Central Dakota German dialect words which contrast with Standard High German/106

3.2 COMPARISON OF A SELECTED INVENTORY OF CENTRAL DAKOTA GERMAN LEXICON WITH THE STANDARD DIALECTAL GEOGRAPHIC WORD-MAPS TO DETERMINE THE ORIGIN OF THE CENTRAL DAKOTA GERMAN DIALECT IN GERMANY/113

3.3 INTERNAL LINGUISTIC EVIDENCE THAT THE CENTRAL DAKOTA GERMAN DIALECT SHOWS OF THE INFLUENCES THE ORIGINAL GERMAN DIALECT UNDERWENT AS A RESULT OF ITS MIGRATIONS/115

   3.3.1 Internal lexical evidence for the external history found in loanwords from French, Russian, Romanian, and Turkish which reflect the immigration to Russia/116

   3.3.2 Internal lexical evidence for the external history found in loanwords from English which reflect the influences resulting from the immigration to the United States/117

3.4 FACTORS FAVORING THE LANGUAGE-MAINTENANCE OF THE CENTRAL DAKOTA GERMAN DIALECT/120

3.5 FACTORS CURRENTLY WORKING TO REPLACE THE CENTRAL DAKOTA GERMAN DIALECT WITH ENGLISH/122

3.6 SOCIOLINGUISTIC FUNCTIONS OF THE CENTRAL DAKOTA GERMAN DIALECT IN CONTEMPORARY LIFE IN THE UNITED STATES/123

3.7 ATTEMPT AT A PROGNOSIS FOR MAINTENANCE OF THE CENTRAL DAKOTA GERMAN DIALECT IN THE FACE OF THE MANY PRESSURES FOR ITS REPLACEMENT BY ENGLISH/124

CHAPTER 4: THE SPIRITUAL LANGUAGE OF A PEOPLE/127

4.0 INTRODUCTION: DER SONNTAG GHERT ZU UNSEREM GOTT 'SUNDAY BELONGS TO THE LORD'/127
    4.0.1 Sources for the Lieder cited/132

   4.1 Der Katechismus nach Luther: Lutheran religion and the language of Luther's church/132
    4.1.1 Kindertaufe: A child's baptism/132
    4.1.2 Konfirmation: Confirmation/134
    4.1.3. Kinder gheren in d'kirche das sie Gottes Wort lernen 'Children belong in the church so they can learn God's Word'/136

4.2 Kirche und Fest: The religious calendar and folk life/139
    4.2.1 Adventszeit: Advent/139
    4.2.2 Der Heiligerobet und der erste und zweiter Christtag: Christmas/141
    4.2.3 Nei johr: New Year/147
    4.2.7 Missionsfest: Mission Festival/155

4.3 Hohezeiten: Celebrations and their function in maintaining family and community ties and language/155
    4.3.1 Hochzeit: Weddings/155
    4.3.2 Leicht: Funerals/161

CHAPTER 5: THE LANGUAGE OF CUSTOMS AND BEHAVIOR/169

    5.0 INTRODUCTION/169

5.1 Worter und weisheiten: Proverbs and sayings, the expression of moral values, ethics, and humor/169

5.2 Brauche: Healing, an expression of folk medicine/188
    5.2.1 Brauche: The art of healing reflected in the verses and psychological insights of the brauchere Friederike Opp/190
        5.2.1.1 Zahnweh: Toothaches, their complications and infections/193
        5.2.1.2 Augeweh: Inflammation and infections of the eyes/194
        5.2.1.3 Mageweh: Stomach flu/195
        5.2.1.4 Darmgichter: Intestinal convulsions/196
        5.2.1.5 Rotlafa und schwulst: Infection with edema and swelling/199
        5.2.1.6 Schussblotter und wilderschuss: Irritations and infections of the eyes/200
        5.2.1.7 Dorweh: Boils and infections from cattle, including ringworms/200
        5.2.1.8 Die rose oder das wildfeier: Very high and rising fever with a spreading rash/201
    5.2.2 Mitweib und brauchere: The art of healing reflected in the verses and medical insights of the brauchere Eva Iszler/207
        5.2.2.1 Schussblotter: Irritations of the eyes/209
        5.2.2.2 Magere: Consumptive diseases/210
        5.2.2.3 Gelsucht: Yellow jaundice/211
        5.2.2.4 Horwurm und ringwurm: Hairworms and ringworms/211
        5.2.2.5 Schweine: Consumption/212
            5.2.2.5.1 Eva Iszler's healing verse/213
            5.2.2.5.2 Württemberg State Museum version/214
    5.2.3 Verzähle: Oral history of brauche incidents/215
    5.2.4 Merseburger Zaubersprüche: The oldest known magic verses in the German language compared with brauche verses/218
    5.2.5 Brauche: Was it magische Heilkunde `magic healing' or hexerei `witchcraft' in Christian communities?/219
    5.2.6 Brauche: An etymological guess/223

5.3 Benennungen der Krankheiten: Old German medical terms preserved by Jacob Grimm in 1835 and still extant in the CDGer.

lexicon/225
5.4 Heilmittel: Folk remedies of the Central Dakota Germans/228
5.5 Aberglaube: Folk beliefs of the Central Dakota Germans/232
5.6 Lieder: Music in folk and family life/237
5.7 Kiche und Hof: Culinary art and the sustenance of daily life/245

CHAPTER 6: CONCLUSIONS/251

6.0 INTRODUCTION/251
6.1 Agrarian society/251
6.2 Common Lutheran religion/252
6.3 Geographical isolation/253
6.4 Previous petrifaction of their language and culture during the Russian period/253
6.5 Homogeneous language and cultural traditions/254
6.6 Conclusion/255

APPENDIX 1: CENTRAL DAKOTA GERMAN FOODLORE/259

APPENDIX 2: MANIFESTO OF CATHERINE THE GREAT/300

APPENDIX 3: AN ACT TO SECURE HOMESTEADS TO ACTUAL SETTLERS ON THE PUBLIC DOMAIN/310

APPENDIX 4: AN ACT TO ENCOURAGE THE GROWTH OF TIMBER ON WESTERN PRAIRIES/315

APPENDIX 5: TREATY OF NONAGGRESSION BETWEEN GERMANY AND THE UNION OF SOVIET SOCIALIST REPUBLICS WITH ADDITIONAL SECRET PROTOCOL/317

APPENDIX 6: MAP SHOWING THE SITE OF THE CENTRAL DAKOTA GERMAN COMMUNITY IN THE UNITED STATES/320

APPENDIX 7: MAP SHOWING THE SITE OF THE CENTRAL DAKOTA GERMAN COMMUNITY IN RUSSIA/321

APPENDIX 8: MAP SHOWING THE ORIGINAL SITE OF THE CENTRAL DAKOTA GERMAN DIALECT OF SCHWÄBISCH/322

APPENDIX 9: MAP SHOWING THE FOUR DISTRICTS OF THE KINGDOM OF WÜRTTEMBERG AND THEIR SMALL COUNTIES OR TOWNSHIPS AROUND 1818/323

APPENDIX 10: DESCRIPTION OF THE RECORDED ORPUS (1984-1987) AND LIST OF THE INFORMANTS CITED IN CHAPTER 3/324

REFERENCES AND SELECTED BIBLIOGRAPHY/326

ABOUT THE AUTHOR/335

Chapter 1: Introduction

1.0 Introduction. In these pages I have tried to describe the Germans of the Central Dakotas. I do so by presenting the history of these people as seen through their language and their culture as they have moved through the pages of European and American history during the past 200 years.

Two hundred years ago, those who are now the Central Dakota Germans were an agrarian people living in southwestern Germany in one of many small independent states that loosely formed the Holy Roman Empire. They were German-speaking, they were predominately Lutheran, and they were grounded in the traditional culture of their ancestors.

They spoke a German dialect known as Swabian. They were staunch German Lutherans who cherished both their secular heritage and their faith. Their culture was family oriented, honoring virtues as old as the German people. Their family life and values were based on reverence for ancestors, a concern for the sort of legacy they would be leaving for future generations, respect and care for living relatives, concern for *freindschaft* `the tribe' or `greater family', a strong sense of duty and family obligation. One had to learn, be knowledgeable, and work hard to be a productive contributor to that society. They also held to the classic virtues of knighthood: to be faithful, loyal, upright, and temperate in all things. They loved music. They loved to sing both their folksongs and the hymns of their church. They celebrated their *hohezeiten* `high occasions' with a drama, ritual, and festivity analogous to those found in the great and ancient legends of the German people.

The language, religion, customs, and traditions of these Swabians live on today in the language and culture of the Central Dakota Germans; still an agrarian society, still a closely knit community of people. The passage of these people over a two-hundred-year period from their original site in Southwest Germany to the steppes of Czarist Russia during the period of the Napoleonic wars, and from the steppes of Russia to the prairies of the great American Plains, while simultaneously keeping the identity and the unity of their society intact, is a remarkable cultural feat and should be to them a source of pride and happiness. The description of this unique cultural achievement of these Central Dakota Germans is the source, inspiration, and content of this volume.

1.1 The Black Sea and Volga Germans. Although this book is about the Black Sea Germans (including Bessarabia) who were Protestant and Catholic, the volume confines itself to describing primarily those Black Sea German Lutherans who immigrated to the Central Dakota region, in order to give as complete a picture as possible of this one group of German emigrants from Russia. It would not have been a manageable project to describe in the same detail all of the Germans who emigrated from Russia to pioneer on the Great Plains of the American West.

However, what is told here about the Black Sea Protestants is, of course, generally applicable to the Black Sea Catholics. It also applies to the Protestant and Catholic Volga Germans who had immigrated to Russia on the issuance of the invitation of Catherine the Great and settled along the Volga River in the east. Their move to Russia was earlier than that of the Black Sea Germans who were invited to Russia by Catherine's grandson Alexander I. The Volga Germans also immigrated earlier to the United States, where they settled in Nebraska and Kansas and southward to Oklahoma and Texas. The Black Sea Germans settled predominantly to the north, in the Dakotas.

Volga Germans who purchased the first edition of this book reported many similarities between their history, religion, and culture and that of the Black Sea Germans described here. In fact, the two groups of Germans from Russia belong to the same historical societies and work together to maintain their history and culture for future generations. They enjoy the same stories and music and their forefathers endured many of the same hardships. Their interests are similar and although their dialects differ, they understand each other very well.

1.2 Divisions of this study. The body of this book consists of four chapters. The first of these, Chapter 2, discusses the political and philosphical situation of Southwest Germany which caused these Germans to move to a new land (2.1), describes their emigration to Russia (2.2), the Black Sea Colonies (2.2.1) and Bessarabia (2.2.2), the places where they settled, and details the reasons for their second emigration, their leaving Russia for the Dakota Territory in the United States (2.2.3). After a brief description of what happened to those who stayed behind (2.2.4), the chapter proceeds to recount their emigration to America (2.3), and the general pattern of their settlement in the Dakota Territory (2.3.1). After this historical review, the chapter concludes with oral history accounts gathered from the Central Dakota Germans themselves. In these sections they relate "the remembered past" (2.3.2) of the years in Russia (2.3.2.1), of one who stayed behind in Russia (2.3.2.2), and of the early years in the Dakotas (2.3.2.3).

Chapter 3 describes the Central Dakota German (CDGer.) dialect (3.1). It contrasts the inventory of the segmental phonemes of Central Dakota German with the segmental phonemes of Standard High German (3.1.1) and then contrasts the Central Dakota lexicon with the lexicon of Standard High German (SHGer.) (3.1.2). In describing the differences in lexicon, the standard word lists and sentences are employed; namely, the Swadesh 100-word and 200-word lists, the norms frequently used by linguistic and cultural anthropologists (3.1.2.1), the Mitzka 200-word list (3.1.2.2) and the Wenker 40 sentences (3.1.2.3), the norms most frequently used by German dialectologists. This section of the chapter also presents a representative sample of CDGer. forms which contrast with Standard High German (3.1.2.4). The second section of the chapter compares a selected inventory of CDGer. lexicon with the standard dialectal geographic word-maps used to determine the source of the CDGer. dialect in Germany (3.2). The forms of the CDGer. dialect are then examined for internal evidence of the emigration from Germany to Russia (3.3.1) and for internal evidence of the emigration of the CDGer. dialect from Russia to the Dakota Territory (3.3.2). The chapter concludes by describing the factors which have favored language-maintenance of the CDGer. dialect (3.4); it identifies the factors currently working to replace the CDGer. dialect with English (3.5), examines the sociolinguistic functions which CDGer. currently performs (3.6), and attempts a prognosis of "language maintenance" for the CDGer. dialect in the face of rising pressures for its replacement by English (3.7).

Chapter 4 describes the interrelationship between the Central Dakota

German dialect and the religious culture of these people, for their language and their religious culture have always been intertwined and mutually supportive. Almost all their festive occasions and celebrations took place within a church context. The chapter describes in detail: Baptism (4.1.1), Confirmation (4.1.2), and the customs surrounding them, the relationships between children and their church (4.1.3), the liturgical year with its religious and secular customs (4.2), e.g. Advent, Christmas, New Year, Easter, Ascension, Pentecost, and Mission Festival. The chapter concludes by describing weddings (4.3.1) and funerals (4.3.2), the two other most important occasions when family and the community united.

Chapter 5 details the language of customs and behavior: the proverbs and sayings which express the Central Dakota German moral values, ethics, and humor (5.1), *brauche* `healing', the expression of their folk medicine (5.2), the old German medical terms preserved by Jacob Grimm in 1835 and still existing in the CDGer. lexicon (5.3), their folk remedies (5.4), folk beliefs (5.5), songs (5.6), and the culinary art and sustenance of daily life by the Dakota German kitchen (5.7).

Chapter 6 summarizes the configuration of traits which distinguished the Central Dakota German community, its language, and culture: (1) agrarian society (6.1), (2) common Lutheran religion (6.2), (3) geographical isolation (6.3), (4) previous petrifaction of their language and culture during the Russian period (6.4), (5) homogeneous language and cultural traditions (6.5), and concludes the description of the Central Dakota Germans language and culture (6.6).

1.3 Ethnographic problems. I have tried to give as complete an ethnography of the Central Dakota Germans as I could, and hope to have succeeded at least to a degree; for the harsh reality is, that if I were to begin again today, this study—whatever its limitations—could no longer be done. The old pioneers who immigrated from Russia and from whom I learned so much, have since died. Even the first generation, those whom I would term the "young pioneers"—for they too pioneered, even though they were born on the land of the old Dakota Territory—are mostly no longer living. Members of the next generation, the second generation, born in the 1930s and 1940s, no longer have the depth of experience to enable them to relate all of the material collected here.

We still know the language, have enjoyed and still enjoy the old customs; but we are of the age when total integration usually takes place in most ethnic groups, the third generation. Members of the fourth generation, who follow, are aware of their heritage but do not understand their heritage as a whole. Their information, knowledge, and understanding are fragmentary at best. Although most of them probably understand Central Dakota German, very few speak it; and fewer yet place value on knowing it. A generational cultural gap has opened; the shift to monolingualism in English has begun.

1.4 Genesis of this research. The genesis of this research was the insight of Dr. Adolf E. Schroeder, who directed me to this project for my Master of Arts degree at Kent State University. He recognized my membership in a unique society, something I had never realized. No research had been done on the topic, and I found I had to go to libraries in Germany to begin. The material I then found (1961-1962) has been substantiated in the years that followed as books were published by groups like the Bessarabian Germans (Kern 1976), and in particular, the three volumes of the Stuttgart Landesmuseum (1987) which used the same source material which I consulted in 1961-1962.

1.5 Persons to whom this research is especially indebted. The success of any collection lies in the informants. Not only were all the Central Dakota Germans whom I interviewed helpful, they were very grateful that somebody cared. Their interest was so sincere and genuine that the whole project captured me completely, and I continued until the work was finished.

My mother, Emma Fischer, was the invaluable key since she was known and respected far and wide among the members of the Central Dakota German community, and could continue to collect and forward material to me for recording and incorporation into this volume.

Dr. Kurt Rein, the noted German dialectologist, gave me the start and advice I needed to begin with a collection of tape recordings of the dialect. These recordings constitute the corpus for Chapter 3. Dr. Rein then confirmed my dialectal findings, which was invaluable in helping me bring this topic to a successful conclusion.

Rebecca Schroeder directed my efforts at collecting the folklore material over a period of many years. If this collection is sufficiently ample and complete, it is due to her advice.

I wish to express my gratitude and appreciation to the Graduate School of Georgetown University for its full Fellowship during the years of graduate study leading to my Doctor of Philosophy degree; and to the members of the German Department, its previous Chairman Dr. Alfred Obernberger and its present Chairman, Dr. Heidi Byrnes.

I would also like to express my gratitude and appreciation to my

Dissertation Committee: to Dr. Alfred Obernberger, Mentor, for his specialized knowledge in dialectology and German minorities; to Dr. John J. Staczek for his interest and knowledge in ethnology and bilingualism; to Rev. Richard J. O'Brien, S.J. for his linguistic advice and editorial assistance; and to Rev. G. Ronald Murphy, S.J. for his insightful suggestions and the encouragement and guidance which helped my years of collection and inquiry become this descriptive account.   Thank You.

Chapter 2: The historical background

2.0 Introduction. In working on this study I have increasingly become aware of a theme that runs through the long history of the Central Dakota Germans. For the history of these people comes alive and one begins to become aware of how they were able to maintain so solid a group identity through two migrations and two centuries of sojourn in lands not culturally German nor German speaking, if one is aware of this basic underlying theme. That theme is their cultural solidarity and group identity as they undertake migration after migration through alien lands and alien cultures, unified and one in both culture and outlook.

Their history begins in Southwest Germany, in particular in Württemberg, a historic area that had changed little until the 1800s when Napoleon changed the lives of its people. These people were Swabians and the Swabians go back to the ancient Germanic tribe of the *Alemannen*. The Swabian dialect which they speak is one of the three dialects of *Alemannisch*. The other two are the *Niederalemannisch* or *Elsässisch*, the dialect spoken in the Alsace region of Germany (today France) and the *Hochalemannisch* or *Schweizerisch*, the dialect spoken in Switzerland and the Austrian province of Vorarlberg.

The Swabian himself, as reflected in his language, had lived in a stable cultural and linguistic situation for centuries. After the Thirty Year's war, which ended in 1648, the area was Protestant, Württemberg itself being Lutheran. In fact, Altwürttemberg, before it received additional territory when its Duke was named King by Napoleon, was the only large state in southern Germany which had remained staunchly Lutheran since the time of Luther's Reformation in the 16th century. (Württembergisches Landesmuseum 1987:323).

The Swabians were known for their strict adherence to tradition. They left Germany without having accepted the Age of Rationalism and the new ideas that seemed to threaten their culture and traditions that were completely bonded with their church and the traditions of their church.

They left Germany and migrated to Russia to escape the burden of the military draft which was being harshly enforced. The newly named King of Württemberg was an ally of Napoleon, and in order to support Napoleon's armies, he supplied him not only with the little that the people owned and grew, but also with their sons to help Napoleon fight his wars.

Their migration was a mass migration in the same sense in which early Germanic tribes moved through Europe during the Great Migration. Similarly, some of these *Württembergers* moved together to Russia, as an extended family, as a tribe. In fact, we find that whole villages left together and then settled together in an isolated area, in a completely new land, Odessa Territory. The villages they formed were made up of Germans only, and their contact with other nationalities was limited. Only in neighboring Bessarabia, to the west, did they have more contact with other ethnic groups. But even there, although different ethnic communities existed together, each group nevertheless lived in separate villages.

The most isolated of the Black Sea villages were those of the Glückstal Region, an area remote and isolated due to mountainous terrain and forests. The Glückstal Region was settled by *Württembergers* who were almost all Lutheran. German families from other parts of South and Southwest Germany who had among them Reformed, Pietists, and Separatists, and many Catholics settled in the Black Sea colonies, too. But in the Glückstal Region lived this most homogeneous group of Lutherans from Württemberg.

The next mass migration was the one from Russia to the United States and Canada, although many settlers also went to South America. The Black Sea Germans and the Germans from Bessarabia, the adjacent area, emigrated in great numbers to the Great Plains area of America, along with other Germans from Russia like the Volga Germans and the Mennonites. The United States census for 1920 records 303,532 Germans who emigrated to the United States from Russia. There were large settlements of these people in the Dakotas, Nebraska, Kansas, Colorado, Oklahoma, Texas, and Montana. The state to receive the most immigrants from the Black Sea colonies and Bessarabia was the state of North Dakota. And, the area of the Central Dakotas from mid-North Dakota to mid-South Dakota formed the largest and most compact concentration. McIntosh County, North Dakota, and McPherson County, South Dakota, are at the center of even this central region.

The Black Sea Germans settled in patterns that reflected the regions they had occupied in Russia; they "stayed together". This "staying together" according to the four regions they had occupied in the Black Sea colonies is really a staying together by the area of Germany from which each had emigrated to Russia and to the Black Sea area. Thus one observes the same people and dialect groups that originally left Germany, now settled together in America.

Again, one cannot help but recall the image of the Germanic tribe, the extended family, "staying together". For whole families either emigrated together or sent for family as they became settled and could invite others to join them.

The Glückstal Region Germans, or *Glückstaler* as they were known to each other, are the Swabians from Württemberg, the Lutherans, who did not accept change to the teachings of Martin Luther. They settled together in the Central Dakota area of the United States of America, still speaking the ancient rhythms of their Swabian dialect that they had maintained through their stay in Russia. They were joined by the Bessarabian Lutherans, and by Lutherans and other Protestant groups from the Grossliebental and Beresan regions, the majority of which were *Württembergers*. Being in the center, they were surrounded in the Dakotas, and even in the Great Plains area, by their own people: fellow Germans from the Black Sea area of Russia and from Bessarabia in the Dakotas, and further to the south in South Dakota, the German Mennonites, the German Hutterites, and then the many settlements of the Volga Germans in Nebraska, Kansas, and Colorado. They had not only remained intact due to isolation and being surrounded by other Germans in the Black Sea area of Russia, but here in America they were again isolated, surrounded by Germans from Russia, safely ensconced in a cocoon in which their language, customs, and culture could remain intact. It took years of research for me to fully realize this, how they could survive the years and the changes and remain culturally and linguistically intact.

2.1 Germany: The political and philosophical situation. As Napoleon with his armies moved eastward across the European Continent at the beginning of the 19th century, the final blow was delivered to the declining Holy Roman Empire, already weakened by the splintering and division resulting from the Treaty of Westphalia in 1648. An arbitrary redistribution of lands and possessions was to strengthen Napoleon's influence across the Continent. The French annexed all territory west of the Rhine River. East of the Rhine, the many small principalities of southern Germany were combined to form the Confederation of the Rhine under the protectorship of the French Emperor. This took southern Germany out of the sphere of influence of Austria.

Following French annexation of the territories on the west side of the Rhine, a French imperial deputation compensated those German princes who had sustained losses there. The result of this *Reichsdeputationshauptschluss* `Principal Decree of the Imperial Deputation', issued at Regensburg in 1803, was a complete remaking of the map of Germany. The secularization, or civil division, of all ecclesiastical territories which had previously been apportioned according to religion, provided the indemnity demanded by the princes of Prussia, Württemberg, Bavaria, Hesse, Baden and Nassau (Reinhardt 1961:I,235). This arbitrary redistribution of lands and possessions signified the destruction of the ancient imperial constitution of the Holy Roman Empire, and furthermore, it brought about a dramatic change from a religious orientation of the territories to a completely civil ownership awarded to the princes.

After the endless religious wars between the followers of Luther and the Pope, the Treaty of Westphalia in 1648 had reaffirmed the right of each prince to choose the religion for the people of his state. This right had already been established in 1555 with the Treaty of Augsburg which decreed, *cuius regio eius religio* `religion according to him who reigns', which was an attempt to bring about religious peace between Catholics and Protestants. In fact, it had only increased religious oppression. Nevertheless, a delicate balance between the religion of the ruler and that of his people had become established. Now all changed again, and the decree of 1803 issued at Regensburg brought Catholics under the rule of Protestant princes and Protestants under the rule of Catholic princes.

The small territories of individual German princes in many ways had constituted some of the last vestiges of feudalism. Their elimination benefited urban dwellers to some extent, but the rural inhabitants of southern Germany resented the changes and the disruptive conditions which brought chaos into their lives and their churches. French rule proved to be oppressive and arbitrary. Taxes were heavy, and young men were conscripted to fight in Napoleon's armies.

In an effort to undermine the economy of England, Napoleon instituted a continental shipping blockade. The effects were disastrous for Germany. The import of foreign raw materials was halted, and shipping activity on Germany's great waterways declined. Merchants and small businesses went bankrupt while unemployment climbed (Flenley 1959:119).

Württemberg was especially vulnerable to this blockade, for the import of foreign raw materials, such as cotton for its weaving industry, was halted. At the same time, demand increased for those goods usually obtained from England in support of the war effort. In Germany, the result of the Continental blockade was unemployment in those industries that depended upon the import of raw material, and an excessive capital investment in war goods production. With the lifting of the blockade, England flooded the European market with its stockpiled goods at prices lower than those of the German producers.

Württemberg was densely populated and, unless a change to a more intensive program of farm management could be made, the land could no longer feed the ever increasing population (Miller 1936:184-218). While it could be said that the old feudal society was breaking up, the new industrial society had not yet emerged. Thus the small scale cottage industry of the area could not compete with the goods manufactured in mass production which were shipped in from elsewhere. Peasant holdings, especially in southwest Germany, tended to be reduced to units too small to support family life (Flenley 1959:199). The almost constant state of war had destroyed farms, crops, and villages; and serious overpopulation contributed to the economic problems. It was against this background of increasingly disturbing political, economic, social, and especially religious factors that a significant migration of southern Germans to the Black Sea area of southern Russia took place.

Emigration was not new to the German people. Eastward expansion had been an element in German history for some time. For example, Germanic tribes had made settlements along the great rivers and reached the Black Sea in the third century. In the 10th century, *Nordmark,* which was to become 'Prussia', began to push out from its eastern boundary on the Elbe, and the *Ostmark,* 'Austria', faced the more difficult task of pushing its boundary down the Danube from Vienna. The era of expansion to the vast lands to the east by future modern states had begun (Flenley 1959:198). Russia, for its part, had a long tradition of seeking contact with the west.

During the time of Napoleon, Swabia was the most populous district of Germany. It lay between Bavaria, Franken, the upper Rhine, and Austria. Covering most of South and Southwest Germany, it was divided into four parts: Württemberg, Baden, Constance, and Augsburg. Württemberg was the largest and most densely populated; it was Protestant and predominantly Lutheran. For years land had been mutually traded between Baden, Württemberg, and Bavaria; the result was fluid and ill-defined borders. This instability was further aggravated by the ways in which despotic rulers wielded their absolute authority in their land. (Leibbrandt 1928:12).

In 1797 Duke Friedrich became the ruler of Württemberg. He immediately ordered universal conscription, a draft that was enforced harshly and ruthlessly. The taxes imposed by Duke Friedrich were oppressive, and the tribute, which had to be paid to the landlords for rent, was indeterminate and arbitrary (Bienemann 1890:3-13). People often did not own their land and were at the mercy of the nobleman to whom the land belonged. Napoleon's troops were stationed or traveled throughout the Duchy. They had to be fed, and they needed support from the farmers in the form of wagons or work. Agricultural production was drastically affected as the land plots began to be "farmed out". The land could no longer be expected to meet the increasing demands of an increasing population dependent on it. The administration of programs was ineffectual and the financial structure of the duchy was weakened. Corruption was rampant. In such times, social justice seemed beyond attainment.

Politically aware by tradition, Swabians had always been independent thinkers. For example, since 1514 the people had possessed the right to own private property, to sell what they owned, and to move to other lands as they wished. Although the theoretical gains of the more liberal institutions were being examined by students and intellectuals in Württemberg, on a more practical level, misunderstandings and mistrust between citizens and administrators grew daily (Leibbrandt 1928:12-35). An examination of the social and other factors that led to the significant emigration of Swabians reveals that, in this period of enlightened rule, the pressures and burdens on the lower classes were intense.

The migration to Russia began in earnest in 1804 and continued in great numbers until 1807 when Friedrich of Württemberg became alarmed at the effect the population loss was having on conscription and tax revenues, and instituted a ban on emigration as part of his Reform measures. Although these restrictions were lifted in the new constitution of 1815, it was stipulated that the emigrant had to pay the government ten percent of all he wanted to take with him. In spite of these restrictions, migration to Russia continued and rose to its highest point in 1818 (Stumpp 1941:7).

The extremely strong religious unrest in Württemberg must be considered a major factor in the mass migration to Russia. Changes taking place in their churches were strongly resisted by the people (Bienemann 1890:3-13). Moreover, under the repressive economic, political, and social conditions existing at this time, the faithful clung more and more to religion as the only stable aspect of their lives. By contrast, during the late 18th century, the nobility and ruling classes of Germany and Austria, as well as those of most of Europe, were strongly influenced by the French philosophers such as Voltaire, Rousseau, Diderot. The religion of the nobility and upper classes became more and more rationalistic and philosophical and tended less toward a personal relationship with God. The official church, which was a state controlled church, became alienated from the needs of the ordinary people.

When new hymnals containing new liturgical arrangements were introduced in the Lutheran church in 1791 and in 1809, many felt their spiritual lives were being intruded upon. They turned away more and more from the rationalistic state church. Introduction of the new hymnals and the official church's drift away from the "word" caused growing numbers to secede from the official state church. They searched for spiritual guidance in the precepts of their traditional beliefs. Up to this point, evangelical devotional piety had exerted a strong influence over the Swabians, but within the framework of the established Lutheran Church (Hoffmann 1905:2). Now, as the people began to break away from the official church, part of the reasoning behind their migration lay in the yearning for a more genuine and visible fulfillment in religion.

Ideas, dreams, and aspirations stimulated by the writings of Jakob Böhme, Johann Albrecht Bengel, and other well-known theologians were readily received by the Swabians. Various quotations from the Scriptures were interpreted and extended to apply to the situation in the world around them. Bengel, whose prophecies two generations earlier in *"The Revelations of Saint John"*, had predicted a great conflict in the last decade of the 18th century, had foretold that the Holy Roman Empire would come to an end and that the King of France would probably become Kaiser. He had further predicted a strong growth of naturalism, philosophical scepticism, and a movement away from religious belief, with people relying more on ethics than on religion. These prophecies seemed strikingly relevant to the events of the day. Bengel had also said, "When the years number 1800, we will not be far from the goal, and our children's children will witness great things" (Stumpp 1941:23). The religious Swabians asked themselves if that time had not come. With Napoleon's armies sweeping across Europe, it seemed that the day of the Antichrist had indeed arrived. Certainly the name "Apollyon" in Revelations 9:11 of the Bible could refer to none other than to Napoleon himself (Baudler 1963:6-9).

Following the defeat of Napoleon in 1815, it was apparent that

Germany had not been able to win her freedom solely by her own efforts. Foreign intervention and aid had been required, above all the help of Czar Alexander I, who had brought Russia and her great military power into the affairs of central and western Europe in a way new to history. On September 15, 1815, the alliance proposed by the Czar to preserve Christian principles in politics and to strengthen the pro-monarchic form of government was completed. This alliance, known as the Holy Alliance, among Russia, Austria, and Prussia, included all Christian monarchs except the King of England (Schaeder 1934:2).

The answer to the economic and social problems of the Swabians seemed to lie in finding both freedom and more land by emigrating to a new country that promised economic self-sufficiency and offered the opportunity to escape the seemingly insurmountable problems which obtained in Germany. The enforced changes in the religious life of the people, and the persecution of those who left the official church contributed greatly to a migration eastward. In addition the required military service which served the interests of the nobility in wars that were of no benefit to the people, was another major factor. Then in 1816, due to government mismanagement and poor weather conditions, there was a massive crop failure in Southern Germany, followed by a year of famine. It seems clear that this "hunger year" provided the final stimulus for the emigration movement (Hoffmann 1905:2f).

In the summers of 1816 and 1817, whole Swabian villages emptied as homes, farms, orchards, and cattle were sold. By barge, by boat, by ox-cart and on foot, men, women, and children followed the course of the Danube River ever southeastward toward the Black Sea. These pilgrims took along few material possessions, but they carried their Bibles and their old traditional hymnals. The established churches do not appear to have opposed the emigration, and in fact some clergymen accompanied the emigrants. (Henne 1932:14)

Statistics for the years 1817-1818, the peak of the exodus, show that the Württemberg districts of Schwarzwald (Nagold and Freudenstadt), Enz (Marbach and Maulbronn), Neckar (Backnang, Brackenheim, Sulz, and Tübingen), Rothenburg, and Alb experienced the greatest loss of people. The Catholic districts of Oberschwaben and Donaukreis sent very few emigrants to Russia (Stumpp 1956:5). It was principally the Protestants of Württemberg who emigrated eastward.

The Catholic colonists who did emigrate to the Black Sea area were from the Rhine Palatinate, from the Alsace, and from Baden. Very few families from elsewhere in Germany joined the migration.

Most of the emigrants were farmers, but artisans of all types, craftsmen, vintners, and professional people, were also included among the emigrants. Russian records show that most of the Black Sea immigrants were by no means destitute but brought with them enough money for a new start (Leibbrandt 1928:52). This is most likely due to the fact that Czar Alexander changed a basic article of his grandmother Catherine's decree when he said that the immigrants must have the material means with which to begin their new life. They left their homes primarily for economic reasons, for the possibility of owning their own land, for freedom of religion, for freedom from military service, and for the desire to establish for themselves a better life (Leibbrandt 1928:52f). Officially they were welcomed and were provided the assistance that enabled them to establish homes for their families. They were able to aid later immigrants who came to join relatives in the Black Sea Colonies, and others who had heard of the opportunities present there.

2.2 Russia: The need for immigrants from the West. Russia had a long tradition of seeking contact with the west. Beginning as early as the 15th century, Russian rulers had turned to western Europe to find a means of stimulating scientific and cultural development in a country long isolated from western civilization. Ivan III who reigned from 1462-1505, invited architects, engineers, goldsmiths, miners, and doctors from Hungary and Italy. Ivan IV dispatched an agent to Germany to induce technicians of all professions to come to Russia. Czar Boris Gudunov, 1598-1605, called upon Germany, Holland, and Denmark to assist him in establishing universities; also Demetrius I favored colonization of Russia from western Europe.

There were periods in which immigration was discouraged; but colonization on a large scale was carried out under the reforms of Peter the Great, who not only sent agents to other countries to induce colonists to settle in Russia in the hope of westernizing his subjects, but in 1679 brought into Russia more than a thousand technicians and military scientists. The Russian Orthodox Church considered these foreigners a menace to the country; but under Peter I persons of every known calling were brought to Russia. Some were even entrusted with diplomatic posts as emissaries to other countries.

The first German settlements in Russia of any significance were those established on the Volga River in the 1760s in an immigration plan conceived and encouraged by Catherine the Great. Herself a German, born Sophia Augusta Frederica of Anhalt-Zerbst at Stettin, a small kingdom on the Oder River in Prussian Pomerania, Catherine had greatly expanded the Russian boundaries during her reign in the latter part of the 18th century (1762-1796). Although Catherine possessed a clear-cut view of Russian society divided among royalty, nobility, and peasants, she espoused liberal ideas and considered herself an initiator of reform in an age of enlightened absolutism (Florinsky 1964:208).

To hold and control the southern areas, designated 'New Russia', or *Novorossija,* had long been a goal of the Czars; however geographic factors made control of the region difficult. The high plains with rivers flowing in all directions had few natural barriers. For several reasons it seemed most practical to settle these newly acquired areas through colonization, particularly since there were not sufficient numbers of Russians. Russian peasants were still in bondage and could not be taken away from the local nobility. Peasants long suppressed and deprived of opportunity, had neither the knowledge nor the means to cultivate new lands (Stumpp 1922:21). As Peter I had done, Catherine turned west for the solution to her problem and began to encourage German colonization of southern Russia.

As early in her reign as December 4, 1762, Catherine issued an invitation to all, except Jews, to settle in her kingdom. The timing of this plan was inopportune and some aspects ill-conceived; for the Seven Years' War, 1756-1763, which involved Russia with Austria and France against German Prussia, was still in progress. Also, she did not at this time guarantee any privileges relating to the personal liberty and religious freedom of settlers. The response to her invitation was discouraging; but Catherine, gifted with tremendous energy and striving to create a new and better Russia, was not one to be easily discouraged.

On July 22, 1763, she issued a second *Manifesto*, which brought such a good response that it came to be regarded as the cornerstone of all colonization programs. (See Appendix 2 for the complete text of her *Manifesto.*) This proclamation, inviting foreigners to settle in Russia, demonstrates the liberal views, the desire for reform, and the foresight that the Empress possessed:

> Anyone who is destitute shall receive money for the expenses of his journey, and shall be forwarded to those free lands at the expense of the crown. On his arrival he shall receive competent assistance and even an advance of capital, free of interest, for ten years. The stranger is exempted from all service, either military or civil, and from all taxes for a certain time. In these new tracts of land the colonists may live according to their own good will, under their own jurisdiction for thirty years. All religions are tolerated (Abbot 1882:147).

The early immigration encouraged by Catherine's *Manifesto* was not an immediate success. The German immigrants who at that time settled in the Volga Region suffered greatly; for conditions were severe, dangers great, and the people generally unprepared for the cruel physical environment and the hardships that awaited them (Klaus 1887:18,182). The oldest complete German settlements in Russia were those established on the Volga 1763-1768. As early as 1765 a minor migration of Württembergers to the Black Sea Region of Russia occurred, but it was not until 1780 that the Russian government had begun active efforts to encourage colonists to settle in the Black Sea Region (Basler 1911:9).

In 1790 Mennonites founded settlements in the Chortiza Region (Lewin 1916:45).

It was not until the beginning of the 19th century, after the accession to the throne of Russia of Alexander I, Catherine's grandson, that conditions in both countries combined to make emigration from Germany to Russia an attractive opportunity for oppressed people who were seeking better opportunities for themselves and their children. The great migration began in 1804. This year marked the beginning of the period of greatest emigration from Germany to Russia. This emigration continued for three years, but declined between 1807 and 1815 because of a prohibitive Württemberg law. It reached its high point in 1818 after a famine in 1817.

During Catherine's reign a series of wars with Turkey occurred which expanded Russian territory in the Black Sea area and had a major influence on the future development of Southern Russia. After a six-year war, the Treaty of Kuchuk-Kainardyhi awarded Russia control of the Sea of Azov, the Black Sea, and protectorship of the Crimea. The Turks, who had for a long time shut off Russia's access to the Black Sea, were finally defeated in 1774.

When the Sultan of Turkey demanded the restoration of an independent Crimea in 1787, war broke out again. Once more Russia was victorious and with the Treaty of Jassy, concluded in the city of Jassy on December 29, 1791, Russia succeeded in expanding her territory in the Black Sea Region by annexing the fortress of Ochakow and gaining control of the Dnieper River (Florinsky 1964:219-225). The Russians were given possession of a large area between the Bug and Dnjestr Rivers. Many Russian generals and officers, who had fought and helped to win the war, were given large properties with the stipulation that they bring Russian people from the heart of the country to these outlying areas and settle them there. This was to make the area a permanent part of Russia and not let it continue as an empty land that the Turks could possibly reconquer. This plan proved unworkable. Most of the Russian peasants were still serfs who as such were not allowed to migrate. Nor did these serfs know how to colonize such large tracts of land.

Catherine died in 1796; and after the five year reign of Paul I, her son, was brought to a violent end by his murder on March 11, 1801, Alexander I ascended the throne. Alexander immediately issued his ascension *Manifesto*, in which he promised to "govern after the laws and heart" of his grandmother Catherine. (Walsh 1958:165).

On February 20, 1804, Alexander issued a decree instructing his ambassador and consuls in Germany to invite selected German farmers and artisans to migrate to Southern Russia. They were to travel in groups, and not more than two hundred families were to be accepted in one year. The agent was to pay only the transportation costs and to issue passports only to those who were considered honest, industrious, and possessed of not less than three hundred rubles in cash or property. Further, the colonists were to be family men (Stumpp 1941:63). Alexander's edict corresponded to the need to settle the vast area conquered from the Turks, and to develop at Odessa, newly founded in 1794, a major seaport and city which would serve to solidify the hold of Russia on the whole of this vast area.

The colonization had a well-developed philosophy and the methods to be utilized had been carefully selected to ensure successful settlement. Alexander's Manifesto Proclamation differed in significant aspects from that of Catherine in that the immigrants were to be selected so that they could "serve as artisans and farmers as examples for the Russian peasant". They were given the necessary assistance, received better land, and enjoyed more favorable conditions than the earlier German settlers during Catherine's reign (Stumpp 1922:44). Their industry and achievements did in fact set good examples for the Russian peasant to observe and imitate, but the peasants lacked the resources to follow the examples.

As early as 1819 Russia tried to check immigration with the Proclamation of August 5, which stipulated that immigrants had to have special permission to enter the country (Stumpp 1922: 50). Although officials were very lax in its enforcement, the Proclamation served to stem the tide somewhat; but for the next twenty-five years the city of Odessa and its colonies continued to grow, and daughter colonies were founded as land ownership continued to increase.

In 1802 the city of Odessa, then with a population of 9,000, was given into the hands of the intelligent and well-educated Duke Richelieu, a French nobleman who served the Czar. In the Edict of October 17, 1803, Czar Alexander commissioned Duke Richelieu to buy land from the nobility in the area around Odessa and to found on it German colonies. He purchased 34,212 *desyatina* which corresponds to 92,372 acres, as one *desyatina* equals 2.7 'acres'. Thus, the Edict of February 20, 1804, which welcomed German colonists to Russia contributed not only to the settlement of the Black Sea Colonies, but also to developing the city of Odessa into a major commercial seaport and a leading city of the Russian Empire. The development of the city and of the Odessa Territory owed much to the capabilities and far-sightedness of Duke Richelieu. Under his perceptive administration the city flourished, and by 1805 it was considered the administrative and commercial center for all of South Russia.

The history of the development of the city of Odessa is an interesting one. Before the time of Christ, a Greek village named Odessos is supposed to have existed just northeast of present-day Odessa. Three to four hundred years after Christ, Odessos as well as other Greek settlements along the Black Sea were destroyed by Asiatic hordes. For about the next 1000 years the area's history is not known. Then it reappears in Polish records in the 14th century as an area belonging to Lithuania. In the 15th century the town of Chadzibej, which was a fortress belonging to the Turks, appeared in the place that was to be Odessa. In 1789 the Russians conquered Chadzibej. They at first planned to make it a settlement for seafaring people, but in 1793 it was decided to build a fortress there. Finally in 1794, Chadzibej was named Odessa, and designated a seaport with the hope of it becoming a major center of trade. The Russian Czars were very interested in its development. In 1800 Paul I gave the city special rights, but it took the talented Duke Richelieu to help realize the Czar's ambitious plans for both the city and its territory (Stumpp 1956).

Some of the first foreign residents were Greeks, Italians, and Albanians, but by 1803 the first German colonists began to arrive. Duke Richelieu made good use of these immigrants. He welcomed them because he needed their abilities as artisans and craftsmen to build the city and he needed their knowledge as farmers to produce food and help develop trade. Two colonies of German artisans developed in the city of Odessa; the Upper Colony, Schmiedestrasse, and the Lower Colony, Handwerkerstrasse (Stumpp 1956).

Additional German colonies were founded on land purchased by Richelieu in the Odessa Territory. From the beginning, until 1834, the German artisans in the city and the German farmers living in the country, each had their own administrations, their own churches and schools, and were under the protection of a Provisional Committee founded by the Russian government. They were always called German colonists, or colonists, even the artisans who lived in the city of Odessa. The city continued to grow with the arrival of the German merchants, teachers, doctors, and persons of other professions.

In 1834 the special privileges of the Germans were withdrawn, and they were accorded only the same rights as other citizens of the city.

The churches represented in Odessa were Lutheran, Catholic, Reformed, Baptist, and the Russian Orthodox Church to which all of the native Russians belonged. Jews were also represented. By 1813, there were 35,000 residents in Odessa, by 1860, 120,000, and by 1873, nearly 200,000. Before the Russian Revolution of October 1917, the city had reached a population of one-half million and was the fourth largest city in Russia. It dominated the whole southwest area of greater Russia from the Romanian border west of Bessarabia to Kiev in the north and to Charkow in the east. It became a leader in exports. In 1822, seven million rubles worth of goods were exported, and by 1888, those exports had reached 324 million rubles (Stumpp 1956). After the Russian revolution of 1917 many of the foreigners living in the city departed and it diminished in both size and importance.

2.2.1 The Black Sea Colonies. The Territory of Odessa, formerly a part of the Province of Cherson and originally settled by the German colonists, was divided into four distinct districts. These four districts or regions are described separately by listing the colonies or communities within each one. The term *Kolonie* `colony' is used throughout to designate what we would term towns or communities. The terms colony and colonists were used by the Germans and the Russians to describe these settlements. A colony includes one town plus all the land that belonged to it. One did not live on individual farms, but lived together in the town or village and farmed the land around. For that reason, when more tracts of land were purchased by the colony and the colony lay too far from the tracts of land, new colonies, called daughter colonies, from which the land could be farmed, were founded. The land purchases were made by colonies that had enough money and could therefore, buy more land from the Russian nobility. The purchases were always large tracts.

Although the German settlers were called "colonists" whether they lived in the city of Odessa or in the villages, among the Germans themselves they were named according to their region. Thus one was a *Liebentaler,* or a *Glückstaler,* or a *Kutschurganer,* or a *Beresaner,* which provided a regional identification. These names continued to be used even after the German colonists settled in America. The identification with one of the four regions of the Odessa Territory extended even further. If you were not from the same *dorf* 'village' in Russia you were not apt to be friends in Dakota. You may know people from church, you may like them, but they were not your friends. Your friends were from your village and your district/region in Russia. This gives an insight into how tightly knit the German communities were and how massive the migration from Russia to Dakota was, to allow this custom to continue. People from the same district/region tended to settle together in the same area, or counties, in Dakota. If one examines the material on the colonies in Russia one finds that there was good reason for this loyalty to one's region or one's town. In Russia, as later in the Dakota Territory, they settled together with people from their own area of Germany who spoke the same dialect and who shared the same faith. In other words, they had loyalty to their own people whom they knew "from home in Germany". The practice continued from Germany to Russia to Dakota.

The following description of the colonies in the Black Sea Area of Russia (2.2.1) is based on the work of Karl Stumpp (1956). Although many have written on this topic in recent years, Stumpp is the prime source on which they all depend. My research shows that Stumpp too, often quoted another prime source, Georg Leibbrandt. Leibbrandt's work in the 1920s seems to have been the beginning of organized research in Germany itself, on the Germans in Russia. For the following description of the four districts or regions of the Black Sea Area and their individual communities, I chose to use an article Stumpp wrote for the *Heimatbuch der Deutschen aus Russland,* because it summarizes much of his own material, and includes work by Leibbrandt. I translated the article and reworked the material, organizing it to make it easier to follow for readers who are unfamiliar with the topic or the area. I made a chart listing each town within each region, giving the name of the town in the order in which it was settled. I computed the 'acres' to the amount of land that the colonists received and purchased, instead of using the Russian *desyatina* figure given in most texts. Although it may not seem important today, I retained the designation of Catholic and Protestant for each town. This becomes relevant when one follows the pattern of settlement in both Russia and the United States, for they always stayed together and settled with the people of their own religion. One has to remember that a war lasting thirty years (1618-1648) was fought in Central Europe over questions of religion until the Peace of Westphalia (2.1) established where each religion would be allowed.

I gave my own insights and explanations where they could add to understanding the text, and the history of the times.

The four regions that made up the Black Sea Colonies, the towns of the region, and their religious affiliation are given below. Following is a description of each region and of each of the towns within it.

(1) **Grossliebental**: founded 1804-1806, 10 colonies,
   6 Protestant and 4 Catholic.
   Protestant: **Grossliebental, Alexanderhilf, Neuberg, Peterstal, Lustdorf, Freudental.**
   Catholic: **Kleinliebental, Josefstal, Mariental, Franzfeld.**
(2) **Glückstal**: founded 1808-1809, 4 colonies,
   4 Protestant, and none Catholic.
   Protestant: **Glückstal, Bergdorf, Neudorf, Kassel.**
   Catholic: none
(3) **Kutschurgan**: founded 1808-1809, 6 colonies,
   6 Catholic and none Protestant.
   Catholic: **Strassburg, Baden, Selz, Kandel, Mannheim, Elsass.**
   Protestant: none
(4) **Beresan**: founded 1809-1817, 11 colonies,
   7 Catholic and 4 Protestant.
   Catholic: **Speyer, Landau, Sulz, Karlsruhe, Rastatt, München, Katharinental.**
   Protestant: **Rohrbach, Worms, Waterloo, Johannestal.**

All the settlements lay within a radius of some 60 miles from Odessa, most within a radius of less than 30 miles. The settlement of the German colonists in Odessa was parallel to the development in the Odessa Territory.

> **(1) Grossliebental Region.** Although there was prosperity and growth, environmental and other conditions were not always favorable in the colonies. In the Grossliebental Region, which had the oldest Protestant and Catholic colonies in the Black Sea area, the land was flat and treeless. Small rivers cut through the area from the north to the south; the Dalnik, Klein-Akerscha, Gross-Akerscha, and Baraboi Rivers. These rivers could cause great damage, even destroying whole villages. It was in this area, particularly in the Baraboi Valley, that Duke Richelieu had been commissioned by the Edict of October 17, 1803, to buy land for the establishment of German colonies in the Odessa Territory, and it was here that the earliest immigrants from South and Southwestern Germany settled in 1804 to 1807 on land purchased from the nobility. Eventually there were eleven colonies established on 92,372 acres.

The first colony, **Grossliebental,** was founded in 1804 on both sides of the Gross-Akerscha River by colonists who were mainly from Württemberg. Grossliebental became the intellectual and economic center of the region. It had a well-known central school, a girls' school, a hospital, an orphanage, an orphanage-fund office, a consumers cooperative, and a court. Every May a bazaar was held in Grossliebental which was attended by all the neighboring villagers.

A Catholic colony, **Kleinliebental**, was founded on the Klein-Akerscha River in 1804, by settlers from the Bavarian Palatinate and from Alsace, or at least settlers who had gathered in Alsace for the journey to Russia.

The favorite rallying places for the emigrants before they departed Germany were at Weissenburg in Alsace and at Karlsruhe in Baden. Both were often listed in the records as points of origin for colonists.

In 1805, the Protestant colony of **Alexanderhilf** was founded on the Baraboi River. The difficulties the first colonists encountered are demonstrated by the fate of the Alexanderhilf colonists who were immigrants from Württemberg and Hungary. Here in 1804, during the three-month period of October, November, and December, 366 people died. In the years 1805-1806, the entire colony with the exception of only a few people, perished. From 1807-1817, and as late as 1825, the empty land claims in Alexanderhilf were resettled by new colonists.

In 1805, **Neuberg** was founded by Protestants from Württemberg. Here, too, death and disease struck, and only twenty-nine of sixty-five families, mostly artisans who had planned to farm, survived.

The Catholic colony of **Josefstal** was founded in 1804 by immigrants who had departed from Alsace. This colony was established in a desolate and bleak area near the Baraboi River. Tree high shrubs, burreeds, and other plants grew on both banks of the Baraboi so that access to the river could only be gained with great difficulty. Wolves, foxes, jackals, and snakes flourished in the area. The Turks had called this area *Burjuboin* which means 'wolf's throat'.

Another Catholic colony, **Mariental,** was founded in 1804 by colonists from Alsace, Baden, Württemberg, and Switzerland.

The colonists who in 1805 founded Protestant **Peterstal** were all Protestants from Hungary.

Hungary at this time was part of the Austro-Hungarian Empire. One can assume that the immigrants from Hungary were ethnic Protestant Germans and Austrians. The Catholic Empress of Austria expelled all non-Catholics, causing Protestants to move eastward to new lands.

The village **Franzfeld** was first settled in 1805-1809 by colonists from the Hungarian towns of Temeswar and Kula. These people later settled in the surrounding Evangelical colonies which made room for new settlers from Alsace and the Rhine Palatinate who were Catholic, thus Franzfeld became a Catholic colony.

An unusual position was enjoyed by the town of **Lustdorf**, founded in 1805 by Württembergers, who were for the most part artisans not interested in agriculture. Lustdorf therefore became a *Kur und Badeort* 'a spa and resort community'. This Protestant colony was noted for its handicrafts. A streetcar connected it with neighboring Odessa.

Freudental founded in 1806, was Protestant. The colonists all came from Hungary, but they came individually unlike the large groups of colonists traveling together from Germany.

In 1828, a daughter colony, **Neu-Freudental** was founded.

> **(2) Glückstal Region.** Glückstal Region consisted of all Protestant colonies. The majority of the colonists were Lutherans from Württemberg. The history of this region can be traced back to the early settlement of the Odessa Territory. Beginning in 1804, families from Württemberg had begun to emigrate to the Armenian town of Grigeriopol close to the Dnjestr River. In 1805, sixty-seven Württemberg families came there, and in 1806, nine German families from Poland joined them, followed in 1807, by twenty-four families who arrived from Hungary. Grigeriopol had been designated for settlement, and it was intended that the settlers blend in with the Armenians already living there. It soon turned out that this plan was not achievable. Duke Richelieu, the Governor of the Odessa Territory, decided to settle the Germans in the Moldavian village of Glinnoi. The Moldavians were taken from Glinnoi and placed in the German homes in Grigoriopol. In this way the first German village in the Glückstal Region, also named Glückstal, was established by 100 German families in 1809.

The village of **Glückstal** had been laid out irregularly by the Moldavians. The huts of clay or earth were narrow and uncomfortable. The Germans planned the area for homes and farms. They soon replaced the huts with homes built of brick. Since the land of the Glückstal Region was very uneven, the colonies were hilly and often had to be laid out unevenly because of it. Glückstal was allocated 20,393 acres of land. The settlers of this colony added to their land by purchase of another 9,315 acres. In 1914 the population was 1,830.

In 1808, some of the German immigrants who also came to

Grigoriopol in 1805, founded the village of **Bergdorf** along with 68 families from Württemberg. Bergdorf was located in the 'Black Valley' or *Schwarzen Tal*. It was a mountain valley with many trees that gave it its appearance and its name. Because of its location between mountains, it was so secluded that a traveler did not discover it until he was directly before it. Bergdorf was the most progressive settlement, culturally and economically, even though it was not as wealthy as Glückstal and Neudorf. Bergdorf owned only the 11,132 acres of land allocated to it. The location of these villages sometimes controlled their size. The land was allocated as a large parcel and in some of the valleys, for instance, in the Black Valley the amount allocated was influenced by the mountains and rivers, which necessarily determined the size of the allocations.

Another village founded in the 'Black Valley', *Schwarzen Tal*, was **Neudorf**, established in 1809. Neudorf received 16,778 acres and bought another 2,505 acres. It was settled by 100 families, mostly from Württemberg and Alsace.

The colony of **Kassel** was founded in 1810, farther to the south. It was similar to the other colonies of its district. Daughter colonies such as **Krontal** and **Kleinbergdorf** were founded when there were too many young people, and the families did not want to break the properties down into little plots as had been done in Germany. Since the families were large, the plots would have had to become smaller and smaller. The colonists helped the small daughter colonies get started, and their own sons would start new farms there. The families benefited individually, and the colonies benefited corporately as the people became more prosperous. For example in 1867, settlers from the Glückstal colonies bought 1,685 acres of land from the crown and founded a small German village called **Krontal** in the far southern corner of the Odessa Territory near the village of Schibka. There were only eleven farms. A year later, settlers from the Glückstal colonies founded the village of **Kleinbergdorf** on a plateau near the town of Grigoriopol. The people of this colony aimed to be more progressive, and were more open to new developments. Farming was carried out with the newest equipment and the most up-to-date methods were employed. One can assume that these were probably children of farmers in the first settlements and that they benefited from their parents experience. Kleinbergdorf had 4,744 acres of land.

(3) Kutschurgan Region. The Kutschurgan is a small river which flows from north to south on the west side of the Dnjestr River and empties into the eleven-kilometer-long Kutschurgan Lake at the village of Baden. It is a *Schilfsee* which means 'the lake is not too deep and has many reeds growing in it'. These reeds were used in many places for roofs of houses. In this river valley four Catholic colonies were founded, all in 1808: **Strassburg, Baden, Selz**, and **Kandel**. Two other colonies were considered a part of the Kutschurgan region, **Mannheim** and **Elsass**, although they were located on another small river, the Baraboi River. Besides being suitable for regular farming, the low-lying land that was half sand was very good for orchards and vineyards. The disadvantage was that sand blown by storms could make large areas unfertile. This disadvantage was not considered during settlement because the main concern had been to place the four villages in a close and secure way so they could help each other in case of danger.

Strassburg settled predominantly by Catholics from Alsace was allocated 9,906 acres and purchased an additional 8,111 acres. In 1915 the population was 1,701.

Baden settled by 53 families, the majority coming from Baden in Germany. This community was allocated 10,055 acres and purchased 3,613 acres. It was noted for beautiful vineyards and for apricot, pear, apple, and cherry orchards. In 1915 there were 1,360 residents.

Selz settled by 100 families, ninety-five of them from lower (north) Alsace. They received 16,929 acres and purchased 13,219 acres. In 1915 there were 2,537 residents. The town of Selz was situated along the shore of the lake and therefore its streets were crooked, not straight as was the case in the other villages. This unusual picturesque town was a favorite for summer vacationers. Only half of the residents farmed land; the other half were artisans who were especially known throughout Russia for making wagons and farm tools such as pitchforks. Their blacksmiths were famous. A bazaar or market was held every two weeks. Twice a year on May 1 and October 8, a fair was held with many visitors attending. It was also the district seat of government and had the court of law.

Kandel, the fourth colony, was founded in 1808 by 98 families of whom 77 were Catholics from Alsace, 13 from Baden. The land allocated the community was 16,783 acres to which purchases added 8,980 acres. Twenty-five per cent of the residents were artisans, blacksmiths, and weavers. The rest were farmers and orchard growers. In 1915 there were 2,522 inhabitants.

The other Kutschurgan colonies on the Baraboi River, also founded in 1808, were settled by colonists who gathered at Lauingen on the Danube. They followed the Danube to Vienna and then took a more northerly overland route to their destination. **Mannheim** was settled by 26 families from Baden, 16 from Alsace, and eight from the Rhine Palatinate. They were joined at the border holding area at Radziwillow by ten German families from Poland. All of these were Catholics who banded together to found this community. They received 10,004 acres and their main occupations were farming, vineyards, and orchards. In 1915 there were 2,076 residents.

The settlement of **Elsass** began in 1808. This land had belonged to a large Russian estate whose owner was named Tscherbanko. For this reason the Russians always called Elsass, Tscherbanko. They were 36 families from Alsace and 21 from Baden plus a few others. They were mainly farmers. The colony was allocated 9,000 acres and purchased 40,500 acres. This large purchase was probably due in part to the availability of land from the Tscherbanko tract, plus the prosperity of this community. In 1915, there were 1,952 residents.

The colonists of the Kutschurgan Region founded two daughter colonies, **Georgental** in 1857 and **Johannestal** in 1864.

The colonies of the Kutschurgan Region were closed Catholic communities, and no Protestants lived there. These colonists left in great numbers for North Dakota when the emigration began.

(4) Beresan Region. The Beresan River is a *steppe* or 'prairie' river that had water only part of the year. The upper part of the river was dry in summer. The Beresan River originated in the colony of Waterloo and flowed south through Speyer, Landau and Sulz. Its valley was unusually productive and for that reason became thickly settled. Most of the German colonists who settled there came from the provinces of the Rhine River which had been devastated by Napoleon. The expeditions of colonists traveled by land from Germany via Bohemia, Silesia, Moravia, and Galizia to the border station of Radzwillow where they rested a month or so. The first column of immigrants arrived in the summer of 1809, and the second in the fall of 1809.

The Catholic colonies of **Speyer**, **Landau**, and **Sulz** were founded in the Beresan Valley. The Catholic colony of **Karlsruhe** was founded in the *Fuchsental* 'Valley of the Foxes' which was a side valley of the Beresan River. In the year 1818, the Catholic colony of **Katharinental** was also founded in the Valley of the Foxes. Catholic **Rastatt** and **München** were founded in the Tschitschekleja Valley.

The two Protestant colonies of **Rohrbach** and **Worms** were founded in another side valley called the Tilgul. In 1820, the Protestant colony of **Waterloo** was founded at the origin of the Beresan River, while the

Protestant colony of **Johannestal** was established in the Sosizka Valley of the small Sasik River. All of this area and its colonies were first a part of the Grossliebental Region, but in 1813 Beresan became the separate Beresan Region with its seat of government at Landau. The region then consisted of 150,111 acres.

Landau was founded in 1809 by Catholic colonists, 66 families from the Rhine Palatinate and 27 from Alsace. Landau had a central school, a girl's school, a hospital, a home for the poor, and an orphans fund. By 1900 Landau had 1,363 residents and owned 24,916 acres.

Sulz also founded in 1809, was primarily settled by Catholics from the Bavarian Palatinate. They were mainly artisans who developed into first-rate farmers. To the 11,885 acres of land allocated to the community, they purchased and added another 108,000 acres of land. The population of Sulz was 1,837.

Speyer was another settlement founded by Catholic colonists in 1809. It was settled by 68 families from the Rhine Palatinate, 23 from Alsace, 10 from the Bavarian Palatinate, 22 from Pirmasens, nine from Baden-Rastatt and two from Bruchsal. They had gathered in Russia from all over southern and southwestern Germany and had been assigned here. They owned 21,319 acres, and had 1,895 residents.

Catholic **Karlsruhe**, in the Valley of the Foxes, was founded in 1810 by 42 families from Baden and 26 from the Bavarian Palatinate. After suffering difficulties at the beginning, Karlsruhe developed into one of the prettiest and richest colonies and even had a men's college and preparatory high school. It received 14,715 acres of land and purchased another 135,000 acres. The town had 1,932 residents.

Between 1817 and 1819 another Catholic colony **Katharinental** was also established in the Valley of the Foxes. It received 15,703 acres of land and had 1,400 residents. The establishment of this community was influenced by Karlsruhe, and the families included 34 from Baden and 17 from the Bavarian Palatinate.

The colonists of Catholic **Rastatt**, founded in 1810, settled in the Tschitschekleja Valley because the Beresan Valley was already settled. These families were from Baden, Alsace and Rhine Palatinate. They owned the original 14,656 acres and had 3,691 residents.

München was founded in the same year as Rastatt, also in the Tschitschekleja Valley, by Catholics from the same areas of Germany. These two colonies had a problem with their water supply. München's location was worse, not only was water a constant problem but in 1825 all cattle died in an epidemic. A total crop loss in 1834 reduced the colony to a penniless state, and in 1838 it was struck by an earthquake. The town owned only the original 7,938 acres allocated and had a population of 1,928. These two colonies in the Tschitschekleja Valley did not experience the good fortune of those in the Fox Valley.

The Protestant colony of **Rohrbach** was established in 1809, the original families being mainly from Baden and Alsace. In 1813, 22 families from Prussian Poland joined them; and in 1817 an additional 16 families from Baden were settled in the community. They had received 23,026 acres, purchased another 4,428 acres, and rented 24,300 acres more. Besides farming they also had large vineyards. Rohrbach had 2,300 residents, but many colonists later moved on when the area of Bessarabia was opened to settlement.

The Protestant community of **Worms** was established in the Zeirgol Valley in 1810. The colonists were from Alsace, Baden and elsewhere in southwestern Germany. They were allocated 10,479 acres of land to which they added by purchasing 15,660 acres more. There were 2,180 residents. The most important institution for the teaching of the deaf at the time, was established in Worms.

The Protestant colony of **Johannestal** was established in the Sosizka Valley of the Sasik River in 1820. It was named 'Johannes Valley', *Johannestal,* in honor of General Insawo whose first name was Iwan, or Johannes in German. The colonists were mainly from Württemberg, primarily Lutherans, with a few members of the Reformed Church. In 1833 the village was moved a few *werst* (3,500 feet in a straight line is a *werst*), to the south because there was not enough water. The community owned 11,245 acres of land and had 1,216 residents. Besides farming they had fisheries that were enclosed by four dams they erected on the river.

The Protestant town of **Waterloo** was settled twice, once in 1819 and again in 1833. Originally in 1819, the colony of **Waterloo** was located eight *werst* to the south of the colony of **Friedrichstal**, and 4 *werst* from the colony of **Stuttgart**. All three had the same problem: no water. They asked the Russian authorities for permission to combine and found a new settlement. They were granted land at **Güldendorf** near Odessa and moved there. Twenty families decided to stay behind. In 1833 they were joined by new families and together they reestablished the community of **Waterloo**. During times of severe water shortage, they had to get their water from **Speyer** which was seven *werst* from Waterloo. They also built cisterns to hold rain water, a method later commonly used by the pioneers on the prairies of Dakota. Most of the colonists in Waterloo were from Württemberg, with a few families from neighboring Baden. The community received 7,454 acres of land, added by purchase 3,456 acres; population 645.

2.2.2 Bessarabia. Bessarabia was not a part of the Black Sea Colonies, but it had a close relationship with these settlements. Not only was Bessarabia located just across the Dnjester River to the west of the Black Sea Colonies, but it was also settled by sons and daughters of people in the Black Sea Colonies, along with a new immigrant wave. Bessarabians were involved in great numbers in the migration from the Black Sea Colonies to America, particularly to the Dakotas. I have not gone into detail about the villages in Bessarabia. All the information on them is contained in a recent book published by the *Landsmannschaft* of Bessarabian Germans, an organization of former colonists who now live in the Federal Republic of Germany. I gave more detail on the Black Sea Colonies because they were the original villages and the original settlements and thus give the flavor for the entire region which includes Bessarabia. Anyone wanting to know more about the German colonies and the unique culture that existed in the land of Bessarabia, can read about it in the book, *Heimatbuch der Bessarabiendeutschen* (Kern 1976).

> Bounded by the Dnjester River on the east, the Pruth River on the west, the Danube River and the Black Sea on the south, a border country throughout its history, Bessarabia became a part of the province of Moldavia in the 14th century when Moldavia became a principality with native rulers. Moldavia reached its height under Stephen the Great, but after his death in 1504 it came under Turkish rule. In a new war with Turkey, which lasted from 1806 to 1812, Imperial Russian troops were able to occupy Bessarabia and the Danube provinces of Moldavia and Wallachia. The peace treaty of May 1812 ceded Bessarabia to Russia (Walsh 1958:169).

The Russian defeat of Napoleon after his attack on Moscow in 1812 proved to be a disaster for the French Emperor. After dominating Europe he had to withdraw and would never again be a threat to the Russian Empire. The Czar could now turn to the settlement of the land won from the Turks.

The invitation to settle in Russia extended by Alexander I was more generous than that extended before by Catherine who had first conceived the idea. In his Edict of 29 November 1813, the Czar invited settlers to southern Bessarabia which then was almost an empty land. His *Manifesto* offered so much that hardly anyone, particularly if he was suffering in his homeland, could refuse such an opportunity for himself and his family. The reasons for leaving their homes given by the people who came to Bessarabia were the same as the reasons given by those who came to the Black Sea Colonies. They did not own their own land, they suffered from wars that went across their farms and destroyed their crops and threatened their ability to survive, they were afraid of paying for more wars and of serving in the armies, and they felt suppressed by the official churches.

Alexander's *Manifesto* stated:
(1) The Russian government gives colonists of the Duchy of Warsaw her special protection and promises them all the rights and conveniences that native Russians enjoy.
(2) From all colonists we expect that they give priority to working toward the improvement of agriculture, horticulture, wine growing, and silk culture.
(3) They will be free from regular taxes and from real estate taxes for 10 years, except for small payments to be made to their Bessarabian landlords.
(4) Poor families will receive 270 rubles from the Crown which do not have to be paid back for 10 years, and others will receive as much as they need to settle there.
(5) Each family will receive 60 *desyatina* (2.7 acres is 1 *desyatina*) of land for personal ownership which is inheritable by their children.
(6) All families that do not have food to eat will receive 5 *kopekes* (1 *kopeke* is 1/100 of 1 *ruble*) sustenance money for each member of the family beginning with the day of their arrival in Russia and ending with the first harvest.
(7) Immigrants and all their generations to follow are now and forever free from being recruited into the military, and they do not have to house or feed military personnel except when troops are marching through their area.
(8) Colonists are free to build the churches their religions require, retain pastors, and to follow their own religious practices.
(9) After the end of the first ten years, colonists will have 10 years to pay back monies borrowed from the government.
(Mutschall 1934:11-12, Kern 1976:10-11).

The people who accepted this invitation of Czar Alexander I to settle on his lands, made their way there in wagons pulled by oxen, or on foot. They found much hardship both along the way and when they arrived. Some of the most serious problems were the communicable diseases exchanged between the arrivals and the local inhabitants. They were often placed in houses together. Communicable diseases were a problem in America too, but never to the degree endured by the early German settlers in Russia.

The settlers began building their own houses when good weather arrived. Here again, the Russian government was active with help even in supplying the wood. By contrast, in Dakota the settlers found no shelter, no trees, and thus no wood and no fuel. One has to reflect to get the full impact of the lack of wood for shelter and for fuel.

In the Black Sea Colonies and Bessarabia the settlers lived together in little villages and farmed their land from the community, while in Dakota, the pioneers lived in isolation, but on their own land.

The similarities were many, the high *Steppengrass* like the high 'prairie grasses', lack of water in places, the use of cisterns to collect rain water, the making of sod bricks, and the vast open expanses.

Western Poland had come under the rule of Prussia in 1795. German settlers had been encouraged to move into Poland, and they had come from north Germany, Prussia, Mecklenburg, Pomerania and from south Germany, Württemberg, Bavaria, and Baden. They had hoped to escape the war and unrest brought to their homes by Napoleon. The Napoleonic War caught up with them again and changed everything when Napoleon defeated Prussia, and gave her Polish provinces into the power of the Polish nobility who had no love for the Germans. When Napoleon invaded Russia in 1812 his armies destroyed crops, confiscated cattle, and interfered with all aspects of a normal existence. Inhabitants were ready to leave, and the Czar's Edict of 1813 was welcomed by them. He even mentioned the people in Poland. More than 1,500 families left for Bessarabia in 1814 and 1815. There were so many that some families had to spend as many as two years living with the Moldavian peasants before the authorities could settle them on their own land (Mutschall 1934:10). The emigration from Poland continued on a small scale for several years.

The first twelve colonies in Bessarabia were settled between 1814 and 1816, mainly by Lutherans. These twelve settlements were named for the battles in the Napoleonic wars, where the Germans and Russians had fought together against the French.

The colonies did not receive the names of battles at their founding. For example in the fall of 1813, 100 families arrived in Bessarabia. Only fifty homes were available, the rest were settled for the winter in the villages of the native Moldavians. In the summer of 1814, houses were built in a colony named **Elizabeth**. It was surrounded by *Steppengras*, there were no trees, and the weather was extreme. This village was then renamed **Tarutino** in 1818, four years after the founding of the colony. It was to commemorate the victory by the Russians over Napoleon at Tarutino on October 18, 1812. Mutschall believes this renaming of the villages was done in connection with a visit by Czar Alexander I to Bessarabia (Mutschell 1934:14).

Following are the German settlements in Bessarabia, listed according to their date of settlement. There is no breakdown by region as was done with the Black Sea colonies, since none existed. The colonists usually settled in a village in which their dialect was spoken. Except for Catholic **Krasna** and Separatist **Hoffnungstal**, all the colonies were Lutheran.

Borodino   (founded 1814)
Tarutino   (founded 1814)
Klöstitz   (founded 1815)
Kulm   (founded 1815)
Leipzig   (founded 1815)
Malojaroslawetz, also called **Wittenberg**   (founded 1815)
Krasna   (founded 1815)
Beresina   (founded 1816)
Arzis   (founded 1816)
Brienne   (founded 1816)
Fere-Champenoise, also called **Alt-Elft**   (founded 1816)
Paris   (founded 1816)

Tarutino became the seat of the *Deutscher Volksrat* 'the Parliament' of all the German settlers in Bessarabia. Here they would make laws for themselves and deal as a united front with the Russian and later the Roumanian (an earlier spelling of Romania), governments.

Kulm and **Leipzig** were unusual in that they were known to have settlers with the north German dialect known as Plattdeutsch.

The main emigration to Bessarabia starting in 1817 and was from Germany itself. Württemberg in particular, sent great numbers of immigrants to Bessarabia. These were joined by settlers from the Black Sea Colonies. In fact the people of Bessarabia and the Black Sea Colonies mixed freely back and forth across the Dnjester River. They were all Germans and basically spoke the same language.

The next twelve colonies established in Bessarabia were:

Teplitz   (founded 1818)
Katzbach   (founded 1822)
Sarata   (founded 1822)
Malojaroslawetz II, also called **Posttal /Alt Postal** (founded 1823)
Neu-Arzis   (founded 1825)
Neu-Fere-Champenoise, also called **Neu Elft** (founded 1825)
Gnadental   (founded 1830)
Friedenstal   (founded 1833)
Lichtental   (founded 1834)

Dennewitz (founded 1834)
Plotzk (founded 1838)
Hoffnungstal (founded 1842)

Hoffnungstal was founded by settlers from the Hoffnungstal district, which was a small area 100 *wersts* (kilometers) northwest of Odessa. Far from the other German Protestants of the Black Sea region, it remained an isolated community, separated by more than distance from the other Protestants, who were mostly Lutherans. The people of Hoffnungstal were Separatists, Protestants who had separated from the Lutheran Church. They were also Swabians from Württemberg. They had received 11,610 acres from the crown in 1818 when the colony was founded. In 1822 they were given another 23,203 acres by the government. All the Separatists were encouraged to settle in this area and give up their plans of religious settlements elsewhere in the realm. Thus in the end there were five settlements:

Hoffnungstal (founded 1818)
Neu-Hoffnungstal (founded 1822)
Neuhoffnung (founded 1822)
Rosenfeld (founded 1822)
Neu-Stuttgart (founded 1831)

According to Mutschall, Separatism eventually died out, but it had lasted for 100 years. In 1934 there were 24 Separatists left in Bessarabia (Mutschall 1934:57).

In the Akkermann district of southern Bessarabia, *Liebentaler*, people from the Grossliebental Region of the Black Sea area, founded two settlements, **Sophiental** and **Chabolat**, with predominantly German and French Swiss colonists. Swiss immigrants, most of whom were French-speaking, also founded the town of **Chabeau** near Akkermann in 1822. They became famous for their vineyards.

Akkermann was a principal city and an economic center in Bessarabia. It was also the location of the university which made it an important center culturally. Akkermann was often mentioned by the Dakota Germans as being a center for them in Bessarabia. Although Kishinev was the capital of Bessarabia (today the capital of Moldavia), most of the German colonies were located to the south of Kishinev.

By 1842 there were twenty-five colonist settlements in Bessarabia, about 10,000 people having settled on 370,000 acres of land between 1814 and 1842. It was a large and fertile area with room for growth. By 1861, it had a population of 33,000, and during the 1860s expansion began anew. Land holdings increased, and 80 daughter colonies were founded. Settlement and the founding of new colonies continued in Bessarabia to the end of the century (Kern 1976:1-21).

In 1859, after the Crimean war (1854-56), the two Danubian principalities of Wallachia and Moldavia united and became the basis for the Romanian nation state. In 1918 after World War I, the allied treaties gave Bessarabia to Romania. In 1940, it was taken again militarily, by Russia.

Ewald Riethmüller (interviewed 1981) reported:

> Many nationalities lived in Bessarabia, the Moldavians themselves, Turks, Bulgarians, Russians, Jews, and Germans. They lived in their own villages but were friendly to each other, enjoying the diversity of their land. In times of crop failure the different nationalities would help each other with loans of grain or share jobs working in the fields during harvest. They would share some of the grain as payment for work. People often came to the Germans asking how they managed their crops and farms.

Catherine and Alexander's plans for development of their country worked. The memories of our pioneers were happy ones. Even the Germans who returned to Germany and were interviewed there, and who had lived through all the hardships of 20th century Russian history, had fond memories of their homes and life in Bessarabia.

2.2.3 Forces behind a new migration to the Dakotas. As the Black Sea Colonies were being established, economic and social changes were taking place throughout Europe that were to have a direct effect on the colonists' future. The growing unrest in the years prior to 1848, and the coming of the industrial revolution brought social changes of great significance. A wealthy class of manufacturers, traders, and financiers was emerging, a new and powerful upper class that could threaten the privileges of the nobility (Flenley 1959:164).

The year of the European Revolution in 1848, was a key point in the history of Europe. The revolution greatly disturbed Czar Nicholas I, who had come to the throne in 1825 and now saw the system in which he had placed his trust being swept away. His impulse for direct and personal intervention against the French revolutionaries was only dampened by the state of the Russian treasury that made any significant action impossible (Walsh 1958:214). The Decemberist uprising in which certain secret societies in Russia mutinied against his regime, and a Polish insurrection, in which Polish insurgents attacked Russian troops stationed in Warsaw, produced serious conflicts in the mind of the Czar. These were subsequently to color his attitude in all questions of policy.

On the one hand he reluctantly realized the necessity for fundamental changes, and on the other he feared that any attempt at reform would lead to a new and perhaps major revolutionary upheaval. In spite of his misgivings concerning reform measures, the Czar's Chancery, an agency which gradually extended its authority over a wide range of responsibilities, succeeded in instituting a number of reform measures, the most outstanding being a codification of laws.

A law of 1842 had provided for the emancipation of the serfs by a voluntary agreement with their masters. Although the law's publication created a stir as a forerunner of emancipation, it was actually rarely used and proved to be inconsequential. (Florinsky 1964:270-275).

Alexander II who came to the throne in 1855, was like Nicholas I aware of the inequities and dangers in conditions in Russia. His belief in the necessity of what came to be known as the Great Reforms was strengthened by Russia's defeat in the Crimean War waged 1854-1856 against France and Great Britian. Incessant peasant unrest and the need for bolstering and modernizing the economy demanded the abolition of serfdom, which was finally achieved on February 19, 1861 (Florinsky 1964:301-308). This great reform only indirectly affected the German colonists; but it set the stage for the future, when Czar Alexander III would begin the russification measures designed to assimilate the colonists into the new Russian peasantry.

The reform under Alexander II which was to have the greatest effect on the status of the German colonists, was the institution of universal conscription in 1874. The condition of the Russian army in the mid-nineteenth century was poor. The burden of "service" which lasted for a period of twenty-five years, was borne exclusively by the lower classes. The nobility, the merchants who paid a special tax, and the German colonists who were exempt by virtue of the decree of Alexander I in 1804, were not obligated to serve in the military. The army reforms shortened the term of service, decreed a more humanized discipline, improved the living conditions of the troops, and modernized the equipment. However, the most basic reform and one that had the greatest impact in altering the conditions of service was the universal conscription law. By virtue of this law, military service became a personal obligation of every male, regardless of social status (Florinsky 1964:301-308). Included in this sweeping change were the previously exempt German colonists.

Although the enactment of the new universal conscription law in

1874, was a move in the direction of social equality, the German colonists felt that they had been betrayed by the government. Military service previously had been optional for them. In the event of war they were required only to house and feed the soldiers in the vicinity of the colony, and if horses or wagons were conscripted the owners received compensation at the end of the conflict.

The Germans who had settled in Russia had a long tradition of anti-militarism. All the other agreements made to them by Catherine the Great and Alexander I had one by one been broken or revoked. The lifting of special privileges had first occurred in 1834 when the colonists had become regular Russian citizens. Then a decree issued in 1871 repealed the provisions regarding the colonists' control of local government. Freedom from military service was the last essential privilege that served to distinguish them, and enabled them to provide for themselves and their families the better life which they had sought.

The war with Turkey that began on April 12, 1877, and ended in 1878, was the first war in which the colonists were involved after the universal conscription law, the draft, was declared in 1874.
(See 2.3.2.1 for an oral history of this war with Turkey.)

In 1881, Czar Alexander III ascended to the throne. Both he and his Danish wife were anti-German. From the beginning of his reign russification of the German colonists received official attention and support. In 1892 all schools, including the colonists' schools, were placed under the control of the government. The German schools, having been private, had resisted the use of Russian as the language of instruction. Now only religion and the German language could be taught in German.   Local government interference had increased.

Those colonists who had felt that they would not always be tolerated as Germans in Russia, that they would be absorbed into the Russian culture, had been proven right. Those who did not want to give up the independence they had, realized the time had come for them to begin another migration in search of freedom from oppression.

2.2.4 The Germans who stayed in Russia. According to Stumpp (1954:14) it has been estimated that in 1938 there were still a million and a half German colonists in Russia, more than the number in the various settlements in the United States (400,000), South America (407,000), Canada (200,000) and Mexico (30,000). What happened to the colonists who did not leave Russia?

The Russian Revolution of 1917 completely changed their way of life. Despite the Revolution, the German farmers remained on their farms until the Civil War in Russia from 1918 to 1920. It was the end of prosperity and independence for the farmer. In 1921-1922 a massive crop failure led to widespread famine and the organization of farms into collective units was halted. Farmers were again allowed to cultivate their own plots of land. But under Stalin in 1928-29 collective farming was firmly established. In 1932-1933 the most rigorous pressure was used to bring individual farmers into the collective farm units. The result was a great famine during a good harvest year. Millions died, including about 350,000 Germans.

Persecution of the Germans was inevitable, and during the years 1936-1938 the leaders and intellectuals were destroyed and many of the men were taken away. By 1940, one-third of the German families were left without a father (Stumpp 1966:32-34). The two pillars of German culture in Russia, the church and the school, were gone forever. When Russia lost Bessarabia in 1918, the 80,000 Germans living there became citizens of Romania. During this period, the settlers heard of the suffering of their families and friends in the Black Sea colonies in Russia, and felt fortunate to be a part of Romania. In 1940, Stalin retook Bessarabia.

The story of Bessarabia is a bitter one. On 23 August 1939, the German Foreign Minister von Ribbentrop and the Soviet People's Commissar for Foreign Affairs Molotov signed a friendship and nonaggression pact on behalf of Hitler and Stalin. (See Appendix for the Treaty of Nonaggression between Germany and the Union of Soviet Socialist Republics with Secret Additional Protocol.) This political event was an attempt by each of them to neutralize the other while they carried on their acquisition of countries and territories.

The special secret agreement or protocol added to the treaty between the two countries did not become known until the Nürnberg trial in 1946. It was the agreement whereby Russia and Germany divided Poland even before the German Army attacked Poland. It also gave Stalin Bessarabia. It did so by stating and recognizing Russia's interests in Bessarabia, while at the same time Germany declared her complete political disinterest. The protocol also provided that Finland, Estonia, and Latvia would be in the Russian sphere of interest and Lithuania in the German sphere (Weinberg: 1954:46-49).

An important part of the nonaggression pact was that there was no provision that the pact would become inoperative if one of the parties attacked a third country. The intentions of the two countries were clear. Germany attacked Poland, and therefore England declared war on Germany on September 3, 1939, beginning World War II. During June and July 1940, the Soviet Union took over the Baltic countries. On 28 July 1940, the Soviet Red Army occupied Bessarabia and northern

Bukovina, which used to belong to the Austrian Empire.

Hitler and Stalin agreed that the 93,000 Germans then living in Bessarabia should return to the German Reich. Every German family was forced to leave all it owned and take part in a mass movement west, settling temporarily in Austria. The men were forced into the German Army, and the next year the older men, the women and children were sent to Poland to work in the fields   (See 2.3.2.2).

In 1941, the Soviet Union was invaded by Hitler's armies. Many German colonists were moved to the far eastern "hunger steppes". However, west of the Urals and beyond the Urals, where in 1918 there were five hundred German villages, the Volga Germans, there was no effort at deportation. Except for those dispersed before the outbreak of the war, no Germans living between the Dnjepr and Dnjestr rivers, the Black Sea Germans, were deported. When the German army retreated from Russia in 1945, many of the Germans moved westward. Of the 350,000 who managed to reach Germany, 250,000 were recaptured by the Soviets (condoned by the Allies as they were considered Soviet citizens) and sent to Siberia. Of the remaining 100,000 about 25,000 to 30,000 emigrated to other countries and 70,000 to 75,000 stayed in Germany (Stumpp 1966:35).

At the close of World War II, the Bessarabians like The Black Sea and other ethnic German people, returned as refugees to the same area in southern Germany from which their forefathers had emigrated. The former province of Bessarabia, is today the independent country of Moldavia. Moldavia which is on the west side of the Dnjester River, includes a strip of land along the east side of the river. This area is controlled by Russia and called Transnistria (also known as Transdniester). Transnistria was the previous location of Black Sea Colonies. The entire beautiful area of Bessarabia and the Black Sea Colonies is still known for its fertile black earth, gently rolling lowlands and good climate, with long warm summers, mild winters, and moderate rainfall.   The villages still exist, but the German settlers are gone, and that part of their history is forever gone.

On December 13, 1955, amnesty was granted to the Germans still in Russia. The official 1959 census of the Soviet Union found that 1,619,000 Germans still lived in Russia (Stumpp 1966:36). No Germans were allowed to live in the former Black Sea or Volga Colonies, but many of those in Siberia moved to the Asian steppes, where they established themselves once again. According to the 1979 census, there were still 1.9 million people who regarded themselves as Germans living in the Soviet Union. This makes them, in terms of population, fourteenth in the list of 118 Soviet peoples. However, there are no

German schools, nor are there any German parishes. The few German newspapers that remain and German lessons here and there contribute little to preserve their language, religion, and culture.

With their colonies dissolved, their churches and schools abolished, the Germans in the Soviet Union have little to sustain them. New Soviet encyclopedias made no mention of German colonization in Russia, an indication that this whole aspect of German and Russian history was officially obliterated.

In 1989 under Gorbachev, and the new openness in the Soviet Union, official recognition of ethnic minorities like the Germans was again allowed. Emigration of Germans from the Soviet Union to the Federal Republic of Germany, termed the *Aussiedler,* was permitted. In 1989 alone, 93,134 German *Aussiedler* arrived in Germany.

2.3 America: Dakota Territory, the call of the empty lands. The call of the empty lands seemed an ideal solution to the problems of the German colonists in Russia. They had the opportunity to own their land, be free of the military draft, practice their religion as they wished, and could retain their language and customs as they had done over their long stay in Russia. They also saw and grasped the historic opportunity of self-determination, the opportunity to be not only the governed, but the government itself.

The following description of Dakota Territory is so carefully and precisely written that I could not improve upon it. Here is the Dakota Territory as described by author and poet Nina Farley Wishek (1941:1-5), who arrived in 1887 to teach school and stayed.

...an unknown country, a stretch of land, a small part of a great whole,
 which lay for ages swept by beating winds and seared by heat and
 drought in the summer suns, or covered by a blanket of snow, frozen
 and silent through long winters. Here were strange prehistoric
 animals, a distinctly different vegetation, and an aboriginal
 people...While centuries rolled away this wild region lay waiting for
 that day when the beating waves of a mighty civilization would roll
 over and across it, developing its fertile soil, creating homes and
 cities, and developing an empire. Then grew the sage brush, blue
 grass, buffalo and bunch grass, and the delicate prairie flowers of our
 present day, covered by an infinite brooding silence...When the very
 earliest explorers began their adventurous trek into the West, they
 necessarily followed the streams as the best means of transportation,
 and so Dakota's early story is closely linked with lakes and rivers,
 such as the Red River of the north, the Missouri and its many tribu-
 taries, the Sheyenne, Mouse, and others. But this particular small

stretch of land of which I wish to write about was not in the path of these early exploring expeditions, it lay too far inland and remote from a large body of water to be connected with the first history...it seemed simply a means to an end, a distance to be traversed in order to reach some other destination usually along the Missouri River. No one thought to tarry here except perhaps to camp overnight or rest and drink at some lake or spring...The present State of North Dakota, together with that of South Dakota, was a part of the territory purchased from France in 1803 by President Thomas Jefferson for the sum of $15,000,000, and the assumption of certain claims held by citizens of the United States against France. This made the purchase, known as the Louisiana Purchase, amount to $27,267,621.98. Strictly speaking only that region drained by the Missouri and its branches was a part of the original Louisiana Purchase, and the Red River drainage area belonged to Canada until 1818, when the present northern boundary of the forty-ninth parallel was fixed by a treaty with Great Britain. In 1804 the Missouri River region of North Dakota was included in the District of Louisiana, which name was changed the following year to Louisiana Territory...The first bills in Congress at Washington regarding Dakota Territory were considered in 1859. The bill for its admission as a territory was passed on February 15, 1861...When first created, Dakota Territory extended from the Red River Valley and the western boundary of Minnesota to the eastern boundaries of Washington and Oregon...during a period of twenty-one years from 1861 to 1882 Dakota Territory underwent several changes in boundaries, and it was not until 1882 that it was reduced to the area now occupied by the two states of North and South Dakota. After Dakota Territory was admitted in 1861, David Jayne of Springfield, Illinois, a friend of Abraham Lincoln, was appointed governor by the martyr president. Other officials were appointed from various eastern states. The first Territorial Congress was elected September 16, 1861, and the first Legislative Session was held at Yankton, March 17 to May 16, 1862. The first land office was established at Vermillion, and the first filings on North Dakota lands were made at that office on July 30, 1861. The Territorial Legislature of 1871 asked Congress for a division of the Territory...An affirmative vote on the question of dividing Dakota Territory into two states finally occurred at the general election in 1887.

North Dakota and South Dakota were admitted to statehood in 1889. They were among the last ten states to enter the Union. The name, Dakota, is taken from the Sioux Indian language and quite eloquently means, `an alliance of friends'.

2.3.1 The immigration of the Germans to the Dakotas

from Russia and their general pattern of settlement. As early as the 1860s some of the young men in the Black Sea German colonies were being encouraged by their elders to make a trip to faraway America and to report back on the conditions there. It was not until two decades later, however, that this dream became a movement. By 1880 many young men had undertaken the arduous journey, traveling by train to North German ports, by ship to America, and then again by train westward across the United States of America to the Dakota Territory. They reported to families and friends at home in Russia that the new territory had land that was free and of almost unlimited availability. The country was as wide as the horizons, almost completely uninhabited, the soil was rich and black (Baudler 1963:8).

The promise of free or inexpensive land of unlimited availability and of such fertility that a large capital investment was not necessary for a new start, was a powerful attraction for the Black Sea German colonists, as it was for all of the agricultural population of Europe. During the 19th century this attraction was to have an enormous impact on the settling of America, as massive waves of immigrants flocked to the newly opened West.

For the Germans from Russia, as for many others, the desire for religious and political freedom, the absence of restrictions upon the development of society, and freedom from military conscription were of great importance in their decision to migrate to America. They left their homes in Russia in groups of twos and fours, of tens and twenties, of families and communities. The exodus began in earnest in the 1880s and went on into the 20th century (Baudler 1963:8).

Along with that of the other major groups of Germans in Russia, the Black Sea German migration accelerated as news of opportunities in the new country spread from colony to colony.

In 1862 Congress passed the famous Homestead Act that gave every man or woman 160 acres of public land for the price of the filing fee, approximately ten dollars. To insure that the land went to actual settlers it provided that the owner must reside on or cultivate the land for five years. An additional 160 acres could be added through a tree claim which meant the settler had to plant rows of trees, called "shelter belts" or "wind breaks". A third portion of 160 acres could be obtained by filing what is called a "preemption claim". This meant that the settler could buy a third portion of 160 acres at the price of $1.25 per acre. Thus each settler could have a 480 acre farm. In point of fact, many who followed from Russia after the first farms were established had to transfer one of the possible 160 acre portions to the relative who brought them from Russia to Dakota. (See Appendices for the complete text of the Homestead Act and for the complete text of the law providing for the planting of trees on the western prairie.)

For many years after the Homestead Act of 1862 the Great Plains resisted settlement. Farmers were unwilling to venture into this great ocean of grass, into this wholly new environment. Few streams ran all year round, and underground water was 30 to 300 feet down. The American pioneer was used to digging 10 to 20 feet into the ground. He was a woods dweller, dependent on trees for fuel, buildings, and fences. On the plains trees were found only in the bottom lands near rivers and even there, they were very sparse. These conditions discouraged settlers (Bragdon & McCutchen 1973). Germans arriving from Russia had seen the steppes become fruitful after their settlements were established. They had dealt with the problems before, although, as they learned later, no one would have ever imagined the ruggedness of this land and the weather conditions which prevailed over these great prairie expanses that prehistorically had been a great glacial ice-field; and which had never before been settled or tilled.

The following quote from writer John R. Milton, substantiates the oral stories of the pioneers about the difficulty of taming this wild land, and it gives an interesting historical perspective.

> The history of the United States is, in a real sense, the history of the frontier. For two-and-a-half centuries that sometimes elusive line between "civilization" and the wilderness moved westward across the continent. At the six locations identified by Frederick Jackson Turner the line was pronounced in varying degrees. In the seventeenth century the natural barrier was the "Fall line", the highest point of navigation on the eastern coastal rivers. A century later it was the Allegheny Mountains. Settlement then progressed rather steadily through the forest lands which now constitute the Midwest until reaching the Mississippi River early in the nineteenth century. By the middle of the nineteenth century the noticeable frontier line was at the Missouri River where its direction is approximately north and south. The fifth line, some twenty-five years later, is the one which most directly affected South Dakota. This line could not be seen as easily as the others, but it came close to paralleling the upper Missouri. Its importance lay in its definition: the line of arid lands. That line if drawn on a map today, would descend through Jamestown, North Dakota; Aberdeen, South Dakota; and Grand Island, Nebraska; and the middle of Kansas. West of this line the rainfall was, and still is, markedly lower than to the east of the line. From here to the Rocky Mountains which was the sixth and final frontier line late in the nineteenth century, lay that Great American Desert mentioned in early reports such as the one by Major Stephen

Long, what today we call the Great Plains. This was long considered the least desirable of all the western lands and was, in truth, the last frontier. Frederick Jackson Turner considered the frontier closed in 1890...(Milton 1977:82)

The line drawn by Turner from Jamestown, North Dakota, descending down through Aberdeen, South Dakota, is the general Central Dakota area under study here.

The railroads advertised to bring people to settle the vast expanses, and to use the trains for transportation of people, and the grains and goods they would produce. Many people believed the picture they presented, and headed west. As one family approached their claim, they remembered some of the railroad advertising.

"The traveler sees with delight the flowering meadow of unimagined fertility stretching out to the faraway horizon, grasses watered by numerous streams near whose banks grow abundant stands of trees." What they found was bleakness, emptiness, darkness falling like a shroud on frightening infinity. The night was filled with the yipping and whining of coyotes. In the morning they found a sense of freedom and the smell of fresh grass, a warm and bright sun, virgin soil under their feet, and nothing but the people themselves to cast a shadow (Milton 1977:86).

The settlement of Dakota Territory followed the rail spurs. Wherever the railroad stopped a community sprang up and settlers poured from the trains into the community and from there out onto the open prairie. The major emigration into the Great Plains began around 1870 when settlers began arriving in Yankton in the southern part of the Territory, where the railroad terminated at that time. The first to arrive were the Volga Germans and the Mennonites who in the 1870s settled primarily in Kansas and Nebraska, spreading into Colorado. The Black Sea Germans began arriving in Yankton in 1873.

The sources used for the following information on settlements were personal interviews and knowledge gained from visits to the different areas, as well as an article by Richard Sallet published in 1931 in the *German-American Historical Review*. All written sources which I reviewed on the settlements of the Black Sea Germans and the Bessarabians, always made reference to this article. By contrast, I was careful not to rely solely on what is basically one man's writing and one article. My own investigations did, however, show Sallet to be a very good source.

The names of the four districts of the Black Sea colonies are given to help locate the origin of the American settlers. When reading the names of the communities it is best not to expect German names. They were generally named by the railroad officials and the politicians, and they often named the counties and the communities after themselves.

Protestants from the Beresan Region, the communities of Rohrbach, Worms, and Johannestal, established homesteads in the area to the north of Yankton in 1873. One group of these Beresan Protestants settled in Sutton, Nebraska, which soon became a major early German settlement. Some later moved on to help establish another major settlement in St. Francis, Kansas.

Bessarabian Protestants began arriving and settled at Russell, Kansas, in 1878, developing another major settlement. Russian Germans moved on into Colorado and Oklahoma, and as far south as Wichita Falls, Texas.

Bessarabian Protestants established homesteads at Parkston in Hutchison County in 1878, and many Mennonites and some Hutterites (1874) settled in the Yankton area during this time. By 1880 most of the available homestead land in southern South Dakota was already settled, with the Germans arriving from Russia established in large numbers in Yankton, Bon Homme, Douglas, and particularly in Hutchison counties. As more and more of the Black Sea immigrants arrived, they found little available land. The Scandinavians too, had arrived in large numbers; with some moving west from Minnesota. They settled in the area to the north of Yankton.

Thus, by 1884, the new Black Sea German arrivals were pushing north from Yankton to Ipswich in Edmunds County, following the railroad which had by then been extended north to Ipswich. The immigration flow and the westward expansion of railroads paralleled each other. The biggest influx of immigrants began in 1884 when the rail terminus was at Ipswich. It reached its peak with the opening of the new rail terminal at Eureka in McPherson County, South Dakota, in 1887. Eureka lay in the heart of an area that was previously cut off and lay remote and undeveloped. This area which I have termed Central Dakota and which lies in the very center of the two Dakotas was not served by roads or rivers. The Old Forts Yates Trail crossed it, but people stayed on the Trail and kept moving on west. Thus the extension of the railroad to Eureka opened up this part of the Territory for settlement. This development coincided with the immigration of the Germans from the Black Sea colonies to the north of Odessa and the German colonies in Bessarabia to their west. Their emigration out of Russia was at its high point and they began arriving in this Central Dakota area by the thousands. Thus we find a historical situation which explains their settlement together in such large numbers and to such a degree, that the central area of the two Dakotas could become overwhelmingly German.

The Black Sea Germans spread from northern South Dakota across southern North Dakota and on into western and northern North Dakota. The settlements went into Canada; the Provinces of Manitoba, Alberta, and Saskatchewan were free and available for homesteading.

The state of North Dakota was to receive the largest number of Black Sea German immigrants to America. Settlements sprang up everywhere, with the former Black Sea colonists attempting to stay together, grouping by religion and regional identity. Thus the Beresan Region Catholics settled together west of the Missouri River in North Dakota, and the Kutschurgan Region Catholics east of the river and in the mid and northern half of North Dakota.

The largest concentration of any group of Germans from Russia were in an area covering south-central North Dakota and north-central South Dakota. These colonists were predominantly Lutheran. The majority were from the Glückstal Region of the Black Sea colonies. This also meant they were largely Swabians from the Württemberg area of Germany. The *Glückstaler* were joined by Lutheran and other Protestant groups from the Black Sea settlements in the Beresan and Grossliebental Regions, and by the Bessarabians who were, except for the Catholic village of Krasna, predominantly Lutheran. Bessarabians from Krasna along with Kutschurgan and Grossliebental Region Catholics also settled in the Central Dakota area as described below.

In 1884 in the Central Dakota area, colonists from the village of Glückstal in the Glückstal Region settled near Hosmer and Bowdle in Edmunds County and in Artas and Herreid in Campbell County, South Dakota. Neudorf villagers from the Glückstal Region settled in Eureka in McPherson County along with colonists from Hoffnungstal in Bessarabia. Bergdorf colonists from the same Glückstal Region settled at Leola and Long Lake in McPherson County, South Dakota.

In 1885, colonists from the Protestant towns of Worms and Rohrbach in the Beresan Region settled at Greenway, McPherson County, South Dakota, their settlements extending as far as Zeeland in North Dakota. By 1889, the year the Dakota Territory was divided into North and South Dakota, the South Dakota counties of McPherson, Campbell, and Edmunds were heavily settled by Black Sea Germans who comprised up to three-fourths of the population. The Black Sea Germans were also present in great numbers in Walworth and Corson counties, and to a lesser extent in Brown County, although Aberdeen in Brown County is today the major city for the Germans living near the North and South

Dakota border.

Eureka in McPherson County, South Dakota, had developed into a major commercial center because of the railroad that brought in the homesteaders and exported their wheat.

> Until into the 1890s Eureka, South Dakota, was the "Wheat Capital of the World", at the farthest end of the new Chicago, Milwaukee and St. Paul Railroad, it became the funnel into which the wheat fields of the Dakotas emptied. Into the prairie terminal came also trainload after trainload of Russian-German immigrants. ...So prosperous was the community of Eureka that 32 commission houses had agents there to buy in the grain crop. With 42 grain elevators handling 4,000,000 bushels a year, Eureka became the Milwaukee's most profitable station with earnings of $100,000 a month (Life Magazine 1937:15-24).

The Glückstal Region colonists moved into McIntosh County in North Dakota, settling first in the Jewell district of the county, which is near Ashley, North Dakota, and directly across the border from the Bergdorf district of McPherson County, South Dakota. They spread across the Ashley area to Wishek; and, as settlement increased, the *Glückstaler* settled Lehr in 1886. McIntosh County became more than three-fourths Black Sea German Protestants, predominantly Lutheran.

In 1886, Kulm in LaMoure County was settled by colonists from Kulm, Bessarabia. Linton in Emmons County was settled in 1889 by colonists from the Grossliebental Protestant town, Neu-Freudental. In 1890, Bessarabian Protestants settled in Fredonia and Gackle in Logan County and in Merricourt and Monango in Dickey County. *Glückstaler* from Kassel settled in Streeter in Stutsman County in 1891. Thus, eventually not only McIntosh County, but also Logan and Emmons County were nearly three-fourths Black Sea German Protestants. The counties of Dickey, LaMoure, Stutsman, and Mercer of North Dakota were each half Black Sea German Protestant.

The Germans from Russia spread north and eventually covered most of North Dakota. Black Sea Protestants had settled at Carrington in Foster County in 1884. By 1896, they were settling at Medina and Windsor in Stutsman County, at Underwood, Washburn, and Garrison in McLean County, in McCluskey and Goodrich in Sheridan County. These settlers were predominantly from the Beresan Region Protestant colonies. The settlement of North Dakota contined.

A few of the Beresan Protestants also settled on the west side of the Missouri River. Colonists from Johannestal settled in Hebron in Morton

County in 1885, while colonists from Worms settled in New Salem in Morton County in 1887. In 1886, Bessarabian Protestants from Leipzig settled New Leipzig in Grant County. The west side of the Missouri was to become the home of the Catholic Black Sea colonists from the Beresan colonies. Catholic Black Sea colonists had began arriving in 1885, somewhat later than the Protestants. The Catholics wanted to stay in their own communities as they had in Russia and in Germany before that. In 1885, Glen Ullin in Morton County was settled by colonists from Speyer. From here the Catholic colonists spread out, settling as far east as Mandan and as far west as Glendive, Montana. Beresan Catholic colonists from Speyer settled in Mott in Hettinger County in 1888. In 1891, colonists from Karlsruhe, Landau and Speyer settled in Richardton in Stark County, while other Beresan Catholics settled in Dickinson in Stark County.

Many more settlements followed and this entire region west of the Missouri was filled in a few years. The majority of the settlers were the Black Sea Catholics from the Beresan Region, who comprised more than half of the population in Morton and Stark Counties and almost half in Hettinger County. These Beresan Catholics came mainly from Speyer, Landau, and Karlsruhe. The Catholics of the Beresan Region came originally from the Rhine provinces of Germany.

Catholics from the Kutschurgan Region of Russia arrived in Ipswich in 1885. They were joined by Catholics from the community of Kleinliebental of the Grossliebental Region of Russia who first settled in Aberdeen, Brown County, South Dakota. Both of these groups then settled in Westport, Barnard, and Frederick in Brown County, thereby forming the only major Catholic settlement in north central South Dakota. Catholics from the Kutschurgan Region also settled in south central North Dakota, forming the only major Catholic settlements there. From 1885 until 1889 they settled in a line from Zeeland in McIntosh County, extending to Hague and Strasburg in Emmons County and to Napoleon in Logan County and Steele in Kidder County. These colonists from Mannheim, Selz and Alsace of the Kutschurgan Region were joined by other Black Sea Catholics. Catholics from Strassburg of the Kutschurgan Region settled Strasburg in 1889; Catholics from Krasna, the only Catholic colony in Bessarabia, settled south of Strasburg; even Catholics from Zürichtal in the Crimea settled in Hague in 1885.

The Kutschurgan colonists moved north and settled in northern North Dakota where they were the dominant Catholic group. In 1892, *Kutschurganer* started settling at Harvey in Wells County. Colonists from Selz, Kandel, and Mannheim in the Kutschurgan also moved north and settled at Orrin, Balta, and Rugby in Pierce County by 1898. Joined by the Catholic *Liebentaler* colonists, the Kutschurgan Catholics settled in Towner and Karlsruhe in McHenry County and Devils Lake in Ramsey County. But it was in Pierce County that Kutschurgan Catholics colonists settled in the greatest numbers.

Many young Black Sea Germans moved on into eastern Montana into McCone, Prairie, Richland, and Dawson Counties. They went there because the land was cheaper; but many returned home to central Dakota after having lost their money with poor crops in a region less fertile than the Dakotas.

From 1904-1910 a large number of Russian Germans migrated from the Dakotas into Canada when the Canadians encouraged settlement with the promise of more homestead land. Saskatchewan drew the largest number of settlers. From there many of the Germans moved on into the western provinces of Canada. These hard working farmers already had capital to invest along with their labor, and thus they helped to establish farming as a viable economic enterprise in the Canadian provinces in which they settled.

Not only did the Germans from Russia settle in the Dakota Territory, Nebraska, and Kansas, and spread into Colorado, Oklahoma, and Texas, they also established settlements in Montana, Idaho, Washington and California. Many settlers moved on from their original stake in the Plains states to the fertile valleys of the state of Washington. By 1890 they were already settling at Odessa, Ritzville, Ralston, Ruff, Lind, Warden, and Marengo, and in Yakima, Tacoma, Walla Walla, Olympia, and Bremerton, Washington.

Lodi, California, became a popular place for Black Sea Germans as long ago as 1897, and remained the most popular city for further migration. Most movement took place during the economic depression of the thirties when many farmers had to give up their land to pay their taxes. They headed west to join their friends and relatives in Lodi.

Today Lodi is the place for vacation or retirement for the Dakota Germans of the older generations, while it still offers opportunity for younger people. When attending church on Sunday in Lodi, it is said that a German from Dakota is apt to find themselves sitting not only next to a fellow Dakota German, but more than likely next to a former neighbor from the Dakotas. The church remains the center of their lives.

In America, the Germans who immigrated from Russia have achieved beyond their expectations the freedom and prosperity they sought. In achieving their dream, they in turn, contributed in a major way to the development of the American West.

2.3.2 The remembered past. What is the "remembered past" of these immigrants? It is the personal perspective on written history. The remembered past or the personal recollections of these historical events has been divided into two sections. The first section (2.3.2.1) reflects the interviews with some of these early pioneers and records their recollections of their life in Russia and their emigration to the United States. The second section (2.3.2.2) reflects pioneer life in the Dakotas as it is remembered by people up to the time of the last interviews in 1987. This is the remembered past to which a Dakotan of today will still relate.

From the many personal interviews I have chosen the following to present places and events which are part of what we call history, but which express it in a personal way, confirming the written histories of the periods.

The materials presented in the remembered past in 2.3.2.1 are my oldest sources, obtained in the early 60's in McIntosh and McPherson Counties with a special purpose. The interviews were conducted only with old pioneers who had actually been born in Russia, and who had come to the United States as adults. At that time I was trying to establish who these people originally were. Their history had not been investigated and the invaluable information I gained from these many interviews was used during a year of research in Germany, following which I wrote my Master of Arts Thesis (Arends 1966).

The most recent information which confirms not only their history but my whole cultural collection is the research which has been done by the Landesmuseum in Stuttgart, Germany. In celebration of the 125 year existence of the Württemberg State Museum, a retrospect of the Napoleonic period in South and Southwest Germany was presented at the museum during 1987. The three volumes covering this exhibition and the collection presented at the museum, are an incredible window into the period of German history which this topic covers.

Migration from Germany to Russia was clearly due to Napoleon's efforts to control the King of Württemberg, who was elevated to this noble height by Napoleon himself after he won dominance over Southwest Germany. Taxes had to be increased, men drafted into the army, and the government's control extended ever deeper into the lives of the people. The King even tried to extend his might over the State Church. The Landesmuseum exhibition covered all facets of the cultural life of the people of that time. The same topics, such as folk medicine and remedies, folk music, literature, and religion; and the same group of people from the same area, and from the same era, are the subject of this book.

My visit to the museum's exhibition in July 1987, and the three printed volumes (*Baden und Württemberg im Zeitalter Napoleons,* 1987) of this exhibition confirmed the value of the materials I collected for this research. It also confirmed a change of viewpoint that I had been undergoing. In Arends (1966) I established they were neither Russians nor Germans, but Germans from Russia, with their own unique culture; and they were not Volga Germans, as they were generally known at that time, but a different group of Germans who had settled in western Russia to the north and west of the Black Sea, rather than in eastern Russia along the Volga River. I have now come to the conclusion that what sets them apart is not the fact that they lived in Russia, as the influence of Russian culture is minimal; nor the fact that they are Black Sea rather than Volga Germans. What makes them unique is the fact that throughout both their Russian and their American experience, they have retained the culture, language, and values of late 18th century Southwest Germany. I have been steadily collecting cultural materials and conducting interviews since 1961 and have found, in examining my data, and in comparing them to the museum collection, that the Central Dakota German culture presents a beautifully preserved relic, a view into a picture of another time.

My cultural collection and language collection along with the Landesmuseum collection show them to be German with incredibly little Russian influence on their language or culture. At first the distinction may not seem that important, but it is significant because there are such misconceptions about them and their existence. It is precisely that little credit is given to these German pioneers for having been a major influence in the settlement of the Great American Plains.

Statistics and their analysis vary according to the interpretation a historian chooses to use. People who arrived at Ellis Island were not asked whether they were native German speakers. Rather they were asked, "where did you come from", and the answer was of course, Russia. Yet, they were not "Russian". They immigrated by way of a long stay in Russia, spanning a period of less than 100 years. They were and are German and they played a major role in the history of the settlement of the American West.

During the German-American celebration of the 300 years of Germans in America, the Germans from Russia were ignored, even though the Germans of the Great Plains constitute one of the largest German settlements in America. Speak with any German national or post World War II German immigrant, they are astounded that there are Germans living in the Dakotas. The contribution made by these German pioneers should not be overlooked by historians.

2.3.2.1 The remembered past of the years in Russia and the immigration to the United States. The personal and family histories of the Germans who migrated from Russia to settle the plains of the Dakota Territory are filled with adversity and disappointment, but reflect an enduring faith and an unshaken hope in the future of their country. They relate reminiscences in the Dakota German dialect. I find that these early interviews provide unique insights since they were with pioneers who were born in Russia and immigrated to the United States as adults.

The oldest living pioneer in the Dakotas in the early 1960s—and certainly one of the best known in both North and South Dakota—was Christian Fischer.

Christian Fischer (interviewed 1961), an officer in the Czar's army, was well-educated, articulate, full of stories. He remained alert and healthy until his death in 1963 at the age of 101. The account he gave of his family history was in many ways representative of reminiscences shared with me by other pioneers. His personal story encompasses the history of these people, and their migration. His information is historically accurate. He was also able to articulate a personal view of the history of the times.

> Johannes Fischer was born in Württemberg in 1832, and in that same year his father, Johannes Fischer, for whom he had been named, took the whole family by horse and wagon along the Danube River to the Bergdorf Colony in Southern Russia (See 2.2.1 for Bergdorf). Included in the family group was the grandfather, himself named Johannes Fischer, who had been born in 1760. The young Johannes Fischer who had been taken as an infant to Russia with his parents and grandfather in 1832, fathered three children: Johannes born in 1860, Christian born in 1862, and Jacob born in 1870. Christian emigrated to the Dakota Territory in 1889 and Johannes and Jacob followed in 1902, bringing their father Johannes with them, one of the only pioneers who had been both in the migration from Germany to Russia and then in the migration from Russia to America. Taken to Russia as an infant, he came to South Dakota as a grandfather following his children and grandchildren to the new land, just as his grandfather had done with him when he went from Germany to Russia.

The cultural continuity of this family is a good example of the nature of their stay in Russia. There was no break in continuity as we see it expressed in the retention of the language and customs of the Dakota Germans.

An old custom of those times was the continued use of the same name by the first born in the family. Here, the eldest child in the family was always named Johannes, and each succeeding generation maintained the name. It was important to know who your family was and your identity was carried by your family.

The Fischer family moved to Russia because of the promise of free land; sixty *desyatina* of good farm land had been promised to each head of the family. Since one *desyatina* was 2.7 'acres', this gave 160 acres to each family. Commissions had been set up by the Russian government to help the German settlers, and the immigrants received what had been promised them. The land proved to be very good for farming, and they had no problem borrowing money at the bank in Odessa. They were able to add thousands of acres to their holdings by buying from the Russian nobility who owned vast tracts of land.

Although the Germans were given very good land, and other inducements to stay in Russia in order to "serve as examples for the Russian peasant", the peasants did not have the means to emulate the models provided for them. Poor beyond belief, with at most five acres of land, they could not obtain credit so they could not buy any land. The Russian peasants lived on *welschkorn* `plain corn', and *mamalek* `bread' which is a form of bread made with primitive hand mills. Their methods of farming were as primitive as their food. They seeded the land by carrying grain in a wooden box and throwing it about as they walked. They were illiterate because their villages did not have schools. Their opportunities for development were very limited.

In 1872, when Christian was ten years old, a railroad linking Poland and Russia was built past his village. It was such an attraction that the young people would walk seven miles to the tracks just to see the trains.

The Germans had their own schools, and Christian attended school from age six through fifteen, as did all the children in the village. School work included religious instruction, reading, writing, and arithmetic. Christian did not regret that he had not studied more subjects. His education had served him well throughout his long life. Both at school and at home the children learned respect for authority and good manners.

By 1880, the Russian government had recognized the value of the education provided by the German schools, and in 1882 required that the Russian language be added to the German schools. This did not please the colonists who were concerned about retaining their own language, customs, and values; nor did they like the fact that all the German children had to be given a Russian name. They saw these actions as a threat to their culture and were more determined than ever to follow their own ways.

Christian's name in Russian became Johannovich since he was the son of Johannes. For Russian usage dictated that the name of the father designated all his sons. Nicholai Alexander II was Czar during this time, and although he did not like having a Russian name, Christian spoke well of the Czar. At the time the Fischer family settled in Russia, in the early 1830s, every Russian child over twelve had to spend four days a week working for a nobleman and two days for his own family. Czar Alexander freed the Russian people from this obligation and also from other forms of servitude.

The German colonists' villages were clean, and they prided themselves on their personal neatness as well as on the cleanliness of their homes and the orderliness of their village. Most of the people Christian knew were Swabian, Saxon, or Bavarian. He observed that as time passed the Germans became wealthy and bought more and more land. Ships from all over the world came into the port at Odessa to bring them foreign goods.

At that time borders were open, Germans and Russians could move back and forth across the borders at will. Even soldiers could leave the country and on Sundays would go on excursions. But when he was eighteen, the borders were closed.

Christian's experience as a young man in Russia was somewhat different from that of the average German pioneer who emigrated to the Dakotas, as most left Russia to avoid military conscription. Christian was drafted in 1883, at the age of twenty-one, and sent to military school for two years. At this time the relationship between Russia and Germany was cordial. Although the border between the two countries had been closed in 1880, this was because the Russians feared trouble with Turkey, not Germany.

In military school Christian was told that Germany and Russia were very good friends, and this was demonstrated when the German Kaiser came for a state visit. He was not only lavishly entertained but was also given his own platoon of guards, made up mainly of Russian German soldiers.

The German colonists had a reputation for scrupulous honesty and were welcome in military school. Christian was told by his commanding officer that the Germans were so honest one could leave his horse in the German village and it would not be taken. In Russian villages a horse could be expected to disappear in seconds. The Russian peasants were thought to be too unschooled to be trainable for military service. So limited had been their educational opportunities that they could only count days of the week; weeks, months, and years were concepts of time beyond their comprehension, Christian was told.

Many of the army officers were from foreign countries. They were welcomed in Russia and often retained their old rank. To serve, they only had to learn the Russian language, but many terms in the Russian military vocabulary were German. Subjects in the military school included Russian, military science, and, above all, mathematics. No one could graduate from the school until he could do all his calculations mentally, since a cannon could not be operated by an officer who could not calculate. The men were also taught how to make their own gunpowder. Christian had learned this so thoroughly that he said he could still make gunpowder in his kitchen if the need arose! The ingredients used included dirt, water, saltpeter, sulphur, and coal.

After graduating from military school, Christian served five years in the army. He was stationed at Fort Ochaknow on the Black Sea, a military compound which encompassed forty acres. Although he had a desk job most of the time, he did serve a six-month tour of duty in Turkey during the Turkish war of 1887-1888, a period he remembered vividly because it had been so terrible. Worst of all, it had taken three weeks to take the fort in which the Turkish General had taken refuge. Men and horses starved because they were too far away for supplies to get to them.

In the Turkish Campaign Christian had found out at first hand, as he said, that war is hell. There was unrest throughout the land, the treasuries were opened, all human and other resources of the country were committed to winning. War was a game of chess.

When Christian left the service, he held the rank of Captain. His uniform had a gold collar, gold bands, and three braids, the decorations of an officer of the Czar. It was a proud uniform that had given him status wherever he went since it showed he was a part of the officer corps.

When inspection came, Christian always did well. When asked what his name was he would reply *Fischer von Sachsen, wo die schöne Mädele wohnen* 'Fischer from Saxony, where the pretty girls live' even though he was from Württemberg. Christian even remembered his draft number, 108, and had a large picture of himself in uniform, with a saber at his belt, hanging in his living room.

After he left the military and returned home, Christian found that six boys from his village had gone to America in 1885. His best friend, Lemmle, was one of them. Up to this time, even the intelligentsia of Russia had known little about America, but around 1886 there was an awakening of interest in the United States. Christian was greatly impressed when on the train, a Russian noblewoman noted the letter from Lemmle he was reading and spoke to him, (which was most unusual), to ask if she could have the stamp from his letter from America.

The young men who had emigrated wrote home about the three quarters of land, 480 acres, to be had free in the Dakota Territory. In

January of 1889, Christian married Friederike Trefz. That same year they left for America. Christian had been given a passport that stipulated that in time of war he would have to return to Russia to train soldiers.

Christian said the prairie was different because it was an untamed place. The wind and storms were free to devastate across a thousand miles. The weather would rage, storms would take away houses and barns and the pioneers would just keep rebuilding. There were still huge chunks of ice on the land in May. In Russia they had stone houses, in America houses of sod and wood.

A vivid view of life in the Russian colonies emerges from stories Christian and other pioneers told. The German colonies usually consisted of less than a hundred families. The head of the family received about 160 acres of land, and in addition land could be rented or purchased from noblemen or from the crown. Villages settled by Germans were laid out in much the same way as they had been in Germany. Although the earliest immigrants to Russia at first lived in huts made of clay with roofs of reed, they eventually had houses of brick or stone and wood in their villages. Houses were spacious and comfortable. The ground floor was divided into several rooms; there was an upstairs and a roof of cane. Behind the house there were the barn, the granary, feedlots, a haystack, and strawstacks. Straw was placed on the floor of the barns to provide warmth for the cattle, calves, horses, pigs, and chickens. It was also put around buildings in the winter time. A village usually had several wells, but if water was easily found at a shallow depth, each family had its own well, dug by hand and lined with rock. The most prominent place in the colony was occupied by the church, and the school and courthouse were nearby. In the larger colonies there was also a market square.

The colonies were kept small, and when one became too large the mother colony would establish a new "daughter" colony on land acquired from the crown or from noblemen. Records were kept on each family in the colony, and these indicated how much property had been brought with them, how much land they received, to what religious faith they belonged, to whom they were married, the number of children in the family, in which house they lived, and what occupation the head of the house followed. German colonists who had become deeply indebted to the Russian government in order to get established became prosperous within a short span of time. A large part of the Russian Empire depended on the food produced by the German colonist, who was an early practitioner of diversified farming, raising horses, goats, sheep, hogs, cattle, and poultry, and planting wheat, oats, corn, barley, millet, and flax. They tended orchards, and harvested garden crops, nuts, fruit, and honey.

The settlers interviewed had different reasons for leaving Russia and coming to America, although those most often given were the desire for more land in a new country and a wish to escape military service. Some said they saw the coming of bad times, a time when they would be forcibly absorbed into the Russian population. These feelings were reinforced when, in 1882, they lost all their old privileges and the Russian language was to be taught in their schools. They felt an unease, a premonition that they would not always be tolerated as Germans in Russia.

Peter Haller (interviewed 1961) was born in Sophiental, in Bessarabia. His family Bible, seen in his home, contained much information: his father immigrated to America on January 29, 1884, and his mother on November 25, 1886, his grandfather had emigrated from Germany to Russia where he died a young man in his forties.

Peter said his grandfather had moved to Russia because Germany had become too overcrowded. The largest city near Sophiental was Akkermann (See 2.2.2 for Bessarabia), which Peter thought compared somewhat to Odessa. The German colonists in his area raised winter wheat, spring wheat, hard wheat, corn, and rye. Jewish merchants (Jewish merchants were also in Dakota, see 2.3.2.2) bought the grain at the farms and Moldavian peasants hauled it by wagon to the train depot in Akkermann. The sacked grain would be piled higher than the houses, waiting for the trains to transport it. Peter estimated that the farmers received eighty cents a bushel for winter wheat.

The *desyatina* `acres' owned by farmers were scattered. Each farmer owned a strip of land bordered on each side by a neighbor's land and then farther away they had another strip. The farmers had each been given land and some had purchased more land. As new land was purchased by the colony, each was allowed to buy an amount proportionate to what he already owned.

Peter Haller attended the German school, and at the age of twenty left for America to avoid the draft and, he confessed, for the adventure of the trip and life in a new land. Russian law stated that, as long as one brother was in the service, the others could stay home until the first was released. Peter traveled by way of Poland and Austria to Germany, where he left by ship from Bremerhaven. After twelve days at sea, he arrived at Philadelphia and continued by train to Eureka, South Dakota, where he was met by friends.

In 1919 he married Mary Heyd from rural Long Lake, South Dakota.

Mary Heyd (interviewed 1961) was born in 1898 in a small village that was a suburb of Akkermann (See 2.2.2 for Bessarabia). Each village had its own church and Mary lived in the Lutheran suburb. Each village also had a city hall and a school and Mary's village had three stores. The cattle were sold in Akkermann and most supplies bought there. Her whole family emigrated to America to avoid having her brothers conscripted. One of the brothers, who lived to be 100, had served for seven years in the personal guard of the Czar. Until his release from the military, the other brothers did not have to serve, as only one son was taken at a time, but they feared what would happen in the future.

The father of another pioneer, Heinrich Roth (interviewed 1961), had also been in the personal guard of the Czar, an honor accorded many of the young men from the German colonies.

The Czar trusted the German settlers. Heinrich Roth remembered there were great celebrations in honor of the Czars that sometimes lasted four to five days. Soldiers would ride through the towns and on one occasion, the lead officer's horse had been trained to bow to people.

Stories of the land and machinery for farming available in America had brought Katherine Linbig (interviewed 1961), born July 2, 1885, and her husband from New Kassel (See 2.2.1 for Kassel, Glückstal), in Russia to North Dakota in 1901. Katherine had lived in the colony of Old Kassel; but it had been flooded by a cloud burst, although there was no stream nearby. She remembered that the climate in Russia could be extreme at times, but generally the weather was very pleasant in the Black Sea Colonies, and there was fruit in abundance. When she and her husband arrived in New York they liked the many trees they saw; but when they got to the Dakotas, they were very disappointed by the hills and rocks and the lack of trees. She vividly remembered the hardships of the early years, and still expressed fear of a tornado that brought a wall of dirt which destroyed everything in its path.

Margaret Opp Hoffman Layer (interviewed 1961), born in 1881, came with her sister Friederike, and their father and mother to join their married sister Rosanne Retzer in 1905. Their father had been a shoemaker in the village of Glückstal (See 2.2.1). He had made high boots for men and very good women's shoes. The girls in the family all had lovely shoes made by their father; but if it rained or was muddy, they would take them off and carry them. The girls spoke

Moldavian and liked to stop and talk to them on market days.

The Moldavians appear often in the stories. They not only hauled the grain and provided transportation links, but they brought food and articles to the markets where the Germans would buy from them. They also had stands along the roads to the markets. As mentioned in 2.2.1 they were living in the area when the German villages were established. Most of the older pioneers spoke not only Russian, but also Moldavian. These Moldavians were like gypsies in the way they moved about and wore colorful dress. All the Germans liked them very much and felt they added to the good memories of their homes in Russia. The Moldavian language is a dialect of Romanian.

Margaret had interesting memories of Russia. She said that the girls had their ears pierced when they were about seven years old. She remembered that in Russia all the dwellings were painted white. A yellow house was a place of ill repute. They all lived in a village and worked on farms, and when their work was done they could work for a nobleman and earn more money. She and Friederike remembered a family story handed down from the days in Germany. The family had come under the rule of a Catholic prince (See 2.1) who had sent his soldiers to search all the houses for the family Bibles, since it was a Lutheran practice to have a Bible in each home. Her family put their Bible inside dough and baked it into a loaf of bread, and the soldiers left without finding it, even though they searched everywhere including in the well.

Mrs. Jacob Bertsch (interviewed 1961), born in 1884 in Neudorf (See 2.2.1 Neudorf, Glückstal) and her sister Mrs. John Wolf, born in 1883, came to America with their family in 1906. Their neighboring villages in Russia had been Bergdorf, Kassel, Glückstal, and Duman. Duman was a Jewish village, one of several in the Black Sea Colonies.

Mrs. John Kalo (interviewed 1961) was born in Borodina, Bessarabia (See 2.2.2) in 1882. She remembered that the city had suburbs populated by Germans, Moldavians, Russians, Turks, and other groups. All national groups had their own village or section of a city, and each area had its own church. In 1897 she and her family auctioned everything they owned except for a few personal belongings. They traveled to Hamburg, where they took a ship to New York, from there they traveled by train to Eureka, South Dakota. At Eureka, they put straw in a wagon they purchased, put their bundles on top and drove out into the empty prairie.

With the harshness of life on the prairie it is not surprising that many of the women remembered their life in the German colonies of Russia as idyllic.

Mrs. Rosina Riedlinger (interviewed 1961), known for her beautiful needlework, was born in Neusatz, Russia, in 1865. She came to America with her husband in 1885 because he wanted to escape military duty. He had been forced to serve three months every summer in the Russian army. Although they were forewarned about the poor conditions in the Dakotas, they felt they had no other choice but to emigrate. On her deathbed Rosina still spoke of her home in Russia with longing. In an interview in the McIntosh County Hospital in 1961 she recounted with great bitterness that the Black Sea colonies had a beautiful climate, fruit grew in abundance, and that there were as many grapes from the vines lying on the ground as there were rocks lying on the land in Dakota.

2.3.2.2 The remembered past as reflected in the oral history of "one who stayed behind in Russia". What happened to the German colonists who did not leave Russia? We have the written history, but what is the remembered past of one who lived through the turbulent times of change in Russia. During World War II the Germans in the old Black Sea colonies and in Bessarabia searched their old family Bibles and records looking for names of relatives who had moved to America. Often they used very incomplete addresses, which nevertheless found their way to relatives in Dakota; correspondence was desperately renewed as the Germans who had stayed behind looked for help. Letters would be brought from one town in Dakota to another where they knew that people of that name lived. Most letters no matter how vaguely addressed, found someone who, even though they were not related, wanted to help a brother. Many packages were sent from America to Germany, especially after World War II, to help these displaced people survive, and start life over again. In our kitchen in North Dakota there was always a large packing carton standing there waiting for family and friends to bring enough flour or coffee or sugar, and warm clothing to fill it. As soon as one box was filled, the money brought together for postage, and the box sent in the mail to one of the relatives; a second box was started. Each relative who wrote received boxes in turn as they were filled. Even years later, those who stayed behind say with tears in their eyes, that this simple way of giving kept them physically alive and gave them the faith to go on.

The following story is the oral history of Emil Bendewald

(interviewed 1962 in Germany). This is his story, the remembered past, of what happened to those who stayed behind.

Emil lived with his family in Bessarabia which was located between the Dnjestr and Prut rivers with its capital at Kishinev. After WWI Bessarabia belonged to Romania, but after 1939 was held by the Soviet Union. Bessarabia was a country with many settlers of many nationalities, and all got along well. The Romanians lived there, Bulgarians, Turks, Germans, and Moldavians (who as Emil states were a product of intermarriage between Italians and Romanians). The different nationalities had their own schools and churches. On July 28, 1940, the Soviet Union occupied Bessarabia. The German Reich's General Ribbentrop and the Russian General Molotov agreed that the Bessarabian Germans should leave (See 2.2.4). When asked who wanted to go, no one volunteered. None of the Germans wanted to leave their home. They had a certain amount of freedom and they liked it where they were. After the Russians occupied Romania they at first ignored the German population. Then they started holding meetings to explain the concept of Communism. They accused the rich of robbing the poor, and said that from now on everyone would own the land together. The situation worsened and the German farmers began to realize they had to leave.

On September 15, 1940, a German commission came to Bessarabia. They evaluated the land of the Germans and asked the Russians to pay the farmers for the land so they could reestablish themselves in Germany. The settlers still had their choice of leaving or staying. After having heard the new Communist theories they decided to leave, although they hated to leave what they considered their home. The women left on October 5, 1940, and the men followed on October 18, 1940. Ninety-two thousand Germans left Bessarabia headed for Germany. They got only as far as Austria where they were routed to Poland. Meanwhile, the Nazis took the land away from the Polish people and sent them to factories in Germany to work. The Germans were then resettled on the Polish farms. The farm work was left entirely to the women and children and all the men were drafted into the German army. The women lived in constant fear of the partisans who were trying to reclaim the land the Poles rightfully owned. The Germans from Russia had been duped into thinking that they were going home to settle on farms that they would be able to purchase in Germany.

On January 12, 1945, the Russians began their big WWII offensive. On January 18, 1945, the mass movement of the Germans fleeing Poland began. The front moved up and caught up with many of the women and children on foot. The Russians shot many and put the rest of them in cattle cars and shipped them to Siberia. Emil's family was able to make it into Germany. All of the Germans living in the east headed west. The men in the family who were drafted into the Wehrmacht also made it to the west. Emil Bendewald spent two years just searching for his family. He found them near Hannover, and they now live near there in Kreis Gifhorn.

The old German colonies are gone forever. Their inhabitants are in East and West Germany and in Siberia. They had tamed the steppes, they had cultivated the fields, drained the swamps, planted orchards and vineyards, helped fight Russia's economic battles, and now they could return from where they came. They left Russia as beggars and undesirables. After World War II there were still nearly two million Germans left in Russia, citizens who had sacrificed their property, their lives, for the country of their birth and had wanted to stay. They were disowned as aliens, jailed as revolutionists, and sent to concentration camps in Siberia as traitors (Baudler 1963:9).

2.3.2.3 The remembered past of the early years in Dakota. There was often a sense of loss among the pioneer women who had left their homes to come to a land that gave them only a life of hard labor under harsh conditions. Emigrants sold and auctioned everything they owned in Russia and took with them only a few bundles of personal belongings, including their bedding and seeds to plant. Most traveled by train to one of the North German ports and then by ship to America. Some remembered that, as they traveled through Germany (1880-1910), they were treated as Russians, encountering hostility from the people whose language and culture they had preserved for so many years in a strange land. Many remembered the voyage by ship to America as the worst experience of the long trip. Some came by sail, and the trip generally took from two to four weeks. After reaching America they boarded trains for the long trip west. Eureka was the end of the railroad line, and after reaching this point, the settlers traveled by oxen or horse and wagon or on foot to their claims.

The men would walk ahead, dressed in sheepskin coats, baggy breeches tucked into highboots, and hats, carrying sacks of seed wheat. The women followed wearing gathered skirts and loose blouses with gaily bordered head shawls loosely tied under their chins, carrying bulky bundles of pillows and feather beds (Brenemann 1936:15).

In spite of the large free grants of land, most of the immigrants expressed the deep feeling of disappointment they felt on first seeing the barren plains of the Dakota Territory. The land was covered with so many rocks that it seemed that rocks grew there. The rock piles are the most vivid memory for they remained there as monuments to the hardships. There were no trees, there was not a single tree to hold back the soil or the wind.

The same picture emerged from each person, no trees, endless prairie with nothing but a howling wind, and land covered with rocks. The wind, they said, was always in the grass. It personified the fact that there was no escape.

Pioneer life on the prairie was bleak, particularly for the women who had to work as hard as the men to establish the farms. The settlers had to clear the rocks from the fields before crops could be planted; and rock piles are to be seen everywhere even today, mute testimony to the labor of the pioneer men and women who cleared the land. It took settlers, whose wives could bear the hardships, to tame the great prairie. Disappointed as many women were in their new surroundings, difficult as life on the prairie was for the pioneer families, a willingness to work to the limits of human strength and to endure the hardships facing them, was all that made it possible even to survive. Many women died in the uneven battle.

The wild land and climate were unlike anything they had seen. The ferocity of the climate was what they remembered most about the early days. They told many stories of suffering from the elements. Rain and wind storms, penetrating cold, unbearable heat and drought, devastating prairie fires ignited by lightning consuming farms and homes, and their only constant, the wind which blew day and night, were all part of the new life on the great American prairie. Many had a hearing problem from the wind, and men grew deaf from its constant whine. Sore eyes were a continual problem. Swarms of flies made life miserable for man and animal, and grasshoppers devoured the crops. Mosquitoes thrived in a land with no water. Thunder and lightning storms were fearful as they lit the great expanse of sky.

The most feared were the blizzards and the tornadoes. Blizzards with fierce winds coming from every direction would punish them, freezing eyelashes, suffocating people caught in the blizzard winds. One step into a blizzard and you are lost to it. No one could ever tell when a blizzard would come raging across the prairie. Ropes were used in the winter to keep a link between the home and the barn. Snow drifts as high as mountains formed, and farms were completely buried in snow. It was a time of confinement. Yet, on a nice sunny day, the horses and sleighs would run on the vast and beautiful frozen sea of ice and snow, as they went to town for supplies.

Hail storms were and are a great menace. Hail usually comes in June and July. Hail can come in round pieces of ice or in just plain large chunks of ice, destroying an entire crop and the year's labor within minutes. It is the single greatest threat to the crops; but for the people themselves, tornadoes were and remain today the greatest threat. Almost everyone has been in one, and those who were in the tornado's storm can never forget the fear—it speaks to you from their eyes as well as from their lips. After a tornado sweeps across the land destroying homes and entire farms, it takes the prairie only a season to reclaim its own; and where once a family lived only the prairie grasses and the blowing wind remain.

Their first homes in America were not at all like the tidy brick or stone houses in the German colonies of Russia. Here they were made of sod blocks, closed with lime, and offered few of the comforts of home. The earth itself, from which the sod blocks were cut, was the only building material on the prairie. There were no trees, and where there are no trees there is no wood. Worse than a sod house were the first homes which were simply dug-outs built into the side of the hill which had a door and one window.

Life in a sod hut was difficult, trying to make a new sod house clean and livable seemed like an impossibility. It was very painful to be called a dirty Russian because you lived in a sod house and did not have anything but what you could make yourself. What a contrast from the stories of the clean villages and their ethnic identity as Germans while they lived in Russia. One way of making the best of things were the many evenings when they sat and visited, talking as they chewed sunflower seeds and spit them on the earthen floor of the sod house. The seeds were left on the floor overnight and in the morning the housewife would sweep the sunflower seed oil left in the spit and shells, across the earthen floor. Thus it helped to give the floor a hard surface which then became as clean and as hard as a wood floor; the whole house was cleaner and less dusty. The major problem with the first sod walls was that vermin lived in the earth; and as they crawled out of the sod they had to be killed, and a constant vigil was necessary. After the "bugs had been worked out" the sod house could be quite comfortable. Around 1908 they began adding wooden floors to the sod houses. The addition of a warm and clean floor made the sod house with its thick walls a very livable home.

The settlers not only did not have wood with which to build, they also did not have wood for heat and warmth. The first stoves were holes in the ground where a fire was built for heat and cooking. Fuel was straw or buffalo chips. The first sod shelters were combination dwelling and barn, for cattle were very important. The heat from the cattle helped to keep everyone warm in winter. Keeping warm in 40 to 50 degrees below zero with a wind chill factor of 100 is not an easy matter even today. Many people still freeze to death if they are caught outside when a blizzard hits and they can not find the warm shelter of a barn or a house.

March blizzards and snow storms were the most feared for you could be caught on a clear day in a sudden storm, with temperatures dropping rapidly. Cattle were blinded as their eyes froze shut from the wet snow and the freezing drop in temperature; confused they starved and died.

Tedious journeys covering fifty or sixty miles had to be made on foot or with oxen in order to bring in supplies. Buffalo bones were sold for about $4 a wagon load to pay for tools with which to work. Wood had to be dragged a hundred miles from the Missouri River. The women were left alone with the children for days while the men went for supplies. The men could be caught in a blizzard and return home only after many days, or never return. It was a life that took its toll. Many pioneer women died young; and the men, needing someone to care for the home and children, married again.

It seems impossible today to heat a house and survive a Dakota winter without fuel. The women remember the planning and work it took throughout the year to keep the family warm, clothed, and fed during the long winter. It was not uncommon to have huge chunks of ice on the land as late as May, and fuel was always uppermost in the minds of the settlers. In the summer, the family picked up all the buffalo and cow chips on the land, and these, along with straw, were used to heat the homes in the early pioneer years. Because the men worked from dawn to dusk in the fields, it was left to the women to get the cattle. They wore huge outdoor aprons and would fill them with dry cow chips from the pasture to take home to put in the box by the stove for cooking fires or to store them in a shed for winter use. One early pioneer, Christian Retzer, who like my father told me much about pioneer life, described the common method of making fuel from cow manure:

> The manure was piled into beds all winter long. In the spring the horses were used to tramp it down until it was very hard. It was dug up in square chunks and stacked in small pyramids to allow it to dry out. When it was dry, it was placed in large stacks; and in the fall it was put into a shed used only for the fuel supply. In the winter, it was brought in as needed and put into a box where it was hammered into smaller pieces that could be used. This fuel burned very well and for

a long time. Only cattle manure could be used as there was no odor in the house from it.

The kitchen cookstove was used not only for cooking and baking, but for heating the house and warming the irons for neatly ironed clothing. Water for all purposes was heated in a reservoir behind the stove. Coal for fuel only became available in later years, but many farmers could not afford it and continued to use the old fuel. They tried planting trees, but a tree could not get started because the soil was too dry and the prairie too hot. The days and evenings of the pioneer family were devoted to taking care of the work that had to be done. A typical day in a farm family started before dawn.

The wife would get up at four in the morning in the summer, at five in the winter time, and build a fire in the kitchen cookstove. She would start it with corncobs and then keep it going with cow or buffalo chips. She would start the coffee and then go out to the barn to join her husband, who had gotten up with her and gone out to start the chores. The husband would have the stalls cleaned and the cattle fed with hay and other feeds, ground barley or oats. The wife would milk the cows. She would feed her chickens, ducks, geese, and turkeys. The husband would be feeding the horses their hay and currying them. He would clean their part of the barn and feed the hogs and sheep. The children would join in the work and do whatever their age and strength would allow. The mother returned from the barn ahead of the rest to make the breakfast. Everyone else helped until each job was done so that the whole family could sit down at the breakfast table together, say their prayer of thanksgiving and eat their meal together as a family. After the breakfast the mother would help the children get ready for school and pack their school lunches, which usually consisted of homebaked bread and homemade butter, or syrup.

In the winter the children went to their school, usually several miles away. Schools had a barn for at least six horses. In cold weather, the children went to school in a buggy or, in snow, in the sled. In good weather the children walked as the horses were needed for the fields. The horse was a most important animal, and families were thought to be well off when they had horses.

The men cleaned out the barns, hauled manure away to use for fertilizer and heat, worked on the farm equipment, tended to their animals, and took care of the chores. Often they went out to trap weasel, muskrat, fox, and rabbit in order to sell their fur pelts. The women did the housework, washing clothes by hand with a washboard, baking bread, making butter, and cooking for the family. They knitted stockings, gloves, and hats with wool yarn. They sewed clothes for the family, using flannel for winter clothing and cotton for summer wear. They sewed all their own clothes including the many underskirts they wore under their long dresses and the aprons which they always wore over their dresses. One sees them on the old pictures always dressed in their good Sunday clothes with the men wearing long sleeved white shirts.

They made their own bedding with flannel, and filled it with goose and duck feathers. They sewed the sturdy white material from flour sacks from their large puchases of flour, into sheets. They took care of the many household chores—filling kerosene lanterns, keeping the cookstove going and a pot of tea or coffee brewing.

It would be getting dark when the children returned home from school. The family would sit down together at about five, pray, and eat their evening meal together. Afterwards the whole family worked at the chores that still had to be done; milking the cows, cleaning the barns, feeding the animals and poultry. Gathering the eggs was the job of the smallest. The work took several hours, and afterwards the children did their homework, the mother knitted or sewed, and the father did whatever needed to be done by him.

One pioneer (Pauline Warner, interviewed 1965) remembered how her parents and others she knew spent their evenings.

> The women would knit and the men would brush the wool until it would give strings to knit with. The father would use a brush with strong bristles, almost like a wire brush, and he would brush and brush the sheep wool until all at once it would give a string. They knit gloves, stockings, sweaters, and other clothes that they wore. Most of the older people had sheep to produce the wool.

In the summer, the children were home to help with the farm work, but the mother also had to work in the field. Even small babies went to the field, where they were put in the shade beside a hay stack or laid in the back of the heather box with the grain and taken along as the field was worked during harvest time. The mother would do her housework, wash clothes, make butter, bake bread, and do other chores at night. Even the large noon meal which had to be served to the hungry workers the next day, had to be prepared the night before. A farm mother never got to bed before midnight in the summer, and she began her work again at four in the morning.

The German women were strong and worked as hard as the men. They were aloof and stayed with their own people. Neither the men nor women married outside of the German community either in Russia or in the United States. In the 1940s change came to the Western settlements; not after World War I as had been the case with most Germans living in the United States. In these communities the changes occurred after World War II. The world came to them; and as they were drafted for the war and left to serve, they became more integrated and more a part of the mainstream of American life.

Many pioneers had stories of the Jewish businessmen of the prairies who for some had made the difference between survival and losing to the harsh life. Although they were not active in the grain business, they were the buyers of cattle, fur pelts, poultry, eggs, and all dairy products. They were the lawyers and professional people, and the trades people. They owned the stores that sold most of the items a pioneer needed to buy, and in addition, they often brought in kosher sausage, olives in barrels, pickled herring, smoked fish, yeast, halva, walnuts and peanuts. Special foods could be ordered and the older pioneer men often ordered tobacco leaves from Russia, which they enjoyed smoking.

The Jewish merchants bought the whole range of products the German pioneers wanted to sell, traveling to individual farms to buy fur pelts and cattle, and offering household items and medicinal products for sale. They were always invited to dinner and always accepted the invitations. The Jewish merchants in the communities extended credit to the farmers who did not have enough money to buy their groceries or have cream or eggs to barter.

Many of the farmers borrowed money from the Jewish businessmen when the banks would not lend to them. It was the only way many pioneers could borrow money since they had no collateral when they arrived. One pioneer in my own family, my grandfather Jacob Fischer, arrived too late to homestead and had no collateral for a bank loan. He and his wife, who had four children, worked for other farmers. One day he drove to Eureka, South Dakota, to see Joseph Bender, a Jewish merchant, to ask him for a loan to buy a farm of his own. Joe Bender gave him the money with only a verbal agreement that it be repaid as he could. Jacob bought a small farm in Greenway, South Dakota, with a sod hut for a home. He repaid the money, sold the farm and bought a larger place in McPherson County that had a wooden house for a family, now consisting of six sons. This was just one of the many stories the pioneers told about the assistance they had received from the Jewish merchants.

The communities of Ashley, North Dakota, in McIntosh County and Eureka, South Dakota, in McPherson County had the largest Jewish populations in the Territory and became major centers of commerce.

The Jewish Congregation in Ashley was very active and maintained one of two Jewish cemeteries in North Dakota. Although the Jewish synagogue in Ashley closed in the 1930s as the tradespeople moved away during the Depression, the names of the store owners and cattle buyers are still well known and remembered with warmth and affection. Every long conversation about the old days brings out a story of kindness and trust, although now only the cemetery remains as a reminder of the unique contribution Jewish businessmen made to the development of the American West.

As the pioneers established homes and farms on the vast and treeless prairies, they clung to the old ways of conduct and dress, many of which persisted into the late 1940s. The women wore dark long dresses, with numerous petticoats, a long apron, and a shawl or a bonnet. The second petticoat always had a pocket where the money was kept, presenting some problems when shopping. They wore high black leather shoes with buttons and loops and long black stockings. Their hair was braided and wrapped around their heads or pinned at the napes of their necks. They wore thin gold earrings in their pierced ears. The custom of piercing girls' ears at age seven had been discontinued in America, and many young American-born women felt their first freedom had been the right not to have pierced ears. The Russian-born women always wore shawls; an everyday shawl of black, a white shawl for bed, and a black embroidered fine shawl for Sundays were part of every woman's wardrobe. Larger heavy shawls had been a necessity when they lived in dugouts or sod homes.

Homes were sparsely furnished; the work was unrelenting. Diptheria and scarlet fever struck families and communities. And yet the memories of the hard times are lightened by the strong sense of family and community that was retained, and the simple pleasures of home and church life.

A mosaic of good memories emerges from the stories. The parents spoke Russian when they didn't want the children to understand them. If you received something new, it had to be worn to church first. They learned little poems and sayings, delighting in the sounds.

In the winter, when the windows were frozen and frost flowers formed, parents taught the children a rhyme:

Blume blühen auf fensterscheiben
sind sonst nirgends aufzutreiben
ja, ja, der winter der ist da.
ja, ja, der winter der ist da.

A favorite tongue twister which delighted children and adults was:

Hinter Heinnes Hannes haus
hängen hundert hasen aus
hundert hasen hingen aus
Hinter Heinnes Hannes haus.

Sometimes older children played tricks by grabbing a younger one's nose and demanding: *Was fressen Gänse?* `What do geese eat?' The answer was *Hafer und Schnee, lass mei Nase geh.* `Oats and snow, let my nose go.'

Many pioneers told of the mischief they as children got into when the parents left for a visit to a neighbor. During the winter they would head for the cream supply being stored for sale and take just enough to make ice cream. The treat would be made and eaten and the children sleeping when the parents returned home. Mothers could usually tell what had happened but would not mention the escapade to the fathers. One pioneer told about a time when he and his brothers made candy while they were home alone. Something went wrong; it was not edible, and so they fed it to the dog. When the parents returned, they found the dog could not open his mouth because his teeth were stuck together with the candy. The boys were punished, but this did not stop them from making goodies in the future. It was only one setback.

The young adults enjoyed the church activities and the barn dances and, above all, they liked to sing, both the religious songs and the "fun songs" learned from the American pioneers, *My Wild Irish Rose, Springtime in the Rockies,* and *The Red River Valley.* Songs of faithful sweethearts and broken hearts alternated with old German folksongs and religious songs. The young people often had parties at different homes where they would play games and sing songs. It was their way of dating and of meeting each other.

It was a hard life but not entirely bleak, for above all, they had the company of their neighbors who shared with them the bond of common memories, handed down from the pioneers to their children. The bond of common memories was strengthened by the Dakota German's love for company and for visiting. When they got together in the evenings they would always sing the old songs, and tell stories.

Storytelling is an art form known to all cultures. Their 'stories' were called *streichle,* and were accounts of adventure in which the hero usually got into some mischief to the amusement of the listeners.

Most families had company once a week during good weather and almost always on Sundays after church. Families drove for miles on

Sundays to go to their church or visit another church that was having a special service. Sundays, going to church and visiting with friends, evoked the most pleasant memories of the pioneer women.

Not only the parents visited neighboring farms, but the children did as well. They could only go away to visit other farms when the moon was full, otherwise it would be too dark to see and much too dangerous. No one wanted to carry a lamp because they were afraid of starting a prairie fire. They walked those miles between the farms and as one pioneer told me:

> *Mir sind wie kleine haifle glofe*
> /mir sin vi glaine haifle glofe/
> `We walked like little piles of people' moving along so tightly pressed together that we were one because we were so afraid of the coyotes who barked in the early evening and howled at night as we walked back home.

The coyotes were very much a part of prairie life, a continual presence, and a continual danger both for people and their animals.

In the Dakotas, although preserving their own culture, the Germans strove to become good citizens of this new land, their adopted country. On voting day they lined up in their buggies at the polling place long before it opened. They did not want to take a chance on not being able to vote. They were so grateful for a government that they themselves chose and of which they were a part. It was the first time they, as many other immigrants, had experienced self-government and the personal rights that come with it.

The Fourth of July was enthusiastically adopted as a holiday, with dances in the streets, new clothes, and fireworks. When dawn broke people were already underway headed to town in their buggies. That this was a most important event can be shown by the fact that one received a new summer dress just for the occasion. The young men worked hard to earn extra money which they were allowed to spend frivolously on this festive occasion.

As the decades passed, many of the settlers became prosperous, rising rapidly in influence, and owning increased material possessions. Most were farmers whose families had tilled the soil for generations, and who passed their frugal ways and love for the land on to their children. Historically conservative and cautious in dealings with those outside his own ethnic group, the Dakota German did not like to entrust his income from the sale of his produce to banks or speculators. He would rather lend his money to his neighbor or buy more land with it.

His honesty was proverbial. Money was loaned on verbal agreement with notes and mortgages unknown. Although inclined to excessive caution, the Dakota Germans were progressive. They were eager to try anything new that would enable them to improve their farming methods, increase crop yield, and expand their holdings. They pioneered in a number of ways, experimenting with cooperative insurance, real estate, building materials, markets, stores, creameries, oil, flour mills, and community granaries (Joachim 1939:14). Many "Yankee" inventions are said to be based on their ideas, including a special crop sieve and coffee mills that were patented by other Americans.

> The size of the family determined the need for land in the mind of the Dakota German farmer, and children were taught to value family achievements and their land. The father worked so that every son could have his own home and farm when he came of age. If a son was physically unable to undertake the strenuous labor required by farm work, he was schooled for a position for which he was fit. However, an able-bodied man who took a white-collar job was not considered as fortunate as those who worked the land with spade and plow.
> They enjoy nothing more than telling a visitor about their family and property. The farmer's eyes sparkle as he speaks of his land, his crops, his livestock. He cannot separate himself as a person from the land for which he has worked. Before he dies he wants to be able to pass it on to his children, all of it, tax-free and debt-free. He cannot bequeath it to his church, to his daughters, or to childless sons. The large holdings will go to the boys with a large family, to the heirs with his name. (Joachim 1939:17)

But all of the children, daughters included, will receive a fair and just piece of land from their father for their children. No one will be left without anything to show that they were members of a good family.

There are now wind breaks of trees called shelter belts to protect fields from blowing away, but the pain and suffering of the pioneer years and of the bad times in the thirties are still remembered. The modern day hard times began with the stock market crash in the fall of 1929 that triggered the great economic depression. The depression worsened, until by 1932 grain prices had fallen so low that a fair crop brought little or no income to the farmer. This was the year that wheat sold for 20 cents per bushel.

Then came the great drought of the 1930s. Year after year crops were seeded and they died. There was no feed for the cattle. There were seven years without rain, when there was no food and no way to earn a living.

It was in this period that the government as an economic measure, paid nominal prices for cattle. They then destroyed and buried them on the spot not allowing them to be used for food. It was a time to try the souls and the courage of the people. The dry earth gave up its top soil to the wind. No human effort could change nature.

Few could pay their taxes so many lost their farms and had to leave their homes to try to reestablish themselves elsewhere. There are many bitter stories about banks and foreclosures. The drought ended, World War II ended, and slowly prosperity returned.

Those who stayed now have modern farms producing the wheat that feeds much of America. But they too, still live with the hardships of the prairie, the constant possibility of seeing lives and crops destroyed by the fierce elements. There are still tornadoes, sudden blizzards, and hailstorms, and it is a rare family that has not experienced the loss of a year's work. Often grain prices were too low to support a family farm.

A recent note received from a county official in Leola, South Dakota, written on a scrap of paper and sent along with a receipt for payment of land taxes, expresses the dependence of the farmers on the weather and shows the incredible community spirit which pervades as "Ed" writes to me, someone he has never met but someone he knows belongs to Dakota through land and family. It is presented the way it was written which reminds one of Haiku poetry.

No Rain So Far
Blowing Dust
  to-day.
So far Seeding hasn't
  Started much
So it's Still Time.
but it sure don't Look good.

Although it didn't look good to the German immigrants from Russia in the 19th century, many of their descendants have seen the prairie yield a bounteous harvest in spite of hardships and setbacks.

I would like to end this chapter with the words of the poet and author Nina Farley Wishek, who arrived in Dakota Territory in 1887, and stayed to make her own contribution to the settlement of the American West, one of the great stories of human history.

> They were a brave, stout-hearted band. It took courage and tenacity of purpose to hold out through the vicissitudes of those hard years and found even this small part of our Great Northwestern Empire.

They fought the cold and storms with poor protection and shabby shelter; they battled prairie fires, hot winds and devastating droughts, when even their small pittance was often swept away by burning winds or fires. They lived through hard times, depressions, poor prices, and sacrifice was their daily bread. They toiled the years away with little mechanical help, and drove those weary miles to market with their little produce, to return with the bare necessities for their existence until another crop. But through all the hard times and deprivations there always hung a thread of mystery and romance in the shimmering atmosphere, along with the mirage in the quivering haze on the far horizon line (Wishek 1941:xi).

Chapter 3: The Central Dakota German Dialect

3.0 Introduction. This chapter presents a general description of the Central Dakota dialect of German (CDGer.). Although there have been descriptions published of the dialects of (1) the German-speaking Swiss Mennonites in southern South Dakota and Nebraska, the Amana Germans, and the German-speaking Hutterites (Rein 1977), (2) the German-speaking Hutterites (Obernberger 1980), (3) the Volga German dialects of Nebraska (Schach 1983 and 1985), (4) and even a description of single German dialects in Russia (Bond 1978), there exists, to date, no published overall description of the dialect of the Black Sea Germans who immigrated from Germany to Russia and then eventually settled in a compact group in the area in the center of the two states of North and South Dakota (for a more exact geographic description of their place of settlement and of their travels since their first emigration from Germany (See 2.2 and 2.3). This speech community I have called the Central Dakota Germans and their dialect, Central Dakota German (CDGer.). I am not attempting to reconstruct the dialect spoken by these Germans while they lived in the Black Sea area of Russia, specifically in the Territory of Odessa and in Bessarabia. Instead, I am presenting this dialect of German as I found it spoken in the Central Dakota area. Specifically, this investigation concentrates on McIntosh County, North Dakota, and McPherson County, South Dakota, the two counties in the center of this central Dakota area.

The German dialects of eastern and southeastern Europe were thoroughly investigated by German linguists and dialectologists, especially during the period after World War I. The best known examples of dialect development in these so called "linguistic islands", the term used by German linguists to describe those areas where

German was spoken in an area surrounded by a major non-German language of the country of residence, are the German dialects spoken among the "Saxons" in Transylvania in Romania or among the "Danubian Swabians" in Hungary, Romania, and Yugoslavia. A selected bibliography of these investigations in this particular linguistic area can be found in the work of Schwob (1971), Wiesinger (1982), and Hutterer (1982).

Linguistic development of the dialects in the German villages of the area north of the Black Sea was paralleled by the linguistic developments in the German dialects in Bessarabia which is located to the west of the Black Sea colonies. Those two dialect areas, the German colonies in the Black Sea Region to the north of Odessa and the German colonies in the province of Bessarabia to the west, were both part of the Southwest Russian Empire. They were settled by basically the same type of settlers from the same regional and social background. The Bessarabian German dialects are among the most thoroughly investigated dialects; the most recent publication being Fiess (1975). Both of these dialect areas, that of the Black Sea Germans and that of the Bessarabian Germans, contributed settlers to the Central Dakota German-speaking area and to the Central Dakota German dialect which is described here.

Like many of the German "linguistic islands" found in Eastern Europe, the language spoken by the Central Dakota Germans is a variety of German that most resembles the German dialects spoken in Southwest Germany. It is a *Westoberdeutsch* dialect variant of German, mainly Swabian. As my description makes clear, this dialect is not the direct counterpart of any dialect spoken in Germany today. It is another variety of German, a dialect unique in itself. It is a new and distinct dialect which German dialectologists would call a `daughter dialect' or *Ausgleichsmundart*, i.e., a newly formed dialect balanced by the mutual assimilation of the speech habits among speakers of the first generation of colonists who went to Russia from different southwest German dialect areas and who immigrated to the United States and settled in the Central Dakota area. A similar kind of mixing of dialects was found in most of the German settlements in eastern and southeastern Europe.

Although to date there is no detailed descriptive grammar and dictionary of this Central Dakota German dialect, for the purposes of this survey it can, nevertheless, be adequately identified and described by the simple expedient of showing that both the sounds of the Central Dakota German dialect (CDGer.) and the lexicon it employs contrast with the sounds and lexicon of Standard High German (SHGer.) (3.1).

After this initial identification of the CDGer. dialect, the chapter compares a selected inventory of CDGer. lexicon with the standard dialectal geographic word-maps for Germany and thus identifies the historical and geographical sources of the CDGer. dialect in Germany (3.2). The chapter then lists the internal linguistic evidence which CDGer. shows of some of the influences the original German dialect underwent as a result of its first emigration to Russia and of its second emigration to the United States (3.3). For internally, in its lexicon, the CDGer. dialect echoes its external linguistic history, the historical and geographical influences this dialect has undergone since its speakers first left Germany for Russia and subsequently immigrated to the United States. This is evidenced in the loanwords of French, Russian, Romanian, and Turkish origin which reflect the influence of French civilization in Southwest Germany and Alsace in the 18th and early 19th century and the dialect's first emigration to Russia (3.3.1), and in the more numerous loanwords of English origin which reflect the result of its second emigration, to the United States (3.3.2).

Next, the chapter lists those factors which have favored language maintenance of the CDGer. dialect (3.4) and those which are currently working to replace the CDGer. dialect with English (3.5). The chapter then identifies and describes the sociolinguistic functions which the CDGer. dialect currently performs in contemporary life in the United States (3.6). The chapter concludes with an attempt at a prognosis of the probability of "language maintenance" for this CDGer. dialect in the face of the rising pressure(s) for its replacement by English (3.7)

3.1. The Central Dakota German dialect (CDGer.).

3.1.0 Introduction. Without a detailed description, the Central Dakota dialect can be adequately identified and described by the simple expedient of showing that both the sounds of the CDGer. dialect and the lexicon it employs contrast with the sounds and lexicon of Standard High German (3.1). The CDGer. dialect is identifiable and can be distinguished from other German dialects by the way it sounds and the lexicon it uses. More precisely, the Central Dakota German dialect can be identified and be distinguished from other German dialects by the set of segmental phonemes which occur in its sound system and the lexical items which constitute its vocabulary. In both of these areas it contrasts with Standard High German.

3.1.1 The segmental phonemes of Central Dakota German (CDGer.) contrasted with the inventory of the segmental phonemes of Standard High German (SHGer.).

Central Dakota German (CDGer.) is a distinct dialect of German and contrasts with Standard High German (SHGer.) as shown by the differences in their phonemic inventories. Table 3.1 displays both the inventory of the segmental phonemes of Central Dakota German and the inventory of the segmental phonemes of Standard High German. A brief inspection of Table 3.1 shows the principal differences between the dialect and Standard High German.

Central Dakota German shows an inventory of 31 phonemes, 11 vowels, 20 consonants, and two diphthongs; whereas Standard High German shows an inventory of 38 phonemes, 16 vowels, 22 consonants, and three diphthongs.

The main difference between Standard High German and Central Dakota German is in the contrasting number of phonemes in their vowel inventory, 11 for CDGer. and 16 for SHGer. Not only has CDGer. five fewer vowels but a distinctive feature has been lost from its vowel system, i.e., CDGer. does not show a structural phonemic opposition between a set of unrounded front vowels and a set of rounded front vowels. Moreover, the choice of symbols I have used to indicate the two lower front vowels in CDGer. reflects the fact that these vowels are consistently represented by lower, more open, allophones than are the comparable vowels in Standard High German.

The consonant system of CDGer. also shows a smaller inventory; 20 consonants vs. 22 consonants in SHGer. Consonant phonemes which are absent in CDGer. but occur in Standard High German are indicated by an ellipsis (...). There are two consonant phonemes of Standard High German which do not occur in Central Dakota German, namely /z/ and / z /with a line on top.

In addition, one may note that the CDGer. shows only two diphthongs, /ai/ and /au/ in contrast to the three diphthongs which occur in Standard High German, /ai/, /au/, and /oi/.

There is a wide range of sub-phonemic realization of the consonants: Liquids can accept syllabic quality, i.e., [r] and [l] mostly in stressed position; nasals in final position tend to be omitted, i.e., machen /maxê/, leaving light nasalizations of the final vowel that can vary widely depending on topic, speed, personal style of the speaker, and other situational factors.

Table 3.1 The inventory of the segmental phonemes of Central Dakota German vs. the segmental phonemes of Standard High German.

	Central Dakota German:						Standard High German:					
	B	LD	A	AP	P	V	G	B	LD	A	AP	P	V	G
Stops:	p		t			k		p		t			k	
	b		d			g		b		d			g	
Affricates:		pf	ts						pf	ts				
Fricatives:		f	s	š		x	h		f	s	š		x	h
		v	..	..	j				v	z	ž	j		
Nasals:	m		n			ŋ		m		n			ŋ	
Laterals:			l							l				
Trill:			r							r				
High:				i:	..	u:					i:	y:	u:	
				i	..	u					i	Y	u	
Mid:				..	..	ê o:					e:	ø:	ê o:	
				ɛ	..	o					ɛ	œ	o	
				ɛ:							ɛ:			
Low:					a							a		
					a:							a:		
Diphthong					..								oi	
					ai	au						ai	au	

B   Bilabial   AP   Alveopalatal   V   Velar
LD Labiodental P   Palatal   G   Glottal
A   Alveolar

Due to typographical limitations the symbol /ê/ is employed to represent the unrounded mid-central vowel (schwa) which is conventionally transcribed /ə/: Likewise /i/ is employed for /I/: /u/ for /U/: and /o/ for /ɔ/.

3.1.2. The lexicon of Central Dakota German contrasted with the lexicon of Standard High German.

That Central Dakota German is a separate and distinct dialect of German can be shown not only by the fact that the inventory of its functional set of speech sounds (phonemes) differs from those of Standard High German (cf.3.1.1), but also by the fact that its vocabulary contrasts with the vocabulary of Standard High German. That the vocabulary, or lexical items, of the Central Dakota German dialect contrasts with that of Standard High German can be shown in more than one way.   Instead of simply listing those words of the Central Dakota German dialect which differ from those used by Standard High German to represent the identical item, it would be useful to employ some standard vocabulary lists which linguists, generally, and dialectologists, more particularly German dialectologists, employ to measure the similarities and differences of languages or dialects.

Three sets of standard lists immediately come to mind: (1) the Swadesh (1950) lexicostatistical word lists (3.1.2.1); (2) the Walther Mitzka (1939) list of 200 German words (3.1.2.2); and, (3) a vocabulary based on the Georg Wenker (1876) set of 40 sentences (3.1.2.3). The Wenker 40 sentences are the most important tool available for the study of German dialects as they have been the standard instrument used for this purpose since they were published in 1881. In hearing the informant responses to standard lists, words appear that seem to the field worker to be especially unique to the dialect. Patterns of usage emerge, even without a formal and exhaustive grammatical study. Under (4) a representative list which seems to characterize the dialect, is assembled. Noted are words that are regarded as "typical" by the speakers themselves. See (3.1.2.4)

3.1.2.1 The Swadesh lexicostatistical word lists. The first set, the Swadesh lexicostatistical word lists, have been the lists probably most widely used by American anthropologists and descriptive linguists, even those not particularly interested in the glottochronological methodology of Morris Swadesh, for the comparative study of languages and dialects. The Swadesh lexicostatistical word lists come in two forms: (1) a 100-word list (3.1.2.1.1) and (2) a 200-word list (3.1.2.1.2). Although almost all of the words that occur in the Swadesh 100-word list also occur in the Swadesh 200-word list, they occur in a slightly different order. Consequently, for the convenience of anthropologists or dialectologists who, for their particular purposes, may prefer to use one list rather than the other, I have included both Swadesh lists. The versions of the two Swadesh word lists employed here are cited from Samarin (1967: 218ff); and, as explained by Samarin the 200-word list actually consists of 218 items.

Through the use of these two lists one can get an indication of difference between the Central Dakota German (CDGer.) dialect and Standard High German (SHGer.), even on the most common and supposedly "culture free" words of everyday life.

This degree of difference between the CDGer. dialect and Standard High German can be expressed in a relationship, between the percent of CDGer. words which are employed by the speakers of the CDGer. dialect and the percent of Standard High German words which they employ. One caution, however, must be mentioned. The fact that speakers of the CDGer. dialect preferred the CDGer. dialect form over the Standard High German form does not mean that they are necessarily ignorant of the Standard High German form or that it is entirely absent from their vocabulary. They may know the Standard High German form from their reading or hearing of Luther's translation of the Bible and retain the form in their passive vocabulary; but the Standard High German form is not the form they normally use in their active vocabulary, for that they use the CDGer. dialect form.

3.1.2.1.1 The Swadesh 100-word list. The following is the Swadesh 100-word lexicostatistical word list which is so often used for language and dialect description and comparison. As presented here the list consists of the item number, then (1) the Swadesh English word which was used to elicit the CDGer. dialect form from a speaker of the CDGer. dialect, (2) the orthographic form of the CDGer. dialect word used to represent the English word, (3) a phonemic transcription of the CDGer. dialect form in response to the English word, and (4) the orthographic form of the word used to represent the English word in Standard High German, a form which may or may not differ from the form elicited from the CDGer. dialect speaker.

No. 'English Word'; Central Dakota German (CDGer.) Dialect Word; /Central Dakota German (CDGer.) Dialect Word Phonemically Expressed/; Standard High German Word (SHGer)

1. 'I' ich /ix/; ich
2. 'thou' du /du/; du
3. 'we' mir /mir/; wir
4. 'this' der, die, das /dêr di: das/; dieser, diese, dieses
5. 'that' seler, seli, sel /sɛlêr, sɛli, sɛl/; jener, jene, jenes
6. 'who?' wer /vɛ:r/; wer
7. 'what?' was /vas/; was
8. 'not' net /nɛt/; nicht
9. 'all' all /al/; all
10. 'many' viel /fi:l/; viele
11. 'one' eins /ains/; eins
12. 'two' zwei /tsvai/; zwei
13. 'big' gross /gros/; gross
14. 'long' lang/ lang/; lang
15. 'small' klein /glai(n)/; klein
16. 'woman' weib /vaib/; Frau, Weib
17. 'man' man /man/; Mann
18. 'person' mensch /mɛnš/; Mensch
19. 'fish' fisch /fiš/; Fisch
20. 'bird' vogel /vo:gêl/; Vogel
21. 'dog' hund /hunt/; Hund
22. 'louse' laus /laus/; Laus
23. 'tree' baum /ba:m/; Baum
24. 'seed' some /so:mê/; Samen
25. 'leaf' blatt /blat/; Blatt
26. 'root' wurzel /vurtsl/; Wurzel
27. 'bark' rinne /rinê/; Rinde
28. 'skin' haut /haut/; Haut
29. 'flesh' fleisch /flaiš/; Fleisch
30. 'blood' blut /blu:t/; Blut
31. 'bone' knoche /knoxê/; Knochen
32. 'grease' fett /fɛt/; Fett
33. 'egg' ei /ai/; Ei
34. 'horn' horn /horn/; Horn
35. 'tail' schwanz /švants/; Schwanz
36. 'feather' fedder /fɛdêr/; Feder
37. 'hair' hor /ho:r/; (Kopf-) Haar
38. 'head' kopf /kopf/; Kopf
39. 'ear' ohr /o:r/; Ohr
40. 'eye' auge /a:g/; Auge
41. 'nose' nas /na:s/; Nase

42. `mouth' maul /maul/; Mund
43. `tooth' zahn /tsa:/; Zahn
44. `tongue' zung /tsu_/; Zunge
45. 'fingernail'/fingernagel/finggêrna:gêl/; Fingernagel
46. `foot' fuss /fu:s/; Fuss
47. `knee' knie /kni:/; Knie
48. `hand' hand /hant/; Hand
49. `belly' bauch /baux/; Bauch
50. `neck' knick /knik/; Nacken/Hals
51. 'breasts'bruscht/brušt/(sg.),brischt/bri:št/(pl.); (weibliche) Brust
52. `heart' herz /hɛrts/; Herz
53. `liver' leber /lɛbêr/; Leber
54. `drink' trinke /drêngkê/; trinken
55. `eat' esse /ɛsê/; essen
56. `bite' beisse /baisê/; beissen
57. `see' gucke /gukê/; sehen
58. `hear' here /hɛ:rê/; hören
59. `know' kenne /kɛnê/; können
60. `sleep' schlofe /šlo:fê/; schlafen
61. `die' sterbe /štɛrbê/; sterben
62. `kill' umbringe /umbri ngê/; töten
63. `swim' schwimme /švimê/; schwimmen
64. `fly' fliege /fli:gê/; fliegen`fly' mucke /mukê/; Fliege
65. `walk' lafe /la:fê/; gehen
66. `come' komme /komê/; kommen
67. `lie' na liege /na:li:gê/; liegen
68. `sit' hocke /hokê/; sitzen
69. `stand' stehe /štɛ:/; stehen
70. `give' gebe /gɛbê/; geben
71. `say' sage /sa:gê/; sagen
72. `sun' sonne /sonê/; Sonne
73. `moon' mond /mo:nt/; Mond
74. `star' sterne /štɛrnê/; Stern
75. `water' wasser /vasêr/; Wasser
76. `rain' rege /rɛ:gê/; Regen
77. `stone' stein /štai/; Stein
78. `sand' sand /sant/; Sand
79. `earth' erd /ɛ:rt/; Erde
80. `cloud' wolke /volkê/; Wolken

81. `smoke' rach /ra:x/; Rauch
82. `fire' feier /faiêr/; Feuer
83. `ash' äsche /ɛšê/; Asche
84. `burn' brenne /brɛnê/; brennen
85. `path' wegle /vɛ:glɛ/; Weg(lein)
86. `mountain' hoher bugel /hohêr bukêl/; Berg
87. `red' rot /ro:t/; rot
88. `green' gre /grɛ:/; grün
89. `yellow' gel /gɛ:l/; gelb
90. `white' weiss /vais/; weiss
91. `black' schwarz /švarts/; schwarz
92. `night' nacht /naxt/; Nacht
93. `hot' heiss /hois/; heiss
94. `cold' kalt /kalt/; kalt
95. `full' voll /fol/; voll
96. `new' nei /nai/; neu
97. `good' gut /gu:t/; gut
98. `round' rund /runt/; rund
99. `dry' trickle /driglê/; trocknen
100. `name' name /namê/; Name

3.1.2.1.2 The Swadesh 200-word list.

1. `all' alles /alês/; alles
2. `and' und /unt/; und
3. `animal' tier, tierle /di:r, di:rlɛ/; Tier(chen)
4. `ashes' äsche /ɛšê/; Asche
5. `at' bei /bai/; bei
6. `back' buckel /bukêl/; Rücken
7. `bad' schlecht /šlɛxt/; schlecht
8. `bark' rinne /rinê/; Rinde
9. `because' wegich /vɛgix/; wegen, weil
10. `belly' bauch /baux/; Bauch
11. `big' gross /gro:s/; gross
12. `bird' vogel, vogele /vo:gêl, vɛgêlɛ/; Vogel(chen)
13. `bite' beisse /baisê/; beissen
14. `black' schwarz /švarts/; schwarz
15. `blood' blut /blu:t/; Blut
16. `blow' blosse /blo:sê/; blasen
17. `bone' knoche /knoxê/; Knoche
18. `breast' bruscht /brušt/(sg.), brischt

/bri:št/(pl.);(weibliche) Brust
19. `breathe' schnaufe /šnaufê/; atmen
20. `brother' bruder /bru:dêr/; Bruder
21. `burn' brenne /brɛnê/; brennen
22. `child' kind /kint/; Kind
23. `clothing' kleider /glaidêr/; Kleider
24. `cloud' wolke /volkê/; Wolke
25. `claw' klobe /klo:bê/; Kralle
26. `cold' kalt /kalt/; kalt
27. `come' komme /komê/; kommen
28. `cook' koche /koxê/; kochen
29. `count' zähle /tsɛ:lê/; zählen
30. `cut' schneide /šnaidê/; schneiden
31. `dance' tanze /dantsê/; tanzen
32. `day' tag /dag/; Tage
33. `die' sterbe /štɛrbê/; sterben
34. `dig' grabe /grabê/; graben
35. `dirty' dreckig /drɛkix/; schmutzig
36. `dog' hund /hunt/; Hund
37. `drink' trinke /dringkê/; trinken
38. `dry' trickle /driglê/; trocknen
39. `dull' trib /dri:b/; trüb
40. `dust' staub /šda:b/; Staub
41. `ear' ohr /o:r/; Ohr
42. `earth' bode /bo:dê/; Boden
43. `eat' esse /ɛsê/; essen
44. `egg' ei /ai/; Ei
45. `eight' acht /axt/; acht
46. `eye' auge /a:g/; Auge
47. `fall' falle /falê/; fallen
48. `far' weit /vait/; weit
49. `fat/grease' fett /fɛt/; Fett
50. `father' vater /fadêr/; Vater
51. 'fear' angst /angšt/; Angst
52. `feather' fedder /fɛdêr/; Feder
53. `few' wenig /vɛnig/; wenig
54. `fight' händle /hɛndlê/; streiten
55. `fire' feier /faiêr/; Feuer
56. `fish' fisch /fiš/; Fisch
57. `five' fenfe /finfê/; fünf
58. `float' fliesst (im wasser) /fli:st
    (im vasêr)/;(oben auf) schwimmen, treiben

59. `flow' fliesse /fli:sê/; fliessen
60. `flower' blome /blo:mê/; Blume
61. `fog' nebel, duft /nɛ:bl, duft/; Nebel
62. `foot' fuss /fu:s/; Fuss
63. `four' vier /fi:r/; vier
64. `freeze' friere /fri:rê/; gefrieren
65. `fruit' obst /obšt/; Obst
66. `full' voll /fol/; voll
67. `give' gebe /gɛ:bê/; geben
68. `good' gut /gu:t/; gut
69. `grass' gras /gra:s/; Gras
70. `green' gre /grɛ:/; grün
71. `guts' därm /dɛrm/; Gedärme
72. `hair' hor /ho:r/; Haar
73. `hand' hand /hant/; Hand
74. `he' er /ɛ:r/; er
75. `head' kopf /kopf/; Kopf
76. `hear' here /hɛ:rê/; hören
77. `heart' herz /hɛ:rts/; Herz
78. `heavy' schwer /švêr/; schwer
79. `here' do /do:/; hier
80. `hit' schlage /šla:gê/; schlagen
81. `hold, take' hebe /hɛ:bê/; halten
82. `horn' horn /horn/; Horn
83. `how' wie /vi:/; wie
84. `hundred' hundert /hundêrt/; hundert
85. `hunt' jachtle /jaxtlê/; jagen
86. `husband' man /man/; Mann
87. `I' ich /ix/; ich
88. `ice' eis /ais/; Eis
89. `if' ob /ob/; wenn
90. `in' in /in/; in
91. `kill' umbringe /umbringê/; töten
92. `knee' knie /kni:/; Knie
93. `know' kenne, wisse /kɛnê visê/; kennen, wissen
94. `lake' lake /la:k/; See
95. `laugh' lache /laxê/; lachen
96. `leaf' blatt /blat/; Blatt
97. `leftside' linkseseit /lɛnksêsait/; linke Seite
98. `leg' schenkel /šɛnggêl/; Schenkel
99. `lie' na liege /na:li:gê/; liegen
100. `live' lebe /lɛ:bê/; leben

101. `liver' leber /lɛbêr/; Leber
102. `long' lang /laɔ/; lang
103. `louse' laus /laus/; Laus
104. `man, male' man /man/; Mann
105. `many' viel /fi:l/; viele
106. `meat, flesh' fleisch /flaiš/; Fleisch
107. `moon' mond /mo:nt/; Mond
108. `mother' mutter /mudêr/; Mutter
109. `mountain' bugel /bukêl/(sg), bigel /bikêl/(pl); Berg
110. `mouth' maul /maul/; Mund
111. `name' name /na:mê/; Name
112. `narrow' schmal /šma:l/; schmal
113. `near' dicht /dixt/; nahe
114. `neck' knick /knik/; Nacken/Hals
115. `new' nei /nai/; neu
116. `night' nacht /naxt/; Nacht
117. `nose' nas /na:s/; Nase
118. `not' net /nit/; nicht
119. `old' alt /alt/; alt
120. `one' eins /ains/; eins
121. `other' andere /andɛrɛ/; andere
122. `person' mensch /mɛnš/; Mensch
123. `play' spiele /špi:lê/; spielen
124. `pull' ziege /tsi:gê/; ziehen
125. `push' dricke /drikê/ drücken
126. `rain' rege /rɛ:gê/; Regen
127. `red' rot /ro:t/; rot
128. `right' recht /rɛxt/; recht `correct' machts recht /maxts rɛxt/; richtig (machen)
129. `rightside' rechte seit /rɛxtêsait/; rechte Seite
130. `river' river /rɛvêr/ Fluss
131. `road' weg /vɛ:g/; Weg
132. `root' wurzel /vurtsêl/; Wurzel
133. `rope' strick /štrik/; Seil, Strick
134. `rotten' verfault /fêrfault/; verfault
135. `rub' reibe /raibê/; reiben
136. `salt' salz /salts/; Salz
137. `sand' sand /sant/; Sand
138. `say' sage /sa:gê/; sagen
139. `scratch' kratze /kratsê/; kratzen
140. `sea' sea /sɛ:/; See, Meer

141. `see' sehne /sɛ:nê/; sehen
142. `seed' some /so:mê/; Samen
143. `seven' siebe /si:bê/; sieben
144. `sew' nähe /nɛ:ê/; nähen
145. `sharp' scharf /šarf/; scharf
146. `shoot' schiesse /ši:sê/; schiessen
147. `short' kurz /kurts/; kurz
148. `sing' singe /singê/; singen
149. `sister' schwester /švɛštêr/; Schwester
150. `sit' hocke /hokê/; sitzen
151. `skin' haut /haut/; Haut
152. `sky' himmel /himêl/; Himmel
153. `sleep' schlofe /šlo:fê/; schlafen
154. `small' klein /glai(n)/; klein
155. `smell' schmacke /šmakê/; riechen
156. `smoke' rach /ra:x/; Rauch
157. `smooth' ebe /ɛ:bê/; eben
158. `snake' schlang /šla_/; Schlange
159. `snow' schnee /šnɛ:/; Schnee
160. `some' ebes /ɛbês/; etwas
161. `spear' speer /špi:r/; Speer
162. `spit' spucke /špukê/; spucken
163. `split' verspalte /feršpaltê/; spalten
164. `squeeze' zusamme dricke /tsamê drike/ zusammendrücken
165. `stab' steche /štɛxê/; erstechen
166. `stand' ufsteh /u:fšte:/; aufstehen
167. `star' stern /štɛrn/; Stern
168. `stick' stecke /štɛkê/; Stecken
169. `stone' stein /štai(n)/; Stein
170. `straight' grad /grad/; gerade
171. `suck' suckle /suglê/; saugen
172. `sun' sonne /tson/; Sonne
173. `swell' schwelle /švɛlê/; schwellen
174. `swim' schwimme /švimê/; schwimmen
175. `tail' schwanz /švants/; Schwanz
176. `ten' zehn /tsɛ:n/; zehn
177. `that' der, die, das /dêr di: das/ (stressed); / dr d(i) `s/ (without being stressed); der, die, das
178. `there' dort /dort/; dort
179. `they' sie /si:/; sie
180. `thick' dick /dik/; dick

181. `thin' dinn /din/; dünn
182. `think' denke /dɛngkê/; denken
183. `this' der, die, das /dɛr di: das/; dieser, diese, dieses
184. `thou' du /du/; du
185. `three' drei /drai/; drei
186. `throw' schmeisse /šmaisê/; schmeissen
187. `tie' binde /binê/ binden
188. `tongue' zung /tsu_/; Zunge
189. `tooth' zahn /tsa:/; Zahn
190. `tree' baum /ba:m/; Baum
191. `turn' drehe /drɛ:ê/; drehen
192. `twenty' zwanzig /tsvansêk/; zwanzig
193. `two' zwei /tsvai/; zwei
194. `vomit' kotze /kotsê/; erbrechen
195. `walk' laufe /la:fê/; gehen
196. `warm' warm /varm/; warm
197. `wash' wäsche /vɛšê/; waschen
198. `water' wasser /vasêr/; Wasser
199. `we' mir /mir/; wir
200. `wet' nass /nas/; nass
201. `what?' was /vas/; was
202. `when?' wann /van/; wann
203. `where?' wo /vo:/; wo
204. `white' weiss /vais/; weiss
205. `who?' wer /vɛ:r/; wer
206. `wide' breit /brait/; breit
207. `wife' weib /vaib/; Frau
208. `wind' wind /vind/; Wind
209. `wing' fliegel /fli:gêl/; Flügel
210. `wipe' abputzen /abbutsê/; abwischen
211. `with' mit /mit/; mit
212. `woman' weib /vaib/; Frau
213. `woods' wald /valt/; Wald
214. `work' schaffe /šafê/; arbeiten
215. `worm' worm /vorm/; Wurm
216. `ye' ihr /i:r/; ihr
217. `year' johr /jo:r/; Jahr
218. `yellow' gel /gɛ:l/; gelb

3.1.2.2 The Mitzka 200-word list. The Mitzka list of 200 words was developed by Walther Mitzka to elicit synonyms of the German dialects, something that he and others thought lacking in the "40 Wenker sentences". The 200-word list has been in use since 1939. It developed into the *Deutsche Wortatlas*, the 'German Word Atlas', which has 22 volumes that took until 1972 to publish. This German Word Atlas was the tool used to identify the historical linguistic home of the Central Dakota German speakers (3.2.). The word atlas is based on the 200 words, the variations of the words, and where these variations occur geographically in German speaking Europe, except for Switzerland. A representative choice of words is made, and each word is located in the word atlas. One then identifies the geographical location where the words are used, drawing the boundaries around the site where the dialect word occurs. By using a representative list of words and by placing the boundaries that are drawn on a series of overlays on top of each other on a scaled map, one can locate the general area where the elements of a particular dialect are to be found in the same combination.

The 200 words or phrases of the Mitzka list given here are followed by the Central Dakota German expression. When the Standard High German word was not known by the CDGer. speaker, an ellipsis (...) is shown in the list. This seemed to occur when a specific bird, insect, or plant was mentioned and may be due to the fact that since the item did not occur in their daily life in the Dakotas, the SHGer. word did not occur in their vocabuary.

No. Standard High German Word(s) (SHGer.); Central Dakota German (CDGer.) Dialect Word; /Central Dakota German (CDGer.) Dialect Word Phonemically Expressed/; 'English Word'

1. Ahorn: ... ... `maple'
2. Ameise: ameise /omaisê/ `ant'
3. Anemone: ... ... `anemone'
4. Augenbraue: augehor /a:gêho:r/ `eyebrows'
5. Augenlid: augedeckel /a:gêdɛkêl/ `eyelid'
6. auswringen: auswringle /ausrɛŋglê/ `wring out'
7. Backenzahn: backezahn /bakêtsa:(n)/ molar tooth
8. Backtrog: backschiessel /bakšisêl/ `kneading-trough'
9. barfuss: barfussig /barfusix/ `barefoot'
10. Bauchweh: mageweh /magêvɛ:/ `stomach ache'
11. sich beeilen: dommelt sich /domêlt six/ `to hurry up'
12. Begräbnis: die leicht /di laixt/ `funeral'
13. Beule: schwer /švɛ:r/ `boil'

14. es blitzt: es tut wetterleichte /ɛs du:t vetrlaixê/ 'it is lightning'
15. Brennessel: brennessel /brɛnɛsl/ `stinging nettle'
16. Brombeere: ... ... `blackberry'
17. Brotscheibe: a brot schnitte /a bro:tšnitê/ `a slice of bread'
18. bügeln: begla /bɛ:glê/, bleta /blɛtê/ `ironing'
19. Deichsel: deigsel /daigsl/ `two horse shaft'
20. Distel: hegsa /hɛksê/ `thistle'
21. Docht: wiche /vi:xê/ `wick'
22. Eichelhäher: ... ... `jaybird'
23. Eigelb: das gehle vom ei /s'gɛ:le vom ai/ `egg yolk'
24. Elster: ... ... `magpie'
25. Ente (männliche): entrich /ɛndrix/ `male duck', Ente: (female): gatsch /gatš/ `duck`, Ente (junge): getschle /gɛtšlê/ `young duck'
26. Erdbeere: strohbeere /štro:bɛ:rê/ `strawberries'
27. sich erkälten: kalt kriege /kald kri:gê/, verkiele /frki:lê/ `catch cold'
28. ernten (Kartoffel): grumbiere raus steche /grumbirê raus šdɛxê/ `harvest potatoes'
29. Euter (der Kuh): kuh eiter /ku aidr/ `cow udder'
30. Euter (allgemein): eiter /aidr/ 'udder'
31. fegen (Stube): ausfege /ausfɛgê/ `sweep'
32. Ferkel: seile /sai:lɛ/ `piglet'
33. Fledermaus: fledermaus /flɛdrmaus/ `bat'
34. Fliege (Stuben): muck /muk/ `house fly'
35. Frosch: frosch /froš/, krot /grot/ `frog'
36. Frühling: frihjahr /fri:jor/ `spring'
37. Gabeldeichsel: beckholz /bɛkholts/ `pair of shafts'
38. gackern: gackse /gaksê/ `cackle'
39. gähnen: maul ufsperre /maul ufšpɛrê/ `yawn'
40. Gans (male): ginserich /ginsêrix/ `goose (male)' Gans (female): gans /gans/ `goose female'
41. Gans (junge): ginsle /ginslɛ/ `young goose'
42. Genick: gnick /knik/ `neck'
43. Giesskanne: giesskann /gi:skan/ `watering can'
44. Glühwürmchen: feierwurmle /faiêrvurmlɛ/ `firefly'
45. Grasschwade: schwade /šva:dê/ `swath'
46. Grossmutter: grossmutter /grosmudr/, ähne /ɛnê/ `grandmother'

47. Grossvater: grossvater /grosfadr/, ahne /a:nê/ `grandfather'
48. Grummet: zweite ernt /tsvaitɛ ɛrnt/ `the second crop'
49. Gurke: gugumere /gugumêrê/ `cucumber'
50. häufeln: heifle /haiflê/ `heap'
51. Hagebutte: hagebutza /hagêbutsê/ `hedge hawthorn'
52. Hahn: hahner /hanêr/ `rooster', Henne: huhn /ho(n)/ `female chicken' hahner /hɛ:nêr/ `chickens' hengele /hingêlɛ/ `young chicken'
53. Handwerker, der Fässer anfertigt: fasbinder /fasbindêr/ `cooper'
54. Handwerker, der Blech am Haus bearbeitet: schmied /šmi:t/ `tinsmith'
55. Handwerker, der Bauernwagen anfertigt: wagner /vagnêr/ `wagonmaker'
56. Handwerker, der Möbel anfertigt: schreiner /šrainêr/, tischler /dišlêr/ `carpenter'
57. Handwerker, der Tontöpfe macht: ... ... `potter'
58. Handwerker, der Vieh schlachtet: schlachter /šlaxtêr/ `butcher'
59. Handwerker, der Fleisch verarbeitet: butcher /butšêr/ `butcher'
60. Hebamme: die hebong /di hɛbong/ /mitvaib/ `midwife'
61. Heckenrose: hagebutzerose /hagêbutsaros/ `hedgerose'
62. heiser: heiser /haisêr/ `hoarse'
63. Henne (brütende): kluck /gluk/ `cluck'
64. Heuschrecke: heischreck /haišrɛk/, grasshopfer /grashopfêr/ `grasshopper'
65. Himbeere: raspberry /rɛsbɛrê/ `raspberry'
66. Holunder: zahringkebaum /tsa:ringkêba:m/ `lilac tree'
67. Hügel: bugel /bukl/ `hill' Hügel: bigel /bikl/ `hills'
68. Hühnerauge: hehnerauge /hi:nêra:gê/ `corn on foot'
69. Hühnerhaus: hehnerstahl /hi:nêršta:l/, hehnerheisle /hinêrhaislɛ/ `chicken coop'
70. Hummel: eme /ɛ:mê/ `bumble-bee'
71. Igel: stachelschwein /štaxlšvai/ `hedgehog'
72. Iltis: stinkkatz /štêngkats/ `polecat'

73. Käfer: kefer /kɛ:fêr/ `beetle'
74. kämmen (Haare): hor strehle /ho:r šdrɛ:lê/ `comb hair'
75. Kätzchen (am Haselstrauch): ketzle /kɛtslɛ/ `cattails'
76. Kalb: hammele /hamêlɛ/, kelble /kɛlblɛ/ `calf'
77. Kamille: kamille /kamilê/ `camomile'
78. Kaninchen: has /ha:s/ `rabbit'
79. Kartoffel: grumbiere /grumbi:rê/ `potato'
80. Katze (männlich): koter /ko:dêr/ `tomcat'
81. Kaulquappe: junge krot /jungɛ grot/ `tadpole'
82. Kleiderhaken: kleiderhänger /glaidêrhɛnkêr/ `clotheshangers'
83. Kleiderschrank: kleiderschank /glaidêršaŋk/ `wardrobe'
84. kneifen: pfetze /pfɛtsa/ `pinch'
85. Knöchel (am Fuss): knechle /knɛxlɛ/ `anklebone'
86. Knospe: blihknopf /bli:knopf/, sie schiessen knepf raus /si ši:sên knêpf raus/ `bud'
87. Kopfweh: kopfweh /kopfvɛ:/ `headache'
88. Kornblume: kornblome /kornblomê/ `corn-flowers'
89. Kreisel: spinner /špinêr/ `top'
90. Kröte: krot /grot/ `toad'
91. Kruste (des Brotes): krust /krušd/ `breadcrust'
92. Laken (für das Bett): leintuch /laindux/ `bedsheet'
93. Lamm (weibl.): lamm /lam/ `female lamb'
    Lamm (männlich): schafbock /šofbok/ `male lamb'
    schäfle /šɛflɛ/ `small lamb'
94. Lappen (Wasch-): wäschlumpe /vɛšlumbê/ `wash cloth'
95. leer: leer /lɛ:r/ `empty'
96. leihen (Geld an jemand): verborge /frborgê/ `loan money'
97. Lerche: lärch /lɛrx/ `lark'
98. Libelle: ... ... `dragonfly'
99. Maiglöckchen: maiglocke /maiglokê/ `lily of the valley'
100. Larve des Maikäfers: ... ... `larva of a beetle'
101. Margerite: ... ... `a daisy-like flower'
102. Maulwurf: maulwurf /maulvurf/ `mole'
103. Meerrettich: meerrettich /mɛrɛtix/ `horseradish'
104. Mistkäfer: stinkkäfer /štingkɛ:fêr/ `dung-beetle'
105. Mohrrübe: gelriebe /gɛlri:bê/ `carrots'
106. Motte: schabe /ša:bê/ `moth'

107. Mücke (Stech-, nicht bes. Art): schnoge /šno:gê/ `mosquito'
108. Mütze: kapp /kap/, peltzkap /bɛlskap/ `cap, fur hat'
109. Mutterschwein: loos /lo:s/ `sow'   : eber /ɛ:br/ `boar'
110. nachharken (Getreide mit grossem Rechen zusammenholen): zusammenschleife /tsusamênšlaifê/`to rake (grain)'
111. Nachharke (das Handgerät dazu): rechl /rɛxl/ `rake'
112. Nachmittag: nachmittag /noxmidag/ `afternoon'
113. Narbe (einer Wunde): narfel /narfl/ `scar'
114. neugierig: neigierig /naiširix/, naseweisig /nasêvaisix/ `curious'
115. nicht wahr?: gell /gêl/ `isn't that so'
116. Ohrwurm: ...... `earwig'
117. Ostern: Ostere /oštêra/ `Easter'
118. Pate: der (tauf)pate /dr daufpadê/ `godfather'
119. Patin: die taufpate /di: daufpadê/ `godmother'
120. Peitsche: beitsch /baitš/ `whip'
121. pfeifen: pfeife /pfaifê/ `pipe'
122. Pflaume: pflaum   /pflaum/   `plum' gwetsche /gvɛtšê/ `dryed plum or prune'
123. pflügen: pflige /pfli:gê/ `plow'
124. Pflugwende (Ackerstelle, wo der Pflug gewendet wird):ende vom glem /ɛnt fom glêm/ `end of claim (homestead claim)'
125. Pfropfen (für die Flasche): stopfer /šdopfêr/ `bottle stopper'
126. Pilz: bilz /bils/ `mushroom'
127. Platzregen: schwere rege /švɛrê rɛ:gê/ `heavy rain shower'
128. Preisselbeere: ...... `cranberry'
129. Pulswärmer (aus Wolle): wolle händschich /volê hɛnšix/ `woolen mittens (wristlet)'
130. Unkraut ausziehen (mit der Hand): unkraut raus ropfe /ungraut raus ropfe/ `pull weeds (by hand)'
131. Werkzeug zum Durchstechen d. Leders: stechnodel /štɛxnodêl/ `awl'
132. die Sense mit dem Hammer schärfen: *die Sens mit dem schleifstei schêrfe* /di sens mitêm šlaifstai šêrfê/ `sharpen the scythe with the whetstone'
133. letzter Wochentag vor dem Sonntag?:   samstag /samšdag/`Saturday'

134. Quecke: quecke (unkraut) /quɛk/ `quick-grass'
135. Rasen: grass /gra:s/ `sod'
136. rauchen (Tabak): pfeif rauche /pfaif ra:xê/ `smoking a pipe'
137. Rauhreif: reiferich /raifêrix/ `hoarfrost'
138. Regenwurm: regewurm /rɛ:gêvorm/ `rain worm'
139. Reifen (am Fass): rempf /rɛmpf/ `barrel rings'
140. Rinde (des Nadelbaums): ... ... `bark of evergreen trees'
141. Rinde (des Laubbaumes): rinne /rinê/ `bark of leaf trees'
142. Roggen: rogge /rokê/ `rye'
143. Rotkraut: s'rotekraut /srotêkraut/ `red cabbage'
144. Sahne (süsse): rahm /ra:m/ `cream'
145. Sauerklee: ... ... `clover'
146. Sauerkraut: sauerkraut /sauêrgraut/ `sauerkraut'
147. schelten: verschelte /fršeldê/ `scold'
148. Schaufel (für Sand usw.): schaufel /šaufêl/ `shovel'
149. Schlüsselblume: ... ... `cowslip, primrose'
150. Schneeglöcken: schneeglocke /šnɛ:glokê/ `snowdrop'
151. Schnittlauch: zwiebelrohr /tsvi:bêlrɛr/ `chives'
152. Schnürband (am Schuh): stiefelschnir /štifêlšni:r/`shoelaces'
153. Schnupfen: schnupfe /šnupfê/ `headcold'
154. Schornsteinfeger: kammee ausputzer / kamɛ: ausbutsêr/ `chimneysweep'
155. Schwalbe: schwalb /švalb/ `swallow'
156. Schwengel: schwingel /švingêl/ `swingbar'
157. Schwiegermutter: schwiegemutter /švi:grmutr/ `mother-in-law'
158. Schwiegersohn: tochterman /doxtêrman/ `son-in-law'
159. Schwiegertochter: sohnerin /tsɛ:nêrê/ `daughter-in-law'
160. Schwiegervater: schwiegevater /švi:gêfatêr/ `father-in-law'
161. Seil (aus Hanf): strick /štrik/ `rope'
162. Sperling: spatzevogel /špatsêfo:gl/ `sparrow'
163. Spinngewebe: spinnewebe /špinêvɛ:bê/ `spiderweb'
164. Stachelbeere: stachelbeer /šdaxêlbɛ:r/

`gooseberry'
165. Star (Vogel): star /šda:r/ `starling'
166. Stecknadel: stechnodl /šdɛxno:dl/ `pin'
167. Streichholz: schwefele /švɛ:fêlɛ/ `matches'
168. stricken: stricke /šdrikê/ `knit'
169. Stricknadel: stricknodel /štrikno:dl/ `knitting needle'
170. Tasse (Ober-, Unter-): tass /das/, plettle /blɛtlê/ `cup, saucer'
171. Tauber (männl. Taube): taubrich /daubrix/ `male pigeon'
172. Tomate: patlatchana /batlašanê/ `tomato' pomadora /bomadorê/ `tomato'
173. Topf: hafe /ha:fê/ `crock' topf /dopf/ `earthen vessel'
174. unfruchtbar (von der Kuh): geltkuh /gɛlt ku:/ `barren'
175. Veilchen (Viola): viola blome /violê blomê/ `violet'
176. veredeln (Obstbäume): ...... `graft'
177. Viehbremse (Insekt): viehbremse /fi:brɛmsê/ `horsefly'
178. Wacholder (Juniperus): ...... `juniper tree'
179. Wanze: wanz /vants/ `bed bug'
180. Warze: warz /varts/ `wart'
181. wenden (Heu): hai umdrehe /hai umdrɛ:ê/ `to turn over hay' (hai umdrehe oder wende mitem drigel)
182. Werktag: werktag /ve:rkdag/, wochetag /voxêdag/`weekday'
183. wiederkäuen: iberkauen /i:brkauê/ `ruminate'
184. wiehern: wengert /vɛngêrt/, grilt /grilt/ `neigh'
185. Wimper (Augen-): augehor /a:gêho:r/ `eyelashes'
186. Zahnschmerzen: zahnweh /tsa:(n)vê/ `toothache'
187. Zaunkönig: ...... `wren'
188. Ziege: geiss /gais/ `female goat' geissbock /gaisbok/ `male goat'
189. er hat den Brief zerrissen: er hat den brief ufgrisse /ɛr hatên brif ufgrisê/ `he tore up the letter'
190. voriges Jahr hat es viel Obst gegeben, dies Jahr wenig: letzt johr war viel obst, des johr ist nix /letšd jo:r var fi:l obšt dis jo:r iš niks/ `last year there was a lot of fruit, this year little'
191. es hagelte vorgestern:
es hat vorgester gschlosst, es hat vorgester

ghagelt /s hat forgɛštêr tšlo:st/ /s hat forgɛštêr
ghagêlt/ `it hailed the day before yesterday'
192. er soll den Wagen ziehen:
er soll der Wage ziege /ɛr sol dêr va:gê tsi:gê/
`he should pull the wagon'
193. da war niemand zu sehen:
da war nemand zum seh /da var nɛmant tsum sɛ:/
`there was nobody to be seen'
194. erst gab es Tränen, dann weinte das Mädchen nicht mehr:
erst hat sie gheilt und nohêr hat sie nimme gheilt
/ɛršt hat si khailt und noxêr hatsê nɛmi khailt/
`first there were tears, then the little girl didn't cry anymore'
195. Junge, halt den Mund, gehorche lieber:
Bub, halt dei maul, horch lieber
/bu:, hal dei maul horx li:bêr/
`Boy, shut your mouth, better (that you) obey'
196. das Kind ist so klein, es braucht einen Sauger: das kind ist so klein, es braucht ein schlotzer
/s kind iš so glai: s braux a šlotsêr/
`the child is so small, it needs a pacifier'
197. den Schornstein fegen: das kammee putze
/das kamɛ: butsê/ `to sweep the chimney'
198. im Nebel war keiner zu sehen:
hast keiner g'seh für lauter nebel/
hošd kanêr tsɛ: fir lautr nɛ:bl/
`in the fog no one could be seen'
199. wir haben oft gewartet:
wir hen schon oft gwart
/wir hɛn šon oft gvart/
`we have often waited'
200. zeigt mir doch den Weg zwischen den Häusern:
weis (zeig) mir den weg zwischer dene heiser
/vais (tsaig) mɛr n vɛ:g tsvišêr dɛnê haisêr/
`show me the path between the houses'

3.1.2.3 List based on the Wenker set of 40 sentences. The third set of lists is the vocabulary list which can be constructed from the 40 Wenker sentences developed by Georg Wenker who began using these sentences in 1876 and worked with them until his death in 1911. They represent his device for collecting the sounds and forms of the various dialects of the German language. His goal was the publication of a large linguistic atlas that would not only describe the dialects, but also allow one to establish the site of all the dialects spoken in Germany. The sentences themselves were first published in 1881 in the *Sprachatlas für Nord-und Mitteldeutschland.* Wenker's 40 sentences became the standard tool that German dialectologists have employed for several generations in their studies of the various dialects of Germany and abroad. The Wenker sentences became, by reason of the continuity of their use for more than 100 years, the most important tool used by German dialectologists.

Consequently, I have used these sentences in collecting data about CDGer. and find that they represent, in my opinion, the most important items of my data collection. They have also been relevant in that the vocabulary and the sentences used are familiar to farming community respondents. I also found that speaking a whole sentence gave a much better insight into the normal way of pronouncing words than by using a simple question asking for a word. Most interesting is that only three foreign words occurred in the entire set of 40 Wenker sentences and these are related to the territory where the Germans lived: *steppe, prairie,* and *farmer.* This would indicate that the CDGer. dialect has kept its identity and its original vocabulary intact.

My investigations have elicited these sentences from 30 different speakers of Central Dakota German, seven of them male and 23 of them female. Moreover, this sample represents four generations of CDGer. speakers ranging in age from 29 years old to 96 years of age. In one family I was able to record the Wenker sentences and the Mitzka 200-word list in three generations. The striking aspect for me was that German was spoken without any trace of an English accent having crept into the German sound system. The names and ages of all the informants for the CDGer. dialect can be found in Appendix 10.

The 40 sentences of Wenker are in Standard High German as shown on line "a". These sentences were presented orally to Central Dakota German dialect speakers who then repeated them in their CDGer. dialect. These utterances in the CDGer. dialect were then transcribed both in the orthography of the CDGer. dialect as shown on line "b", and also in a phonemic transcription of the CDGer. dialect, shown on line "c". All three of these versions, that is, a, b, and c, are presented here together with my English translation of Wenker's Standard High German sentences given on line "d".

In these sentences, as in the Swadesh and Mitzka lists, one can note the differences between the Standard High German forms and the Central Dakota German forms. In the Wenker sentences one can also notice the differences in the patterns in which these forms occur, namely, the intonation and coarticulation due to German syntax.

The Wenker set of 40 Sentences

No. (a) Standard High German Words (SHGer.); (b) Central Dakota German (CDGer.) Dialect Words; (c) /Central Dakota German Dialect Words Phonemically Expressed/; (d) English Translation of the Wenker Sentences

1a.	Im Winter fliegen die trockenen Blätter in der Luft herum.
1b	Im winter fliegen die trukene bletter in der luft rum.
1c	/ɛm vindr fli:gên di drukênê blɛtr indr luft rom/
1d	`In winter the dry leaves fly around in the air.'

2a	Es hört gleich auf zu schneien, dann wird das Wetter wieder besser.
2b	Es hert gleich uf zum schneie, noh werds wetter wieder besser.
2c	/ɛs hɛ:rt glaix uf tsum šnaixê, no vɛrts vɛtr vidêr bɛsr/
2d	`It will soon stop snowing, then the weather will get better again.'

3a	Tu Kohlen in den Ofen, dass die Milch bald an zu kochen fängt.
3b	Tu kohle in der ofe, das die milch bald kocht.
3c	/du kolê in dr o:fê, das di milix bal koxt/
3d`	Put coal in the stove, so that the milk will soon begin to cook.'

4a	Der gute alte Mann ist mit dem Pferde durch's Eis gebrochen und in das kalte Wasser gefallen.
4b	Der gute alte man ist mit dem Pferd durchs eis broche und ins kalte wasser falle.
4c	/d'gu:di aldi man iš mitêm pfɛrd durixs ais broxê und ins kaldê vasêr falê/
4d	`The good old man broke through the ice with the horse and fell into the cold water.'

5a	Er ist vor vier oder sechs Wochen gestorben.
5b	Er ist schon vor vier oder sechs woche storbe.

5c /êr iš šun for fi:r odr sɛks voxê štorbê/
5d `He died four or six weeks ago.'

6a Das Feuer war zu stark, die Kuchen sind ja unten ganz schwarz gebrannt.
6b Das feier war so heiss, das die kuche une ganz schwarz brennt sind.
6c das faiêr var so hois, das di ku:xê unê gants švarts brɛnt sin/
6d `The fire was too hot, the pies were burned really black underneath.'

7a Er isst die Eier immer ohne Salz und Pfeffer.
7b Er est die eier immer ohne saltz und pfeffer.
7c /er ɛst di aiêr ɛmr u:nê salts un pfɛfêr/
7d `He always eats eggs without salt and pepper.'

8a Die Füsse tun mir weh, ich glaube, ich habe sie durchgelaufen.
8b Die fiss tun mir so weh, ich denk ich han sie wund glofe.
8c /di fi:s du:n mir so vɛ: ix dɛ_k ix han sɛ vund glofê/
8d `My feet hurt me, I believe I've walked them through.'

9a Ich bin bei der Frau gewesen und habe es ihr gesagt, und sie sagte, sie wollte es auch ihrer Tochter sagen.
9b Ich war bei dem weib und hans ihr sagt, und sie hat sagt sie mechts a ihrer tochter sage.
9c /ix var bai dêm vaib un hans êr tsa:kt, un si hat tsa:kt si mɛxts a: i:rêr doxtêr sa:gê/
9d `I was at the women's place and I told her, and she said she also wanted to tell it to her daughter.'

10a Ich will es auch nicht mehr wieder tun.
10b Ich will es a nimme tun.
10c /ix vil ês a: nime do:/
10d `I don't want to do it ever again.'

11a Ich schlage dich gleich mit dem Kochlöffel um die Ohren, du Affe!
11b Ich schlag dich gleich mit dem kochleffel ans ohr, du aff!

11c c/ix šlag dix glaix midm koxlefl ans o:r du af/
11d `I'm going to hit you about the ears with the cooking spoon, you monkey.'

12a Wo gehst du hin, sollen wir mit dir gehen?
12b Wo gehst du nah, sollen mir mit dir geh?
12c /vo gɛ:š du na:, solên mir mit dir gɛ:/
12d `Where are you going, should we go with you?'

13a Es sind schlechte Zeiten!
13b Es sind schlechte zeite!
13c /ɛs sin šlɛxtê tsaidê/
13d `These are bad times.'

14a Mein liebes Kind bleib hier unten stehen, die bössn Gänse beissen dich tot.
14b Mei liebes kind bleib drunte steh, die bäse gäns beissen dich tod.
14c /mai li:bês kint blaip drunê štɛ: di bɛ:se gɛns baisn dix dot/
14d `My dear child stay down here, the mean geese will bite you to death.'

15a Du hast heute am meisten gelernt und bist artig gewesen, du darfst früher nach Hause gehen als die andern.
15b Du hast heit das mehrste glernt und bist antlich (ordentlich) gwese so kannst du freher heim geh wie die andere.
15c /hašd haid s'mɛršdê glɛnt un bišd antlix gvɛ:sê so kanš du fri:r hoim gɛ: vi di andêrê/
15d `You have learned the most today and have been very good, you may go home earlier than the others.'

16a Du bist noch nicht gross genug, um eine Flasche Wein auszutrinken, du musst erst noch etwas wachsen und grösser werden.
16b Du bist noch nit gross genug zum a flasche wein trinke, du muss erst noch ein bissle wachse und greser werde.
16c /du bišd nox nêt gro:s gênuk tsum a flaš vai dringkê du muš ɛršt nox a bislê waksê/

16d 'You are not yet big enough, to drink a bottle of wine, you still have to grow a little and get bigger.'

17a Geh, sei so gut und sag deiner Schwester, sie solle die Kleider für eure Mutter fertig nähen und mit der Bürste rein machen.
17b Geh, sags deiner Schwester sie soll die kleider fer eire mutter fertig nähe und mit der berst putze.
17c /ge sags dainr šveštêr si sol di glaidêr fir aiêr mutr fɛrdix nɛ:ê un mit dêr bɛršd butsê/
17d Go, be so kind and tell your sister, she should finish sewing the clothes for your mother and clean them with the brush.

18a Hättest du ihn gekannt! dann wäre es anders gekommen, und es täte besser um ihn stehen.
18b Hetst du ihn kennt dann wers anderst komme und noh deht es besser mit ihm stehe.
18c /hɛdšd du ên kɛnd dan vɛrs andêršd komê un no dɛt ês bɛsr mit ɛ:m šdɛ:/
18d 'Had you known him, then things would have been happened differently, and it would be better for him now.'

19a Wer hat mir meinen Korb mit Fleisch gestohlen?
19b Wer hat mir mei karb mit dem fleisch stohle.
19c /vɛr hot mir mai karb mitêm flaiš šdo:lê/
19d 'Who stole my basket of meat?'

20a Er tat so, als hätten sie ihn zum dreschen bestellt; sie haben es aber selbst getan.
20b Er hat so tu wie wann sie ihn zum dresche bstellt hen, sie hen es aber selber tu.
20c /er hat so g'do: vi van sê ên tsum drɛšê bšdɛlt hɛn si hɛn's abêr sɛlbêrt do:/
20d 'He acted as if they had asked him to do the thrashing, but they did it themselves.'

21a Wem hat er die neue Geschichte erzählt?
21b Wem hat er die neie geschicht verzehlt?
21c /vɛ:m hat ɛr di naiê tšixt fêrtsɛ:lt/

21d 'To whom did he tell the new story?'

22a Man muss laut schreien, sonst versteht er uns nicht.
22b Mir muss laut schreie sonst versteht er uns nit.
22c /mê mus laut šraiê sunš frsdɛːd êr uns nɛt/
22d You have to speak loudly or else he won't understand us.

23a Wir sind müde und haben Durst.
23b Mir sind mid und hen dorst.
23c /mê sɛn miːd un hɛn doršt/
23d 'We're tired and thirsty.'

24a Als wir gestern abend zurück kamen, da lagen die andern schon im Bett und waren fest am schlafen.
24b Wann mir gestrobed zureck komme sind, dann waren die andre schon alle im bett und hen fest schlofe.
24c van mir gêšdroːbêt tserik koma sin, dan varên di andrê šon alê im bɛt un hɛn fɛšd tšloːfê/
24d 'When we came back last night, the others were already lying in bed and were fast asleep.'

25a Der Schnee ist diese Nacht bei uns liegen geblieben, aber heute Morgen ist er geschmolzen.
25b Der schnee ist letzt nacht liege bliebe aber heit morge war er aller vertaut.
25c /dr šneː iš lɛdšt naxt liggê bliːbê abr haid margê išêr fêrdaut/
25d 'The snow stayed on the ground last night, but this morning it had thawed.'

26a Hinter unserm Hause stehen drei Äpfelbäumchen mit roten Äpfelchen.
26b Hinter unserm haus stehn drei schene äpfelbämle mit rote äpfele drah.
26c hindêr unsêrm haus stɛhn drai šɛːnɛ ɛpflbɛmlê mid roːdê ɛpfêlɛ draː/
26d 'Behind our house there are three small apple trees with red apples.'

27a Könnt ihr nicht noch ein Augenblickchen auf uns warten, dann gehen wir mit euch.
27b Kennt ihr nit a kleines weile warte, noh gehn mir mit euch.
27c /kɛnt ir nit a glainês vailê vardê, no gɛn mir mit aix/
27d `Couldn't you wait a second, then we'll go with you.'

28a Ihr dürft nicht solche Kindereien treiben.
28b Ihr sollt nit so kindisch sei.
28c /ir sold nɛt so kindiš sai/
28d `You aren't allowed to do such childish things.'

29a Unsere Berge sind nicht sehr hoch, die euren sind viel höher.
29b Unser bigel sind nit so hoch, eure sind viel heher.
29c /unsêr bikêl sɛn nɛt so hox, airê sɛnd fi:l hɛxêr/
29d `Our mountains are not so high, yours are much higher.'

30a Wieviel Pfund Wurst und wieviel Brot wollt ihr haben?
30b Wieviel pfund wurst und brot willst han?
30c /vifi:l pfunt voršt und brot vilšd han/
30d How many pounds of sausage and bread do you want to have?

31a Ich verstehe euch nicht, ihr müsst ein bisschen lauter sprechen.
31b Ich versteh euch nit, ihr missen ein bissle lauter verzähle.
31c /ix fêršdɛ: aix nɛt ir misn a bislɛ laudr frtsɛlê/
31d `I don't understand you, you have to speak a bit louder.'

32a Habt ihr kein Stückchen weisse Seife für mich auf meinem Tische gefunden?
32b Hen ihr kei stickle weise seif uf meim tisch funde.
32c /hɛn ir kai šdiglɛ vaisê soif uf maim diš fonê/
32d Didn't you find small piece of white soap on my table for me?

33a Sein Bruder will sich zwei schöne neue Häuser in eurem Garten bauen.
33b Sei bruder will zwei schene neie heiser in eurem garte baue.
33c /sai brudr vil tsvai šɛ:nɛ naiɛ haisêr in airêm gartê bauê/

33d   'His brother wants to build two nice new houses in your garden for himself.'

34a   Das Wort kam ihm vom Herzen!
34b   Das Wort kommt vom herz.
34c   /dɛs vort kumt fom hɛrts/
34d   'The words came from his heart.'

35a   Das war recht von ihnen!
35b   Das war recht von ihne.
35c   /dɛs var rɛxt fon ɛ:nê/
35d   'That was the right thing for you to do.'

36a   Was sitzen da für Vögelchen oben auf dem Mäuerchen?
36b   Was fer kleine vegel hocken uf dem kleine mauer?
36c   /vas far glainê fɛ:gl hokn uf dr glainê maur/
36d   'What kind of little birds are sitting on top of the small wall?'

37a   Die Bauern hatten fünf Ochsen und neun Kühe und zwölf Schäfchen vor das Dorf gebracht, die wollten sie verkaufen.
37b   Die farmer hatten fenf ochse und nei kih und zwelf schefle ins dorf brocht, sie willen sie verkafe.
37c   /di farmer hadn finf oksê un nai ki: un tsvɛlf šɛflɛ ins dorf broxt si vɛlên si frka:fê/
37d   'The farmers had brought five oxen and nine cows and twelve lambs to the village, they wanted to sell them.'

38a   Die Leute sind heute alle draussen auf dem Felde und mähen.
38b   Die leit sind alle draus uf der stepp und tun die ernt schneide.
38c   /di lait sɛn alɛ draus uf dr šdêp und dun di ɛrnt šnaidê/
38d   'People are all out in the fields today mowing.'

39a   Geh nur, der braune Hund tut dir nichts.
39b   Geh nomme, der braune hund macht dir nichts.
39c   /gɛ nomê, dêr braunê hunt maxt dir nix/
39d   'Go ahead, the brown dog won't do anything to you.'

40a Ich bin mit den Leuten da hinten über die Wiese ins Korn gefahren.
40b Ich bin mit dene leit da hinte eber die prairie ins korn g'fare.
40c /ix bin mit dɛni lait da hindê ibr di brɛri ins karn farê/
40d `I drove with the people back there, over the meadow to the grain field.'

3.1.2.4 Representative sample of Central Dakota German dialect words which contrast with Standard High German. In this representative sample of words characteristic of the Central Dakota German dialect, I would like to include words that have not necessarily occurred in the standard dialect studies, but are simply words that occur in the CDGer. vocabulary and when used by CDGer. speakers, identifies them as persons who truly know the dialect and appreciate its beauty of expression. As Staczek (*GURT 1988*:283) succinctly puts it:

....I believe there is a need to celebrate linguistic heritage, to rediscover it, and to restore, as a richness of human resource, what is retrievable linguistically and culturally. It was in the preface to the first edition of Haugen's *The Norwegian Language in America* that I found encouragement about how such personal "...homely materials could become the subject of scientific study..." (1969:ix).

One phenomenon I have noticed is that many Germans who became United States citizens after World War II and who, of course, speak both fluent German and good English, include in the midst of their German speech many English words pronounced as in American English, that is, with American English phonemic sounds. By contrast, the CDGer. speaker is a true bilingual who uses only one language at a time and does not insert English words into his German sentences. If an English word is used, the word is pronounced as a German word, i.e. with the phonemics of Central Dakota German and as part of the CDGer. vocabulary and not as a cited English word, pronounced in an American English manner. If the bilingual CDGer. speaker does use both languages in the same sentence, it occurs as an instance of "code switching". He comes to a word like *beer/bier*, which is pronounced nearly the same in both languages; and, although he may have begun the sentence in German or English, when he comes to the word *beer/bier*, he may switch to the other language. Topics may cause a language change. If the topic is more easily discussed in English, he may make a complete switch to English rather than use many English words in a German sentence. Such a speaker then switches back to

German once the discussion of the "English" topic has been completed. Thus, he might discuss a new tax law in English, but switch back to German to discuss the plight of the poor and what the new tax law will mean to them, and to his audience.

Poplack (*GURT 1988*: 90-118) speaking on language status and language accommodation found that bilingual proficiency has the further function of keeping one from language borrowing. She found "code switching" to be a bilingual ability, and "borrowing" acquired behavior, not part of a lexical need.

In Central Dakota German the social class effect, an important factor in the use of words not belonging in a language, is absent. There are simply not enough CDGer. dialect speakers who go on to study Standard High German and who, when returning to the dialect community, can show educated status by use of it.

On the tapes of the informants I noticed that they tried very hard in answering the questions to find the correct dialect word. They felt badly if they didn't know a word or have it in their vocabulary. Then they would try to give me the word in Standard High German. They did not resort to reporting on the English word nor did they try to identify the word by discussing it in English. They would simply say, *das wort hin mir gar nit* 'we don't have that word'.

It became clear to me both in speaking with the informants and in listening to my tapes that their language is a serious matter to them, and that they are very aware of the language they employ. They view language as the vehicle with which they relate to people, and the correct word or the expression used is of great importance. They are always careful to observe the conventions of the language; thus, even though they live in the American culture where *you* is simply *you* for everyone, they still carefully follow the old German usage of *Ihr* 'you' as a term of respect and *du* 'you' as a term used only for children and very close friends and for relatives who are younger. They would never address even the dearest aunt with *du*; they treat a grandmother or grandfather similarly. The form *Ihr* does not connote distance or the distinction between friends and acquaintances such as one generally finds in the use of the Standard High German *Sie* versus *du*.

Ihr is simply, a sign of respect for the person addressed.

A good example of a firm CDGer. language taboo is the expression for 'you are lying' SHGer. *du lügst* or *sie lügen*; it is never used. You can paraphrase and get your meaning across, but you may never accuse someone of lying. Nor may you ever challenge God or fate with language; you will suffer for that act. If someone curses you, it is viewed with great seriousness and dread that the curse will come true.

How do the informants themselves describe their dialect? The best description was:

> *man muss langsam und leicht spreche,*
> *und es muss schen klinge.*
> 'You have to speak slowly and with a light touch, and it has to sound nice.'

This is an insightful comment, supported by linguists like Nida (1988: p. 242-49) who finds that today style and aesthetics are most often overlooked and language is expected to be merely a display of logic.

The Central Dakota German speaker finds the Standard High German speaker's enunciation "too crisp" and his vowels "too taut".

The strength of the CDGer. dialect always amazes those knowledgeable about German dialects and of the facts concerning German language speakers who have emigrated to the United States.

In discussing CDGer. vocabulary, the words for foods are the words which first come to mind, for they are the words most generally known and the ones remembered the longest. Here we find such words as *knepfla* /knepfla/ for any small pieces of dough prepared in a multitude of ways, *kremela* /grimêla/ for small crumbs of dough generally put into a good soup broth, *schupfnuddle* /šupfnudlê/ for dumplings made of dough, *kiechla* /ki:xla/ for sweet dough fried, *strudel* /štrudêl/ for dough rolled very thinly, and *stampfetz* /štamfɛts/ for mashed potatoes. *Schmagets* /šmagêts/ means a plant that `smells good'. A rare and old German word is *peterling* /pɛtêrliŋ/ for `parsley'. Every Central Dakota German is *daheim* /dahaim/ `at home' and not *zuhause*; he always has a *sommerkiche* /somêrkixê/, a kitchen outside the main house where everyone gathers and all the cooking is done except in the winter. There he visits with his friends in an exercise called *maistube mache* /maišub maxê/ `making a May visit', which could be an expression which refers to the difficulty of visiting during the winter months when one waited with expectation for the beautiful month of *Mai* `May'. More interesting is that in Middle High German the word *majen* /maiên/ means `to visit'. Thus, this Central Dakota German expression could reflect back to the Middle Ages.

Vocabulary words which to a native speaker immediately identify the Central Dakota German dialect, are words found in the following list. These lexical entries are often instances that simultaneously show the influence of the Swabian dialect.

No. Central Dakota German (CDGer.) Dialect Word; / Central Dakota German (CDGer.) Dialect Word Phonemically Expressed/; 'English Word'; (Standard High German Word)

1. *schaffe* /šafê/ `to work' (*arbeiten*)
2. *daheim* /dahaim/ `at home' (*zu Hause*)
3. *raus ropfe* /raus ropfê/ 'to pull out' (*heraus ziehen*)
4. *durmel* /durmêl/ `idiot' (*Idiot*)
5. *er ist soffe* /erštsofê/ `he's drunk' (*er ist betrunken*)
6. *dommelt sich* /domêlt six/ `to hurry' (*sich beeilen*)
7. *gell* /gêl/ `don't you think so too' (*nicht wahr?*)
8. *bub* /bua/ `boy' (*Junge*)
9. *dapfer* /dapfêr/ `quickly' (*schnell*)
10. *butzig* /butsix/ `tiny' (*winzig*)
11. *base* /bas/ `aunt' (*Tante*)
12. *hocke* /hokê/ `sit' (*sitzen*)
13. *mannsleit* /manslait/ `men' (*Männer*)
14. *weibsleit* /waibslait/ `women' (Frauen)
15. *nalege, nagehe, nahocke* /na:ligê/ /na:gɛhê/ /na:hokê/ `lie down, go there, sit down' (*hinlegen, hingehen, hinsetzen*)
16. *arg* /arg/ `very' (*sehr*)
17. *uf* /uf/ `on, upon' (*auf*)
18. *wiedig* /vi:dix/ `mad' (*wütend*)
19. *heilt* /hailt/ `crys' (*weint*)
20. *leicht* /laixt/ `funeral' (*Begräbnis*)
21. *gestrobet* /gêštrobêt/ `last evening' (*gestern Abend*)
22. *vaterschwestersohn* /fadêršvɛstêrso:/ `cousin' (*Cousin*)
23. *tochterman* /doxtêrman/ `son-in-law' (*Schwiegersohn*)
24. *duft* /duft/ `dew' (*Tau*)
25. *vieliche* /fi:lixê/ `many' (*viele*)
26. *schwätzen* /švɛtsên/ `to speak' (*sprechen*)
27. *hebe* /hɛ:bê/ `hold' (*halte*)
28. *ich han* /han/ `I have (*habe*)' *mir hin* /hin/ `we have' (*haben*)
29. *gucken* /gukê/ `look' (*schauen*)
30. *nomma* /noma/ `taken' (*genommen*)
31. *lauter* /lautêr/ `many' (*viele*)
32. *nimme* /nimɛ:/ `not again' (*nicht mehr*)
33. *bikel* /bikêl/ `hills' (*Hügeln*)
34. *hor* /ho:r/ `hair' (*Haare*)
35. *grundbiere* /grumbi:rê/ `potatoes' (*Kartoffeln*)
36. *gelriebe* /gêlri:bê/ `carrots (*Mohrrüben*)'
37. *schabe* /šabê/ `moths' (*Motten*)

38. *neigirich* /naiširix/ 'curious' (*neugierig*)
39. *henschich* /hinšix/ 'gloves' (*Handschuhe*)
40. *nasetichle* /na:sdi:xle/ 'handkerchief' (*Taschentuch*)
41. *grilt* /grilt/ 'loud irritating voice' (*Geschrei*)
42. *sei Weib* /sai vaib/ 'his wife' (*seine Frau*)
43. *verzähle* /fêrtsɛ:lê/ 'to tell' (*erzählen*)
44. *verrisse* /fêri:sê/ 'torn' (*zerrissen*)
45. *mir* /mir/ 'we' (*wir*)
46. *nix* /niks/ 'nothing' (*nichts*) *nit* /nɛt/ 'not' (*nicht*)
47. *peterling* / pɛtêrliŋ/ 'parsley' (*Petersilie*)
48. *mädle* /mɛ:dlê/ 'girl' (*Mädchen*)
49. *bissle* /bislɛ/ 'a bit' (*bisschen*)
50. *strele* /šdrɛ:lê/ 'comb' (*Kämmen*)
51. *gugumere* /gugumêrê/ 'cucumber' (*Gurke*)
52. *hochzeit* /hoxtsix/ 'wedding' (*Hochzeit*)
53. *freundschaft* /fraindšaft/ 'relatives' (*Verwandtschaft*)
54. *sehnerin* /tsɛ:nêrê/ 'daughter-in-law' (*Schwiegertochter*)
55. *weisen* /vaisê/ 'to show' (*zeigen*)
56. *versteckelt* /fêrštɛglt/ 'to hide' (*Verstecken*)

There are old words in the dialect such as *strel* /sdrɛ:l/ 'comb' (*Kamm*); *peterling* / pɛtêrliŋ / 'parsley' (*Petersilie*); and *duft* /duft/ 'hoarfrost' (*Rauhreif*) which could make an interesting etymological study.

According to Rein the use of the Swabian word *tochterman* /doxtêrman/ 'son-in-law' contrasts with the usage of most other German dialect speakers in the United States (such as the Hutterites who were from Austria, the Amish from the German Palatinate, the Texas Germans and the Amana Germans in Iowa who came from Hesse) and represents an archaic standard.

There are usages and expressions which are unique, such as: *die hin dich a immer diene wolle* /di: hin dix a imêr di:nê volê/ 'they always wanted to hire you' (*die haben dich immer anstellen wollen*).

Words like *weib* /vaib/ 'woman' (*Frau*) which in modern Standard High German are found to be either amusing or derogatory have retained their original meaning in Central Dakota German. The word *weib*, in fact, means more than just 'woman or wife'. It denotes respect and affection for you are the *weib* 'wife' of your husband just as was true in Middle High German usage: *sin wip* was a most important designation. To the Central Dakota German speaker the Standard High German word *Frau* means 'a woman who lives in the city'. An instance, which I recorded, shows how the old usage has been retained and how beautiful the expression can be:

> Dem Tschetter sei weib ischt storbe. Ach nei, doch nit die Bertha!
> 'Andreas Tschetter's wife has died. Oh no, not Bertha!'
> (*Die Frau vom Tschetter ist gestorben. Ach nein, doch nicht die Bertha!*)

The word *weib* is also used in *mitweib* /mitvaib/ 'midwife' (*Hebamme*) which literally means the 'woman with you'. Here the CDGer. word *mitweib* is a loan word from the English word 'midwife'. They use a unique and beautiful expression to describe what a midwife does: *sie empfängt's kind* /sie emfingts kint/ 'she receives the child'.

There are words and expressions such as *hingele* /hingêle/ 'a small chicken', or, 'someone who easily gets sick'. *Das ist ein durch triebener* /das iš a durx dribênêr/ 'someone who is possessed, over-active, apt to cause mischief'. The worst vice is to be stingy, for then one becomes *a geitsiger hund* /a gaitsigêrhunt/ 'a stingy dog'. This comes close to cursing someone, but cursing is left to others, *er flucht wie ein Türk* /er fluxt vi: ai turk/ 'he curses like a Turk'.

Grimm (1849:668f) complains that not only have Latin words replaced the old German words describing illnesses, but illness itself is now called *Krankheit* which formerly signified a disease. He lists the forgotten terminology for illnesses and they are the very expressions used in the Central Dakota German dialect. (See 5.3).

God is always addressed in Standard High German as *unser Herr Gott* or in what the Central Dakota German speakers believe to be Standard High German as they try to use it in sacramental language. When they speak the word for baptism, *taufen*, they invariably say /daufê/; but if I point this out they deny it and say in perfect Standard High German /taufên/. Children are allowed to speak to God in the most familiar way saying, *Abba lieber Vater Amen* /a:ba li:ba va:têr a:mên/ 'Dad, dearest father, Amen'.

Finally, I would like to submit the following list that impressionistically, to me at least, gives a rather good idea of the pronunciation of Central Dakota German, and represents some of the striking phonemic features.

No.   Standard High German Word (SHGer.); Central Dakota German Dialect Word (CDGer.); /Central Dakota German Dialect Word (CDGer.) Phonemically Expressed/;   English Word

1. *mein: mei* /mai/ `mine'
2. *beissen: beisse* /baisê/ `to bite'
3. *hinaus: naus* /naus/ `to go out'
4. *Taube: taub* /daub/ `dove'
5. *aufmachen: ufmache* /ufmaxê/ `open'
6. *neue Häuser: neie heiser* /naiê haisêr/ `new houses'
7. *Haus: haus* /haus/ `house'
8. *Schnee: schnee* /šnɛ:/ `snow'
9. *hoch: hoch* /ho:x/ `high'
10. *Haufen: haifle* /haiflê/ `pile'
11. *Höhe: heh* /hɛ:/ `height'
12. *heissen: heisse* /haisê/ `named'
13. *Heute: heit* /hait/ `today'
14. *Baum: baum* /ba:m baum/ `tree'
    Bäume: bäme /bɛ:m/ `trees'
15. *Dienstag: Dienstag* /dinšdag/ `Tuesday'
16. *Dunst: dunst* /dunšt/ `vapour'
17. *rein: rein* /rai/ `clean'
18. *einkaufen: einkaufe* /aika:fê/ `to buy'
19. *Sohn: sohn* /so:(n)/ `son'
20. *etwas: ebas* /ɛbês/ `something'

Throughout the Central Dakota German dialect one finds contraction and assimilation. Thus words given in the lists may vary in normal pronunciation because the dialect speaker normally uses them in context and there they are subject to the influence of contraction and assimilation. In this process the word accent is likely to shift or be altered. Some of the most frequent instances of contraction and assimilation are the article and the following noun, e.g. *die sonne* and contractions and assimilations that occur in verb forms e.g. *der isch*.

die Sonne: die sonne /tsonê/ `sun'
das Knie: das knie /skni/ `knee'
der ist: der isch /dêrš/ `he is'

Another example of the influence of contraction and assimilation is the pronunciation of /e/. Normally the dialect speaker uses a moderately open version of that vowel, namely, /ɛ/ (more open than in Standard High German). This open quality can be slightly changed into a more closed one due to sentence stress or to stress on one word:

gestern Abend: gestert Abend /gɛštro:bêt/ `last night'

There are also conditions in which /e/ becomes more closed, lengthened, and nasalized. The final nasal /n/ is dropped. Part of its nasal quality is preserved in the pronunciation of the preceding vowel, thus the loss of final nasal causes the preceeding vowel to nasalize. Depending on context, this quality varies with the pronunciation. In single words it appears strongest. In the transcriptions this nasalization is expressed by putting the nasal in brackets.

Stein: *stein* /stai(n)/ `stone'
klein: *klein* /glai(n)/ `small'
Zahn: *zahn* /tsa:(n)/ `tooth'

3.2 Comparison of a selected inventory of Central Dakota German lexicon with the standard dialectal geographic word-maps to determine the origin of the Central Dakota German dialect in Germany. The two hundred word list developed by Walther Mitzka (3.1.2.2) contains synonyms which help to identify the geographic location of the dialect. These words are contained in geographic word maps that detail the locations in which each synonym of a word is found. The technique involves using a number of transparent overlays that display the locality in which a particular dialect word occurs. By tracing onto transparencies the location of several words that are unique to a particular dialect, a pattern begins to emerge which indicates the origin of a particular dialect. These transparencies are placed on the properly scaled map of Germany. Thus, the general location and source of the dialect can be determined.

The source of the Central Dakota German dialect can be interpreted through the word maps to have the following characteristics:

(1) The change from the stop /k/ to the fricative /x/ has taken place since the CDGer. dialect uses the SHGer. *machen* and the SHGer. *ich*. Its location is south of the Benrather and Uerdinger lines on the German dialectological maps; that is, it is south of the *machen/maken* line and south of the *ich/ik* line.

(2) It has undergone the process of sound change /p/ > /pf/ (Grimm's law 1822) in that it contains the affricates /pf/ as in *apfel* `apple' and *pfund* `pound'; it is south of what is known in German as the *apfel/appel* line, the dividing line between the use of the stop /p/ versus the affricate /pf/. This sound change appears to be partial as CDGer. consistently uses /b/, /d/, and /g/ instead of the post-sound change /p/, /t/, /k/ in the initial and medial positions. (It is not a Palatinate dialect like the Pennsylvania Amish dialect.)

(3) It is part of the Swabian dialect because of the special Swabian features in the combinatory system, e.g., *st* becomes *št* in all positions. Standard High German *ist* /ist/ corresponds to Swabian *ischt* /išt/ `is', *fest* /fest/ corresponds to *fescht* /fɛšt/ `firm', *gestern* /gêstêrn/ corresponds to *geschtern* /gɛštêrn/ `yesterday'. *Gestern* is one example of pretonic vowel > /ge/ becomes /g/ at the beginning of words such as *gehört ghert, gefahren, gfahrê*, but not in the case of those words where the stem also begins with /g/ as in *gegangen* which becomes *gange* rather than *ggange*.

(4) A notable change from Standard High German to Swabian is the exclusive use of the diminutive affix *-le(in)* for the Standard High German diminutive affix which can be either *-chen* or *-lein*.

(5) It has a northwest Swabian characteristic in the dropping of the *n* /n/ as in *machen* /maxê/, while southeastern Swabian adds a *t* /t/ to *machen* /maxênt/.

(6) It is not central Swabian: Central Dakota German has /wɛ:/ for *weh* `sore, hurt' whereas central Swabian has /wa:i/, CDGer. has *schnee* /šnɛ:/ `snow' and central Swabian employs /šna:i/. CDGer. retains the *n* /n/ before *s* /s/ as in /gans/ for *gans* `goose', while central Swabian drops the *n* /n/ and the word occurs as /gais/.

(7) It may perhaps be possible for a German dialectologist, using the materials I have collected, to make a further statement on localization of the dialect. Within the scope of this study, it is safe to say: Central Dakota German is a somewhat archaic variety of what is termed *Honoratioren-Schwäbisch*, that is, a hybrid of Swabian used primarily by educated Swabians (e.g., clergymen, officials) and understood by everyone throughout the Swabian-speaking dialect area.

The completed picture of the "source dialect" which the geographic word maps attest to identifies Central Dakota German as *oberdeutsch* `upper German' (meaning the higher region geographically which is southern Germany), more specifically, a Swabian compromise dialect found in southwest Germany. The Swabian compromise designation is due to the strong influence on the dialect from reading the Bible and other religious teachings, such as the liturgy and song books, which are all written in Standard High German. (See Appendix for map with location of German dialects.)

The following are words in the *Deutscher Wortatlas* `German Word Atlas' which were used to determine the historical and geographic home and origin of the Central Dakota German dialect. Both the atlas volume number and the map number are listed for each word to facilitate reference. A *Deutscher Wortatlas* (DWA) map of Germany then shows the location of the source of the Central Dakota German dialect when the transparent overlay drawings from the word maps are placed on the correctly scaled map of Germany.

No. (Standard High German word) / Central Dakota German (CDGer.) word: *German Word Atlas* **volume and map number**

1. *(auswringen) / ausringeln*: DWA vol. 4/Map 7
2. *(Fliege) / Mücke*: DWA vol. 1 / Map 9
3. *(Frühling) / Frühjahr*: DWA vol. 4 / Map 15
4. *(hageln) / schlossen*: DWA vol. 4 / Map 8
5. *(Junge) / Bua*: DWA vol. 4 / Map 23
6. *(kehren) / fegen*: DWA vol. 3 /Map 1
7. *(Mädchen) / Mädle*: DWA vol. 4 / Map 30
8. *(Mutterschwein) / Loos*: DWA vol. 4 / Map 31
9. *(Pate) / Patt(e)*: DWA vol. 4 / Map 33
10. *(Rinde) / Krust*: DWA vol. 4 / Map 28
11. *(Roggen) / Rogga*: DWA vol. 4 / Map 42

The *German Word Atlas* (DWA) also includes large format maps that show the large general areas in which some words occur, whereas the regular maps just listed give the more precise and specific location for each word. I chose the following five words from the large-format maps as being representative of the CDGer. dialect:

1. *(Frosch) / Krot*: DWA vol. 13 / Map 13
2. *(Kartoffel) / Grundbiere/Erdäpfel*: DWA vol. 11 / Map 18
3. *(Maulwurf) / Maulwerfer*: DWA vol. 3 / Map 16
4. *(Mutterschwein) / Loos*: DWA vol. 8 / Map 17
5. *(schimpfen) / schelden*: DWA vol. 2 / Map 8

3.3 Internal linguistic evidence that the Central Dakota German dialect shows of the influences the original German dialect underwent as a result of its migrations. The CDGer. dialect shows internal linguistic evidence of the influences the original German dialect underwent as a result of the migrations of the Central Dakota German dialect speakers. Presented here is the internal lexical evidence of the external history found in loanwords from French, Russian, Romanian, and Turkish that reflect the influences resulting from its first emigration to Russia; and the internal lexical evidence found in loanwords from English which reflect the influence resulting from its second immigration from Russia to the United States.

3.3.1 Internal lexical evidence for the external history found in loanwords from French, Russian, Romanian, and Turkish which reflect the immigration to Russia. The foreign words found in the Central Dakota German lexicon appear to be words that were learned at the market where the German immigrants had contact with people who were not Germans from their villages. Indeed, they were so segregated from the Russians that only Germans lived in the German villages. In Russia, there were no other nationalities living in their communities as there were subsequently in the United States. The words listed are not the only foreign words learned by the Central Dakota Germans during their stay in Russia, for almost all of the immigrants spoke some Russian and many also spoke Romanian or what they called Moldavanisch (Moldavian).

Russian was the language used for more formal situations such as seeking employment from a Russian nobleman or selling goods and products to them. It was also the language needed for the government and the military. Indeed, Russian was taught as a language in their German schools. Moldavia, on the other hand, was the language used by people who moved around, who went from market to market with their products, and thus the German colonists spoke the local Moldavian in the market places.

The words I have listed are simply a sample of those foreign words which found their way into the Central Dakota German dialect and took their place in the CDGer. dialect as a part of its lexicon.

No. 'English Word'; Foreign Word; / Foreign Word Phonemically Expressed by Central Dakota German (CDGer.) Dialect Speaker/, Country of Origin

1. `tomato' *baklaschana* /baklašanê/, Russian for `eggplant'
2. `tomato' *pamidory* /pomadorê/, Russian and Romanian
3. `lilac tree' *zahrinkebaum* /tsa:rinkêbo:m/, Russian & German <Rus. *Zahrinke* CDGer.*baum*, `little Czarina's tree'
4. `storage building' *magazin* /magasa(n)/, French
5. `ducks' *gatscha* /gatša/, Polish
6. `watermelon' *arbuse* /arbusê/, Russian
7. .`melon patch' *bastan* /bɛšdan/, Russian
8. `turkey poults' *boggerla* /bogêrla/, Romanian

9. `corn' *kukuruza* /kukɛruts/, Turkish
10. `beets & vegetable soup' *borscht* /boršt/, Russian
11. `a filled turnover' *placenta* /blagêndɛ/, Romanian, Russian
12. `filled cabbage leaves' *haluptsy* /haluptsê/, Ukrainian
13. `steppe' *stepp* /šdep/, Russian 'prairie'
14. `tall weeds' *buryan* /burion/, Russian

3.3.2 Internal lexical evidence for the external history found in loanwords from English which reflect the influences resulting from the immigration to the United States. English has had a much greater influence on the language than Russian. While in Russia, the Germans lived in a rather isolated way in their own villages; in the United States, they were neighbors of other Americans who were English speakers. It was the English language that was used as their common language, a common occurrence for language groups in the United States. While the original generation of immigrants did not have the opportunity to attend schools where they would have learned English, the first generation attended the rural farm schools and did learn English. Nevertheless, the Central Dakota German dialect was very strong in resisting English influences. It took English words and ideas and incorporated them into the dialect. The switching back and forth between German and English and the great use of English words and sounds one would expect, did not occur.

This can be attributed to a tendency of petrifaction that generally takes place in the language and in other cultural behavior, of isolated speech communities, at least during some early periods (see Schwob, Obernberger, Rein). For during the time the Central Dakota German dialect was spoken in the Russian Empire, its speakers became accustomed to having other languages spoken around them, but they remained self-contained and did not easily accept many foreign words and influences. This was made easier because of the diversity which existed in the Russian Empire, the many languages used by the many different peoples who lived there, and the acceptance of this situation by the Russian government. There was never any `melting pot' as we know it. Thus, when the speakers of the Central Dakota German dialect came into contact with the English speakers who surrounded them in their new setting, and with schools where only English was used, and a situation where the only instruction in the German language was that given in the confirmation classes of their own churches (which at first were only German-speaking and only later became partially German-English), their language was prepared to live in this environment without changing its structure and lexicon.

The changes which did occur in the Central Datkota German dialect are interesting indeed, and I have divided them according to the different types of "language change" customarily classified by linguists, such as Haugen 1969, Hockett 1958, or Bloomfield 1933.

A language that is intact and strong takes in foreign words and assimilates them into its own sound system, and they then become "loan words". A good example of this is the English word *store*. The English phonemes of this word are unacceptable as German phonemes and the word can only be incorporated if the English /st/ becomes German /št/ as in *stube* /štubê/ `sitting-room' or *stein* /štain/ `stone'. The word store changes from /stor/ to /štor/. The word *upstairs* takes on somewhat the same characteristics as it becomes /opštɛ:s/, rather than the English *upstairs*. The words retain their English meaning but they have been incorporated into the Central Dakota German phonemic sound system. Thus we find words like *buggy* /bogi:/, *homestead claim* /das glêm/, *butcher* /butšêr/, and *pantry* becomes /pindrɛ/.

The borrower may not accept the donor language words along with the cultural item. Instead, he adapts the material to his own language. A new lexical item arises, and since it arises under the impact of another linguistic system, it is a "loanshift". Thus we have the German word *gleich* which means `to like something'. It comes from the influence of the English word *liking* and the SHGer. word *gleichen* which means `to liken or to compare'. Thus we have a change from the meaning `similarity' to the meaning `attitude'. Another good example of this adaptation is the use of the Central Dakota German word *meint* instead of SHGer. *bedeutet*, for the `meaning' of something; thus Central Dakota German *meint* is used when English *mean* would be used in the sense of `signify'. It is interesting how such adaptations can be repeated. For instance, *gleichen* appears in Pennsylvania German although they had no contact with the Central Dakota Germans.

According to Hockett (1958: 408-416) all borrowing can be a phase of what anthropologists call "diffusion". The acquisition of loanshifts is an instance of the particular kind of borrowing called "stimulus-diffusion". A member of a borrowing community gets the general notion for something from the donor community, but works out the details for himself. Hockett says that good nonlinguistic examples are to be found in the history of writing. The Latin alphabet spread into England and was adapted for the writing of English in the 7th century; this was "ordinary diffusion". The same can be said for Central Dakota German and its use of the Latin alphabet instead of German Gothic script (Fraktur). Capitalization of nouns, which is the practice in Standard High German, was dropped when the writing system used was no longer the old German script but the `same writing as the English use'. This meant that they took over the whole English system and only employed upper case or capital letters where English used upper case or capital letters.

"Loanblends" are new forms developed in the borrowing situation, when both the `loanword' and the `loan shift' mechanisms are involved. The borrower imports part of the foreign model and replaces part of it with something already in his own language. Thus we find in Central Dakota German the word *strohberry* which means literally `strawberry' while the standard German word for the berry is *Erdbeere*.

We also find mixed words that are half Central Dakota German and half English in: *zurickbecke* (<Ger. *zurick* `go back', verb + *becke* <Eng. *backup* (a car), verb) which is either German *zurückfahre* or English *back-up* (verb) but here becomes a mixture of the two. Another example is *hehnerfence* `chicken fence' which is neither German *Hühnerzaun* nor English *chicken fence*.

Interference is found in an expression like *kalt kriege* which means 'catch a cold' using the stem *kalt* combined with *to get* instead of the German word *erkälten*. *Ausgewore* means `worn out' using the German *aus* for *out*, while the German prefix *ge-* is affixed to English *worn*. Just as they neatly add the Swabian version of the diminutive /le/ to *feierwirmle* `firefly' as discussed below. They follow the Swabian practice of retaining only the /e/ at the end of a word and dropping the /n/ even when borrowing a word like *worn*. In a different type of interference English *raspberry* interferes with the SHGer. word *Himbeere* and we have Central Dakota German *raspbeere*.

A "loanblend" can also be the addition of a German suffix to the imported English word. For example the English word *used* becomes the Central Dakota German word /gust/ by adding the standard German prefix *ge-* to *used* and then dropping the `e' as the Central Dakota German dialect does for all *ge-* prefixes and we have the Central Dakota German *gused*. The English word *grasshopper* becomes the Central Dakota German word *grashopfer* even though the SHGer. word *Heuschrecke* is known to them.

Another type of loan is simply a new "coinage". The SHGer. word *Hebamme* is the equivalent of English *mid-wife*. The Central Dakota German employs the `loan translation' *mit-weib* `mid-wife'. They do not use the SHGer. word *Hebamme*, although they know what it means. They respond by saying they do not use this word, but it means *hebong* `delivery' a word they appear to have coined themselves.

Often "coinage" can lead to an entirely new word, e.g. Central Dakota German *sonnerose* /so:nêro:sê/ (literaly: `sun' + `rose') 'sunflower' although Standard High German had *Sonnenblume* available, a form which is the equivalent of English *sunflower*. Nevertheless, Central Dakota German. coined *Sonnerose*. Another such instance is Central Dakota German *Christtagbaum* /grišda:kbaum/ (<SHGer. *Christ* `Christ' + *Tag* `day' + *Baum* `tree') rather than the SHGer. word *Weihnachtsbaum* (<SHGer. *Weih* `bless' + *Nacht* `night' + *Baum* `tree').

They developed new words using their own vocabulary; the SHGer. word *Glühwürmchen* became Central Dakota German *feierwirmle* which is an adaptation of Eng. *firefly*. The Central Dakota German form showing the neatly added Swabian diminutive *-le*.

3.4 Factors favoring the language-maintenance of the Central Dakota German dialect. Many factors have favored the language maintenance of the Central Dakota German dialect, but clearly the most important one is the value placed on the language by the community. The second most important factor was the support the language received from the religion of the community. The Luther Bible, the Luther Catechism, and the Lutheran hymnal were the basis upon which the Central Dakota German dialect of German was maintained. The Lutheran religion supported the language and the language supported the religion and in this interlocking relationship lay the strength needed for language maintenance. In an isolated and remote area of the United States their importance for language maintenance could only be heightened further.

If one accepts the theory of the "petrifying tendency" of a dialect in isolation, then one can view these kinds of linguistic groups as mobile cultural islands that could sustain themselves in most situations, irrespective of the precise location. The very fact that their dialect had already experienced consolidation with other German dialects in Russia and had reached and maintained a "language balance" further supports the hypothesis. The dialect had, in and of itself, created its own form of language maintenance since it had already incorporated the speech of different immigrant German dialect groups into its language balance.

Arends' hypothesis accepts and expands this theory by stressing the Great Plains environment, and the complete isolation of such a large number of people as a major factor. Also, they must be reckoned with as a formidable group if one considers their impact in numbers since they constituted approximately 75% of the adjoining counties of McPherson, Campbell, and Edmunds in South Dakota, and McIntosh, LaMoure, Emmons, Logan, and Dickey counties directly across the border in North Dakota. These same Germans spread North and West through most of North Dakota and on into Canada, and South through South Dakota, joined by the Volga Germans in Nebraska, and Kansas. But, the compact ethnic core was the central area in the heart of North and South Dakota, the area under study here. A map of the Dakotas shows that this area has no major highway running through it and no major river. The area lies between the Missouri River on the west and the James River on the east. It lies to the east, west, south, and north of the main highways, the paved roads leading to the major routes which cross the United States. It is an area compact and isolated. A trip across gravel and dirt roads to the major cities of Aberdeen, South Dakota, and Bismarck, North Dakota, was a major undertaking and an event reserved for the heads of the family. It was a trip undertaken only once or twice a year to Aberdeen, and perhaps once in several years to Bismarck. Thus, in my view, the Central Dakota Germans were doubly isolated, isolated in the remote Dakotas and isolated within the Dakota Territory. In addition, there was a very large buffer zone of German speaking peoples surrounding them in this Great Plains environment.

An additional important factor to bear in mind is that we are investigating an agrarian society and agrarian societies are almost always conservative and self-contained. The people raised their own food, and preserved it, and were in control of their own destiny as they prepared themselves for the unbelievably extreme weather conditions. The climatic conditions were beyond anything they had experienced during their centuries in Europe. The key to their survival was their reliance on themselves and their relatives and neighbors. The relatives and neighbors were Germans from Russia, speaking the same dialect and having the same cultural heritage, the same beliefs and behavior system, holding the same common traditions.

If the Central Dakota area was not on the main system of roads and rivers, in the region, it certainly was not in the mainstream of American life. Teachers who taught in the small one-room school houses were members of their own group who had finished high school. Ministers who served in their German churches and later in their German/English churches were also of the same group. They studied at the same Lutheran seminaries and they returned to the Dakotas to minister to their bilingual parishes. Indeed, there was no higher calling for a young man than to study and return as a pastor.

The strength of family and community ties, the agrarian nature of the society and its isolation within an isolated area of the United States, the long and sustaining relationship with a religion in which the German language played such a large part and, above all, the value placed on the language in and by the community, sustained the Central Dakota German dialect and made it another instance of language maintenance in the United States.

3.5 Factors currently working to replace the Central Dakota German dialect with English. There are many factors working to replace the Central Dakota German dialect with English, but the most important one is that the individual identity is no longer tied to the group identity of being a German from North or South Dakota. Young people still realize that they have a German heritage, but they no longer feel that they are a part of a unique group of people tied together by a common cultural identity.

There are many factors at work, which I will describe, which favor the replacement of German with English even as the language of the home and of religion; but the most important factor and one with which many sociolinguists may disagree, is the influence of television. If television can influence every facet of American life throughout the United States, it should come as no surprise that it is irrevocably changing the way members of ethnic groups view themselves. Every child wants to identify with the other American children on television. Stories that grandmother tells them are nice; but what is their relevance for today? Why should someone learn a second language or be bilingual when no value is placed on it in our society? Value is accorded to knowing only English, and someone who is bilingual appears to know "less". As Staczek (*GURT 1988*:284) says there is a flight of bilinguals from bilingualism. The choice has been made and the shift from Central Dakota German and English bilingualism to English monolingualism is in progress.

What are some of the more important reasons for this language shift? The final curtain on maintaining bilingualism in the Central Dakota German communities was lowered with the decision to hold church services only in English with a German service on rare occasions. The interlocking relationship of language and religion which had maintained and sustained both was broken, and the Central Dakota German dialect suffered.

Another curious factor is the lack of German instruction in foreign language programs in the schools. German is taught in the colleges, but not in the high schools. With the church no longer supplying the reading materials in German, the schools might have filled the gap, although they would be teaching Standard High German, not the Central Dakota German dialect. A common view held that one should rid oneself of the German dialect since it appeared to be an impediment to the acquisition of good English. Learning German in high school will not cause anyone to have a German accent. On the contrary, knowledge of the dialect and familiarity with its sound system would be a great help in learning to speak Standard High German with proper intonation and without an English accent.

Other factors which have contributed to language switch are the consolidated large schools, as contrasted with the small rural schools. The one-room schoolhouse was recognized as culturally important for many reasons. For ethnic groups such as these, the one-room schoolhouse, as social center and center for learning, was the glue that held the community together.

Economic changes on the farms affected both rural and community life. In the fifties, rural electrification brought the modern world to the farms of the Dakotas. It was a boon and a change for the better; but it also changed the simpler ways of rural life. Farms became more modern and in the process less self-sustaining. There are now dairy farms, wheat farms, cattle farms, where before there were small farms which had dairy cattle, geese, chickens, wheat, flax, hay, etc. The era of large farms and specialization reaches into the Dakotas as well.

Education and moves to the city are now the normal course for Dakota young people. They know they will not be remaining on the family farm. As they become educated and move to the city they intermarry with other young people who are not of German descent and who do not speak German. Their children no longer hear German unless it is on a visit to their grandparents. If they marry another Dakota German and stay within the Dakotas they do maintain the language and have fun speaking to friends and relatives on their visits home.

Central Dakota German is still commonly spoken and heard on the streets and in the stores of the Central Dakota area. Young people still acquire the language but not so actively; they know it more in a passive sense. They still learn it because it is all around them; but they no longer attempt to learn to speak it well and to express themselves in it fully. I believe it will still be a viable language for yet another generation, but the process of dying has begun and the final passing of the Central Dakota German language as an active living language of expression to a passive language with limited expression will occur when the people who are now aged fifty and above are no longer there.

3.6 Sociolinguistic functions of the Central Dakota German dialect in contemporary life in the United States. The Central Dakota German dialect very clearly still performs a major role in the life of the communities of the Central Dakota region and has important sociolinguistic functions. It holds everyone together as members of one large family. The beauty of retaining an old form of speech which has held a group of people together over a 200-year period of migrations and in different social conditions is the sense of belonging which each member of the group feels. Their cultural heritage is intertwined and its expression occurs through a common language. The Central Dakota German dialect makes the dialect speaker a member of a very large and supportive family. When entering one of their communities or stopping at one of their farms, there is immediate acceptance when the stranger speaks in the Central Dakota German dialect. An opening question then inquires where you are from, and then what is your family name. One is then "placed" and they know who you are and want to be helpful to someone they trust.

There is a unique sense of belonging that everyone feels even if they no longer live in the Dakotas. It is a feeling of acceptance; you simply "belong" through the use of language. This interrelationship of language and the world, the concept of language as a social interpersonal code, becomes clearer as one studies and employs this language that has held people together for such a long time.

3.7 Attempt at a prognosis for maintenance of the Central Dakota German dialect in the face of the many pressures for its replacement by English. What is the prognosis for maintenance of the Central Dakota German dialect in the face of the many pressures for its replacement by English? All signs indicate that the prognosis is not good. The first positive sign which might indicate a retardation in the present rate of decline would be a reversal in the attitudes of the younger Central Dakota Germans themselves, such that they would come to value their dialect of German as an old and beautiful dialect worth preserving, rather than just a variety which is of lesser value than Standard High German.

Although strong German language programs in the local high schools would be of assistance, the variety of German which would be presented there would be Standard High German. This would give value to the skill of knowing and speaking German, but in the long run would probably not check the decline of dialect use. What a strong German language program would do is produce first class German linguists who have benefitted from the German language present in their families and communities.

As for the Lutheran churches which previously were a support for maintenance of the language, their switch to English services merely reflects the fact that they are being true to their primary commitment, which is the preaching of the Gospel, not language instruction or maintenance. In the early 1940s, certainly by 1950, the Lutheran churches, recognizing the increasingly bilingual make-up of their congregations, switched from exclusively German services to having both a German service and an English service. After the switch about 40% still attended the German services exclusively. Then, in about 1982, the main Lutheran church in Ashley dropped the German service completely to the sorrow and anger of many of the older people who still preferred to attend the German service. Many of them felt at the time and still feel that, in the interest of the Gospel, the Lutheran church should continue to provide them with their traditional Lutheran liturgy in German.

In1988, we estimated the monolingual speakers of German to be less than 10%, all of whom are in their eighties. Middle-aged people are bilingual German-English; younger people tend to be monolingual speakers of English with limited knowledge of German.

Given this rather unpromising prognosis, what might those interested in the Central Dakota German dialect do before this variety of German disappears completely?

(1) A series of descriptive studies should probably be initiated as quickly as possible. Its minimum objective would be a descriptive sketch of the grammar of the language and the production of lexicon with both Standard High German and English words. Needless to say, the descriptive grammar should contain as full and illustrative a sketch of the phonology, morphology, and syntax of the dialect as time permits; and this descriptive sketch should be accompanied by recordings of the examples cited in the text of the sketch. Such grammatical and lexical studies would be of great worth to future historians of the German language and those attempting to codify its dialectal varieties.

(2) If the decline of this dialect should continue, a careful description should be kept of the process. For just as from the careful study of terminal illnesses and death we can learn much about the biological and physiological processes which constitute health and life, so from a careful study of the gradual disappearance of a dialect we can learn much about the linguistic and sociolinguistic processes at work in all languages.

(3) Whatever happens to this Central Dakota German community, that story cannot but be of instructive interest to the cultural anthropologist who here has a perfect laboratory in which to observe the various forces and types of cultural and social change, the factors which affect such changes, and the values and entities which survive.

Chapter 4: The spiritual language of a people

4.0 Introduction: Der Sonntag ghert zu unserem Gott `Sunday belongs to the Lord'. When Sunday morning came the bell in the steeple invited all to attend the worship services.

The importance of the church was established early in the life of the Dakota German child, for his parents wanted him to have a thorough religious education. The Lord's Day was a holy day, and on Saturday evening Sunday clothes were laid out, the body was bathed, and the face shaven. The women, mothers and daughters, put the home into holiday dress and prepared a meal for the Sunday dinner (Joachim 1939:18).

Church services were held every Sunday in the German language. As late as the 1940s, Sunday School was held in German every week. During the hour when the children were attending Sunday School, parents visited, outside in good weather or in the back of the church on cold days. There were many such cold days on the Dakota prairies, and the grown-ups' loud whispering often filled the church. The children, even as adults, still remembered the "shshsh"' noises that accompanied their Sunday School lessons. The women carried leaves of a fragrant plant, a variety of mint, that grew wild on the prairie, which they called *schmackgets* `something that smells good', and they waved and shook them as they talked, so that the scent filled the whole church.

The typical minister was responsible for four different churches and could visit each only once a month. In the pastor's absence, either a school teacher or a deacon would read the sermon at the worship service. The church itself was built by the pioneers as soon as possible after they reached their settlement site. To build it, they all worked together. Until the church was ready they met for the Sunday worship in their homes with their neighbors. The settlers generally managed to stay together in religious communities. The Lutheran Church predominated in the center of the Dakota Territory. The only large concentration of Catholic families in the Central Dakotas was in the Hague-Zeeland-Strasburg area of North Dakota, with a large number of Catholics also present in Napoleon. Although only the customs and practices of the Lutherans are reported here, similar practices obtained for the settlers who came from other German Protestant groups in Russia, such as the Reformed, the Evangelicals, and the Baptists. As my informants explained to me, there was a fluidity among the German Protestants. By this I mean there was a lot of intermarriage and changing from one of the Protestant religions to another. It was also the practice that if you lived on a farm surrounded by neighbors of one of the Protestant religions who met together and built a church together, you were apt to join that church rather than drive a great distance with horse and carriage to attend a different church. This spirit prevailed and is the reason why everyone followed certain basic religious customs. The Catholics having settled together remained intact.

My informants said that the Reformed and Lutheran churches barely differed. This becomes self-evident in that they joined together and formed one church in Germany. This occurred in Baden and Württemberg in the year 1821. One of the outcomes of the Enlightenment period was this blending of the two faiths. But, it was also part of the reason many people objected to what was being done to their church. Many Lutherans did not want to change their liturgy or sacraments to suit this union. The leaders of the movement for change wanted to develop a new catechism which would be more a good teaching manual rather than a catechism representing the old Lutheran traditions. In the new church union individual ministers were to be able to make changes in the liturgy. The basic point of theological difference between the old Lutherans and the Reformed church concerned the manner of Christ's presence in the Eucharist. According to the Reformed theology, the bread and wine were a visible sign and symbol of Christ's unseen forgiveness and represented the good that flows from it. Communion showed remembrance, public expression of ones Christian belief, and was an act of love. In contrast, the Lutherans believed the bread and wine to be the body and blood of Christ. The Communion of the Lutherans represented forgiveness of sin, renewal of faith, imparting of strength, joy at the prospect of death in the Holy Spirit, and the hope for eternal life. Thus, when we state that many left due to changes in the liturgy and in their church, this must be understood as encompassing changes in the theological views about the nature of the sacraments, theological views which were at the very heart of their religion and sacramental beliefs. Thus one can see how very central and basic these differences were. Those who left for Russia stayed in the separate churches which they had belonged to in Germany; those who stayed behind in Germany became members, in July 1821, of the new combined church, the Evangelical-Lutheran Church (Württembergisches Landesmuseum 1987:301).

The Central Dakota German Evangelical and Baptist churches appear to have been very much alike. They both believed in the need to be saved. The Baptists alone baptised adults rather than children. The Baptists also believed in total emersion.

Although I do not have statistics on the religious groups in the Central Dakotas, the following statistics from Russia for the year 1897 give an indication of the religious situation. Official statistics for the 1,790,489 Germans living in Russia, including the Baltic, are broken down in the following chart (Stumpp 1966:20) to show the number of each religion and their total percentage.

Lutherans: 1,360,943 or 76.0%
Roman Catholic: 242,209 or 13.5%
Mennonites: 65,917 or 3.7%
Reformed: 63,981 or 3.6%
Baptists: 19,913 or 1.1%
Greek-Orthodox: 13,360 or .7%
Other Christians: 1,411 or .1%
Jewish: 22,855 or 1.3%
  (This figure includes all non-Christians.)

Thus customs presented in this religion chapter are Lutheran customs which seem to have been accepted and practiced to some degree by all the German Protestants in the Central Dakota area. This is not surprising when one considers the large majority the Lutherans must have been. In the songs one can see the cross-over between the religions as we find Baptist songs very popular with the special singing groups, in particular at the Lutheran funerals.

There were no organs or pianos in the early churches; but there was always much singing, for the people loved music and delighted in singing the old familiar songs. In church, women and girls sat to the left, men and boys to the right, a custom observed in the Dakota German Protestant services whenever German services where held.

After church on Sunday, people lingered to visit for an hour, at least; women talked, children played. Afterwards, men hitched the horses, in summer to the buggy, in winter to the sled. During the winter months heavy blankets and footwarmers were a necessity. The footwarmers were of metal, filled with briquet coal which had been heated ahead of time. Some people heated large stones or bricks in their cook stoves and used these for footwarmers. There were always invitations from relatives and neighbors for Sunday dinner, which traditionally featured a rich noodle soup, cooked with a whole chicken, prepared the day before. Other dishes, such as sauerkraut, spareribs, ham, and mashed potatoes, were winter favorites for Sunday dinner, as was *halupsy*, cabbage leaves filled with ham bits and rice. *Knepfla*, the usual accompaniment for sauerkraut, was never cooked on Sunday because dough could not be made on this holy day. *Kuchen*, the dessert, was always prepared the day before and was served with tea. The Sunday dishes were chosen from those which could be prepared the day before and then reheated for Sunday dinner. Traditional German food lent itself well to this practice.

On Sunday afternoon there were prayer meetings held by the deacons, and religious instruction for the young. This practice of meeting on Sunday afternoons was one of the distinguishing features of the Pietist movement which was a moving force in the emigration from Württemberg. Pietists were those Germans who advocated a revival of the devotional ideal in the Lutheran church. Sunday was also the time when baptisms, marriages, and funerals were held.

Although one was allowed to feed the cattle, no other work was permitted on Sundays. One could not even cut with a scissors. Even today one does not see the Dakota German farmer working in his fields on Sunday.

Church services were also held in the evening, from 7:00 p.m. to 8:00 p.m. Afterwards, the older people went visiting and some of the young people went to barn dances in cleanly swept hay lofts where they waltzed or danced the polka to the accompaniment of an accordion or a harmonica. Dances were over by 10:30 p.m.; at that time all the young people had to go home.

The church was named for the farmer whose property lay closest to it. For example, four churches in one district of the Ashley, North Dakota, area were the Schmidt Kirche, the Schumacher Kirche, the Quashnick Kirche, and the Biederstedt Kirche. The minister's call to a community was usually for life, particularly in the pioneer years; and he was the representative of the Lord there. He traditionally lived in his own home until the time when parsonages were built. He received a salary and the special contributions connected with his office. In addition, he was given sausages made by the parishioners as well as chickens and garden produce. Sharing the best one had with the minister was the custom.

The minister's duties were demanding, for he was responsible for advising and counseling all his parishioners. Everyone went to him for help and for mediation of their problems. If neighbors argued, the minister would have to make a just settlement of the dispute, for church members could not go to Communion if they had an unsettled argument in the family or with a neighbor. Business arrangements were not written agreements or handled by lawyers. A man's word was enough. This explains the taboo that one could never call someone a liar. The need for the minister as mediator is understandable.

A case in point is an incident that occurred in the 1920s as told by Margaret Hoffmann. Gottlieb Bendewald had an argument with another farmer over whether or not payment had been made to him for threshing a field. The case was taken to court, where it was tried through interpreters since neither one spoke English, and Gottlieb lost. However, he would not give up because he believed he was in the right and a man had to be as good as his word. He appealed to the State Supreme Court, where he again lost. He lost more money on the trials than the case involved; but worse for him and his family was the fact that he could not attend Communion for almost three years. Nor, according to the law of the church, could the other farmer. Then Gottlieb's opponent became ill. The minister called Gottlieb to the deathbed of his opponent, and the sick man confessed that he had never paid his debt. Gottlieb forgave him; and thus the two men received communion together before the neighbor's death. The emotional content and the deepest meaning of Christianity had been preserved.

The Dakota German from Russia adhered very strictly to the tenets of his faith. Even in the modern American setting, with the hardships of pioneer life largely past, he is a faithful attendant at church service, an enthusiastic singer of the hymns, and a good listener who enters wholeheartedly into the spirit of the church service (Joachim 1939:19).

One of the customs was that of kneeling and praying to thank for deliverance. In a time of crisis for her family a woman would say, 'Please, dear God, help us in our hour of need and I will pray to you before the church forever'. If her prayers were answered, she would always kneel and pray when she arrived at church on Sunday. You would see the old pioneer women wearing their shawls on their heads, kneeling and praying many many years afterwards. They never forgot their commitment. Life on the prairie made a relationship with God a very close and personal one.

Being able to worship in the German language is very important to the old German pioneer. His church is his link to the past. His forefathers managed to preserve the religious practices of their ancestors after leaving their homes in Southern Germany. In Russia and in the Dakotas his church and his language gave him a center for his life and an identity. He has tried to hold fast to a familiar liturgy and his traditional language of worship. Consequently some have felt forgotten by their church as their opportunities to worship together have become few.

4.0.1 Sources for the Lieder cited. This chapter and Chapter 5 cite hymns, songs, and carols which the Central Dakota Germans call by the generic name *Lieder*. The sources employed for each of these *Lieder* are cited in parentheses beneath each title in an abbreviated format. Full bibliographic information for each volume of *Lieder* is given in the general bibliography.

The sources and their abbreviations are:

Evangelium Lieder. 1897 (EL)
Liederschatz. 1914. (LS)
Evang.-Lutherisches Gesangbuch für Kirche, Schule und Haus
'Lutheran hymnal'. [no date, in use since 1908]. (LH)
Neue Glaubernsharfe. 1916 (GH)
Oral tradition. (OT) [name of person if song is no longer known by the majority of the Central Dakota German community]

The sources for *Lieder* are cited by their number in the hymnal rather than by page. The text of these *Lieder* were also checked against the following three hymnals published in Germany in order to ascertain whether they were common Lutheran hymns in Germany: *Gesangbuch* of 1753 (Ga), of 1823 (Gb), and of 1855 (Gc).

4.1 Der Katechismus nach Luther: Lutheran religion and the language of Luther's church. The rites of the church are still an integral part of the pattern and rhythm of the Dakota German's life, and he takes part in all church ceremonies. These people left Germany because they could not accept changes in Luther's church. They wanted the language and ritual of the church to remain the same. In their religious traditions it is this adherence to old customs that makes them also quite unique, although not in the same sense as the well-known religious communities like the Amish or the Hutterites.

4.1.1 Kindertaufe: A child's baptism. Baptism marks a child's formal acceptance into the congregation and is a special occasion not only for the family but for the community. In the early years two women and one man, either relatives, neighbors, or friends, served as sponsors for the baby. A hymn traditionally sung at Baptisms was:

Liebster Jesu, wir sind hier
(LH 289, GH 75, Ga 556, Gc 185)

Liebster Jesu, wir sind hier,
deinem Worte nachzuleben;
dieses Kindlein kommt zu dir,
weil du den Befehl gegeben,
dass man sie zu dir hinführe,
denn das Himmelreich ist ihre.

Ja, es schallet allermeist
dieses Wort in unsre Ohren:
Wer durch Wasser und durch Geist
nicht zuvor ist neugeboren,
wird von dir nicht aufgenommen
und in Gottes Reich nicht kommen.

Darum eilen wir zu dir,
nimm das Pfand von unsern Armen,
tritt mit deinem Glanz herfür
und erzeige dein Erbarmen,
dass es dein Kind hier auf Erden
und im Himmel möge werden.

Following the baptism there was a big feast for the family and sponsors to which at least twenty guests were usually invited. The finest food was served on this occasion. Noodle soup as the first course, followed by stuffed goose, duck or chicken accompanied by baked potato slices and baked rice. *Kuchen* was a tradition for all special occasions, and certainly a `must', as the Dakota German says, for the celebration of a baptism.

4.1.2 Konfirmation: Confirmation. Dakota German children attended Sunday school and church every Sunday, and each summer they attended an all-day Bible school for a month. The three years of instruction preceeding Confirmation were a requirement, and no matter what the family situation, children simply could not be kept from school to work at home. These classes formed the basis of a continuing religious heritage as well as the continuation of German as the language of religion. Children studied the German Bible and learned to read and write German. This continued until age twelve or thirteen. Then they were ready for Confirmation classes, also in German, which were conducted by the pastor.

It was the wish of every German mother to have her children confirmed by age 14. The course of religious instruction leading to Confirmation was difficult, especially for children learning English in school; and the parents worked hard to teach them the required Bible lessons. Teaching always emphasized the holiness of Sunday and included instruction on activities that were not allowed on Sunday.

Confirmation was always a time of great celebration for the family. It held a special significance for both the child and his family because it meant that their faith and language had been maintained through a long sojourn in Russia and resettlement in the United States.

The ceremony was held each spring, on Palm Sunday, and a beautiful ritual marked the Confirmation in the early days in Dakota. A path of sand was made to the church door, and the boys scattered *maiblume* or *haseblume* which are blue and white flowers very much like crocuses, upon it. The girls were dressed in white and the boys in navy suits with white shirts. The children to be confirmed walked down the path to the church by two's, girls in front, to the church. As they went they sang the song:

Jesu geh voran
(LH 464, LS 175, GH 327, EL 296, Gc 223)

Jesu geh voran auf der Lebensbahn
und wir wollen nicht verweilen,
Dir getreulich nachzueilen,
führ uns an der Hand bis ins Vaterland.

Soll's uns hart ergehn, lass uns feste stehn
und auch in den schwersten Tagen
niemals über Lasten klagen;
denn durch Trübsal hier geht der Weg zu dir.

*Rühret eigner Schmerz jemals unser Herz,
kümmert uns ein fremdes Leiden,
O so gib Geduld zu beiden;
richte unsern Sinn auf das Ende hin.*

*Ordne unsern Gang, Jesu, lebenlang.
führst du uns durch rauhe Wege,
gib uns auch die nötige Pflege.
Tu uns nach dem Lauf deine Türe auf.*

After these verses of the song, when they came to the last phrase 'Tu uns nach dem Lauf deine Türe auf', asking that the doors of heaven be opened to them, the doors of the church signifying the doors of heaven were opened to them and they entered both realms. The children recited the appropriate Bible verses they had learned which referred to this solemn occasion; then the pastor proceeded with the Confirmation. It was the child's acceptance into the Faith and into the fellowship of the congregation as an adult with full rights, the most important of which was the right to receive Communion. Two songs were always sung for the Communion, the first one before Communion and the second one during Communion.

Jesu nimmt die Sünder an!
(LH 379, EL 144, Gb 215, Gc 216)

*Jesu nimmt die Sünder an!
saget doch dies Trostwort allen,
welche von der rechten Bahn
auf verkehrten Weg verfallen.
Hier ist, was sie retten kann:
Jesus nimmt die Sünder an!*

Schmücke dich, O liebe Seele
(LH 300, GH 506, Ga 619, Gc 194)

*Schmücke dich, O liebe Seele!
Lass die dunkle Sündenhöhle,
komm ans helle Licht gegangen,
fange herrlich an zu prangen;
denn der Herr voll Heil und Gnaden
will dich jetzt zu Gaste laden;
der den Himmel kann verwalten,
will jetzt Herberg in dir halten.*

Eile, wie Verlobte pflegen,
deinem Bräutigam entgegen,
der mit süssen Gnadenworten
Klopft an deines Herzens Pforten.
Eile, sie ihm aufzuschliessen,
wirf dich hin zu seinen Füssen,
sprich: Mein Heil, lass dich umfassen;
von dir will ich nicht mehr lassen.

It was not so many years after Confirmation that young people began to think about marriage and establishing a home of their own. Although marriage was a Christian celebration, and the wedding, if it was at all possible, always took place in the church, secular traditions were very much an element of marriage, so much so that one is reminded of the marriage of Kriemhild in the ancient saga of the *Nibelungenlied*. These marriage customs are described in 4.3.1.

4.1.3. Kinder gheren in d'kirche das sie Gottes Wort lernen `Children belong in the church so they can learn God's Word'. From their earliest years children were trained as before them their parents and grandparents had been, in the religious life and practices of their family. There were prayers for every occasion, and religious worship was a daily ritual for the family. The most important prayer that each child learned was of course, The Lord's Prayer. Prayers were said at every meal and were usually carefully chosen so as to have meaning for the young. After the head of the family, the father, said the prayer, all the children chorused in unison, *Abba, lieber Vater, Amen*, the words of Jesus in the Garden of Gethsemane. Romans 8:15 says, `the spirit that makes us sons enabling us to cry Abba, Father'. *Abba* is the Hebrew word for the familiar form of `Father', the equivalent of English `Dad', an informal way to address God the Father. It was so familiar that only Christ himself could say it. Here we find it used by children in what must be an old oral tradition. The innocence of a child allowed him to speak to God as `Dad' and also gave him a feeling of love and closeness to God along with his awe of the deity.

Two of the favorite table prayers were prayers that are well known table prayers in German:

Komm Herr Jesu
Sei unser Gast
und segne alles, was
Du uns aus Gnade bescheret hast.

'Come Lord Jesus,
be our guest
and bless all
that you through your
grace, have bestowed
upon us.'

and:

Komm Herr Jesu
segne diese Speise
uns zur Kraft
und Dir zum Preise

'Come Lord Jesus,
bless this food
for our strength
and for your glory.'

Daily evening prayers always included the Lord's prayer, and in addition:

Christi Blut und Gerechtigkeit
das ist mein Schmuck und Ehrenkleid
damit will ich vor Gott bestehen
wenn ich im Himmel werde eingehen.

'Christ's Blood and
Righteoues, that is my
adornment and garment
of honor, with them I
will face and sustain
God's test to enter the
realm of heaven.'

There were also traditional bedtime prayers for the very young child:

Engele komm und
mach mich fromm
dass ich zu Dir
in den Himmel
(her)rein komm.

'Little angel come
and make me holy,
so that I to you
in heaven may come.'

To all their prayers the children always added:

Abba, liebe(r) Vater, Amen.

'Dad, Dearest Father, Amen.'

Another favorite child's prayer was:

Ich bin klein,
mein Herz ist rein
es darf niemand drin wohnen
als Jesus allein.
Abba, liebe(r) Vater, Amen.

'I am small,
my heart is pure,
no one may live in it
but Jesus alone.'
'Dad, Dearest Father,
Amen.'

A more modern child's evening prayer was:

Müde bin ich, gehe zu Ruhe
schliesse meine Äuglein zu.
Vater, lass die Augen Dein
über meinem Bette sein.
hab ich Unrecht heut getan,
sieh es, lieber Gott, nicht an.
Deine Gnade und Christi
Blut,   macht ja allen
Schaden gut.

'Tired I am, I lay down
to rest and close my
little eyes.
Father, let your eyes
keep watch over my
bed.
If I did something
wrong today,
don't look at it,
Dear God.
Your grace and Christ's
Blood will surely make
all my mischief good.'

Both daily prayers and Bible reading were an important part of family life. All the family gathered around and ended the day together with the father reading to them from the family Bible.

This Bible also contained all of the family history. Births were recorded, then Baptism, Confirmation, Marriage, births of the children of the marriage and then their further history, and finally the date of death and the favorite Bible verses a person wanted associated with his memory. It was the only family history and record.

Many people have had to rely on this record when they applied for social security or, for instance, passports. Indeed, this record is still accepted by our government with the word of two witnesses, since this old tradition was the only record made during the early years on the prairie. When one considers how recent the history of the Dakota Territory is, one realizes that many of the older people on social security today have only this record for their date of birth.

Religion and faith were not Sunday events, but rather permeated all

THE CENTRAL DAKOTA GERMANS / 139

of their lives, their way of thinking. In their religion and in the sacraments which marked the milestones of their lives, was contained their view of the world, their sense of community, their relationship with each other, with the world of nature, and with the world of the hereafter.

4.2 Kirche und Fest: The religious calendar and folk life. The description of the liturgical year can be summarized under its principal festivals: (1) Advent (4.2.1), (2) Christmas (4.2.2), (3) New Year (4.2.3), (4) Easter (4.2.4) (5) Ascension (4.2.5) (6) Pentecost (4.2.6), and (7) Misson Festival (4.2.7).

For the Dakota German, church and school life were closely related. In Russia, instead of public schools, the schools had been run by the church and had been important in holding the people together and teaching them their German language and culture. In America, for the first time, children attended public schools along with children who were not German. And, for the first time, German was not taught in the schools. The majority of the Dakota German children attended isolated rural schools where they were usually taught by a fellow Dakota German. The language of instruction was English; but since the students, parents, and teacher were so isolated, the culture changed little. German remained the language of the home. Many children experienced great difficulty in making the transition from the rural school to high school; and, of course, many children were denied the opportunity of attending high school. Their school situation and their continued use of German as the language of the home, family, neighbors, friends, and the church, formed and maintained their culture. This culture, the folk life of these people, continued to follow its ancient flow, directed by the seasons, and encompassed by the liturgical calendar.

4.2.1 Adventszeit: Advent. Advent, those weeks of preparation for Christmas, presented its own series of rituals and festivities.

Education brought the Dakota Germans into American culture, and one of the adopted American customs became a part of the Christmas season. This most popular event took place a few weeks before Christmas, when the different little country schools would have their annual Christmas programs. The programs were very well attended, and the schools packed with parents, family, and other relatives and friends.

One custom of the American pioneers that proved very popular was for young girls of about sixteen to nineteen to bring baskets of food for lunch to be auctioned off at the school Christmas program. The baskets held homemade sausage, bread, cookies, and apples. One basket usually contained something like a pig's tail and added to the laughter of the evening. The young men were very nervous and eager about which basket they would get in the auction, since they would eat lunch with the girl who had brought it. It was supposed to be a secret who brought which basket, but the boys would try very hard to find out to whom the baskets belonged before the bidding began. Proceeds from the auction were given to the individual schools.

4.2.2 Der Heiligerobet und der erste und zweiter Christtag: Christmas. The three days of Christmas were observed with daily church services. The Christmas Eve program was the event of the year for the children. Each child had a Bible verse or religious poem he had learned, and even the smallest would come to the front of the church and say his piece or sing a little song. These seem to be the most treasured of the childhood memories.

Songs that were sung by everyone in the congregation included, *Oh, du fröhliche, Ihr Kinderlein kommet, Stille Nacht,* and *O, Tannenbaum*. At the end of the service, each child received a paper bag filled with fruit and nuts, a real treat to the prairie children who did not have these foods available to them the rest of the year. The family rode home from church on a sleigh; it was not until the 1930s that cars made their appearance. Waiting at home was a box, previously hidden by the parents. This was the family Christmas present. It was filled with wonderful treats, oranges, apples, figs, dates, nuts, and *bock hörnli* `a hard sweet shaped like a horn'. Everything was equally divided among the children. They would sometimes trade nut for nut for their favorites and then either eat their share or store it in a secret place. Of course, brothers and sisters who had eaten their candy would try to find that belonging to the child who had frugally saved some for the future. It was a game of wits to hold on to one's Christmas treats.

The children's prayer on Christmas Eve was a special one and filled with humor:

Engele(in) komm und mach mich fromm dass ich zu Dir in den Nussesack komm.	`Little angel come and make me holy, so that I into your sack of nuts may come.'

This was their evening prayer, which usually ended with 'so that I to you in heaven may come'. *Dass ich zu Dir in den Himmel herein kom.*

For Christmas day a tree had been decorated with real candles, and pies, cakes, and cookies had been baked for this special holiday. The traditional Christmas dinner was goose. The children rarely received toys, but there was always good food and lots of visiting, all of which made it a truly wonderful time of the year for children.

The best loved Christmas songs of the German pioneer children were sung at church, at home, and at family and community gatherings. Everyone had his favorite Christmas carol. The following were some of the most popular and well-known German songs. They reflect a continuing contact with German culture through music, as well as a maintaining of much of an older era's religious piety.

Alle Jahre wieder
By Wilhelm Hey, Friedrich Silcher
(OT, Well known verse)

Alle Jahre wieder
kommt das Christuskind
auf die Erde nieder,
wo wir Menschen sind.

Kehrt mit seinem Segen
ein in jedes Haus,
geht auf allen Wegen
mit uns ein und aus.

Ist auch mir zur Seite
still und unerkannt,
dass es treu mich leite
an der lieben Hand.

O Tannenbaum
By Ernst Anschütz

0 Tannenbaum, 0 Tannenbaum,
wie grün sind deine Blätter.
Du grünst nicht nur zur Sommerszeit,
nein auch im Winter, wenn es schneit!
0 Tannenbaum, 0 Tannenbaum,
wie grün sind deine Blätter.

Freuet euch, ihr Christen alle
(Ga 23, OT verse)

Freuet euch, ihr Christen alle,

freue sich, wer immer kann!
Gott hat viel an uns getan.
Freuet euch mit grossem Schalle,
dass er uns so hoch geacht,
sich mit uns befreundt gemacht.
Freude, Freude über Freude!
Christus wehret allem Leide:
Wonne, Wonne über Wonne!
Jesus ist die Gnadensonne.
Halleluja! Halleluja! Halleluja!

Weihnacht ist heut
(LS 167)

Weihnacht ist heut'
Wir sind erfreut,
Dass der Herr Jesus Christ,
Zur Welt geboren ist,
Dass der Herr Jesus Christ,
Zur Welt geboren ist.

Hörst du den Klang,
Den Engelsang?
Betend die Hirten knien,
Weil unser Heil erschien,
Betend die Hirten knien,
Weil unser Heil erschien.
Komme auch du,
Mein Kind, herzu,
Dir auch wird ewiges Heil,
Friede und Gnade zuteil,
Dir auch wird ewiges Heil,
Friede und Gnade zuteil.

Horch, wie die Schar der Engel singt!
(LS 168)

Horch, wie die Schar der Engel singt!
Horch, wie die Luft zusammenklingt!
Sieh, wie da droben Licht erglüht!
Sieh, wie's den Erdkreis hell umzieht!

Ob heller leuchte dieser Strahl,
Ob heller töne der Choral,
Wer sagt mir das? Der Hirten Chor,

Der ist auf einmal Auf und Höh'r!

Von Engelscharen her erschallt's,
In Hirtenherzen widerhallt's:
Dem droben in der Höh' sei Ehr',
Auf Erden Frieden wiederkehr'.

O du fröhliche
By Johann Daniel Falk
(LS 165, GH 103, EL 291)

O du fröhliche, O du selige
gnadenbringende Weihnachtszeit!
Welt ging verloren, Christ ward geboren:
Freue, freue dich, O Christenheit!

O du fröhliche, O du selige,
gnadenbringende Weihnachtszeit!
Christ ist erschienen, uns zu versühnen,
Freue, freue dich, O Christenheit!

O du fröhliche, O du selige,
gnadenbringende Weihnachtszeit!
Himmlische Heere jauchzen dir Ehre:
Freue, freue dich, O Christenheit!

Stille Nacht
By Johann Mohr, Franz Gruber
(LS 164, GH 102)

Stille Nacht, heilige Nacht!
Alles schläft, einsam wacht
nur das traute, hochheilige Paar;
holder Knabe im lockigen Haar,
schlaf in himmlischer Ruh,
schlaf in himmlischer Ruh!

Stille Nacht, heilige Nacht!
Hirten erst kundgemacht,
durch der Engel Halleluja
tönt es laut von fern und nah:
Christ, der Retter, ist da,
Christ, der Retter, ist da.

Ein Kinderlied auf die Weihnachten vom Kindlein Jesu
By Dr. Martin Luther
Dakota Germans know this hymn as:
Vom Himmel hoch da komm ich her
(LH 117, Ga 38, Gc 58)

*Vom Himmel hoch da komm ich her,
ich bring euch gute neue Mähr,
der guten Mähr bring ich so viel,
davon ich sing'n und sagen will.*

*Euch ist ein Kindlein heut geborn
von einer Jungfrau auserkorn,
ein Kindelein so zart und fein,
das soll eur Freud und Wonne sein.*

*Es ist der Herr Christ, unser Gott,
der will euch führn aus aller Not.
Er will eur Heiland selber sein,
von allen Sünden machen rein.*

*Er bringt euch alle Seligkeit,
die Gott, der Vater, hat bereit,
dass ihr mit uns im Himmelreich
sollt leben nun und ewiglich.*

*So merket nun das Zeichen recht,
die Krippen, Windelein so schlecht;
da findet ihr das Kind gelegt,
das alle Welt erhält und trägt.
Des lasst uns alle fröhlich sein
und mit den Hirten gehn hinein,
zu sehn, was Gott uns hat beschert,
mit seinem lieben Sohn verehrt.*

*Merk auf, mein Herz, und sieh dort hin:
was liegt doch in dem Krippelein?
was ist das schöne Kindelein?
es ist das liebe Jesulein.*

*Bist willekomm, du edler Gast,
den Sünder nicht verschmähet hast,
und kommst ins Elend her zu mir:
wie soll ich immer danken dir?*

Ach Herr, du Schöpfer aller Ding,
wie bist du worden so gering,
dass du da liegst auf dürrem Gras,
davon ein Rind und Esel ass.

Und wär die Welt vielmal so weit,
von Edelstein und Gold bereit,
so wär sie doch dir viel zu klein,
zu sein ein enges Wiegelein.

Der Sammet und die Seiden dein,
das ist grob Heu und Windelein,
drauf du, König so gross und reich,
herprangst, als wärs dein Himmelreich.

Das hat also gefallen dir,
die Wahrheit anzuzeigen mir:
wie aller Welt Macht, Ehr und Gut
für dir nichts gilt, nichts hilft, noch tut.

Ach, mein herzliebes Jesulein,
mach dir ein rein sanft Bettelein,
zu ruhen in meines Herzens Schrein,
dass ich nimmer vergesse dein.

Davon, ich allzeit fröhlich sei,
zu springen, singen immer frei
das rechte Susannine schon,
mit Herzenslust den süssen Ton.

Lob, Ehr sei Gott im höchsten Thron,
der uns schenkt seinen eigenen Sohn;
des freuen sich der Engel Schaar
und singen uns solch neues Jahr.

The preceding hymn is a good example of Martin Luther's poetry. He uses simple rhyming verses together with beautiful words to tell the story of the Baby Jesus. He presents the Christmas story in a very familiar vocabulary which everyone even the children, can understand.

Ihr Kinderlein kommet
By Christoph v. Schmid, J.A.P. Schulz
(LS 166)

Ihr Kinderlein kommet, o kommet doch all,
zur Krippe her kommet in Bethlehems Stall.

Und seht was in dieser hochheiligen Nacht,
der Vater im Himmel für Freude uns macht.

O seht in der Krippe im nächtlichen Stall,
seht hier, bei des Lichtleins hellglänzendem Strahl
den lieblichen Knaben, das himmlische Kind,
viel schöner und holder als Engelein sind.

Da liegt es, das Kindlein, auf Heu und auf Stroh.
Maria und Josef betrachten es froh.
Die redlichen Hirten knien betend davor,
hoch oben schwebt jubelnd der Engelein Chor.

O beugt wie die Hirten anbetend die Knie,
erhebet die Hände und danket wie sie.
Stimmt freudig, ihr Kinder,
wer wollt' sich nicht freun,
stimmt froh in den Jubel der Engel mit ein!

Walking through the snow to the children's Christmas Eve program is still a tradition for the Dakota Germans. The children still receive the traditional paper bag with fruit, nuts, and candy at the service. Although Christmas gifts are now more like those given and received in the rest of America, they are still opened on Christmas Eve after church. The foods served at Christmas time are the same as in years past, and singing the old Christmas songs is still an important part of the celebration of the Holy Season. Christmas is still a wonderful and holy time for every child and adult in the community.

4.2.3 Nei johr: New Year. The beginning of the New Year was an event to be celebrated with an awareness of the presence of God in the lives of the pioneers, and church services are still held on December 31st and January 1st.

New Year's also has its secular traditions, however, and after the New Year's Eve church service, the rest of the evening and night are spent celebrating. At midnight the town fire whistle blows and all the church bells ring. The men of twenty-one to about forty are already on their way to the homes of friends and acquaintances to "shoot in the New Year". They knock until someone opens the window, even though most people have been out for New Year's Eve, they hurried home to wait for the knock. When the window is opened the men recite the following New Year's wish. It was given to me by several of my informants and is presented here in Standard High German.

Weil das neue Jahr ist gekommen
Hab ich mir es vorgenommen
Euch zu wünschen in der Zeit
Friede, Freude, Seligkeit.
So viel Sandkorn in dem Meer,
So viel Flöcklein in dem Schnee,
So viel Tröpflein in dem Regen,
So viel Glück und so viel Segen
Soll euch Gott, der Höchste, geben
Er gebe euch Glück in allem Stück
Und wirft das Unglück weit zurück.
Und mit der Zeit gegen Himmel schweben,
Halleluja!

After reciting this verse in unison, they all fire their shotguns into the air and yell, *frohes neues johr!* `Happy New Year!' The revelers are invited in to eat and drink, and then they proceed to the next house. Housewives cook whole hams and bake kuchen to have plenty of good food. For not just one group appears at each house; rather many groups of ten or twelve young men are about. This continues all night and is still one of the best loved events of the year.

The next morning while the adult population is asleep, the children are out going from door to door. Each child goes alone to relatives and neighbors and says the following Central Dakota German verses:

Ich wensch eich a glickliches neies johr
viel gesundheit, langes lebe
will der liebe Gott eich gebe.

`*Ich wünsche euch ein glückliches Neues Jahr*
Viel Gesundheit, langes Leben
will der liebe Gott euch geben.'

`I wish you a Happy New Year,
good health, a long life,
as the dear Lord wants to give you.'

Some parents teach the child to add another line to the verse, one they have made up to be humorous. One such verse was:

Ich wensch eich a glickliches neies johr
viel g'sundheit, langes lebe
und ein bub mit rote hor.

*'Ich wünsche euch ein glückliches Neues Jahr
Viel Gesundheit, langes Leben
und einen Sohn mit rotem Haar.'*

'I wish you a Happy New Year
good health, long life
and a son with red hair.'

The preceding was a wish certain to wake the recipient! The children were given a dime or a quarter to be on their way, and they continued on, waking all the grown-ups on New Year's morning.

One German pioneer, Jacob Nitschke, remembered a long poem that was recited to wish a good New Year to neighbors years ago. In its verses one sees again the great preparations for the Christmas season. Foods not normally available, such as fruits and sweets, were ordered through the grocery store, the Christmas goose fed and raised, the New Year's ham smoked and hung in the grainery to preserve it, cookies and cakes baked, verses and poems learned and recited, songs and hymns practiced and sung—to show the love and appreciation for family and friends as were the gifts of the Magi to the small baby Jesus. All of these good wishes for the coming year are summed up in this old poem, commonly recited during this period.

*Weil das neue Jahr ist gekommen,
hab' ich mir es vorgenommen
euch zu wünschen in der Zeit,
Friede, Freude, Seligkeit.*

*So viel Flocken in dem Schnee,
so viel Tropfen in dem Regen,
so viel Glück und so viel Segen
soll der liebe Gott euch geben.*

*Nahrung, Kleider auch dazu,
bis wir kommen in die Ruh'
dort in jenem Freudensgarten
müssen wir die Zeit erwarten.*

*Ach, Herr Jesu, mach es wahr,
diesen Wunsch zum neuen Jahr.
Das alte Jahr wir beschliessen,
das Neue wir euch anschliessen.*

Das wünsch ich euch und euren

Söhnen und Töchtern zum Gefallen,
und daraus solls Pulver knallen,
voll Fried und Freude immerdar.

Der Herr wacht über Gross und Klein,
durch seine liebe Engelein,
dass uns nichts Böses widerfahre
in diesem ganzen neuen Jahre.

Sollt aber sich in eurem Hause,
womöglich Trauer stellen ein,
dann sucht den Trost in Jesu Worte,
und Friede kehrt im Herzen ein.

Gott lass uns viele Jahre leben,
und endlich nach dem Himmel schweben.
Gott gebe uns Glück in jedem Stück,
halte Unglück weit von uns zurück.

Herr Jesu mach doch alles wahr,
was ich euch wünsche zum neuen Jahr.
Da sollt ihr alle glücklich sein,
und selig macht euch Gott allein.

Wenn kehren wir zum Himmel ein,
besinn dich Mensch, das Jahr ist rum,
wer weiss, ob du oder ich noch bin,
wenn wieder zwölf Monate sind dahin.

Das wünsch ich euch zum ewigen und seligen Leben,
und daraus solls Feier geben. Amen.

The favorite New Year's song was:

Das alte Jahr vergangen ist
(LH 576, Ga 44)

Das alte Jahr vergangen ist;
wir danken dir, Herr Jesu Christ
dass du uns in so gross Gefahr
so gnädiglich behüt dies Jahr.

With attendance at church on January 6, *Heilige Drei Königs Tag* `the feast day of the three kings' the Christmas season was brought to its formal close.

4.2.4 Ostere: Easter.

The whole Lenten and Easter season was observed very strictly and with many rituals, some of which have Catholic and even Old Testament origins.

Fasenacht `Shrove Tuesday' the housewife was always certain to serve *schlitz kiechla*. This was a pastry of unusual shape. An oblong piece of rolled-out dough was cut through with three diagonal slices. Then the extreme corners of the oblong were each pulled through the cut nearest to it. Then the entire pastry was deep-fried. A familiar saying was:

Kiechle raus oder a Loch ins Haus   `Either a kiechle appears or a hole in your house will appear.'

Prunes were cooked and served with the *schlitz kiechla*. No meat was eaten, but a hot potato salad was prepared.

On Shrove Tuesday (the day before Ash Wednesday) it was customary to eat without a light burning at the evening meal to signify that the days would begin to get longer and it would be possible to eat in daylight. A verse was said before the meal:

Marie lichtmess   `Maria, at Candlemass,
spinne vergess   spinning forget
und bei tag   and by daylight
nacht ess.   night meal eat.'

To the Lutherans of the Central Dakotas the old Catholic meaning of some of these customs is lost. For instance, *Marie Lichtmesse* refers to the Catholic Feast of the Purification which commemorates Mary's visit to the temple for her ritual purification, the occasion of her meeting with Simeon and his prediction of the sorrows she would encounter (cf. Luke 2:34,35). The feast was also called *Candlemass Day* from the custom of blessing all the candles which would be used throughout the coming year.

According to the Dakota German verse on *Marie lichtmess* one can forget spinning, one of the daytime occupations of winter for a family which spins its own yarn to make their clothing. At this time of year one could put aside such tasks, and eat the evening meal in daylight.

In Russia the important day for the hiring of farm-workers for the coming season was *Marie Lichtmess* on February 2nd. These workers would then complete their employment on St. Michaels Day, September

29th, the day the workers left again. The return of more hours of daylight on *Marie Lichtmess* meant the return of the yearly planting season for which preparations had to be made. Light has an important role to play in the cycle of life for people who are tied to the rhythms of nature.

Aschermittwoch `Ash Wednesday', the first day of Lent, was the beginning of a period of frequent church attendance with services Wednesday evenings as well as Sunday mornings and evenings. In the farming community, it was also the day on which ashes were put in the chicken barns because this would keep out lice, a folk custom many people followed.

The meal was a simple one, no meat was eaten, a hot potato salad was served. There was no dancing, card playing, or public amusement of any kind during Lent; and no weddings were held during this period. Confirmation was always held on Palm Sunday.

Every Sunday during Lent after the Second Lesson of the morning service, the following songs were sung, (also as part of the liturgy).

O Lamm Gottes unschuldig
(LH 152 & 170a, GH 139, Ga 106, Gb 94, Gc 180)

O Lamm Gottes unschuldig,
am Stamm des Kreuzes geschlachtet,
allzeit funden geduldig,
wiewohl du warest verachtet:
all Sünd hast du getragen,
sonst müssten wir verzagen.
Erbarm dich unser, O Jesu!
(Repeat verse three times and conclude the third repetition with:)
Gib uns den Frieden, O Jesu.

Christe, du Lamm Gottes
(LH 151, Gc 187)

Christe, du Lamm Gottes,
der du trägst die Sünd der Welt
erbarm dich unser!
(Repeat verse three times and conclude the third repetition with:)
Gib uns deinen Frieden!

This song is a German translation of the *Agnus Dei* `Lamb of God' from the Roman Catholic Latin liturgy.

Gredonnerstag `**Maundy Thursday**' was always observed as a holiday, with church services held in the morning. All work and preparation for Good Friday had to be done Thursday afternoon and evening. Even the cattle were fed on Thursday evening, for on Friday only the most necessary work was allowed, such as milking the cows. On Thursday night the men shaved, women washed their long hair, and baths were taken.

Karfreitag `Good Friday' was a day of quiet prayer and church services. The robes worn by the minister were entirely black; the altar and the cross were covered in black. The church had no flowers.

In the homes boiled eggs which had been prepared ahead were served and the traditional dish for dinner was homemade noodles with either stewed raisins or prunes. No meat was eaten.

Ostersonntag `Easter Sunday' was a very happy occasion. Children took hats and filled them with wild flowers. Then on Easter morning these Easter baskets would be found filled with dyed eggs, licorice, and peppermint candy. After church services the children would open gifts received from their baptismal sponsors. This was the day on which the married children and their families came to their parents' home for dinner, to visit, and to attend church with their family. Photographs would usually be taken of the family gathering. One of the favorite songs sung on Easter Sunday was:

Ein Lämmlein geht
(LH 181, Ga 76, Gc 98)

Ein Lämmlein geht und trägt die Schuld
der Welt und ihrer Kinder;
es geht und träget mit Geduld
die Sünden aller Sünder;
es geht dahin,
wird matt und krank,
ergibt sich auf die Würgebank,
entzieht sich aller Freuden;
es nimmet an Schmach,
Hohn und Spott,
Angst, Wunden, Striemen,
Kreuz und Tod,
und spricht: Ich will gern leiden.

The traditional family Easter dinner which took place after the church service, was noodle soup, chicken and potatoes, and *kuchen*. Family rituals were followed closely and one felt a sense of peace.

Ostermontag `Easter Monday' had a holiday aspect for the women. There was church in the morning. Then in the afternoon they would go to the village to sell cream and eggs and do some shopping.

4.2.5 Christihimmelfahrt: Ascension. On Ascension day all work ceased and people attended church. This was another traditional day for visiting relatives. The hymn always heard this day was:

Himmelan geht unsre Bahn
(LH 473, GH 403, LS 112, Gc 561)

Himmelan geht unsre Bahn,
wir sind Gäste nur auf Erden, bis
wir dort in Kanaan
durch die Wüste kommen werden.
Hier ist unser Pilgrimsstand,
droben unser Vaterland.

4.2.6 Pfingste: Pentecost. The first Sunday and Monday of Pentecost were holidays and no work was done. A great deal of baking was done in preparation for Pentecost. It was a time when farmers looked for omens for their new crops. Old sayings insist that rain on Whitsunday meant good crops:

Pfingsten regen ist alles gelegen.	`Rain on Whitsunday makes all things favorable.'
Pfingsten regen bringt viel segen	`Rain on Whitsunday brings many blessings.

4.2.7 Missionsfest: Mission Festival. A longstanding tradition at the end of the harvest is the *Missionsfest* 'Mission festival' held once a year in the fall by each church to collect money to send to missionaries. Every member of the congregation invites guests from other churches, and all the families look forward eagerly to *Missionsfest* and often travel many miles to several different churches to attend each one on its special day. The sermons were special, often with a guest pastor being present in addition to the regular pastor. In the early years it was an opportunity to see friends and relatives rarely seen because the distances were so great. Everyone would be invited to dinner at someone's home. Even strangers who attended would be welcomed to a home for dinner. People gathered outside the church after the services to visit, and no one left alone without an invitation to a home for dinner.

The hospitality of the Dakota Germans is renowned. They feel that a stranger must be welcomed and food and water provided him, for the stranger may be the Christ child come again and who again may find no welcome on earth. Church services are held in the morning and afternoon, and today the custom is that the women of the congregation bring hot food to the church to be served to the visitors between the morning and afternoon services. Everyone has the opportunity to visit together, and even today people still come from far away to attend.

4.3 Hohezeiten: Celebrations and their function in maintaining family and community ties and language. The principal individual celebrations and gatherings of a particular year were weddings (4.3.1) and funerals (4.3.2); and each of these occasions functioned to maintain community ties and friendships.

4.3.1 Hochzeit: Weddings. Engagements were not the practice among the Dakota Germans until the 1930s, when they adopted this new tradition. In earlier times, the courtship itself was conducted with circumspection and great ceremony. Women married young as a rule. Although the young man had perhaps been seen with the young woman or had called at her home, his intentions were not officially known by others. Traditionally he did not speak to his father directly on so delicate a matter. He confided in his mother; she, in turn, would take the message to the father, who was the head of the house, and all would await his reaction. If it was favorable, the father would find a match-maker, usually a relative, and arrangements would be made for a formal meeting with the future parents-in-law and the bride. In the event that the parents of the girl had no objection, the bride-to-be was called in, and the matter laid before her. As soon as her consent for the marriage was obtained, arrangements for the wedding got underway.

In some cases a young man did not have a particular girl in mind, and the services of a *kuppelmann* `match-maker', were necessary. The young man would make a list of girls, and then he and the match-maker, accompanied by the father, or a relative or friend of the father, would dress themselves and their horses in their Sunday best. Many gay ribbons were added to the horses' bridles, and the mission of the colorful group was immediately apparent to all. It was customary for the group to begin at the top of his list of eligible girls and go to each girl's home in succession until the proposal was accepted. The girls, of course, could see the purpose of the ceremonial visit as soon as the young man and his two companions approached.

The *kuppelmann* was not very popular with the young women because they wanted more freedom of choice and more time to choose. A favorite saying was:

Jedem kuppler ein paar schuh, und dann den teufel dazu.
`For every matchmaker a pair of shoes, and then the devil along with them.'

Matchmaking, however, remained a practice in the communities of the Germans from Russia until well into the 1920s.

One lovely old pioneer lady interviewed on this topic had one of those great marriages one seldom still encounters, a touching lifelong deep love and affection for her husband, and they were brought together exactly in the tradition described above. Mary said it was a beautiful ritual, and she still remembers the horses and ribbons and the drama of the occasion.

Invitations to the wedding were extended to relatives and friends from far and near. They were extended personally where possible, by either the bride and groom or by his best man and the bridesmaid. In whatever fashion they were extended, the wedding invitations were always extended personally, usually by visiting neighboring farms on foot or on horseback or by buggy. Sometimes invitations were extended after church services when friends and neighbors were always seen as they gathered and spoke to each other after the services. Letters were written only to relatives who lived at a distance.

Wedding expenses were shared by the parents of the bride and the groom. In the early days the church wedding and the celebration which followed lasted three days and longer. This included a day of preparation, the day of the wedding, and sometimes as many as two more days of dancing, merriment and socializing. Some guests had come a long distance for the wedding; for this occasion was a great social event for family, neighbors, and friends. Everyone would talk of the occasion for many years afterwards and in memory relive again and again the great celebration.

Two songs were always sung at the wedding ceremony:
Jesu geh voran
(LH 464, LS 175, GH 327, EL 296. Gc 223)
Jesu geh voran auf der Lebensbahn,
Wir wollen nich verweilen
Dir getreulich nachzueilen,
Führ uns an der Hand bis ins Vaterland.

So nimm denn meine Hände
(GH 399, EL 218)
So nimm denn meine Hände und führe mich,
bis an mein selig Ende und ewiglich.
Ich kann allein, nicht gehen, nicht einen Schritt;
Wo du wirst geh'n und stehen, da nimm mich mit.

The wedding ring was a narrow band of silver, and the bride usually wore a white dress or a pretty blue dress that she could use afterwards. A common head-dress was a pure white crown of beeswax laced with flowers. Old pictures show that the groom had a big bow ribbon with long streamers on his lapel, sometimes with flowers tucked in at the top. In the winter flowers for the bride and groom were made of crepe paper. In the summer, marigolds and small yellow prairie flowers were used. Ribbons were an important part of the decorations in all marriage ceremonies.

The ritual singing of the Confirmation song *Jesu geh voran* at the wedding ceremony, makes one wonder if perhaps the Lutheran wedding ceremony at one point included Holy Communion which it no longer does.

In the early times the day on which the wedding was held was considered holy. The ceremony could only be held on Sunday, Tuesday, or Thursday since the other days were considered to be unlucky. After the marriage, the rest of the day was spent dining or talking.

On the second day the couple visited neighbors or wandered about, taking a new look at their world. Then there was dancing for the young people from three in the afternoon until midnight. All the furniture in the house had been put into one room and the rest of the space was used for dancing to the music provided by a small orchestra. Ribbons were hung throughout the house and all of the wedding party and guests, including the musicians, wore ribbons. Only the bride and groom wore none at this time. Young girls were dressed in white, and their dresses decorated with ribbons.

Various schemes were used to raise money for the newlyweds as one pioneer mother, Clara Erlenbusch, remembers:

> They sold dances at weddings as long as I can remember ... it's old. The late ones now don't ... do it any more. They even stole the shoe from the bride and sold it. If they had a chance they also stole the bride, then they would collect money and when they had as much money as the ones wanted that stole the bride, the bridegroom could buy her back.

Pieces of the wedding cake were also auctioned, and in the evening on the last day of the celebration the cooks would cover their arms and heads with bandages and ask for donations for their work in the kitchen. Contributions, of course, were for the bride and groom. It was not easy to establish a new household, and the substantial sums raised by these traditional practices were needed and appreciated. Wedding gifts were usually items such as knives, flatware, dishes, and other every-day necessities.

In later years the wedding in the church and the celebration were often held on the same day. Rose Schauer remembers:

> They always had the wedding at the church in the morning at ten or eleven o'clock. They served noodle soup and chicken for dinner, and for supper they served *halupsy*, sausage, and sometimes they had baked ham. For drinks besides coffee and tea, they had homemade wine and beer and schnaps that they brewed ... If they had any noodle soup left from noon they served it at midnight with the rice. They had the dance in the afternoon. The older people didn't dance in the evening but in the afternoon everyone danced. The young people danced in the evening too, while the older people sang songs. They sang all kinds of songs, good and bad called *schätzlieder*. It was all so much fun.

Two of the popular *schätzlieder*, 'songs that tease and amuse', that were sung at weddings, are the following which were tape recorded with Eva Iszler, age 96, singing. (All the songs are presented in Standard High German.)

Auf dem Dach da sitzen Tauben
(Oral Tradition: Eva Iszler)

*Auf dem Dache da sitzen Tauben
dass ich dich lieben tu, das kannst du glauben,
aber Du alleine bist meine Freude
und sonst auch keiner mehr auf dieser Welt.*

*Vor der Hochzeit da gibt es Kuchen
nach der Hochzeit da kommt das fluchen,
aber Du alleine bist meine Freude
und sonst auch keiner mehr auf dieser Welt.*

*Vor der Hochzeit ein holder Engel
nach der Hochzeit ein grober Bengel,
aber du alleine bist meine Freude
und sonst auch keiner mehr auf dieser Welt.*

*Vor der Hochzeit ein Turteltäubchen
nach der Hochzeit ein schlimmes Weibchen
aber du alleine bist meine Freude
und sonst auch keine mehr auf dieser Welt.*

*Vor der Hochzeit ein Stall voll Rinder
nach der Hochzeit ein Haus voll Kinder,
aber du alleine bist meine Freude
und sonst auch keine mehr auf dieser Welt.*

Mädele schick dich dazu
(Oral Tradition: Eva Iszler)

*Da nimmst du dir den Schusterbub
der macht dir Schlappen und Schuh
aber die Schustersweiber müssen's Leder schneiden
lieber will ich ein Pastor nehmen
gehe ich in Sammet und in Seide
aber die Pastorsweiber müssen sich schön putzen
lieber will ich ein Kaufmann nehmen
fahre ich mit der Kutsche
aber die Kaufmannsweiber müssen Butter wäge
lieber will ich ein Bauer nehmen
fahre ich mit dem Wagen
aber die Bauersweiber müssen die Wäge schmieren
lieber will ich ein Soldat nehmen
kann ich brav marschieren
aber die Soldatsweiber müssens Brot weit holen
lieber will ich ein Bäcker nehmen*

aber die Bäckersweiber müssen Teig gern machen
ach lieber will ich ein Gastwirt nehmen
aber die Gastwirtsweiber müssen die Flasche füllen
ach dann will ich ein Mädchen bleiben
habe ich meinen Willen nur.

Another custom is remembered by Eva Iszler and Clare Erlenbusch. Years ago at twelve o'clock midnight on their wedding day, the groom had to sit on a chair with the bride on his lap. The wedding guests formed a ring, men and women holding hands, with the groom and bride in the middle of the ring. The guests sang the following song.
Oh Ihr auserwählten Kinder 'Oh You Chosen Children'.

Oh, Ihr auserwählten Kinder,
Ihr Jungfrauen allzumal,
wisst Ihr nicht, was Euch gebühret
und was Euren Brautstand zieret?
Wachet, wachet, kaufet Öle,
nahe ist die Mitternacht
Schmueckt die Lampen Eurer Seele
habet auf den Bräutigam acht,
Er wird kommen,
hört Ihr Frommen,
was die Friedensboten sagen,
jetzt erscheint der Hochzeitswagen.

Ei, wie lieblich wird's da klingen
in der seligen Ewigkeit.
Engel werden mit drein singen,
die sich längst darauf gefreut,
da sich scharen Paar bei Paaren
werden Ihre Harfen rühren
und die Hochzeit kräftig zieren.

Rühme, jauchze, lebe fröhlich,
Zion, Braut und Königin,
Deine Freude währet ewig
in dem Chor der Seraphim
da Du weiden sollst mit Freuden
in viel tausend Lieblichkeiten,
lass Dich wohl dazu bereiten.

Then the bridesmaid took off the bride's veil and her crown, and they were now man and wife. The song was sad, and the women would weep.

This song and tradition are a significant piece of oral history. I have not been able to find any written source for this. However a song which is somewhat similar is found in the *Liederschatz* (LS 197), a book of Lutheran folksongs. Professor G. Ronald Murphy, S.J. who helped me make many biblical connections, suggests it could be a reference to the parable of the ten virgins Jesus spoke of in Matthew 25:1-13, saying five were wise and prepared for the Bridegroom's coming, and five were foolish and unprepared. Many remembered this ritual from their own wedding and treasured it.

After this ceremony was completed the cooks would invite everyone to eat the traditional dish of rice cooked in milk with cinnamon, sugar, and raisins. Besides the noodle soup and chicken which traditionally followed the morning wedding, and the rice with cinnamon, sugar, and raisins which ended the celebration, there were other favorite dishes served at the wedding feast; *halupsy*, homemade sausage, and as was the case on all festive occasions, plenty of *kuchen*.

For the wedding the bride and groom either purchased a buggy for four or borrowed one. Colorfully decorated by local craftsmen, it had bells fixed to the wheels, and you could hear them wherever they went. The horses were covered with ribbons and flowers. In later years automobiles, also decorated, replaced the horse and buggy. In the buggy, they drove off to their new, already chosen home and prepared to begin their new life as man and wife.

There was a system of gift giving to the bride and groom from their parents. Each child in the family received a *mitgift* or `a gift to take with them from home', as they put it. This included land and cattle. No child was expected to begin life without support as the interest always lay in the preservation of the family.

4.3.2 Leicht: Funerals. Funerals have an important function in maintaining the sense of community. When a member of the Dakota German community dies, the church bell is immediately rung. It is rung three times, short rings for children, long rings for adults. The people recognize the sound of each of the bells and know to which church the person belonged. From this they attempt to learn who has died. I remember the bells ringing, how someone would say *horch* `listen', and we would strain to hear which church had bells ringing and how long. A death is a tragic event for the whole community especially for such closely knit people. However, the presence of death as a part of the community life was never denied; and death, too, had its traditional rituals. Grieving for the person was accompanied by the celebration of his entry into the Promised Land. Many of the hymns commonly sung when friends gathered were those associated with dying, its incredible sadness and loss, and the rebirth and the joy of being transformed in the realm of heaven.

In the early years the body was washed with alcohol, formaldehyde, and alum, and placed in the coffin. The coffin was kept at the home; and during the days before the funeral, visitors called to pay their respects and pray with the family. The coffin was kept open during this period both night and day. During the night, two men, either friends, relatives, or neighbors, kept watch all night so the family could rest. The deceased person was never to be left alone. He was attended with love and affection as if he were there.

Funerals were usually held on Sunday, but this was not always possible because the body could not be kept for more than three days.

The funeral procession was an early tradition. The coffin was carried on the shoulders of six bearers and followed by flower girls, the children of relatives or very good friends, whose duty was to carry the flowers. There were at least two flower girls, or as many as were needed to carry all the flowers.   In the winter the flowers were made of crepe paper.

The procession, a long line of mourners, with the coffin positioned in the middle, would stop at every corner on the way from the house to the church, and at each stop a song would be sung. The bells of the church rang as the procession walked along, but would stop when they were singing. Everyone was dressed in black except for the flower girls, who were usually from twelve to seventeen years old, and were considered too young to have to wear black. In the summer girls wore white at the funerals or a pastel color.

When the procession reached the church, the minister would enter first, then the pall-bearers with the casket, followed by the flower girls and the relatives. The song *Näher mein Gott zu Dir* `Nearer my God to Thee' was always played as the procession entered the church. The flower girls stood next to the casket until the undertaker took the flowers from them and laid them on the casket. They then sat on the side of the church with the pallbearers. In warm weather funerals were often held outside, since the church was often not large enough to accommodate all who attended. There were special hymns for this milestone in the religious life. I give their texts so that the reader may have a feeling for the spiritual language of the Dakota Germans.

Christus, der ist mein Leben,
Sterben ist mein Gewinn
(LH 639, GH 590, Ga 1160, Gb 451)

Christus, der ist mein Leben,

*Sterben ist mein Gewinn;
dem thu ich mich ergeben,
mit Fried fahr ich dahin.*

*Mit Freud fahr ich von dannen
zu Christ, dem Bruder mein,
auf dass ich zu ihm komme
und ewig bei ihm sei.*

*Ich hab nun überwunden
Kreuz, Leiden, Angst und Not,
durch sein heilig fünf Wunden
bin ich versöhnt mit Gott.*

Three other favorites were:

Wer weiss wie nahe mir mein Ende
(LH 623, Ga 1193, Gb 621, Gc 541)

*Wer weiss, wie nahe mir mein Ende!
hin geht die Zeit, her kommt der Tod.
Ach, wie geschwinde und behende
kann kommen meine Todesnot!
Mein Gott, ich bitt durch Christi Blut,
machs nur mit meinem Ende gut.*

*Es kann vor Nacht leicht anders werden,
als es am frühen Morgen war;
denn weil ich leb auf dieser Erden,
leb ich in steter Todsgefahr.
Mein Gott, ich bitt durch Christi Blut,
machs nur mit meinem Ende gut.*

Alle Menschen müssen sterben
(LH 647, GH 593, Ga 1158, Gb 478)

*Alle Menschen müssen sterben,
alles Fleisch vergeht wie Heu;
was da lebet, muss verderben,
soll es anders werden neu;
dieser Leib der muss verwesen,
wenn er anders soll genesen
der so grossen Herrlichkeit,
die den Frommen ist bereit.*

Drum so will ich dieses Leben,
wann es meinem Gott beliebt,
auch ganz willig von mir geben,
bin darüber nicht betrübt;
denn in meines Jesu Wunden
hab ich schon Erlösung funden,
und mein Trost in Todesnot
ist des Herren Jesu Tod.

Was Gott tut, das ist wohlgetan
(LH 453, GH 370, Ga 534, Gb 531)

Was Gott tut, das ist wohlgetan,
es bleibt gerecht sein Wille;
wie er fängt meine Sachen an,
will ich ihm halten stille.
Er ist mein Gott, der in der Not
mich wohl weiss zu erhalten;
drum lass ich ihn nur walten.

Was Gott tut, das ist wohlgetan,
er wird mich nicht betrügen;
er führet mich auf rechter Bahn,
so lass ich mich begnügen an
seiner Huld und hab Geduld.
Er wird mein Unglück wenden;
es steht in seinen Händen.

A special singing group, or choir, usually sang at the funerals. There were favorite songs for these special choirs, and they were generally not from the Lutheran hymnal. They were of an oral tradition or from books like *Liederschatz*, considered to be Lutheran folksongs, and *Glaubensharfe*, Baptist songs. Two favorites were:

Die Pilger zur Heimat der Seligen ziehen
(GH 618)
Die Pilger zur Heimat der Seligen ziehen,
wo Tränen nie werden geweint,
wo himmlische Rosen unsterblich erblühn,
weil da Jesus als Sonne stets scheint,
keine Nacht kann da sein,
keine Nacht kann da sein,
weil da Jesus als Sonne stets scheint,
weil da Jesus als Sonne stets scheint.

Another beloved song with beautiful four part harmony was sung not only at funerals, but when friends gathered.

Meine Heimat ist dort in der Höh
(Oral Tradition, EL 52)

Meine Heimat ist dort in der Höh:
Wo man nichts weiss von Trübsal und Weh (in der Höh)
Wo die heilige unzählbare Schar,
Jubelnd preiset das Lamm immerdar (in der Höh).
Chorus:
in der Höh (in der Höh) meine Heimat ist dort
in der Höh (in der Höh),
in der Höh (in der Höh)
in der Höh (in der Höh)
meine Heimat ist dort in der Höh.

Viel Geliebte sind dort in der Höh,
Wo ich sie einst verklärt wiedersehe (in der Höh)
Und dann bleiben wir immer vereint,
Dort wo ewig die Sonne uns scheint (in der Höh).
Chorus:
in der Höh (in der Höh) meine Heimat ist dort
in der Höh (in der Höh),
in der Höh (in der Höh)
in der Höh (in der Höh)
meine Heimat ist dort in der Höh.

Three other favorites often offered by these funeral choirs are given below. The same spirit of friendship that was felt when they sang these songs together on many an evening, was felt as they sang them now to say good-bye, farewell, we will meet again.

Sehen wir uns wohl einmal wieder
(LS 30, GH 639)

Seh'n wir uns wohl einmal wieder
Dort im hellen ew'gen Licht,
Wo kein Schmerz uns mehr drückt nieder,
Dort vor Jesu Angesicht.
Seh'n wir uns, seh'n wir uns, seh'n wir uns,
Seh'n wir uns wohl einmal wieder
Dort im hellen ew'igen Licht.

Lebt wohl, lebt wohl, mein Morgen tagt
(GH 594)

Lebt wohl, lebt wohl
Mein Morgen tagt,
Lebt wohl, ich geh' zur Ruh!
Der Kampf ist aus,
Mein Morgen tagt,
Der Meister winkt mir zu.
Lebt wohl, lebt wohl,
lebt wohl! ich geh' zur Ruh!
Lebt wohl, lebt wohl!
ich geh' zur Ruh!

Gott mit Euch, bis wir uns wieder sehen
(LS 251, GH 641, EL 151)

Gott mit euch, bis wir uns wiederseh'n!
Mog' Er ratend ob euch walten,
Euch bei Seiner Herd' erhalten!
Wiederseh'n (Wiederseh'n)
Wiederseh'n (Wiederseh'n)
Einst vor Gottes Thron wir steh'n!
Wiederseh'n! (Wiederseh'n!)
Wiederseh'n! (Wiederseh'n!)
Gott mit euch, bis wir uns wiederseh'n!

The service at the church always ended with the beautiful song, *Let me go, let me go*. Its words: 'Let me go, let me go, that Jesus I might see. My soul is filled with desire to embrace him for eternity, and to stand before his throne.'

Lasst mich gehen, lasst mich gehen
(LS 130, GH 621, EL 217)

Lasst mich gehen, lasst mich gehen,
dass ich Jesus möge sehen.
Meine Seele ist voll Verlangen
Ihn auf ewig zu umfangen
und vor seinem Thron zu stehen,
und vor seinem Thron zu stehen.

With the plaintive *lasst mich gehen, lasst mich gehen* 'let me go, let me go', the service came to a close. The casket was opened for the family's last farewell. Everyone then went to the cemetery. The minister read from the Bible and concluded with a final prayer. Flowers were laid on the casket; and as it was lowered, the Minister put earth on the casket saying, *erde zu erde, und asche zu asche* `earth to earth and ashes to ashes'. The funeral ended with the following hymn sung at the graveside:

Wo findet die Seele die Heimat, die Ruhe
(LS 128, GH 617, EL 249)

Wo findet die Seele die Heimat, die Ruhe
Wer deckt sie mit schützenden Fittichen zu,
Ach bietet die Welt keine Freistatt uns an,
Wo Sünden nicht locken, nicht schaden mehr kann,
Nein, nein, nein, nein, hier ist sie nicht,
Die Heimat der Seelen ist droben im Licht.

At children's funerals, girls from the class were chosen as flower girls; and classmates of the child sang a hymn at the service. One song often used for this was: *Ach wäre ich doch schon droben* `Oh, were I already there'.

Ach wäre ich doch schon droben
(LS 143)

Ach wäre ich doch schon droben
Mein Heiland wär' ich da
Wo Himmelsscharen loben,
Wo's schallt Halleluja!

Relatives and friends served as pallbearers. In early times, a baby's casket was usually carried on the head of a young girl. There were no flowers at a baby's funeral.

It was taken as a matter of course that Dakota German children attended and took part in the traditional funeral ceremonies. Included in every aspect of church and family life, they were not shielded from death, which was ever present on the prairie, especially during those early years.

Often family and friends, including the children in the community, gathered around the open casket at the home for a last photograph with a loved one before he was taken to his final resting place. There is hardly a family who does not have such a picture, or a picture of a relative in his casket. These are treasured by a people whose ties to the past and to those who have gone before are very strong.

The custom of the funeral procession to the church and the attendance of the flower girls continued to about 1940. Displaying the deceased in the home continued another few years. Now the coffin is viewed in the funeral home, and it is no longer opened for the family after the service. The service itself is very much the same. The Dakota German cemeteries, seemingly bare and windswept have their own stories to tell, and a history of a community can be traced there. Names, dates, and pictures of the dead are on the gravestones along with favorite verses from the Bible. In a back corner of the cemetery may be found the graves of those who have committed suicide. When a member of the church takes his own life, his body is not taken into the church for the funeral, but a service is held for him, and he is buried apart from the other graves.

The funeral celebration like the marriage celebration has its own traditions. The importance of the deceased person, his life, and the situation of his death, whether he died honorably and whether he was accepted for his deeds and the way he led his life, or whether his life was a loss; whether he died too young with tasks unfinished, whether he left behind a young family that still needed his care—all of these considerations so often find their expression in the funeral service by the way those left behind celebrate a funeral. If his wife should stand at his grave without tears then it is known how this man treated his family and what lay in his heart. There are bereaved family members at every funeral, but when the funeral is for someone who dies too young before a full life could be realized or leaves behind a young family, the whole community grieves. Thus, the funeral is a very important part of the community life.

Although many of these religious and secular customs have been somewhat eroded over the years, the church and religious holidays still provide the traditional center for the Dakota German communities.

Chapter 5: The language of customs and behavior

5.0 Introduction. This chapter describes the language through which the Central Dakota Germans expressed their customs and behavior. The account of their language, their customs, and their behavior is divided into seven sections: (1) *Worter und weisheiten:* Proverbs and sayings, the expression of moral values, ethics, and humor (5.1), (2) *Brauche:* Healing, the expression of folk medicine (5.2), (3) *Benennungen der krankheiten:* Old German words for medical terms preserved by Jacob Grimm in 1835 and still existing in the Central Dakota German lexicon (5.3), (4) *Heilmittel:* Folk remedies (5.4), (5) *Aberglaube:* Folk beliefs (5.5), (6) *Lieder:* Music in folk and family life (5.6), (7) *Kiche und Hof:* Culinary art and the sustenance of daily life (5.7)

The subtitles of the major divisions of this chapter are given in Central Dakota German and manifest the conventions of the Central Dakota German orthography. These Cental Dakota German (CDGer.) expressions are accompanied, where necessary, with English words.

The reader will notice that the *Lieder* cited in 5.6 occur in only one of the two orthographies: that is, the hymns and standard folk songs which they learned from printed song books show only the conventions of Standard High German orthography.

5.1 Worter und weisheiten: Proverbs and sayings, the expression of moral values, ethics, and humor. Proverbs contain not only the distilled wisdom of a people but offer a key to their character and nature. The proverb offers the means by which complex feelings and deep-seated beliefs can be expressed briefly and succinctly. The proverbs of the Dakota Germans reflect their austere environment as well as their wit and humor. Included also are sayings that were commonly used. Not only were they a part of the culture and an expression of moral values, but they were also used to teach traditional values to the young. The down-to-earth explanations reinforced the meaning in the child's mind. To show his intelligence and common sense, he too used the proverbs. These are a wonderful window into the Dakota German culture and value system. People who don't work hard, who don't know anything, or who are lazy are not respected as members of the community; nor are the immoral or those who presume to be more than they are. Whatever the topic, the wit and humor of the Dakota Germans finds expression. Proverbs and sayings reflect an enormous amount of psychological analysis and provide descriptive insights into human nature and the human condition.

Each of the proverbs and sayings is presented as follows: (1) in the orthography the Central Dakota Germans employ, (2) in the orthography of Standard High German, (3) with an English word, and (4) with a brief semantic explanation wherever the point or significance of the item may not be immediately apparent to the reader.

One will immediately note the differences between the orthographical system of the Dakota Germans and that of Standard High German. As we have previously noted, for the Dakota Germans, the conventions for capitalization are identical to the conventions for capitalization which occur in English. Whether this represents the more recent influence of the English-speaking schools or is the result of their departure from Germany before the standardization of the orthography of Standard High German requires further investigation. It would seem that early 16th and 17th century German texts do not uniformly show the current Standard High German orthographic practice of capitalizing all nouns.

These proverbs have neither come from printed sources nor been compared to printed sources. I have simply presented them as a collection of oral traditions from the Dakota Germans whom I have interviewed.

Wer einmal liegt dem glaubt man nit und wenn er gleich die wohrhait spricht.
Wer einmal lügt dem glaubt man nicht und wenn er gleich die Wahrheit spricht.
'Someone who lies once is not believed even if he then speaks the truth.'

Wer nit wenig ehrt, isch viel nit wert.
Wer nicht das Wenige ehrt, ist des Vielen nicht wert.
'He who does not honor the little, is not deserving of a lot.'

Fir nicks isch der tod, und der koschts lebe.
Für nichts ist der Tod, und der kostet das Leben.
'Nothing is free but death itself, and that costs your life.'

Friher morge rege und ein altweibertanz halt nit lange.
Früher Morgenregen and ein Altweibertanz halten nicht lang.
'An early morning rain and old women dancing, don't last long.'

Es bleibt nichts unbelohnt. Jeder mensch kommt an sein ziel.

Es bleibt nichts unbelohnt. Jeder Mensch kommt an sein Ziel.
'Nothing stays unrewarded. Every person reaches his goal.'
   (This means, what you sow is what you reap.)

Den stei(n) wo am weitschde fort schmeischt, holsch am erschte zurick.
Den Stein den du am weitesten weg wirfts, holst du als ersten zurück.
'The stone you throw away the farthest, is the first one you retrieve.'
(Children who may reject their parents and say they no longer need them, come to their parents first when they are in need.)

Ausse wie a lamm, inne isch ein reissender wulf.
Aussen wie ein Lamm, innen ist ein reissender Wolf.
'A lamb on the outside, but inside, a raging wolf.'

Lieber einmal gut gelebt als immer so verstumme.
Lieber einmal gut gelebt als immer so verstummen.
'Better to have really lived well once, than always so restricted.'

Ihr isch t'sonn ufgange am andere eck vom haus.
Ihr ist die Sonne aufgegangen am anderen Eck vom Haus.
'The sun has risen for her, on another corner of the house.'
(If a woman who is a traditional wife and mother, becomes successful at something else too. One could say the sun has shone on a second career for her.)

Sie isch lauter gift und zorn.
Sie ist lauter Gift und Zorn.
'She is made up of venom and wrath.'
(Not only is she unpleasant, she has the qualities of a witch.)

Klane kinder klanes kreiz, grosse kinder grosses kreiz.
Kleine Kinder kleines Kreuz, grosse Kinder grosses Kreuz.
'Small children, small cross to bear; big children, big cross to bear.'
(Problems one encounters with older children, are of a greater magnitude than the simpler problems of the little ones.)

Was versparst an deinem mund, das fressen katz und hund.
Was du ersparst von deinem Mund, das fressen die Katze und der Hund.
'What you save from your own mouth will be eaten by cats and dogs.'
(It doesn't always pay to save and be frugal, for what you have saved

often goes to others, such as your own children, who will not appreciate it.)

Von reiche leit lernt man spare.
Von reichen Leuten lernt man sparen.
'One learns how to save from rich people.'

Was eingeht, macht dich nit unrein, aber was ausgeht.
Was eingeht, macht dich nicht unrein, aber was ausgeht.
'What you eat and drink does not make you unclean, but what you speak can make you impure.' (Mark 8:15)

Jedes dierle sucht sei nahrung.
Jedes Tierlein sucht seine Nahrung.
'Even the littlest animal looks for sustenance.'
(All people search for human contact and need sustenance.)

S'haus verliert nicks.
Das Haus verliert nichts.
'The house does not lose anything.'
(Usually said to children who have misplaced something, and are encouraged to keep looking for it must still be there.)

Was, du hast sie gefüttert und gewässert, und weisst nicht wo sie stehen?
'What, you gave them food and water and you don't know where they are?'
(How can you lose something if you yourself were responsible for it, and were the last to have worked with it? This verse was identified by the informant, Nathaniel Miller, as being Kaschub German, a low German dialect spoken by people in Bessarabia who were from the north near the Baltic Sea; and thus it was learned in the language they shared, Standard High German.)

Das weib wo pfeift und die huhn wo kreht, kehren beide das gnik rum dreht.
Ein Weib, das pfeift und ein Huhn, das kräht, gehört beiden das Genick umgedreht.
'A women who whistles and a hen that crows, both need to have their necks wrung.'

Unkraut verderbt nit.
Unkraut verdirbt nicht.

'Weeds don't deteriorate.'
(Bad people always survive just as weeds do.)

Der wulf verliert die hor aber nit die nicke.
Der Wolf verliert die Haare, aber die Nicke nicht.
'A wolf loses his hair but not his desires.'
(A man may age and lose his hair, but he still has the same desires. This can be derogatory, as in 'old fool'.)

Brauchst dich nimme dummle, der hase isch schon eber'm bukel.
Du brauchst dich nicht mehr beeilen, der Hase ist schon lange über dem Hügel.
'You no longer need to hurry, the rabbit has long since disappeared over the hill.'

Zieg dich nit aus eb schlofe gehsch.
Zieh dich nicht aus, bevor du schlafen gehst.
'Don't give up your inheritance to others until you go to sleep (die).'

Wann's eim zu wohl isch noh geht mir ufs eis und brecht sich die fiess.
Wenn es einem zu wohl ist, geht man aufs Eis und bricht sich die Füsse.
'If things are going too well, we go out on the ice and break a leg.'

Weibersterbe macht dem bauer kei verderbe, aber pferde verrecke das macht schrecke.
Weibersterben macht dem Bauer kein Verderben, aber Pferdeverrecken das macht Schrecken.
'When women die there's no loss to the farmer, but when horses die, that scares him.'
(This was meant as a good natured joke.)

Du tragst den krug lang an der brunne, aber endlich verstosst du ihn doch.
Du trägst den Krug so lang an den Brunnen, aber endlich zerbrichst du ihn doch.
'We carry the pitcher often to the well, but finally we do break it.'
(If you commit evil acts one of the acts will finally show you up.)

Es isch kei kessele so krumm das kei deckle nuf passt.
Es ist kein Kessel so krumm, dass kein Deckel passt.
'There is no kettle so crooked that you can't find a cover to fit it.'

(There is no one so unusual that they can't find a mate.)

Jedes kessele hat sein deckle.
Jeder Kessel hat seinen Deckel.
`Every little kettle has its little cover.'
(Every girl can find a mate.)

Ram uf, die soldate kommen.
Räum' auf, die Soldaten kommen.
`Put things away, the soldiers are coming.'
(Probably said in the days when soldiers in Germany came to your house to search for something they wanted to take from you. Now said with humor when there is an anticipated visit by grandchildren who will probably break things not put away.)

Der eigener lob stinkt.
Eigenes Lob stinkt.
`Self praise stinks.'

Wer nit hert, muss fiehle.
Wer nicht hört, muss fühlen.
`Who doesn't listen, must feel.'

Wer nit zu zeit fortkommt, kommt a nit zu zeit heim.
Wer nicht zur Zeit fortkommt, kommt auch nicht zur Zeit heim.
`Who doesn't leave on time, will also not return on time.'

Junges blut hopst gern.
Junges Blut hopst gern.
`Young blood likes to jump about.'

Mit der gabel esse isch a ehr, aber mit der hand kriegt ma meh.
Mit der Gabel essen ist eine Ehr, aber mit der Hand kriegt man mehr.
`To eat with the fork is polite, but you can get more with your hand.'

Die kirchig isch kei grot, sie hopst nit fort.
Die Kirche ist keine Kröte, sie hüpft nicht fort.
`The church is not a frog, she won't hop away.'
(Said by someone who is too lazy to go to church and he wants to postpone it to another Sunday.)

So wie einer esst, so schafft er ah.
So wie wir essen, so arbeiten wir.

'The way we eat is the way we work.'

Wo die liebe na fallt da bleibt sie liege, und wanns gerade im misthaufe isch.
Wo die Liebe hinfällt, dort bleibt sie liegen, und wenn es gleich im Misthaufen ist.
'Where love falls, there love stays lying, and if it is right in a heap of manure.'
(People 'fall in love' and go ahead with their wishes no matter how wrong.)

Es isch kopst wie tsprunge.
Es ist gehüpft wie gesprungen.
'Hopping is like jumping.'
(No matter how you do it, the result is the same, bad.)

Alt wie a kuh und immer noch lerne dazu.
Alt wie eine Kuh und immer noch lernen dazu.
'Old as a cow but still learning.'

Noch dem ungewidder scheint die sonne wieder.
Nach dem Ungewitter scheint die Sonne wieder.
'After the storm the sun shines again.'
(You can be sad, but you will be happy again.)

Spare in der zeit noh hasch's in der not.
Spare in der Zeit, dann hast du in der Not.
'Save in time and you have when in need.'

Feg erscht der dreck vor deinere dir, noh kommst und fegst bei meiner.
Fege erst den Dreck vor deiner Tür, dann kommst und fegst vor meiner.
'First sweep the dirt before your door, then you can sweep before mine.'

Wer nit kommt zur rechte zeit, muss esse was ebrig bleibt.
Wer nicht kommt zur rechten Zeit, der muss essen was übrig bleibt.
'He who doesn't arrive on time has to eat what is left.'

Rege macht sege.
Regen macht Segen.

'Rain gives the blessing.'

Der wind heilt, er will rege.
Der Wind heult, er will Regen.
'The wind is crying, he wants rain.'

Zum a grober sack mussch a grober bindel han.
Zum groben Sack muss man grobe Bänder haben.
'A coarse sack needs to have a coarse tie.'
(Rough people can only be dealt with in the same manner.)

Wann die maus satt hat noh ischs mehl bitter.
Wenn die Maus satt ist, ist das Mehl bitter.
'When the mouse is full, the flour is bitter.'
(When you're not hungry, then you may not like what has been cooked.)

Man soll der tag nit lobe vor em obedt.
Man soll den Tag nicht loben vor dem Abend.
'You shouldn't praise the day before evening falls.'
(The day can still turn out badly.)

Die hett mir nit besser zusamme dricke kenne mit dem schupkarrich.
Die hätte man nicht besser zusammen drücken können mit dem Schubkarren.
'They could not have been pressed together any better with the wheelbarrow.'
(They fit so well together in a negative way, each being lazy.)

So jung kommen mir nimme zusamme.
So jung kommen wir nicht wieder zusammen.
'We'll never be together this young again.'
(We will all be older next time we meet.)

Wer sich noch der decke streckt, dem bleiben die fiss ungedeckt.
Wer sich nach der Decke streckt, dem bleiben die Füsse unbedeckt.
'He who reaches up too far, leaves his feet uncovered.'

Wann man den hund muss uf die jagd trage, fängt er keine hase.
Wenn man den Hund auf die Jagd tragen muss, fängt er keine Hasen.
'If you have to carry the dog to the hunt, he won't catch any rabbits.'
(If you have to show someone exactly how to do a job, you might as well do it yourself.)

Macht nicks aus in wellem finger das dich schneidscht, es blit und schmerzt alle weg.
Einerlei in welchen Finger du dich schneidest, es blutet und schmerzt.
`It doesn't matter on which finger you cut yourself, it bleeds and causes pain.'
(Each child in the family must be treated the same as the other children in the family.)

Wer kei knoblich fresse hat, der stinkt a nit.
Wer keinen Knoblauch gefressen hat, der stinkt auch nicht.
`Who doesn't eat garlic, doesn't stink.'
(If your behavior is above suspicion you will not be suspected.)

Wann der mantel passt, noh zieg ihn ah.
Wenn der Mantel passt, dann ziehe ihn an.
`If the coat fits wear it.'
(Some people refuse to accept a criticism even though it obviously fits them. Often used in describing a reaction to a sermon.)

Wanns nit regert, noh trepfelts.
Wenn's nicht regnet, dann tröpfelt es.
`If it's not raining, then at least it's coming down in little drops.'
(Working at little jobs and earning a little bit keeps the family sustained even during hard times.)

Jeder mensch versteht sei liederlichkeit.
Jeder Mensch versteht seine Liederlichkeit.
`Every man understands his own weaknesses.'

Ein esel nennt der andere langeohr.
Ein Esel nennt den anderen Langohr.
`A donkey calls another long ears.'
(He's calling someone else what he himself is.)

Der verdreht die auge wie a verschossener stier.
Der verdreht die Augen wie ein geschossener Stier.
`He twists his eyes like a steer that's been shot.'
(He can't give you an honest straight look in the eye.)

Trett dem hund nit uf der schwanz sonscht beisst er dich.

Tritt dem Hund nicht auf den Schwanz, er beisst dich.
'Don't step on the dog's tail; he'll bite you.'
(If you don't want trouble, don't start trouble.)

Der hat lieber a leerer darm als a meeder arm.
Der hat lieber einen leeren Darm als einen müden Arm.
'He'd rather have an empty gut than a tired arm.'

Zu gut isch a stick liederlichkeit.
Zu gut ist ein Stück Liederlichkeit.
'Too good can be a vice.'
(If you are too good to people and always give without return, you only make them weaker and less able to return.)

In der nacht sind alle katze schwarz.
In der Nacht sind alle Katzen schwarz.
'In the night all cats are black.'
(It doesn't matter if you marry a homely woman as long as she's a good wife and mother.)

Morge, morge, nur nit heit, sagen alle faule leit.
Morgen, morgen, nur nicht heute, sagen alle faulen Leute.
'Tomorrow, tomorrow, just not today, is what all lazy people say.'

Er hat katz im sack kauft.
Er hat die Katze im Sack gekauft.
'He's bought a cat in a sack.'

Du kannst die ochse zum wasser fihre, aber saufe kannsch sie nit mache.
Man kann den Ochsen nur zum Wasser führen, saufen muss er selbst.
'You can lead an ox to water, but he must drink himself.'
(You can ask someone to do something, but you cannot force him.)

Wer der kopf gwäsche han will, der muss selber dabei sei.
Wer den Kopf gewaschen haben will, der muss selber dabei sein.
'Whoever wants his hair washed, has to be there.'
(If you want something done for you, you'd better be there yourself.)

Mit dem mass wo du mesch, wird dir wieder gmesse.
Mit dem Mass, mit dem du misst, wird dir wieder gemessen.
'With the measure you use to measure others, you too will be measured.'

Wer lange schläft, den Gott ernährt. Wer früh aufsteht, sein Gut verzehrt.
Wer lange schläft, den Gott ernährt. Wer früh aufsteht, sein Gut verzehrt.
`He who sleeps long, God nourishes; he who gets up early, consumes his wealth.'

Wer kei arbeit hat, macht sich's.
Wer keine Arbeit hat, macht sie sich.
`He who doesn't have work, makes work.'

Kommt mir eber der hund, noh kommt mir a eber der schwanz.
Komm ich über den Hund, komm ich auch über den Schwanz.
`If I can get over the dog, I can get over the tail.'
(If you have worked and suffered you are prepared for future hardships too, and they will become less difficult for you to overcome.)

Fang die katz und hock sie vors loch.
Fang die Katz und setz sie vor das Loch.
`Catch the cat and put her in front of the hole.'
(Let's get down to business.)

Mit gwalt reisst mir dem hund der schwanz raus.
Mit Gewalt reisst man dem Hund den Schwanz aus.
`Too much force pulls the dog's tail out.'
(When too much force is applied things have to break.)

Wer was kann, den hält man wert, und wer nicks kann, den niemand begehrt.
Wer etwas kann, den hält man wert, and wer nichts kann, den niemand begehrt.
`He who has ability is held in esteem, and he who knows nothing, no one respects.'

Lieber a laus im kraut wie gar kei fleisch.
Lieber eine Laus im Kraut als gar kein Fleisch.
`Rather a louse in the cabbage than no meat at all.'
(If someone owes you something, it's better to accept a small sum at a time than to get nothing at all.)

Tanzt er nit, noh guckt er zu, verreisst kei strumpf und spart sei schuh.
Tanzt er nicht, dann sieht er zu, zerreisset keine Strümpfe und spart seine Schuh.
`If he doesn't dance, then he can watch; he won't tear his stocking or ruin his shoes.'

Er tretts geld mit die fiss naus.
Er tritt das Geld mit den Füssen hinaus.
`He kicks his money out with his feet.'
(A wasteful person who spends everything and quickly.)

Schad fir der hieb wo nebe nah fällt.
Schade für den Hieb, der daneben fällt.
`It's a pity for the blow that misses.'
(Spare the rod and spoil the child.)

So wie du dich bettscht, so mussch a liege.
So wie du dich bettest, musst du auch liegen.
`As you make your bed, you have to lie in it.'

Erfahrung macht glick.
Erfahrung macht Glück.
`Experience makes luck.'

Der faule tragt sich tot, und der fleissige springt sich tot.
Der Faule trägt sich tot, und der Fleissige springt sich tot.
`The lazy person drags himself to death, and the industrious person runs himself to death.'
(The lazy person wants to walk less and carry more, while the ambitious person is willing to run back and forth. Either way we work toward the end goal, death.)

Eberall ischs gut, aber daheim ischs am beschte.
Überall ist's gut, aber daheim ist's am besten.
`Everywhere is good, but home is the best.'

Viel rutsche macht blede hose.
Viel Rutschen macht blöde Hosen.
`A lot of sliding wears out your pants.'
(If you move too often or change jobs too often, you end up with nothing.)

Der apfel fallt nit weit vom stamm.
Der Apfel fällt nicht weit vom Stamm.
'The apple does not fall far from the trunk.'
(The word *stamm* has a double meaning, it means family and tribe as well as trunk of the tree. Thus the use of the word *stamm* rather than *baum* 'tree' creates a double emphasis. The father, family, all the relations are responsible for each child and its upbringing.)

Von nicks kommt nicks.
Von nichts kommt nichts.
'Nothing creates nothing.'
(With no effort, there is no accomplishment.)

Es gebt kei fleisch ohne knoche.
Es gibt kein Fleisch ohne Knochen.
'There is no meat without bones.'
(There is no life that is only good or easy. There are difficult periods for everyone.)

Unter eim alte baumstumpf lässts sich gut ruhe.
Unter einem alten Baumstumpf lässt sich gut ruhen.
'You can rest well under the trunk of an old tree.'
(If a woman marries someone older she will have security and need not work so hard.)

Gesegnet sei das ehebund, verheiratet sind die dumme hund.
Gesegnet sei der Ehebund, verheiratet sind die dummen Hunde.
'Blessed is the state of matrimony, married are the stupid fools.'

Was ich nit weiss, macht mich nit heiss.
Was ich nicht weiss, macht mich nicht heiss.
'What I don't know, won't make me angry.'

Borge macht sorge.
Borgen macht Sorgen.
'Borrowing causes worries.'

Der wurde ein aug dran gebe, wann der andere eins verliert.
Der würde ein Auge daran geben, wenn der andere eins verlieren würde.
'He would give up one eye if the other person would lose one too.'
(He would be willing to suffer just to see his enemy suffer.)

Ein blindes henle findt als mal ah ein kernle.
Ein blindes Hähnchen findet auch als mal ein Körnchen.
`Even a blind chicken sometimes finds a kernel.'
(Everyone has good luck sometime.)

Wanns uf die grosse ankommt, kennt man mit die kih ah hase fange.
Wenn's auf die Grösse ankäme, dann könnte man mit den Kühen auch Hasen fangen.
`If it were a matter of size, then one should be able to catch rabbits with cows.'

Wo nicks isch, da hat der Kaiser sei recht verlore.
Wo nichts ist, da hat der Kaiser sein Recht verloren.
`Where there is nothing, that is where the Kaiser has lost his authority.'
(The Kaiser is always supreme; if he does not exercise his rights, it is only where there is nothing to claim.)

Wann der bettler ufs ross kommt, reitet er scharfer wie der edelmann.
Wenn der Bettler aufs Ross kommt, reitet er schärfer als der Edelmann.
`When the begger gets on the horse, he rides harder than the nobleman.'
(People who gain power are more cruel to people like themselves than a nobleman born to privilege would be.)

Bettelleit hins gut, es bricht ihn kei ochs kei horn und frisst ihne ah kei maus kei korn, bettelleit hins gut.
Bettelleute haben es gut, es bricht ihnen kein Ochs ein Horn und frisst ihnen auch keine Maus ein Korn, Bettelleute haben es gut.
`Beggars are well off, their ox won't break it's horn, no mouse will eat their corn, beggars are well off.'

Nicks han isch a ruhiges lebe.
Nichts haben ist ein ruhiges Leben.
`To have nothing is a quiet life.'

Ein geschenkter gaul guckt mir nit ins maul.
Einem geschenkten Gaul schaut man nicht ins Maul.
`Don't look a gift horse in the mouth.'

Miehle warm und der ofe warm macht den reichste farmer arm.
Mühle warm und Ofen warm macht den reichsten Bauer arm.
'Mill warm and oven warm makes the richest farmer poor.'
(Farmers cannot afford luxury. They must live frugally. This verse is unusual because of the use of the word farmer. This occurs only here, in every other case they use the German word *bauer*.)

Das vegele wo drin isch, will raus; und das vegele wo draus ist, will nei.
Das Vögelein, das drinnen ist, will heraus; und das Vögelein, das draussen ist, will hinein.
'The bird who is in wants to get out, and the bird who is out wants to get in.'
(Girls that are married envy girls who are single and free; while girls who are single envy the girls who are married. Note the use of the diminutive of 'bird' *vegele* whenever the subject is a girl, otherwise the regular noun for 'bird' *vogel* is used.)

Wo der deifel nicks nimme ausricht, da schickt er ein altes weib nah. Wo der Teufel nichts mehr ausrichtet, da schickt er eine alte Frau hin.
'Where the devil no longer can accomplish his purpose, he sends an old woman'.
(Refers to old women gossiping and all the trouble this can cause. It is said in good humor.)

Lustig glebt und selig g'storbe hat dem deifel die rechnung verdorbe. Lustig gelebt und selig gestorben hat dem Teufel die Rechnung verdorben.
'Living merrily and dying holy cheats the devil of his reckoning.'

Die ganz woch kranke leit im haus, und wann der Sonntag kommt sind keine zu vergrabe.
Die ganze Woche kranke Leute im Haus, kommt Sonntag, sind keine zu begraben.
'The whole week there are sick people in the house, but come Sunday there is no one to bury.'
(Sunday was the traditional day for funerals.)

Arbeit macht das leben siss, aber faulheit stärkt die glieder. Arbeit macht das Leben süss, aber Faulheit stärkt die Glieder.
'Work sweetens your life, but laziness strengthens the limbs.'

Dem beser hund gibt mir immer zwei stickle brot.
Dem bösen Hund gibt man immer zwei Stück Brot.
`One always gives the meanest dog two pieces of bread.'
(When people are mean you have to try twice as hard to get along with them. This is the best solution for you, since you can't be meaner than the meanest dog.)

Es gebt nit immer jagdtage, es gebt ah fangtage.
Es gibt nicht immer Jagdtage, es gibt auch Fangtage.
`There are not always days of hunting, there are also catch days.'
(After the game has been successfully hunted, it must also be prepared and preserved which is an enormous amount of work. There are not just good days in life, but also difficult days when you must preserve and prepare.)

Geld wie mischt und keins in der kischt.
Geld wie Mist, und keines in der Kiste.
`Money as available as manure, but none saved in a chest.'

Ein junger baum kann man biege.
Einen jungen Baum kann man biegen.
`A young tree and a young person can be shaped.'

Eine kuh deckt alle armut zu.
Eine Kuh deckt alle Armut zu.
`One cow covers all poverty.'
(No matter how poor if you have a cow you are always well off. The cow provides most of what one needs to live such as milk, cream, butter, cheese, cottage cheese, yoghurt, or buttermilk.)

Wo nicks isch geht a nicks verlore.
Wo nichts ist, geht auch nichts verloren.
`Where there is nothing, nothing can be lost.'
(If you don't own anything such as land or cattle, you can't lose it.)

Ohne versuch schmeckt nicks.
Ohne Versuch schmeckt nichts.
`Without trying you cannot taste anything.'

Wer sich hitt vor Märze wind, bleibts ganze johr a schenes kind.
Wer sich hütet vor Märzwind, bleibt das ganze Jahr ein schönes Kind.

'Who protects himself from the March wind, will remain a lovely child for the rest of the year.'

Das erschte isch vergange.
Das Erste ist vergangen.
'The beginning is past.'
(A second husband or wife can never be the same as the beginning of a first marriage.)

Er isch a haus deifel und a gasse engel.
Er ist ein Hausteufel und ein Gassenengel.
'He is a house devil and a street angel.'
(A man who is mean at home but always shows his best face to the public.)

Schulde sind kei hase, die laffen nit weg.
Schulden sind keine Hasen, die laufen nicht fort.
'Debts are not rabbits, they won't run away.'

Reiss der grot hoor raus wo keine sin.
Reiss der Kröte die Haar heraus, wenn sie keine hat.
'You can't pull hair from a frog if it hasn't any.'
(If someone owes you money and he hasn't any, you can't collect.)

Kaft und gmesse, isch bald fresse.
Gekauft und gemessen, ist bald gefressen.
'What is bought and measured, is soon eaten.'
(You save by not spending in the first place.)

Im grab kenn mir schlofe.
Im Grab kannst du schlafen.
'You can sleep in the grave.'

Dem isch keine gut genug, dem missen mir a neie backe.
Für den ist keine gut genug, dem müssen sie eine Neue backen.
'No one is good enough for him, they have to bake him a new one'

Der isch doch nebers nescht falle.
Der ist doch neben das Nest gefallen.
'He fell out of the nest anyway.'
(You climb too high and think you're too much, and then you fail.)

Er isch so langsam wie siebe tage regewetter.
Er ist so langsam wie sieben Tage Regenwetter.
'He is as slow as seven days of rain.'

Herr was bin ich gworde, und Herr was wills noch were.
Herr, was bin ich geworden, und Herr, was wills noch werden.
'God what have I become, and God what will still become of me.'
(If you have reached great heights you must remember what you were, for you could still become even less than you were at the beginning.)

Es isch nit Gottes armut, es isch dem deifel sei liederlichkeit.
Es ist nicht Gottes Armut, sondern des Teufels Liederlichkeit.
'It is not God given poverty, rather it is the devil's laziness.'

Er kommt hinne noch wie's femfte rad am wage.
Er kommt hinten nach wie das fünfte Rad am Wagen.
'He follows along behind like the fifth wheel of the wagon.'
(He is pretty useless.)

End ohne schrecke isch besser wie schrecke ohne end.
End ohne Schrecken ist besser als Schrecken ohne End.
'An end without sorrow is better than sorrow without end.'

So wie sie pfeift, muss er danze.
So wie sie pfeift, muss er tanzen.
'He has to dance to her tune.'

Wer hoch nuf kommt, fällt hoch runter.
Wer hoch hinauf kommt, fällt hoch herunter.
'When you climb high you fall from a greater height.'

Er fihrt sie hinterem licht rum.
Er führt sie hinter das Licht.
'He is leading her behind the light.'
(Thus she cannot see the truth.)

Noch wulf kommt bear.
Nach dem Wolf kommt der Bär.
'After the wolf comes the bear.'
(If you cannot get along with someone, expect that the person who follows them will be even worse.)

Den hat der blitz aus der wand tschlage.
Den hat der Blitz aus der Wand geschlagen.
'He was struck from out of the wall by lightning.'
(He was not born of a woman rather he was created by lightning and appeared from out of nowhere. The saying is used to describe a child who continually misbehaves and no punishment frightens him, or to someone who simply cannot fit in.)

Er hat kei femf cent fir a grot vorlocke.
Er hat keine fünf cent, um eine Kröte hervorzulocken.
'He does not have five cents with which to entice a frog.'
(People who act important but have nothing.)

Alles was kei verstand hat, sage die wohrheit.
Alles was keinen Verstand hat, sagt die Wahrheit.
'Everything that has no sense, tells the truth.'

Der reisst lieber alles tsamme wie das er sei zorn gibt.
Er reisst lieber alles zusammen als dass er seinen Zorn gibt.
'He would rather destroy everything than give up his wrath.'

Das isch a schlechter augespiel.
Das ist ein schlechtes Augenspiel.
'That was a poor mischief.'

Er hat a wieder in'dt flasch gwillt.
Er wollte auch wieder in die Flasche hinein.
'He wanted to get back into the bottle too.'
(If you want something that is not possible.)

Dort isch er naus, er hat a hitle uf.
Da ist er hinaus, er hatte ein Hütlein auf.
'There he went out, he had on a little hat.'
(If someone is told something and keeps wanting it repeated, this phrase is used instead.)

Wo gehscht du nah? Ins loch, bohne lese.
Wo gehst du hin? In das Loch, Bohnen lesen.
'Where are you going? Into the hole to pick beans.'
(A non-answer given when you don't want to say where you are going or what you are up to.)

The Dakota German proverbs and sayings are filled with magic. There are wolves and frogs and little people. It is the stuff of a Grimm fairy tale, and seen in the light of the Grimm collection, has an authenticity and relationship to the thinking of late 18th and early 19th century Southwest Germany before the Dakota Germans moved on into another time and another age.

5.2 Brauche: Healing, an expression of folk medicine. This section discusses what in Central Dakota German is called *brauche* 'the art of healing' as it was practiced in the Central Dakota German communities. Indeed all of the German words employed in this section, with the exception of Standard High German (SHGer.) *magische Heilkunde* 'magic healing' and *Merseburger Zaubersprüche* 'Merseburg charm or magic verses' are Central Dakota German words. In Standard High German *Brauch* (pl. *Bräuche*) or *Gebrauch* (pl. *Gebräuche*) m. mean 'use, custom, rite, ceremony, ritual'. The Central Dakota German word *brauche* (no pl.) refers to what I have translated here as 'healing' or 'the art and practice of healing'. Cognate to this form is *brauchere* 'healer' f. *Brauchere* means *a weib das brauche kann* (CDGer.) 'a woman who is able to do *brauche*'. This role in their society was almost exclusively female, although Emma Fischer and Eva Iszler did remember a Jacob Hoffmann as the sole instance of a man being engaged in *brauche* (5.2.5). *Brauche* was practiced by Lutherans.

In discussing *brauche*, I shall describe (1) *brauche*, the art of healing reflected in the verses and psychological insights of the *brauchere* Freidricka Opp (5.2.1), (2) *mitweib und brauchere*, the art of healing and medical insights of the *brauchere* Eva Iszler (5.2.2), (3) *Merseburger Zaubersprüche*, the oldest known magic verses in the German language (5.2.3), (4) *verzähle*, oral history of *brauche* incidents (5.2.4), (5) *brauche*, was it *magische Heilkunde* 'magic healing' or *hexerei* 'witchcraft' in a Christian community (5.2.5), (6) *brauche*, an etymological guess (5.2.6).

Among the original settlers who emigrated from Germany to Russia there were probably no pharmacists or doctors. Some colonists had gained a good practical knowledge of medicine, and there were midwives in every village. It was not until years after the first colony was established that the Russian government decided to provide medical care for the new settlers. Itinerant doctors, often largely self-trained, would make the rounds of the villages to sell books, provide medical advice, prepare prescriptions, and instruct in the proper mixtures of roots, powders, and plants for various ailments. Their fee was considered reasonable: a night's lodging and a meal. At least one of the books purchased in this way, *Lehrbuch der Geburtshülfe für Hebammen* by Dr. Franz Karl Nägele (Heidelberg: Akademische Verlagsbuchhandlung von J.C.B. Mohr, 1854), made its way to America. It belonged to Mrs. Katherine Ehley, one of the several midwives in Ashley, North Dakota.

The Dakota German pioneers could rarely seek a doctor's advice, and in the early days many settlers including hundreds of children died from diphtheria, scarlet fever, and smallpox, the three biggest dangers. The most common diseases along with these three, but not as life threatening, were measles, German measles, strep throat, pneumonia, and ulcers, both interior and exterior. Convulsions in babies were dangerous and feared. Tuberculosis, although not one of the more common diseases, was also present on the prairie and took many lives. Many mentioned the flu epidemic of 1918 in which hundreds of Dakota Germans died.

Neither as colonists nor as pioneers did these settlers have the opportunity to go for medical care as there was no modern medical health care system to rely upon. They did have their ancient traditions and their own understanding of how to maintain good health. This helped them little when an illness struck. Their greatest fears were of the infectious diseases which could kill many of the people in a family or community, and for which there was no medical cure. They could only trust in God and console themselves with the fact that no one could hinder what God had ordained.

Many small abrasions or simpler problems such as colds in different parts of the body were dealt with by folk remedies and with the advice of practioners of folk medicine or simply by taking advice from the grandmother of the family. But the more serious problems and the life threatening illnesses needed the healing efforts of the *brauchere*. The *brauchere* had the ability to heal the sick.

This tradition, rooted in German history, had been taken by the Germans to Russia and was then again transplanted to America. It is an aspect of *magische Heilkunde* 'magic healing', known for a thousand years by the German people. Although it has generally died out in recent years in Dakota, this does not mean that it has fallen into disrespect; it only means that there are now doctors available in the communities who can help the sick. In the culture of the Dakota Germans *brauche* was not the practice of magic healing, but a desperate attempt to cure or help one's sick when there were no other means available. These healers who could only inherit their power from their mother, are still thought to have done their best to care for the sick and are still held in high regard today.

5.2.1 Brauche: The art of healing reflected in the verses and psychological insights of the brauchere Friederike Opp.

In *brauche* it was believed that in order to help people who were seriously ill and in their hour of need, of helplessness, and of pain, the *brauchere*, or 'healer', had to have the power of healing which she gained through inheritance. But also the *brauchere* had to have developed a great personal inner strength and source from which the sick person could draw. The firmness of her belief and her faith in God was most important for it supported the belief of the sick person in the ability of the *brauchere* to help marshal the forces needed to gain superiority over the illness.

The people who were able to do *brauche* were mostly women, but this is not unusual, for in ancient Germanic tribes women were the ones who had the powers over the sacred (Grimm 1835:225).

The healer's strength lay in her hands and in her ability to pass her faith and strength on to the sick person. Nowhere are feelings of hopelessness and insecurity stronger than in the sick. Without the belief and faith of the sick person in the healing and in the healing strength of the *brauchere*, the sick person could not be helped. His own belief gave him new strength and hope within himself which supported his body in the struggle against the disease. Not science but feelings, faith, and believing were the reality.

Modern medical doctors have recognized that a person's will to get well and his belief in his ability to get well help him to recover from serious illnesses. It is a very open question as to what happens in the human mind and body to conquer disease.

In *brauche* we find the words *hope, belief, strength* pitted against the words *need, helplessness, hopelessness*, the language of insecurity. People had nothing but their will and the strength of their beliefs, and it is in this context that one can understand the power of healing. *Wer in tiefer not ist, bangt nach Hilfe* 'Whoever is in great need longs for help' (class notes from course, *Magische Heilkunde*, taught by Professor Dr. Kurt Ranke, Göttingen University, 1961-62).

The secrets of *brauche* were kept within the family of a healer through generations. When the healer reached the twilight of her life or the end of her strength, the secrets and the power were passed on upon an oath of secrecy, to only one of her daughters, the one chosen. It was believed that the secrets of *brauche*, if told to others, lost their healing power.

The following collection was made possible when the doors were opened by my mother who did not see the need to carry on the tradition of *brauche*, feeling it was a practice no longer needed. She did, however, want to see it preserved and remembered for the important role it did play.

Emma Fischer, my mother, whose maiden name was Bendewald, received the verses and the *brauche* tradition from her mother, Friederike Opp whose married name was Bendewald. Friederike brought them with her when she immigrated from Glückstal, Russia, in 1905. Friederike practiced as a full-time *brauchere* when she arrived in 1905 until she married in 1908. She remembered being picked up by horse and buggy or sled in winter, often in the middle of the night and in bad weather, to be taken to heal someone. As will be shown, time is of the essence. After her marriage Friederike moved out of the town to a farm in McIntosh County. She then no longer made house calls, but people would still come to her farm for healing. In the last years of her life, when she again lived in town, crippled by rheumatism and confined to a wheelchair because of the extreme hardships and cold she had endured as a pioneer wife on the Dakota prairie, people still kept coming to her for healing. She felt she was too old and weak to impart strength to them, but many still wanted her help. She no longer felt she could take payment for healing but she insisted that they make a special offering to the church instead. For Friederike believed that if no payment was made for the *brauche* the sickness would strike back at her. The danger was great and the ritual had to be exact.

She was not only a healer of physical illnesses; her opinion was sought for personal problems and family disputes which she was called upon to settle. Two members of a family would come to her individually and tell their problem and she would give the fair judgment of what had to be done to heal the hearts and souls of the people involved. It was frequently a question of differences between marriage partners or a question of fairness to the step children or adopted children of whom there were many due to the deaths of so many women from the hardships.

I spent the first 14 years of my life sitting on the floor next to her wheelchair, hidden in her long skirts, and was a part of the visits, the coming and going of the many, many people who came to see her. When she died in 1951 at the age of seventy-five, many members of her community felt a great sense of loss, for a warm human being, to whom many had come for comfort and advice, was gone.

Brauche can only be done when the moon is new or in its ascendency, never to a full or waning moon. The philosophy of *brauche* is that as the light appears and 'increases', *nimmt zu*, the strength in the healing is increasing while the sickness or disease is 'decreasing', *nimmt ab*.

Ideally one looks to the moon as the first sliver of light appears across the bottom of the moon and any time thereafter, while it keeps increasing up to a half moon. It is the power of the increasing new light of the moon versus the disease which must decrease. (*Was ich seh nimm zu, was ich greif nimm ab* `May what I see increase, what I grasp decrease'.)

First you must believe, then faith is strengthened by the form-rhymes which are repeated so that all thought and concentration becomes a rhythm. In all *brauche* or `healing', the number which has power is the number three. *Die drei höchste namen* `the three holiest of names' God the Father, God the Son, and God the Holy Ghost invest the number with its power. Each verse of the cure is said three times. The hand of the *brauchere* is formed into a fist and then turned so the back of the hand faces the area causing the pain; gently, as close to the surface as possible, it moves in a circle during the entire time the verse is said. When the three holiest names, *Gott Vater, Gott Sohn, Gott Heiliger Geist*, are said, the back of the hand touches ever so gently three times, once with each holy name, the surface of the face or the area of pain if it is part of the face. The healer then blows on the area three times. Every cure is secret and is said under one's breath and inaudibly; only the three holy names are said audibly. Thus, we find things always in three's whether the verse, the breath, or the three holiest of names. There is always movement with a well-defined rhythm and the movement is done so the bad is moving away from you. Even the hand position is warding off the disease with the hand not only not open, but turned so that only the back of the hand faces the disease. The blowing is also a blowing away of the disease. Further on in the remedies (5.2.2) it will be shown that the "bad thing" is buried, or burned, or sent away; just as in *brauche* the rhythm and movement are to move it away from the affected person, and from the *brauchere* who stands in danger for the disease may strike back at her.

In a day when medicine had not yet discovered the power of germs, the *brauchere* was already wary. Friederike did not allow people to touch her, and she constantly washed her hands even if someone only shook them in greeting. She did want to be kissed, as was the custom.

The ritual behavior described above was employed in the verses cited in the section that follows, along with the ritual described for each verse.

Breath as the life force was a part of Germanic belief. One believed that the vital force was contained in the breath, and this force was therefore located in the head. It was believed that when a man died this vital force, the breath, withdrew into his head, but could thereafter re-emerge (Hackmann 1971:163). We also find breath as the term for life in *Genesis* 2 where in ancient Hebrew the Bible speaks of "the breath of life". This is probably the symbolism for blowing three times onto the sick person. The number three is not only the holy number of Christianity, but it was a holy number for the ancient Germanic people even before they were Christianized. For them the number three had always been imbued with magical properties.

Words used are important. For earlier peoples the word was often viewed as being somehow identical with the thing itself. Words were considered to have the power over external affairs and even to control them. That is why many words were secret or even taboo, for their use could represent the use of power over external affairs themselves.

All of the verses and procedures are repeated three times over a period of time.

The *brauche* verses are cited in the following manner. The original verse is in Central Dakota German (CDGer.) dialect form, second the verse is translated into Standard High German form (SHGer.), and third, the verse is translated into English.

5.2.1.1 Zahnweh: Toothaches, their complications and infections. Toothaches were the cause of much pain and many complications in pioneer times. The healer rotates the back of her hand continuously on the affected cheek, while speaking the verse under her breath.

Zahnweh
Zahneschmerzen kleines licht
fir die rose und für die gicht
fir die rose nicht allein
auch für die kleine wirmelein
was hier steckt in dem gebein.

Gott Vater, Gott Sohn, Gott Heiliger Geist.
(Blow gently three times on the affected area)

`Zahnschmerzen kleines Licht*
für die Rose und für die Gicht
für die Rose nicht allein
auch für die kleinen Würmlein
die hier stecken in dem Gebein.

Gott Vater, Gott Sohn, Gott Heiliger Geist.'

'Toothache little light
for the rose and for the pain
not for the rose alone
also for the little worm
stuck here in the bone.

God the Father, God the Son, God the Holy Ghost.'

The word *wirmelein* (SHGer. *Würmlein*) does not necessarily mean `little worm'. The word *wurm* `worm' can mean anything hidden. This includes bad spirits. According to Grimm, `...disease was regarded as a spiritual-animal...And they likewise were imagined in the form of butterflies or worms, which caused gnawing pains and swellings in the joints of hands and feet...' (Stallybrass 1883 translation of *Teutonic Mythology* by Jacob Grimm, Vol. III:1156 which includes quotes from another source, Joh. Weyer's *Arzneibuch* `medicine book' published in 1515 and again in 1588). The word *die rose* is more fully explained in Section 5.2.1.8. Here it simply means red and inflamed. Although the word *gicht* is retained in this old verse, it is no longer common in the Central Dakota German dialect. (For an explanation of *gicht* see Section 5.3.) *Gichter* are `convulsions' in Central Dakota German (see 5.3), *gegicht* is gout, and *gebein* is a very old German word they still use for `bones' or `skeleton'.

This is an interesting verse with many possibilities. The *wirmelein* certainly points to the cause of the pain inside the tooth. The *kleines licht* `little light' is the healing burning power aimed at the *wirmelein*.

5.2.1.2 Augeweh: Inflammation and infections of the eyes. Eyes can become inflamed from either infection or from cold. The prairie wind made this a serious problem. The thumbs of the healer are put on the infected eyes and the verse is said.

Du hast das blut
dafür sind meine
daumen gut.

Gott Vater, Gott Sohn, Gott Heiliger Geist.
(Blow gently three times towards the infected eye so the air is moving over and on past the eye.)

`*Du hast das Blut*
dafür sind meine
Daumen gut.

Gott Vater, Gott Sohn, Gott Heiliger Geist.'

`You have the blood
and for that my
thumbs are good.

God the Father, God the Son, God the Holy Ghost.'

5.2.1.3 Mageweh: Stomach flu. This verse was for stomach flu or other stomach disorders in children, especially with *auszehrung* `dehydration and weight loss from diarrhea and high fever'.

A string was wrapped around the stomach three times. This measured string, which had to be in one piece, was then wrapped crisscross around a raw egg. The egg was thrown into an open fire and stirred until completely burned while the following verse was said. (There is no other way to do this verse, but with an open burning flame consuming the egg).

*So wie du verbrennst
so soll das fieber
von dem kind
sei mage abnehme.*

Gott Vater, Gott Sohn, Gott Heiliger Geist.

`*So wie Du verbrennst
so soll das Fieber
von dem Magen des Kindes
abnehmen.*

Gott Vater, Gott Sohn, Gott Heiliger Geist.'

`As you burn
so shall the fever
in the child's
stomach decrease.

God the Father, God the Son, God the Holy Ghost.'

The oldest meaning of the word *monat* `month' is measurement of the moon's cycle, the `moonth'. The meaning is therefore tied to the moon. Thus we have measurement of the person as a corrolary to lunar cycles. The moon plays an important role in the whole concept of *brauche* and is an integral part of it. In the New York Museum of Natural History exhibition (December 1986) which depicted European culture in the Ice Age 30,000 years ago, the symbol of the moon is the thread which runs through the entire 30,000 years of human history on the European continent, along with the symbol of the womb. Both of these two ancient symbols signify renewal. The use of the moon in *brauche* is most natural, and the authenticity of verses such as these would be suspect without the influence of the moon as an integral part.

The measuring of the child's stomach obviously has something to do with his ability to overcome the fever and sickness of his stomach. Again the ritual itself indicates that the "unwanted" should decrease as the moon increases, and be destroyed by burning. According to Grimm, measurement was an ancient custom used for healing and to determine if the evil was growing or receding. In Kings I:17,21 and II:4,34 Elias and Elisa measure their child and bring it back to life (Grimm 1835:675).

This was my favorite *brauche* as a child, for I loved the ritual, the measuring of my stomach, the wrapping of the string around a raw egg, and the excitment and drama of stirring the burning egg in the open flames while the *brauche*, Friederike, said the magic verses under her breath. Each step of the ritual done thoughtfully, with deliberation, the ceremony was most impressive. I knew, without a doubt, that I would get well. This shows how effective a "distractive" rite was in getting a child's mind focused on getting well rather than on being sick.

5.2.1.4 Darmgichter: Intestinal convulsions. This ritual was used for treating convulsions in babies and young children. Here the child's convulsions were located in the intestines, *gedarm* `intestines', and *gichter* `convulsions'. I was told we are speaking here of a life-threatening situation. Convulsions were the unexplained death, and this was an attempt to help. Fascinating is that the child himself cannot help the process along since he does not have the understanding. The *brauche* is working alone, which means there is more implied in this than simply helping a sick person to gather his resources to fight the disease.

Darmgichter
Es stehen drei jungfrauen
an dem sand
die haben das gedarmverrenk
an der hand

eine zu der rechte
und die andere links
und die andere gerade aus.

Gott Vater, Gott Sohn, Gott Heiliger Geist.
(Blow gently on the child's face three times.)

`*Es stehen drei Jungfrauen*
an dem Sand
die haben das Gedärmverrenk
an der Hand
eine zu der rechten
und die andere links
und die andere gerade aus.

Gott Vater, Gott Sohn, Gott Heiliger Geist.'

`There are three virgins
standing on the sand
they have the entrails
in their hand
one to the right
and the other to the left
and the other straight ahead.

God the Father, God the Son, God the Holy Ghost.'

The three virgins in the verse above, standing to the right and to the left and the third straight ahead holding the dislocated entrails, could well be the three Fates in classical Greek and Roman mythology who determine the length of the thread of life of each of us. Clotho who spins the thread of life, Lachesis who draws out the thread, and Atropos who cuts off the thread of life. This same concept appears in Grimm (1835:405-408) as a part of Germanic mythology and here it is even closer to the verse above, almost an identification of the verse as early Germanic. In Grimm the three women are called *norns* or *nornir*. The oldest is named *Urthr* `what was, the past'. The middle one is *Verthandi* `what is, the present'. The third one and youngest is *Shuld* `what shall be, the future'. These three virgins allot to every man his term of life. The *norns* spin the threads of fate, and they stretch the golden cord; one *norn* to the east, another to the west, a third to the north (Grimm 1835:405-408). Compare this to the three virgins in the verse, *eine zu der rechte, und die andere links, und die andere geradeaus;* `one to the right, and the other to the left, and the other straight ahead.'

Why are they standing on the sand? Is it the sand of the desert or could it be sand of the bank by the water, where there are tides that are controlled by the moon; again bringing in the moon as part of the effectiveness of the verse?

The *gedarmverrenk* is the intestinal length but with a serious twist in it. Thus the child who had intestinal convulsions had a serious twist in the intestional system itself. The verse acknowledges that the three Fates or Norns will decide if the child lives, and this very acknowledgment of their power is most likely the way to ask them for mercy for the child.

Murphy thinks this may be an ancient Germanic verse to which the line about the Father, Son and Holy Ghost might have been added at a time after the Christianization of the early Germanic tribes. The beautiful text of the *Heliand,* probably written in the year 840 A.D., was used to bring Christianity to the German people (See Murphy for a poetic transcription of this single most important work, from the old Germanic alliterative verses into Standard High German and English).

The source used by Grimm is the *Edda* which records the oldest oral stories of the Germanic people, the Germans and the Scandinavians. The *Edda* were written in the 13th and 14th century in Iceland; but the oral stories contained therein date to the years 800 or 900 A.D. and before. The *Edda* contain sagas, stories of heros and gods told in beautiful prose and poetry. They also contain *Spruchdichtung*, verses similar to the ones being studied here.

In this unique source, it is said that there are more *norns* both good and bad; but both types cause their effect through resorting to things in three's (Grimm 1835:411). This concept of the good and bad *norns* has come down through the centuries and finds expression in the belief that there are witches, *hexe*, who commit evil; but there are also good *norns*, women who have the knowledge and gain the power to use it for good purposes only. Even in the German fairy tales which give us insights into their culture and thinking, there are always the good and the bad fairies. The good fairy does not take on the bad fairy, for her evil is too powerful; but she finds a way through her "wisdom" of outdoing or moderating the evil spell. *Brauchere* ward off the evil of disease through their own wisdom and power.

Grimm writes about the reverence the Germanic tribes had for women which was also emphasized by Tacitus, the historian of ancient Rome (55 ca. 117 A.D.). Tacitus wrote that the old systems of law, especially Alemannian (forbears of the Central Dakota Germans) and Bavarian law, made the compensation for injury double for a woman, unless she had taken up man's weapons (Grimm 1835:397).

Grimm, in his commentary, continues on about the importance of women. There were half-goddesses, handmaidens to the upper Gods who were men. These handmaidens were the revealers, or prophets, a role reserved for men in the Jewish and Christian faith. For the Germanic tribes, men earned deification by their deeds; but women by their wisdom. Interestingly in American history, women are almost deified when the story of the pioneer woman is told. Here women were the key element in the settlement of the great American West, our own saga and ballad of heroism and beauty of human purpose.

5.2.1.5 Rotlafa und schwulst: Infection with edema and swelling.
Rotlafa is a sickness which occurs when a part of the body becomes red from infection. *Schwulst* means `swollen, filled with liquid'.

Rotlafa und schwulst
Rotlafa und schwulst und schmerzen
sollen weichen
wie die sterne
am himmel streichen.

Gott Vater, Gott Sohn. Gott Heiliger Geist.
(Blow gently three times on the infected area if it is on the face, if not then blow gently three times on the face.)

`*Entzündung und Schwellung und Schmerzen*
sollen weichen
wie die Sterne
am Himmel streichen.

Gott Vater, Gott Sohn, Gott Heiliger Geist.'
`Infection, swelling, and pain
should soften and lessen
just as the star's light diminishes
as it streaks across the heavens.

God the Father, God the Son, God the Holy Ghost.'

Here we again find mythological terminology. The three symptoms of the disease should lessen and give way in the same way that stars streak through the heavens in a stream of light, and then fall and disappear.

5.2.1.6 Schussblotter und wilderschuss: Irritations and infections of the eyes. *Schussblotter* are similar to a sty, or any irritation in the eye. *Wilderschuss* has elements of *rotlafa* and *schwulst*. It is an infection with both redness and swelling. Thus we find the verse is also basically the same.

Schussblotter und wilderschuss
Schussblotter und wilderschuss
sollen weichen
wie die sterne
am himmel streichen.

Gott Vater, Gott Sohn, Gott Heiliger Geist.
(Blow toward and moving past the eye.)

`*Fliegender Kern und wilder Spross*
sollen weichen
wie die Sterne
am Himmel streichen.

Gott Vater, Gott Sohn, Gott Heiliger Geist.'

`The rushing kernel and the wild sprout
should soften and lessen
just as the star's light diminishes
as it streaks across the heavens.

God the Father, God the Son, God the Holy Ghost.'

5.2.1.7 Dorweh: Boils and infections from cattle, including ringworms. This boil or sore comes from cattle and keeps enlarging if not treated. It is a type of ringworm of the head and scalp. This same cure could be used for other forms of ringworm which appeared as lumps under the skin. After the verse was said, when she had finished, the *brauchere* put a ring of ink around the *dorweh* to keep it from spreading.

The healer had to hold the sore firmly and look at the moon when it was a half moon and getting to be a full moon. Anyone with this problem had to wait for the right period for the treatment, as it would only work during the correct period of lunar time.

Dorweh
Was ich seh
nehme zu

*und was ich greif
nehme ab.*

Gott Vater, Gott Sohn, Gott Heiliger Geist.

`Was ich seh
nehm zu
und was ich greife
nehm ab.

Gott Vater, Gott Sohn, Gott Heiliger Geist.'

`May what I see
increase
and what I grasp
decrease.

God the Father, God the Son, God the Holy Ghost.

An interesting note to add here is that in his translation of Grimm's collection of Teutonic Mythology, Stallybrass mentions a verse which Grimm believes to be a relic of ancient moon-worship. It can only be said while looking at the moon as it is a half moon turning toward a new moon. He stands with his face to the new moon and crys, `may what I see increase, and what I suffer cease' (Stallybrass 1883:715) (Grimm 1835:408). This is the same ritual and is almost the same verse as the Central Dakota German verse cited above, i.e., *was ich seh, nehm zu, was ich griff, nehm ab* `may what I see increase, what I grasp decrease'. (A remarkable comparison.) Grimm thought that the turning of the face to the moon was the key element relating to antiquity and moon-worship. Since moon worship as a cultural heritage can be traced back 30,000 years to the European Ice Age, there is no telling how old such a verse and ritual really might be.

5.2.1.8 Die rose oder das wildfeier: Very high and rising fever with a spreading rash. *Die rose* was the term used for an ailment in which the face was swollen, very red, and covered with a rash. The illness was marked by a very high fever, and this is the reason why it was called *das wildfeier* `the wild fire'. Fire could be considered a personification for it was uncontrollable once it was raging and wild.

Die rose oder das wildfeier
*Du hast den kalten
und warmen brand
der Herr Jesu
ging ibers land
da kam ein mann
der ging nach Jeriko
der nahm den kalten
und warmen brand
mit nach Jeriko.*

*Gott Vater, Gott Sohn, Gott Heiliger Geist.
`Du hast den kalten
und warmen Brand
der Herr Jesu
ging übers Land
da kam ein Mann
der ging nach Jericho
der nahm den kalten
und warmen Brand
mit nach Jericho.*

Gott Vater, Gott Sohn, Gott Heiliger Geist.'
`You have the cold
and warm burning fire
our Lord Jesus
walked across the land
there came a man
he went to Jericho
and took the cold
and warm burning fire
along to Jericho.

God the Father, God the Son, God the Holy Ghost.'

Time was of the essence and *die rose* had to be discovered in time for the treatment by the *brauchere* to be effective, otherwise the person would surely die. The cure for *die rose* could never be spoken or told, or in any way be given to someone directly. It could only be written down and hidden. The person chosen to become the next in the line of *brauchere* had to find the verse. This cure, was written down by

Friederike for her daughter Emma, who did not find the small piece of paper until 15 years after Friederike's death, even though it was hidden in the family Bible which she used regularly. It was believed that the verse lost its power if ever given directly to another person. The new *brauchere* had to find it for herself. In that sense this verse was unique for it was the only verse treated in this fashion. All other ritual verses were passed on directly. It is also the only verse that uses clearly Christian language, *der Herr Jesu* `our Lord Jesus' appears in the body of the verse and not just in the refrain. Could it be that you had to gain self-knowledge and find and nurture your spiritual self, before you could find the verse?

Die rose, so feared by the Dakota Germans, is listed in the Essex Pharmacological Atlas of Dermatology (Shering Corporation, USA, 1978):

> Erysipelas, also known as *Die Rose* and St. Anthony's fire. It is most common in infants, young children, older age groups, and particularly in debilitated individuals. Within a week after a superficial scratch or abrasion, there is an abrupt onset of symptoms and an area of painful erythema develops; this spreads rapidly, becoming an edematous, hot, bright red, tense plaque with a characteristic advancing, elevated and well-demarcated border. Vesicles and bullae may develop. Facial erysipelas usually spreads on both cheeks and nose; there is usually a marked edema of the eyelids. The face, scalp and lower legs are most often affected in adults. In children the trunk is often involved.
>
> The symptoms are pronounced from onset. There are chills, headache, malaise, vomiting, and a high fever. The edematous plaque is painful to the touch. The well-defined red edematous plaque accompanied by high fever are clues to the diagnoses of *Die Rose*, which results from a hemolytic streptococci infection of the skin. This same germ, when it enters the throat, is the cause of scarlet fever. If *Die Rose* remains untreated it may result in complications such as endocarditis, meningitis, nephritis, and pneumonia. Locally there may be suppuration and gangrene. The treatment is with penicillin.

But in those days there was no penicillin. Indeed we can now readily see why time was of the essence when we know what the disease involved and how deadly the disease's complications were. Scarlet fever was one of the major deadly diseases in the age before penicillin was discovered. A superficial scratch or abrasion would be a common occurrence working on the land.

What does the symbolic language of the verse tell us? Is Jesus on his way to Jericho, the city in the Bible or is there something more? The Venerable Bede, for some the father of English literature, in the 8th century wrote:

> The 'certain man' is the human race in Adam, 'Jerusalem' is the heavenly city of peace, from which Adam went down to 'Jericho', that word meaning 'the moon' according to some early commentators, signifying the world with its changes and its wanderings (Browne 1930:252-253).

The connection is made between the moon and Jericho. In the previous verses also we have seen the importance of the moon, and we know that the position of the moon was the key to the verses. In the verse for *die rose* the moon was not mentioned, but we find that the word Jericho means the moon. The moon clearly remains a key to all of the verses.

The word *die Rose* is still known and used in modern German, thus, it was a possible connection one could make in researching *Spruchwörterbücher*, books containing German sayings. In one book of old German sayings appeared a verse called a *Heilspruch gegen die Rose*, which is a healing verse for *die Rose* (Lipperheide 1935:1035). Most interesting was the designation of it as a verse for *Wunden* 'wounds'. What could have been more important in the days of battles with spears and swords than to have a verse against the infection of an open wound. Once again we see the importance of time before infection and gangrene set in. The Lipperheide verse is the following:

Unser Herr Christus führ über das Meer,
Stach sich am Speer,
Das schwoll nicht, Das quoll nicht,
Es kam kein Eiter, Es kam kein Blut
Aus seinen heiligen fünf Wunden rot.

'Christ Our Lord rode over the sea,
pierced himself on a lance,
the wound did not swell, it did not gush,
there came no pus, there came no blood,
from his five Holy Wounds so red.'

The book does not give any information about the verse, how or why it was used.

In the famous medieval story of Parzival, the knight who sought the

Holy Grail, we are told that the knight Gawan knew the *Wundsegen* 'wound blessing', and Parzival did not (Wolfram von Eschenbach circa 1200 as presented by Stapel 1984:262). Parzival was the knight born to be heir to the Holy Grail, the chalice of Christ, which serves as a *motif* 'symbol' for Christ.

In the story Parzival searches for the good King Anfortas, the holder of the Holy Grail. When he finds him, he follows all the correct procedures for courtly behavior, exhibiting all the virtues of knighthood. Yet, he fails to be found worthy of the Grail. He is turned away, condemned to a harsh life, because he did not possess the inner spiritual knighthood in Christ which would make him worthy of his inheritance. He did not ask at the right hour about the wound and the pain of King Anfortas.

Parzival was unable to show Christian concern for the suffering of his fellowman. His progress towards a synthesis of knightly virtues and service to God takes him through many trials and experiences. His life in search of inner knowledge and spiritual greatness, makes him worthy to become the holder of the Holy Grail and the new King.

Interesting in this beautiful old saga, is its description of the King's wounds and of *Wundsegen* 'wound blessing'. The words used to describe the king's wounds were *heiss, kalt, warm, mond, brand* 'hot, cold, warm, moon, fire or burning fire, or another meaning for the word *brand* 'gangrene'. The Central Dakota German *brauche* verse for *die rose,* uses these very same words.

Timing in the art of *brauche* was of greatest importance and in the verse, *die rose,* it was of utmost importance. *Wildfeier* 'wild fire' gives the imagery of urgency. This urgency turns into symbolism in the Parzival story as we read:

Es handelt sich also weniger um die Beweggründe der Frage, als um den rechten Zeitpunkt (Kairos), um die metaphysische Stunde, die der "richtig" handelnde Mensch nicht verpassen darf. (Wolfram von Eschenbach circa 1200 as presented by Stapel 1984:249).

`Here the question is less one of the reason for acting, than of acting at the right time, the right metaphysical hour, which the person who acts "correctly" dare not let pass.'

The quotation marks around *richtig* in the text, as in the person who acts `correctly', are interesting.

But what of the fact that *die rose* could never be mentioned, that the verse could never either be told, or even directly given to another? This taboo, I believe, is similar to the one mentioned in a footnote to Wolfram's text when it describes the moment when Parzival first meets the wounded King Anfortas (Stapel 1984:124).

Andere Handschrifen haben statt Ungnade d.i. Unheil als Strafe Gottes, Ungenande, d.i. Krankheit, deren Namen zu nennen man sich scheut, Wundbrand.

`Other handwritten versions use the word *Ungenande* `the unnamed', that is, the sickness which one fears to name, wound gangrene; instead of using the word *Ungnade* which means `out of God's Grace' to show punishment from God.'

Was there magic healing in the Parzival story, or were the healers influenced by this wonderful story written in 1200 and possibly known to many people of the German speaking region? Is the verse for *die rose* of a different genre than the other *brauche* verses? Unanswerable questions, it does show how much of culture we can view through the beautiful words of its writers. But even more important it shows that culture lies in its people and it lives in them.

The danger for a *brauchere* was great, but that danger was not just the danger a modern would think of, namely, danger from contact with disease and infections. The *brauchere* was afraid of the personification of the disease. Disease was viewed as having a will and a power of its own; it could strike the *brauchere* if everything she did were not absolutely correct. The correctness of the ritual was important, but most important of all the *brauchere* could have no doubt. Any doubt and her powers were ended. Her belief had to be strong enough to conquer the disease in its personification. The great fear was that it would strike back and consume her. This concept of facing danger for the benefit of others is beautifully expressed by a phrase in Parzival:

Wer immer dahinkam, ritt der Gefahr entgegen; denn niemals nehmen sie Sicherheit, sondern sie wagen ihr Leben gegen das Leben des anderen' (Stapel 1984:253).

`Whoever came there, rode toward danger, for they never seek security for themselves, rather they risk their life for the life of another.'

We remember that Friederike believed that payment for *brauche* had to be made. After her physical strength had waned she felt she could no longer accept this payment, but a payment had to be made or the disease could strike back at her. Friederike solved this dilemma by having the person make a special donation to a church as the payment.

As the well-known researcher and folklorist, Professor Kurt Ranke said (class notes, Göttingen 1961-62), the deliverance from the powers of nature, from disease and sickness, is the redemption sought by all peoples; it is the deliverance from the struggle for existence. We try to overcome the forces of nature, of our very existence, with our will. This battle of man with the forces of nature, with nature itself, and with the supernatural, is the very essence of the folktales and beliefs. Ranke also said there are some humans who through their will and their very strong beliefs can attain magical power. A part of this is the art of magic healing known through what he called, more than a thousand years of German history.

In *Culture, Language, and Personality*, Edward Sapir (1956:202) clarifies the role of people like the *brauchere*.

> In spite of the often assorted impersonality of culture, the humble truth remains that vast reaches of culture, far from being in any real sense "carried" by a community or a group as such, are discoverable only as the peculiar property of certain individuals, who cannot but give these cultural goods the impress of their own personality. With the disappearance of such key individuals, the tight, "objectified" culture loosens up at once and is eventually seen to be a convenient fiction of thought.

5.2.2 Mitweib und brauchere: The art of healing reflected in the verses and medical insights of the brauchere Eva Iszler. There were many midwives and medical practitioners among the Dakota Germans. The most well known throughout the Central Dakota area was Eva Dockter Iszler, who lived until 1985. Eva was different from Friederike in that she was a *mitweib* (CDGer.), *Hebamme* (SHGer.), `midwife', and she was trained in the practical medical tradition by her mother. Eva was not only a midwife; she also had a great knowledge of herbs and medications, she knew massage and physical therapy, and she knew healing. She had learned *brauche* from her mother. It seems everyone agrees that one *brauche* could not work with all diseases. There appear to have been almost what one would view today as `branches of medicine'. Most of the midwives did not do more than deliver babies. They did a good job and were well known in the communities; some of them were Mrs. Pfahl, Mrs. Hartner, Mrs. Schock, Mrs. Guttmiller, and Mrs. Nitschke.

The Germans, while living in Russia, had their own very good school system. They also had the opportunity of learning a trade or for women, of learning how to be a midwife, a profession now coming into its own in the United States. Eva Iszler nee Docktor said that her mother was chosen from her school along with five other young women in her town and was given the opportunity for medical training. She said the choice was made based on the size and tenderness of their hands, how well they could stomach illnesses, and how easily they could learn to become a midwife. They were given small books with descriptions of different sicknesses, that they had to be able to diagnose.

Many of the older women mentioned the work of Mrs. Martha Leiske of the Kulm area, who was a midwife, medical practioner, and *brauchere*, a combination like that of Eva Iszler. Friederike Opp did only *brauche*, and what we could call analysis or counseling. She was known for her insights into good and evil, and seemed to be able to see into the nature of things. Mrs. Gustof Gunst of Ashley could do *brauche* for consumption (a popular name for tuberculosis) and was a well-known *messerin* `a woman who measures'. When one informant's brother died of tuberculosis, Mrs. Gunst appeared at their door, and asked to measure the two younger children of the family. Their mother agreed, and Mrs. Gunst proceeded to do exactly what Grimm describes in his book, which I quote here in translation by Stallybrass.

> A village has its *messerin*, always an old woman. When she is asked to say whether a person is in danger from consumption, she takes a thread and measures the patient, first from head to heel, then from tip to tip of the outspread arms; if his length be less than his breadth, then he is consumptive: the less the thread will measure his arms, the farther has the disease advanced; if it reaches only to the elbow, there is no hope for him. The measuring is repeated from time to time: if the thread stretches, and reaches its due length again, the danger is removed (Grimm 1835:676) (Stallybrass 1883:1165).

Mrs. Gunst found then to be in danger and their measurement short. She returned three times, each time she measured them and said the *brauche* verse for her speciality, consumption. The measure of their arms lengthened and she was relieved to have saved them from the disease.

At this point I would like to present the *brauche* verses of Eva Iszler. Eva had her own unique way of when she said the verses.   She could say it once and have the patient return two more times with a couple of days between, or on a specific day, until the verse had been done three times in total. She would just lay her hands lightly on the affected area and let them slide down on the body while saying the verse silently. Also, she seems to have a theme running through her verses; they treat mostly consumptive diseases; and, the diseases are asked to fly in the wind so as never to enter another human body. She says the three holiest names with a slight difference.

The verses were given to Eva by her mother who got them in turn, from her mother. They were written down by her daughter and heir to the verses, Helen Iszler Frisch. Neither Helen nor her sisters were chosen to be a *brauchere*. Eva did not believe that they had the gift.

5.2.2.1 Schussblotter: Irritations of the eyes.

Schussblotter
*Schussblotter ich drick dich
aus dem auge
schussblotter ich strick dich
aus dem auge
schussblotter flieg in dem wind
das dich kein menschen auge mehr findt.*

Gott der Vater, Gott der Sohn, Gott der Heilige Geist.
(Blow gently three times.)

*`Fliegender Kern ich drücke dich
aus dem Auge
Fliegender Kern ich stricke dich
aus dem Auge
Fliegender Kern flieg in den Wind
dass dich kein Menschenauge mehr findet.*

Gott der Vater, Gott der Sohn, Gott der Heilige Geist.'

`Rushing kernel I am pressing you
out of this eye
rushing kernel I am snaring you
out of this eye
rushing kernel fly in the wind
that no human eye will find you again.

God the Father, God the Son, God the Holy Ghost.'

During the recitation of the verses the thumbnails are pressed against the eyelids, rather firmly. The *brauchere* would then blow into the eye from the side of the nose toward the side of the head, so that the breath would pass off to the side of the head and away from the eye, three times. This verse was for an eye irritation or infection.

5.2.2.2 Magere: Consumptive diseases. The following verse is for diabetes, and for any diseases which are of the wasting variety. The verse mentions *geschwulst* `swelling', *rotlafa* `infection', *wassersucht* `dropsy', *gelsucht* `yellow jaundice', *gichter* `convulsions'.

Heit ist Freitag
esst der Jude kein schweine fleisch
trinkt er kein roter wein
magere las dein beissen sein.
geschwulst rotlafa wassersucht
gelsucht und gichter
geh aus dem kirber.

Gott der Vater, Gott der Sohn, Gott der Heilige Geist.

`*Heute ist Freitag*
isst der Jude kein Schweinefleisch
trinkt er keinen roten Wein
Magere, lass dein Beissen sein.
Geschwulst, Entzündung, Wassersucht
Gelbsucht und Zuckungskrampf
geht aus dem Körper.

Gott der Vater, Gott der Sohn, Gott der Heilige Geist.'

`Today is Friday
the Jew does not eat pork
he does not drink red wine
meagerness stop your sting.
swelling, infection, dropsy,
yellow jaundice, and convulsions
go out of this body.

God the Father, God the Son, God the Holy Ghost.'

For this verse she only saw the patients on Fridays. They had to come to her on three consecutive Fridays. It is interesting that one of the Germanic goddesses was Freya who lived on into the Christian era when a day of the week was named after her, *Freitag* `Friday'.

I believe this could be two verses put together. The first four lines appear to me to be the original verse with the last three lines added on to name the diseases which go with the verse.

5.2.2.3 Gelsucht: Yellow jaundice. A verse for *wildfeier* `wild fire' which was a fever running wild, *flu* `flu', and *gelberknopf* `yellow knot'. Eva's use of the English word *flu* is the only example of a foreign word creeping into the *brauche* verses. It appears to have been inserted into the verse as it breaks the rhythm. The word *flu* itself is a modern word, short for *influenza*.

Eva said that this is a verse she asked for and received from Friederike. Emma says her mother, Friederike, hated to give a verse even with just the word *wildfeier* in it (even though it was not the verse *die rose* itself) to someone directly. But Eva needed this verse to help with her work with the diseases mentioned in the preceeding verse. It's an example of how different *brauchere* knew who had the right to *brauche* and how they received respect from one another for their specialties.

Name: (use name of sick person)
wildfeier und flu und der gelberknopf
und was sich noch dazu findt
und die schindel fliegen im wind.

Gott der Vater, Gott der Sohn, Gott der Heilige Geist.

`Wildfeuer und Grippe und die Gelbsucht
und was sich noch dazu findet
und die Schindel fliegen in den Wind.

Gott der Vater, Gott der Sohn, Gott der Heilige Geist.'

`Wild fire and flu and the yellow knot
and whatever else finds itself too
and the shingles fly in the wind.

God the Father, God the Son, God the Holy Ghost.'

5.2.2.4 Horwurm und ringwurm: Hairworms and ringworms. This verse is used the same way for both hairworm and ringworm. The verse is the same for both, but you must use the correct word.

Horwurm eins
horwurm zwei
horwurm drei
horwurm drei
horwurm zwei
horwurm eins

Gott der Vater, Gott der Sohn, Gott der Heiligen Geist.

`Haarwurm eins
Haarwurm zwei
Haarwurm drei
Haarwurm drei
Haarwurm zwei
Haarwurm eins

Gott der Vater, Gott der Sohn, Gott der Heilige Geist.'

`Hairworm once
hairworm twice
hairworm thrice
hairworm thrice
hairworm twice
hairworm once.

God the Father, God the Son, God the Holy Ghost.'

As mentioned before, *wurm* `worm' does not necessarily mean a worm. In Grimm we find the expression *haarwurm*. He says the people thought that elves under the spells of witches went into the muscles of the hands and feet and caused pain and swelling. Since this was like arthritis, and difficult to cure, the people attributed it to witches spells. This was called *haarwurm* `hairworm' in Germany and *springende gicht* `jumping pain' in Holland (Grimm 1835:672).

5.2.2.5 Schweine: Consumption. The verse for *schweine* is most interesting. A 1987 exhibition at the State Museum in Stuttgart, covered the Napoleonic period in South and Southwest Germany at the turn of the 19th century. At this time the Central Dakota Germans still lived there. The museum exhibited two verses (1987: Katalog Band 1.2, p. 2292). These two verses had been taken from a book published by the Württemberg State Church, *Glaube, Welt und Kirche im evangelischen Württemberg* (1984:206). One of the two verses was very similar to a *brauche* verse, while the other verse was somewhat different. One of the differences is the rhyming of the verse. The *brauche* verses are not rhyming verses, but are like the old German poetic *Stabreim* `alliterative verse'.

The verse very similar to a *brauche* verse is the second of the two verses which follow. The more unrelated rhyming verse with an English word added, follows immediately. I presume the +++ means the three holy names.

Ich stand auf Holz und seh' durchs Holz
und durch die grünen Zweigen
der liebe Gott nehm mir mein Geschoss
und auch mein heilig Leiden. + + +

`I stood on wood and saw through wood
and through the green branches
dear God take from me my pain
and also my holy sorrow. + + +'

The museum verse that I found to be very similar to a *brauche* verse, turns out to be literally the same verse for the same disease as that given and described by Eva Iszler. This would mean that her verse was known to a woman in her family as long ago as the late 1700s while they still lived in the same area of Southwest Germany from which the museum verse also originates, and of course, probably much longer. This is a unique substantiation of the art of *brauche* indicating how old it is, and how the secrets were truly passed on, retained, and used through many many generations. If we connect this with the Grimm analysis of one of the verses Friederike used as being from the time of moon worship, then we are speaking of a period of time which indeed stretches far back into history.

I will first present Eva's verse and her explanation of the disease, followed by the verse from the Stuttgart museum exhibition and the explanation of this disease given in a German dictionary. Interestingly, the word that Eva uses, *die schweine* `consumption', and the word the museum uses *die Schwinde* `consumption', are the same disease according to the Stallybrass translation of Grimm's *Teutonic Mythology*. Stallybrass lists as one disease: *Lungensucht* `pneumonia', *Schwinge*, or *Schweinichen* or *Schwinde* or in Austria *der Schwund* or *die Schwindsucht* (Stallybrass 1883:1158).

5.2.2.5.1 Eva Iszler's healing verse. Schweine is in the bones and limbs, and as she said, *Sie werden immer weniger* 'they become less and less' *und vertrocken* 'and dry up'. The person loses weight and becomes very thin. His limbs and his nerves dry up. The person suffers from *auszerung* 'consumption'. She begins her verse with the question 'do you have consumption in your skeleton' and then she goes on with the verse.

Schweine
Hast du die schweine in deinem gebein
schweine aus dem mark
schweine aus dem knoche
schweine aus dem fleisch
schweine aus der haut
flieg in den wind
dass dich kein menschen kirper mehr find.

Gott der Vater, Gott der Sohn, Gott der Heiligen Geist.

`Hast du die Schwinde in deinem Gebein
Schwinde aus dem Mark
Schwinde aus dem Knochen
Schwinde aus dem Fleisch
Schwinde aus der Haut
flieg in den Wind
dass dich kein Menschenkörper mehr findet.

Gott der Vater, Gott der Sohn, Gott der Heilige Geist.'

'Do you have consumption in your skeleton
consumption out of the marrow
consumption out of the bone
consumption out of the flesh
consumption out of the skin
fly in the wind
that no human body will find you again.

God the Father, God the Son, God the Holy Ghost.'

5.2.2.5.2 Württemberg State Museum version. The verse from the museum text (18/19th century) is the following. The explanation of the word *Schwinde* in the Cassell German dictionary (1939:532) is that 'one becomes less, shrinks, wastes away, a drying up', and that *die Schwindsucht* is 'consumption'. Note the museum calls it a

Zauberspruch `magic verse'.

Zauberspruch gegen die Schwinde
Schwinde aus dem Mark
Schwinde aus dem Bein
Schwinde aus dem Nerv
Schwinde aus dem Fleisch
Schwinde aus dem Blut
Schwinde aus dem Haut
Schwinde aus dem Haar
Gott der Vater schwindet nicht
Gott der Sohn schwindet nicht
Gott der Heilige Geist auch nicht.

(Samstag 3 mal zu sprechen
gegen der morgen Sonn zu
schauen, unbeschauen.)

Magic verse against consumption
Consumption out of the marrow
Consumption out of the bone
Consumption out of the nerve
Consumption out of the flesh
Consumption out of the blood
Consumption out of the skin
Consumption out of the hair
God the Father is not consumptive
God the Son is not consumptive
and neither is God the Holy Ghost.
(Say the verse 3 times on Saturday
looking at the morning sun, yourself unseen.)

5.2.3 Verzähle: Oral history of brauche incidents. Eva Iszler decided to stop her work of healing for the same reason that Friederike Opp stopped. They both felt they no longer had the physical strength for the battle; and most of all, they no longer had the strength in their hands. Physical strength and power centered in the hands were key qualities needed for their work. In 1985, while speaking in a taped conversation in answer to questions I had about *brauche*, Eva said that there were no doctors and that the midwives, the medical practitioners who knew herbs and medicines, and the *brauchere* filled this void by doing the best they could do to help people in need. She said some people think it is wrong to use the three Holy names in *brauche*, but she felt not; for they were not being used lightly and they were being used by people who believed in God. The *brauchere* were Lutherans, but they had many patients who were Catholic. Eva said Catholics believed, and thought they would begin to get well as soon as they were touched. The Baptists were hesitant about coming; when nothing else helped, they too would come, but they expected an instant cure.

Of the many stories of the *brauchere* Friederike Opp the most dramatic healing remembered was that of Mrs. Jacob Lux. It was spring and Mrs. Lux came to see Friederike at her house in Ashley. She needed help badly; she had *die rose* and *das wildfeier*. Her whole face and head were swollen and thick with a red rash. Her eyes were almost closed and her hair was so thick with the rash that she could not even comb it. She was very hot, burning with a high fever; she had the fire that burns, *wildfeier*. She came in the morning and Friederike said she had to stay with her all day so she could do the *brauche* three times. You cannot do the *brauche* three times in a row. Normally the patient returned on three consecutive days, but Mrs. Lux was in such bad shape that Friederike kept her and took a chance doing the *brauche* three different times in one single day. Mrs. Lux wore a huge shawl with which she covered her head and face. Cold air only made it worse. By evening Mrs. Lux's daughter was able to take her home again. She had slowly improved over the day as the intense heat left and her fever diminished. She still had the rash for a few more days, but the improvement had set in when they conquered the fever. *Das weib isch binah verbrennt* `the woman almost burned up' is how it was dramatically described, and *wann es nei schlagt, dann musch du sterbe* `if it strikes inward, than you must die'.

Eva Iszler told a story about a Seventh-Day Adventist who came to her with *schingles*. *Schingles* is a rash which begins simply; then in her words, *es geht ganz darum* `spreads around the whole body' *kommt zum kreuz* `has reached a point of no-return when it covers the back' *noh gehts ins blut* `for then it goes into the blood' *geht nimme weg* `it will never go away again' *noh isch es vorbei* `then it is all over' *du musch sterbe* `you must die'.

The *Sabbater* as she called him, came to her because he believed she could help him. She rubbed his body with special herbs and she did *brauche* for him. Her treatments healed him and he became well again. Then his wife got the same disease, and the husband gave his wife the medication to rub on herself. It did not help her. She went to Eva Iszler and told her about it and said the medicine did not help her and she does not believe any of this *brauche*. Eva said, `Well, then I can't help you'. The woman left and tried to get medical help. She was not helped and a few days later she came back and said, `Say and do to me what you will,

I believe you can help me, please rid me of this terrible disease'. Eva treated her over several days and she got well.

Eva said that in the middle 1970s, a Mr. Nies went to Dr. Fleck in Ashley with this same disease, *schingles*. (Eva had never known this name for the disease; another local medical doctor, Dr. Oja, told her its name. To her, it was a form of *die rose*, but without *wildfeier*.) Dr. Fleck told him it was too far along and he could not help him. Dr. Fleck suggested he go to Mrs. Iszler and he did. He was cured; he had not gotten there too late. This story is taken from a taped conversation of several women including Eva Iszler and Emma Fischer.

When Eva Iszler was asked about the moon, she also said what Emma had stated, that the four quarters of the moon were important and the *brauche* had to be done as the moon was gaining *neu licht* 'new light', and not when the moon was full or getting less. She also said that your belief is everything: *so wie du glaubst, so geschiehts dir* 'as you believe, so will it come to pass for you'. A very powerful statement.

Psalm 91 verse 7 was said for children who had convulsions, according to Eva Iszler. She would wrap the child in the mother's bridal veil or wedding gown, and lay it in warm water, saying the verse.

Ob tausend fallen zu deiner Seite, und zehn tausend zu deiner Rechten, so wird es dich doch nicht treffen.

'If a thousand shall fall at thy side, and ten thousand at thy right hand; it shall not come nigh thee.'

Emma Fischer, daughter of Friederike, says that Psalm 91 is important for anyone in danger, whether caught in a war or in an epidemic or just by a serious sickness that has befallen you. The Psalm is called *Trost in Sterbensgefahr* 'comfort in death's danger'.

Eva Iszler said that, as a midwife, she often had to baptize a newborn baby in danger of dying. She put water on its forehead and made a cross and said, *Ich taufe Dich im Namen Gottes, der Vater, der Sohn, der Heiligen Geist. Amen.* 'I baptize you in the name of God, the Father, the Son, the Holy Ghost. Amen.' This could only be done for a newborn baby.

As a *brauchere*, she very often encountered convulsions in babies. If the baby's convulsions were very bad, it would turn black as coal: and they would run and get the Pastor so he could baptize the child. Only this could save the child and make it get well again.

The general belief was that whenever a child became very sick and was not baptized the Pastor had to be called quickly to baptize the child so it could get well. They believed that if a child should die who was not baptized, it could not go to heaven. This was a great sin which "fell" upon the parents of the child.

Diseases and illnesses became personified as they brought death and destruction to helpless people, families, and communities. They seemed to come secretly at night. Through faith and through their belief people tried to keep the dread visitors away. Persons who are evil, they believed, would suffer; for they have no protection. They did not know the origin of suffering, pain, sorrow, and grief; but through religion they tried to find the answers to these questions which have plagued mankind from the beginning. They turned to their beliefs to alleviate suffering. In many ways their methods demonstrated a heroic contest of human will against the sicknesses of the body in the drama of the struggle for human survival.

The concepts of Medical Anthropology were developed because of increasing awareness of the role of culture in health problems. It is a field which studies human confrontations with diseases and illnesses and the adaptive arrangements made by human groups for dealing with them. This seems to have been intuitively known to the Germans from Russia who practiced healing in the Dakotas.

5.2.4 Merseburger Zaubersprüche: The oldest known magic verses in the German language compared with brauche verses.

The oldest known *Zaubersprüche* `magic verses', and the ones known to most Germans, are the two Merseburger *Zaubersprüche*. They were found in the church library in Merseburg, written onto the empty front page of a church missal in the 10th century. They are a pre-Christian form of blessing in time of need, and are given in *Stabreimen* `alliterative rhyme'. Murphy noted that the *brauche* verses were similiar to the *Stabreim* verses and to the *Merseburger Zaubersprüche*. He encouraged me to make a study of the *brauche* verses pointing out their historical and cultural value. This encouragement brought me back into contact with Eva Iszler who proved to be an invaluable informant. Another window to the past was closed when she died.

According to the *Geschichte der deutschen Literatur* (Grabert-Mulot-Nürnberger 1983:10), the first of the two *Merseburger Zaubersprüche* was for the safe release of prisoners from their enemies. The second verse which applies here, was for healing. This healing verse also gives an insight into the ancient Germanic gods as it calls upon them to try to heal the dislocated leg of a horse. The god Wotan finally is successful, and why, because he knew what to say; he knew the magic healing verse. The entire verse including the situation presented in the first five lines is given in Standard High German. The last four lines believed to be the actual magic or healing verse, are given again in the original Old High German. This is followed by the English words.

Vol und Wodan fuhren zu Holze.

Da ward dem Balders-Fohlen sein Fuss verrenkt
Da beschwor ihn Sinthgunt, Sonne ihre Schwester
Da beschwor ihn Frija, Volla ihre Schwester,
Da beschwor ihn Wodan, er der's wohl konnte.

Wie die Beinrenke, so die Blutrenke
So die Gliedrenke
Bein zu Beine, Blut zu Blute
Gliede zu Gliede, wie wenn sie geleimt sei'n.

sose benrenki sose bluotrenki
sose lidirenki
ben zi bena bluot zi bluoda,
glid zi geliden, sose gilimida sin!

`As the leg violently twists so the blood twists
and the limb twists
leg to legs, blood to blood
limb to limb, bonded they shall be.'

As always, there is mystery, the mystery of who knows the incantation and who has the power to use it.

The verb *verrenken* `twist, dislocate, sprain' is the same verb used to describe what occurs in the *brauche* verse for *darmgichter* (5.2.1.4).

5.2.5 Brauche: Was it magische Heilkunde `magic healing' or hexerei `witchcraft' in Christian communities?

In concluding this account of *brauche* `healing' and of the *brauchere* and her function in the Central Dakota German communities, one might ask quite bluntly whether this represents a type of prairie sorcery or domestic witchcraft practiced among these Dakota Germans who were staunch Lutherans and maintained and followed an orthodox Christian creed.

According to five of my informants, a witch was something quite different:

A witch is a person who runs around with married men and then blackmails them. She is a fiery person who, through her manner of speaking, is always able to tell people what to do and to control, in particular, men. She is capable of great evil, she can curse you and cause you to become sick or crippled.

There were, they say, verses which could be used against such *hexe* `witches', but no one remembered them. One person remembered an end fragment of such a verse: *verrechsch, verrechsch, nit mir* `die, die, like an animal, not we'.

Many said there were *hexe* `witches' years ago, but they were not around any more. The placing of the broom across the door when you went away, so that witches could not enter your home, was not taken lightly. This was a serious belief and you were foolish indeed, if you did not take this precaution.

Eva Iszler gave me an example of the difference between a *brauche* verse and what its counterpart would be in *hexerei* `witchcraft':

Three riders are riding past. A *brauchere* would then say this verse:
Vorder reiter
hinter reiter
und der mittler
nehm die warze
alle weiter.
Gott der Vater, Gott der Sohn, Gott der Heiligen Geist.

`Front rider
rear rider
and the one in the middle
take the warts
all farther along.
God the Father, God the Son, God the Holy Ghost.'

The verse of *hexerei* `witchcraft' would be:

Vorder reiter
mittler reiter
der hintere reiter
soll deine warze kriege.

`Front rider
middle rider
the rear rider
should get all your warts'

In the first verse, which would be the way a *brauchere* would say it, three riders come along: the first rider, the last rider, and the middle rider; and they should take all the warts further along the way with them and away from us. The verse ends with the pronunciation of the three holiest names.

In the second verse, a technique typical of witchcraft appears. The first rider, the middle rider, and the poor last rider who is commanded to get all the warts himself. She curses him with the warts and thus has him take them away. In other words you have done something bad to someone, caused them harm, put an evil on them. Nor is it even necessary that the witch previously knows them or they her. The evil is done by the witch's effective word when she curses you, and there is no blessing at the end of the verse.

Friederike Opp, who spent the last fourteen years of her life totally crippled, was convinced that she had become crippled due to a curse thrown at her by a woman she believed to be a witch. The woman, who was visiting at Friederike's farm became angry when Friederike caught her doing evil. She stood tall and straight, arm and forefinger pointing at Friederike and, with her eyes blazing she screamed, ...*du wirst verkrüppeln!* `...you will become crippled'.

Eva said that she used to be able to do the same *brauche* that Jacob Hoffmann did for *dorweh* `ringworms', but she had to stop because she was afraid it gave the impression of witches to some people. Jacob, because he was a man, could do it. He said his *brauche* verse and he had a special method for grasping and killing the ringworm and, more important, he had a method for stepping on the ringworm and killing it. The worm spot would become smaller and smaller and disappear while he was stepping on it. These actions of firmly grasping and of stepping down hard on a part of the human body were the things that gave the impression of witches. A *brauchere* did not need to be physical. Eva said a woman who was not a Lutheran or a Catholic, once asked her, *Sind ihr die frau wo hexe kann?* `Are you the woman that can do witchcraft?' Eva said she answered, *Wann ich hexe kennt, deht ich nimme schaffe.* `If I could do witchcraft, then I would not have to work anymore.' Eva said that a witch, through her spells, made others do her bidding, and thus witches did not need to work hard. In contrast the job of a *brauchere* was probably the hardest in the world.

These remarks show that the *brauchere*, who were the practitioners of *brauche*, considered that what they were doing was quite different from `witchcraft' as that term is commonly understood.

In ancient times the women of the Germanic tribes were the ones who knew healing and who bound the wounds of the warriors, as was also true in old Norse sagas (Müllenhoff 1900:206). Women were also relied upon to be the *Wahrsagerin* `truth tellers' or people who could tell past history and predict future events. They had to be poets who could tell a story in verse form and who could make predictions with authority and facility of language (Müllenhoff 1900:210-211). In my opinion the emphasis on witchcraft and sorcery was a part of the dark history of the Middle Ages. Women were given a lesser value and could no longer be poets, or doctors, or intelligent observers of events.

What, then, was the real source of *brauche* and what sort of people were the *brauchere* who engaged in such practices?

If we consider the *brauchere* themselves, they were really a self-effacing and compassionate lot. They do not ever even appear to have functioned for personal gain. Whatever they did accept seems to have been more to save the self-respect of their clients and to follow the ritual procedure. They were not jealous either of their "powers" or of each other. If they felt another could afford more comfort for a particular malady, they seem to have been quite quick to refer their patients elsewhere. When the era of modern medical assistance came, they quietly and serenely withdrew. In the practice of their art they were clear-eyed about the responsibility and burdens they assumed in being so concerned about the ills, sicknesses, worries, and tragedies brought to them by those whom they did not and conscientiously would not solicit, but never turned away. They assumed a public professional burden, and bore it continuously, steadily, unselfishly, year in and year out. Nor did the Lutheran pastors, who certainly did not hesitate to speak out on other matters, criticize them or object to their work. Moreover, according to their accounts some of the Roman Catholic Germans also had recourse to their services, and there is no evidence that the Catholic priests objected to this practice.

What they really offered to all who came was a hope based on their own unshakable faith in God. In the modern day, it seems that their rituals were carefully staged momentary distractions from incessant pain, deep human suffering, and the manifold miseries which accompanied a life already hard in itself, but which in addition, in that era, neither provided nor could afford any other source of solace, relief, or cure. What, in fact, they did was compassionately try to help relieve the almost unbearable and murmur repeatedly the name of God the Father, Son, and Holy Spirit. What else can one do for another human being in his time of trial but that, and, to help them gather both strength and confidence to fight the illness that could be overcome.

All of this occurred in the era before modern pharmacology and modern medicine. They could describe and distinguish one malady from another, but specific drugs and cures were for all practical purposes almost nonexistent. One could consider *brauche* to be, in practice, a part of that continuing scientific search which attempts to learn more about medicine and cures for illnesses.

If the modern mind surrounded by its technological resources finds all of this odd or quaint, these old Dakota Germans would be no less puzzled to notice that so many moderns do not seem to realize that even the most advanced surgery is really naught but intelligent wounding and that healing, health, and the real forces of life remain almost as mysterious today as they were to them.

5.2.6 Brauche: An etymological guess. Murphy contributed the idea of investigating the etymology of the word *brauche*. He noted that although the CDGer. meaning given the word was unknown in German, a similar word with a possible related meaning was known in the Spanish language; that word was *bruja*, and its etymology in Spanish is unknown. This section is a follow-up of Murphy's insight.

The German dictionaries do not list any entry for the word *brauche* as we have been using it. The *Etymologisches Wörterbuch der Deutschen Sprache* (Mitzka 1960:96) does not give any meaning even vaguely related to *brauche*. The word is simply not known for the meaning given it by the Central Dakota Germans. The closest one can come to a hint of how the CDGer. meaning could have evolved is found in *Trübners Deutsches Wörterbuch* (1939:412) which says that the form is an old West Germanic word, originally unknown in the north; that the old version of the modern usage of *Gebrauch* was *Brauch* `use, custom, rite, ceremony' which used to mean also *Verwendung* `our use'. *Trübners* gives two interesting quotes.

Diesen Sinn(von Verwendung) hat es auch in Goethe's Zauberlehrling:

> ``*Seine (des Hexenmeisters) Wort und Werke merkt ich und den Brauch."*
> 'His (the witchmaster's) word and work I noted and the custom.'

> *Bei Uhland steht es auch für "Tun, Handeln"*: ``*Nie schlummernd, nie erschrocken, war Retten stets dein Brauch..."*
> 'By [the poet] Uhland it also means `to do, to act': "never resting, never afraid, deliverance was your custom."'

In Spanish, `witch' is *bruja*, in Catalan *bruixa*, in Portuguese *bruxa*.

The word is not listed as occurring in French or Italian, which suggests that it does not have a Latin origin or it would appear in more of the Romance languages including French and Italian. Moreover, the *Romanisches etymologisches Wörterbuch* of Meyer-Lübke fails to mention the word. Nor does an etymology appear for the word in the Juan Corominas' Diccionario Crítico Etimológico. Thus, for *bruja* `witch' no scholarly etymology has been proposed; and the possibility of a Germanic etymon for the Romance word appears to have been overlooked. Several of the articles mentioned are even written by Germans and they too have not considered German as a possible lexical source in this instance.

Since the word is found only on the Iberian peninsula it could very possibly be a Visgothic word left from the invasion of the Visigoths, the Germanic tribe of the *Westgoten* `West Goths', that settled there from 419 to 711 A.D. The Trübner reference said the word was West Germanic which would include the West Goths of the Iberian peninsula. The Gothic word was written: *brukjan*.

This could prove to be an interesting problem for historical linguists. (1) Could the Dakota German word *brauche* be related to the Visgothic word for `witch' and (2) could this practice and its verses be very old. (3) Could Spanish *bruja* `witch' possibly include within its meaning both the evil German *hexe* `witch' and a good counterpart, the CDGer. *brauchere* `healer'? It is also interesting to note that the CDGer. *-re* suffix of *brauchere* is quite distinct from the *-in* suffix which SHGer. assigns to *Zauber* to form *die Zauberin* `witch' and closer to the final suffix of Span. *curandera*.

In an award-winning book by Rudolfo A. Anaya, *Bless Me, Ultima*, set in the Spanish community of Santa Rosa, New Mexico, the main characters of the book are a young boy and a *curandera* `healer'. The story tells how the *curandera* opposes the evil of the *bruja* and how she heals people. She is greeted as *Médica* `healer' and everyone speaks of how she cures. I shall list some of the interesting points in the description of the *curandera*. I am not suggesting that the *bruja* and the *curandera* are parallel to the *hexe* and the *brauchere*. I am asking only that this parallel be examined.

> ...the *curandera* was a woman who knew the herbs and remedies of the ancients, a miracle-worker who could heal the sick. And I had heard that Ultima could lift the curses laid by *brujas*, that she could exorcise the evil the witches planted in people to make them sick. And because a curandera had this power she was misunderstood and often suspected of practicing witchcraft herself (1986:4).'

``La *curandera*,'' they would exchange nervous glances. ``*Hechicera, bruja*,'' I heard once (1986:30).

It was truly the work of a *bruja* that was slowly killing my uncle. ...it was decided to hire the help of a *curandera* (1986:77).

``They let him go too long,'' she said, ``it will be a difficult battle...''(1986:90).

``A *curandera* cannot give away her secrets,'' she said, ``but if a person really wants to know, then he will listen and see and be patient. Knowledge comes slowly...''(1986:31)

My grandfather stepped forward and handed Ultima (the *curandera*) the purse of silver which was required by custom (1986:96).

The comparisons are multiple. The *curandera* was a very devout Christian, a Catholic. She was known by all for the good she could do to protect them against sickness and evil. I have given only a few quotes to show why I thought the parallel ought to be examined. According to Michael Rempfer (written communication), the art of the *curandera* is still practiced in the rural communities of northern New Mexico.

5.3 Benennungen der Krankheiten: Old German medical terms preserved by Jacob Grimm in 1835 and still extant in the CDGer. lexicon. Jacob Grimm decries the fact that at the time of the writing of his book in Göttingen in 1835, the German words which conveyed the names and meanings of sicknesses and which the people knew and used, had been driven from the language by the medical learned and replaced with Greek and Latin words. He goes on to say that for this reason he has to list the older German names which have represented the vocabulary of diseases and healing to people since ancient times (1935:670). He goes on to name the most common words and their meaning (1935:670-674). I am presenting here a representative sample of the basic common vocabulary of diseases he chose and am comparing it with the Central Dakota German words.

Grimm begins with the word *krank* `sick'. He says that in Middle High German it meant only being debilitated or infirm and thus sick. It did not include `problems' by which he means `diseases'. For diseases, they used the word *sucht* `disease' which now is used to designate `addicted'. Thus the old German words for diseases generally have the suffix *sucht*. *Sucht* was considered in the Christian sense to be `God's will'; in pre-Christian understanding it was the work of `spirits'. This belief in the working of `spirits' is what caused diseases to become personified: They attack, they grab at you, they overcome you. In ancient times people considered themselves to have fallen prey to disease. *Sucht* was like *tod* `death' and *schicksal* `destiny'. The word *fieber* `fever' was known in the Middle Ages as *rite*. Thus we find the words *suht* for *sucht* `disease' and *rite* for *fieber* `fever' in the old texts. Words had their personification and thus the Central Dakota German word for *fieber* `fever' is *wildfeier* `wild fire'.

According to Grimm, the personification extended to the idea that *würmer* `worms' and *schmetterlinge* `butterflies' caused swelling and pain in the body, especially with arthritis. Thus we find the CDGer. verses use the expression *wurm*. We now use `scientific names' but we still do not know how arthritis starts nor how it can be stopped.

Grimm begins his list of diseases with *gicht*. What English word can one use for this word? It covers quite a multitude of problems because it can move, it can turn, it can tear and pull, and throb with pain. In the Central Dakota German *brauche* verses the usage is the same. In Standard High German *die Gicht* means `gout' which is not reflected in any meaning the CDGer. would attribute to the word. But *die Gicht* (SHGer.) also means convulsive fits. Those fits could be the *gichter* `convulsions' of CDGer. except that in CDGer. `convulsions' *gichter* symbolize a plural personification of the word which again seems to be more in line with what Grimm says is *gicht* which also means `spirits' or `things' moving around in the body. He mentions *darmgicht* saying it is probably *colik* `colic'; the CDGer. meaning is `intestinal convulsions'. The difference is probably one of severity of the colic.

Die fallende sucht `epilepsia' is known in CDGer. as *die fallige krankheit*. The Latin word *epilepsia* is recognizable in both English and Standard High German. The standardization of medical terminology was probably the reason the Latin words, which Grimm decries, were used to describe the diseases. I find it interesting that the odd names for diseases one finds in the CDGer. language are not odd names at all, rather old German expressions retained in the language because the Central Dakota Germans left Germany before the Latin medical terminology was adopted. The Grimm explanation of disease names is important in trying to understand the verses of the *brauchere* and the diseases she is trying to heal.

Under the word *ruhr* `dysenteria' Grimm says it is also called *darmgicht* which is more serious than the colic he previously mentioned and is closer to the seriousness of the CDGer. word *darmgicht*.

Lungensucht `pneumonia' is also called *schwinge, schweinichen,* and *schwindsucht* all of which we have encountered in the *brauche* section

(5.2). *Schwindsucht* in CDGer. is tuberculosis.

Herzgespan `cardialgia' is also known as *herzweh* `heart pain'. In CDGer. we find not only a similar term *herzsperle* `little closing of the heart' but we even find a *brauche* verse to heal it. The verse is said when one has pressure in the rib cage or when it seems one's heart is under pressure. The *brauchere* rubs from the top of the chest down, pressing with her fingers, doing this three times, while saying the following verse which asks the `little closing of the heart to sink itself' or in other words, that the pressure should move on down and away from the heart.

Herzsperle sinke dich
Herzsperle sinke dich
Herzsperle sinke dich.

Gott Vater, Gott Sohn, Gott Heiliger Geist.
(Blow gently on the person three times.)

For *gelasucht*, Grimm gives several meanings including *die rose* and *das laufende feuer*. Here CDGer. does not agree with Grimm on what the sickness is. He calls it `elephantiasis'.

Central Dakota German has the disease *die gelsucht* `yellow jaundice' which was very common. In *gelsucht* the white of the eyes turns yellow, then the face turns yellow, then the hands, and if it progresses further, one dies. There was also a cure, albeit a difficult one, for this. The *brauche* had to shock the disease. She stood before the sick person then suddenly spit in his face three times and said, *du teufel hast gelsucht* `you devil have yellow jaundice' then quickly said the three holiest names.

Nachtgrif, according to Grimm, is a sickness that you can get from `spirits of the night'. CDGer. does not have that exact expression, but people believe that *nacht luft ist giftig* `night air is poison' and one must protect against it by not leaving the windows open at night.

The vocabulary like CDGer. *rotlafa* `running red with infection' and Grimm's *rothlauf* are both similar. There were also old concepts such as *messen* `measurement' which Grimm said originated in a very early German era. The Central Dakota Germans used `measurement'. The body was measured in different ways to determine the progress or regression of a disease. Grimm also discusses the practice of the `transference' of the illness away from the sick person.

He mentions not only the Parzival story in connection with healing as I concluded, but also Tristan and Isolde. *Isoten* had the knowledge of herbs and pharmacology. He says that the heros of the sagas were involved with medicine and healing, but mainly this function was the calling of women, from the half-gods, to the queens, to the wise woman. The key was to have the knowledge and the power. Grimm and the *brauchere* speak of *die kraft* 'the power' to heal. Did knowledge bring power or was the power its own element?

5.4 Heilmittel: Folk remedies of the Central Dakota Germans. In addition to *brauche* there were many folk remedies which used ingredients at hand in the pioneer home and which were considered by many to be truly therapeutic. These were the days before modern medicine and these home-made remedies were attempts to relieve human suffering and save life.

Camomile tea (CDGer. *kamille tee*, SHGer. *Kamillentee*) was very popular as a medicine in the Dakotas. The camomile plant is thought to have been brought there from Russia, just as it was brought to Russia from Germany, where it is a very well known medicinal tea even today. One thing is certain: the pioneer women planted it everywhere and used it a great deal. One pioneer, Christina Walz always carried camomile seeds in her apron pocket and she threw them into the air wherever she went. Many people today still tell me that she is responsible for the camomile which grows on their farms and which they still use for tea. One pioneer mother remembers:

Kamille tee was mixed with spirits, alcohol that was a hundred and ninety proof home brew. This was always given to women in childbirth to keep them from getting blood poisoning or infection. They gave that to me and I still think that saved my life. Also when a child was born everyone brought hot noodle soup made from mature chickens that were saved for soup and that were only used for special occasions. They also brought a gift for the new mother.

Another remembers:

Grandma always made some *kamille tee*. She would strain it and put the leaves in a rag, then she put it on our eyes. It was very good for sore eyes. If you had the flu and couldn't eat, you had to drink tea. This was such a popular and effective remedy that drinking kamille tea is even used in our hospital today. Kamille tea comes from the camomile plant. It has to be picked when in bloom. You pick off the tops, the flowers, and lay them on a piece of paper and dry them for at least a week. They are then stored in jars. To use it, put 1 teaspoon in a cup and fill the cup with boiling water. You can add sugar if you like it sweet.

The pioneers made many home remedies from plants which grew wild on the prairie. Here are some passed on from local folk medicine practitioners:

Cook *wermut*. It is a lime green plant that grows wild on the prairie. It smells bad and is very bitter. Burn brown sugar: just put some white sugar in a pan and keep mixing it until it gets brown, and then add boiling water to it. Mix the wermut juice, the brown sugar, and the hundred ninety proof home brew. This was taken by diabetic people.

You can also pick a weed that is high and has yellow flowers. It looks just like a small cabbage head. Cook this for diabetics. Some still cook this. (This could be the plant Arnika.)

Some people still cook larkspur which are also called delphiniums, and use it for a bad cough. We used it for whooping cough or 'the blue cough' as we used to say.

Die sonnerose grow wild. They look the same as the sunflower but the inner core of the flower does not produce seeds as the sunflower does. The *mark* 'marrow' of the stalk is mixed with soot and rendered lard or unsalted homemade butter and put on the *dorweh* 'ringworm'.

An important plant mentioned by several informants was 'elvira', a plant which grows indoors. It expands and keeps on growing continuously renewing itself. You can also replant it continually. It was cooked for medicine and put on sores, cuts, and burns. It is still a very popularly used plant because it heals effectively.

Eva Iszler used the 'elvira' plant a lot, and she always had some on hand. She said the stems of the Elvira plant which were called *gichtersteckle* 'convulsion stems' because the juice of the stem was given to small children having convulsions.

Other home remedies were made from materials that were available to the settlers. The following remedies were collected from various Dakota German pioneers.

When our Dad had a bad cough he put a handful of salt in a small tub or dish pan and hot water as hot as he could stand it and enough water so it would cover his feet to the ankles. He believed this helped his cough. I know people still do this today. Our uncle always just took kerosene when he had a cough. He just took a tablespoon full. He told my mother about it. He said you can add sugar to it.

When father had an ear ache he would cook an onion on hot ashes then he would squeeze the onion and let the drops fall into his ear. He said that would help an ear ache.

Emma Roeszler uses a recipe from Mrs. Harter for curing *dorweh* `ringworm'. You put copper pennies in water and set it in the window so the sun hits the water leaving it until the water turns blue/brown. You put this liquid on the ringworm.   It always works.

This one I can still remember. Mrs. Lux always used to do it for my mother when she was sick with her kidney stones. They would put barley in a kettle and heat it, then they put it in a sack and put it wherever she hurt. My mother really believed this helped.

My mother would dig out parsley roots and cook them in water, and let it set; she would then drink that juice.   She said it helped her with her kidney stones.

Our mother said they would blow smoke into a sore ear and then close it with cotton.

When we had a sore throat they would rub you good and then they would take your stocking and wrap it around your neck. By morning you would have relief.

When people had hang nails they would dunk the finger into boiling water 3 times. This cured it.

A cloth soaked in vinegar was laid on your forehead to lower the temperature of a fever. (This is still recommended for bringing down a high fever.) It was also used on joints pained with arthritis.

Mustard packs were put on the painful area to help with kidney ailments.

We used mentholatum as a remedy for all cold ailments. It was also rubbed on the udders of cows to relieve pain from the cold.

Some of the older folks ate raw garlic which was supposed to prevent high blood pressure. (This is still popular in France and Italy today.)

A common laxative was made by boiling a gallon of water and when it boiled add 1/2 to 1 pound of Epson salt, depending on the strength wanted. It was boiled for 15 minutes and then poured into a jug which was kept closed and used as needed. A new kettle had to be purchased for cooking it and could not be used for anything else.

Two common remedies, remembered by many people, were used to cure *schwere* 'boils' and infections. Axle grease from the horse drawn wagons was smeared on the boil or infection which caused the boil to draw to a head. The grease had to have been used and taken directly from the axle.

In the second one, bread soaked in very warm milk was squeezed out and placed on a cloth. This cloth was laid on the infection or boil. It caused the swelling to go down and the pus to come to a head. This remedy is still used and is as effective as ever.

Wermut schnaps was kept on hand by some as a medicine. It was given even to sick children and it always helped. It was very bitter and you only had to drink a little glass of it.

Schmieren (CDGer.), *das Massieren* (SHGer.) 'massage' was the best thing for a sore throat when you had lumps that you could feel with your hands. They rubbed mentholatum or anything like it on your throat and they massaged it until the lumps became smaller. A warm cloth was then tied around your throat. They did this every day until the lumps went away.

They would boil potatoes with jackets on and then mash the potatoes and put them in a rag, and then put them on your stomach, as warm as possible.

There were many cures for stomach ache. Contributors told of some of the old remedies. Every home had peppermint drops. When you got sick with a stomach ache they took a teaspoon and put sugar on it, then added a few drops of peppermint. You had to take that, and wash it down with water. I bought two bottles of peppermint today and am sending them to my daughter to use for the grandchildren when they get stomach aches. My daughter Violet says it really helps, as I can remember it has always helped.

Some of the folk remedies included elements of magic. Carolina Hoffmann said her aunt told her this remedy.

Throw a handful of barley into an open fire like the fire in a coalstove, when someone is sick. As it burned you got well.

Carolina Hoffman also said that if you had a sore on your bones or if your bones hurt you, you had to find a bone from the *vieh weid* `the cattle meadow' as the informant said, `out by the fence' which was as far as the farmer's land went and as far as his cattle could roam. There were usually bones to be found along the fence when you went to get the cattle. The bone had to be found. You then had to throw this bone away over your shoulder without looking to see where it landed and your own bone would heal. Any kind of bone healed; it even helped if you had hurt your ankle. Only the person with the aching bone could do this; no one could do it for you.

A horse hair was used to tie off warts or moles, a remedy that really worked.

Emma Reuther said that if you had a wart or a black spot on skin, you had to rub a piece of *speck* (CDGer.), *der Speck* (SHGer.) `slab bacon' from a pig on it and bury it, and then you had to forget it.

Emma Reuther also related that you could cut a piece of the skin surrounding a ham being sure to include some of the ham fat with it, and lay it in the back of the cookstove inside the smouldering ashes. As it burned the *wartz* `wart' would disappear.

Everyone knew this one, we still do this. If a person has a sore in his mouth, like a canker sore, he has to spit into an open fire three times and the sores will go away. This must be done three times in one day.

5.5 Aberglaube: Folk beliefs of the Central Dakota Germans.

Zeichen lesen war teil der Kultur, immer da. Die schriftlich fest gelegte Sprache konnte dann Begriffen wie Wille, Gerechtigkeit, Freiheit abstrakte Bedeutung geben, aber es gab noch vieles, Unerklärtes, das nicht in linguistischen Zeichen zu fassen war (König 1978:29).

`The ability to read signs was always a part of the culture. The written language could give an abstract meaning to concepts like will, justice, freedom, but there was so much more; there were unexplainable phenomena that could not be captured in linguistic signs.'

In other words there is much about our world that cannot be captured in language. It exists in the collective consciousness of a people. The Dakota Germans believed in reading signs. They thought only a very foolish person would not read signs, nor accept them. After all, one had to be able to read the signs of nature and of the weather. Their very survival depended on the ability to read and act upon those signs.

You can tell a lot about people if you really watch them closely, really listen to what they have to say, and really observe their behavioral patterns. How much of this do we still do in our day? Since our urban societies have changed so much, grown so restless, it is more difficult for us to notice signs and use our intuition because we have moved out of the close-knit societies that would allow such insights and provid time for such reflection. This is why we find old beliefs hard to accept. Nature, the overriding master in earlier civilizations, to some extent, has been brought under control. In any case, we no longer look to nature for signs. We no longer judge by the shape of the moon, by the unusual light of the sun, the fur on the animals. In contrast, we turn on the weather report and have an efficient reading of the signs presented to us.

As mentioned when describing funerals (4.3.2), how you die, how you leave this world was a subject of the greatest importance to the Central Dakota Germans. Their belief in being responsible not only for themselves but also for their children's children is expressed with Old Testament overtones, in their saying:

Es schlagt zurick bis ins dritte und vierte glied.
`It will strike back into the third and fourth generation'.

If a man does something very wrong, the effect of this sin falls on all the men for three to four generations; if a woman does something wrong, the effect of the sin falls on all the women for three or four generations, until the sin is finally expiated and the suffering ended.

We find the Dakota German believes one inherits the intuitive traits just as one inherits a talent for particular tasks. The expression used is not the talent to do something, but rather that he or she has the ability in their hands, *sie hats in den händen*. If a woman can sew well, or cook or bake well, especially make dough well, she has this ability in her hands. If a man has carpenter skills or can play a musical instrument well, he has this ability in his hands.

Just as most abilities are inherited so are *leid* `suffering' and *schicksal* `destiny'. The expression of folk beliefs, whose original significance has long since been forgotten, give us an insight into another world.

For example, one of the beliefs of the Central Dakota Germans was that a woman who has given birth must remain in bed until the ninth day which is the day her muscles and bones return to their normal pre-birthing position. Why would they chose exactly the ninth day? The early Germanic tribes had a nine-day rather than a seven-day week (Müllenhoff 1900:236). Could this have been the measure used for deciding that nine days was the necessary length of time for the recuperation of the mother?

The ancient Germans also had a tradition that a child could be *verstossen* 'denied by his father' (Müllenhoff 1900:314). That meant almost certain death for the child, for he would then also be denied by the tribe. Could this insight into the past be the basis for a child staying with his mother, the mother keeping to her bed and nurturing her child until he was nine days old and safe from harm? We do not know the answer, but we can try to look into the past by studying what we now still know.

Another belief of the Dakota Germans was that one could not eat animals with feet that were not split, that did not have cloven hooves. Such animals were the horse, the mule, and some of the small wild animals. Water fowl like ducks appear to have feet that are not split, but this is not true. For although ducks have webbed feet with tissue growing between the toes, the toes are nevertheless split. I do not know what this tells us, but I suspect it reflects either a fear of witchcraft, or the use of a belief as a way of preserving animals valuable to man for his survival. On the other hand, it may simply reflect the Law of the Old Testament (Deuteronomy 14:6).

The old Germanic word for horse, *das ross* (MHGer.) is still the word used in Central Dakota German. A horse was the most valuable possession one could have from the time of the ancient Germanic tribes who revered horses, until the advent of the automobile.

How beliefs start is an interesting topic. I found that, in addition to the folk beliefs the German pioneers brought with them to Dakota, they also perhaps began a new bit of folklore from their experience of the prairie wind. They personified the wind *der wind* (CDGer.). Repeatedly, in every interview, whatever the topic, the wind was mentioned; the wind, the hardship, and the devastation it brought. The wind is always there, waiting low in the prairie grasses, moaning, and then, in full force, driving the prairie fire, the blizzard, the tornado, howling in all its fury. Even the expression concerning waiting for much needed rain is phrased:

Der wind heult, er will regen
'The wind is crying for rain.'

This is a new personification and a bit of folklore.

Folk beliefs and superstitions explained occurrences of daily life, while providing a common bond among this people. The following are some of the folk beliefs collected from the Central Dakota Germans.

If a hen crows someone in the family will die. The hen must be killed immediately.

If a glass in a cupboard cracked, or if the glass in the kerosene lamp cracked, people were afraid: for this was a sure sign that something terrible was going to happen.

When people left their house for a visit or a trip to town, they placed a broom across the door. People could step over it but a witch would never cross a broom. Thus, the home was guarded and witches could not gain entry.

If a person is lying in bed and hears someone calling, or if he hears someone knock only once, it means there will be an accident, illness, or death in the family.

Cats are healthful to have near sick people. They can also help to draw out a fever.

A ring around the moon shows a coming storm.

The number of stars in a ring around the moon shows the number of days before a coming storm.

Thunder shakes up the ground and makes things grow better.

Rain without thunder does not make the crops grow as well.

When the sky is filled with lightning unaccompanied by thunder, the lightning is cooling off the sky. The next day will be cool.

When it thunders the Heavenly Father is scolding naughty children.

If you see the Northern Lights in the summer in a blaze of light, there will be an incredibly strong wind storm the next day.

When the sun in the winter has white light on each side of it, it is called *bisonne* (CDGer.) and means it will be very very cold.

When the right hand itches company is coming.

A cat washing its face means company is coming.

A dropped spoon, knife, or fork means company is coming. (Each object has a special meaning. A teaspoon is a girl, a large spoon is a woman, a fork is a boy, and a knife is a man.)

When the left hand itches money can be expected.

When the nose itches something new will be heard.

Whatever is thought of while sneezing will come true.

It is a sin to cut with scissors on Sunday.

It is a sin to work in the fields on Sunday even if there will be a loss to the farmer. He can milk the cattle and feed farm animals.

Girls' ears were pierced to prevent them from getting sore eyes.

'Thunder in March portends hunger (a poor crop).' *Friher donner, später hunger* (CDGer.).

'A red sky in the evening portends a dry earth. A red sky in the morning means a wet earth.' *Obedt rot meint trockener bode, morgens rot meint nasser bode* (CDGer.).

'A good rain on Pentecost meant a good crop that year.'
Pfingst rege isch alles gelege (CDGer.).
Pfingst rege bringt viel sege (CDGer.).

'A clear New Year's Eve signifies a good crop year.'
Der Himmelhell und klar macht a gutes fruchtbares johr (CDGer.).

And finally, for a sense of humor: You should not praise your own children to others, and if others praise your children too much to you, then you have to negate the negative effect this will have on them by saying under your breath at the same time as you are hearing the praise,

lechs am ärschle, lechs am ärschle
`lick his little behind, lick his little behind'

Good omens were always welcomed by the hard-working pioneers. Great attention was paid to omens about the weather and each pioneer farmer would sniff the air and check the wind and sky for signs. The weather, nature, was an integral part of life.

The following quote is a good summary of the Dakota Germans' viewpoint of their own beliefs (in CDGer. language).

Sie hin a grosse glaube ghabt an allem, und es war auch immer wohr 'They had a great faith in all things, and it was always true.'

5.6 Lieder: Music in folk and family life. The German pioneers loved to sing and were known for their musical ability. Parents encouraged their children to be musical, to sing or play a musical instrument. They sang the most intricate melodies with two and four part harmonies without the aid of a piano or a book. Very early, pedal organs found their way into most homes; pianos followed. Older people sang the favorite songs from their church and their youth; and the younger generation, those who were born in America, loved to sing the songs popular with the other young pioneers. They thought they were happy risqué songs about lively women and lost loves. This was their country and they wanted to be a part of its cultural life too, while preserving their own. In Russia the lines had been drawn and you never crossed them. Each ethnic group kept to itself. In America it was different. We were all here together to form a great country.

Young people loved the old melodic church songs too, and even today an evening get-together among friends usually ends with the singing of the old familiar hymns and other favorites. The theme running through these German songs is one of hard work and total faith in God and the life hereafter; friendship, fellowship, and love. They had complete faith in the rightness of things and realized that the culmination of a life of faith and work was not necessarily given an earthly reward. It was in their songs, in which language, music, religious feeling and the bond of common memories combined to evoke a long and loved past.

This section does not include many songs since they have already been included in the appropriate religious occasions or celebrations. The song is an important part of ritual and thus, the correct song must be sung on the proper occasion. For that reason I have included the songs in their ritually correct place rather than in this general section of *Lieder*. There are many more songs, particularly *schätzlieder,* which could and should be recorded. This would be an interesting study for a musicologist. Many of the Central Dakota Germans know, just as my father Christoph Fischer did, a very great number of songs which they can not only sing but play on a number of musical instruments,

including the piano, peddle organ, banjo, guitar, harmonica, accordion.
Following are some of the Central Dakota German's favorite songs. They are cited in the Standard High German.

Auf, denn die Nacht wird kommen

Auf, denn die Nacht wird kommen,
Auf mit dem jungen Tag,
wirket am frühen Morgen
eh's zu spät sein mag.
Wirket im Licht der Sonne,
fanget bei Zeiten an,
Auf denn die Nacht wird kommen,
da man nicht mehr kann.

Schön ist die Jugend bei frohen Zeiten

Schön ist die Jugend bei frohen Zeiten,
Schön ist die Jugend sie kommt nicht mehr,
Ja Ja sie kommt nicht mehr
Sie kommt ja nimmer mehr,
Schön ist die Jugend sie kommt nicht mehr.

Wer Gott vertraut, hat wohl gebaut

Wer Gott vertraut, hat wohl gebaut
im Himmel und auf Erden;
wer sich verlässt auf Jesum Christ,
dem muss der Himmel werden.
Darum auf dich all Hoffnung
ich ganz fest und steif tu setzen;
Herr Jesu Christ, mein Trost du bist
in Todes Not und Schmerzen.

Fang dein Werk mit Jesu an

Fang dein Werk mit Jesu an,
Jesus hats in Handen;
Jesum ruf zum Beistand an
Jesus wirds wohl enden.
Steh mit Jesu Morgens auf,
geh mit Jesu schlafen;
führ mit Jesu deinen Lauf,
lasse Jesum schaffen.

Gott ist die Liebe

Gott ist die Liebe,
lasst mich erlösen,
Gott ist die Liebe,
er liebt auch mich.
Darum sag ich's noch einmal,
Gott ist die Liebe,
Gott ist die Liebe
Er liebt auch mich.

Lasset uns mit Jesu ziehen

Lasset uns mit Jesu ziehen,
seinem Vorbild folgen nach,
in der Welt der Welt entfliehen
auf der Bahn, die er uns brach,
immerfort zum Himmel reisen,
irdisch noch, schon himmlisch sein,
glauben recht und leben fein,
in der Lieb den Glauben weisen.
Treuer Jesu, bleib bei mir,
gehe vor, ich folge dir.

Mir ist Erbarmung widerfahren

Mir ist Erbarmung widerfahren,
Erbarmung deren ich nicht Wert,
Das zähl ich zu dem wunderbaren,
mein stolzes Herz hats nie begehrt,
nun Weiss ich das und bin erfreut
und rühme die Barmherzigkeit,
und rühme die Barmherzigkeit.

Der Himmel steht offen

Der Himmel steht offen.
Herz weisst du warum,
weil Jesus gekämpft und geblutet darum,
weil Jesus gekämpft und geblutet darum.

Wie lieblich ist's hiernieden

Wie lieblich ist's hiernieden,
Wenn Brüder treu gesinnt,
In Eintracht und in Frieden
vertraut beisammen sind,

In Eintracht und in Frieden
vertraut beisammen sind.

Dort oben im Himmel

Dort oben im Himmel
dort haben wir's gut,
Wer's glaubt und beherzigt
dem wächset der Mut,
Dort sagt uns der Heiland,
ererbet das Reich,
der Vater gab mir es,
ich gebe es euch.

Die Heimat fällt mir immer ein

Die Heimat fällt mir immer ein,
ach wann erreich ich sie,
Ich möchte gern im Hinmel sein
mit Kinder Gottes im Verein,
In seliger Harmonie,
In seliger Harmonie.

Der beste Freund ist in dem Himmel

Der beste Freund ist in dem Himmel,
auf Erden sind die Freunde rar,
denn bei dem falschen Weltgetümmel
ist Redlichkeit oft in Gefahr,
drum hab ichs immer so gemeint
mein Jesus ist der beste Freund.

Ich bin im Himmel angeschrieben

Ich bin im Himmel angeschrieben,
und Gottes Kinder zugezählt,
mich hatte schon sein brünstig Lieben
von Ewigkeit dazu erwählt.
Nun ruhe ich in seinen Armen
mein Vater blickt mich freundlich an,
ich weiss von nichts als von Erbarmen,
dadurch ich ihm gefallen kann.

Immer Fröhlich

Lasst die Herzen immer fröhlich
Und mit Dank erfüllet sein!

*Denn der Vater in dem Himmel
Nennt uns Seine Kinderlein.*

*Chor. Immer fröhlich, immer fröhlich
  Alle Tage Sonnenschein.
  Voller Schönheit ist der Weg des Lebens;
  Fröhlich lasst uns immer sein!*

*Gott führt uns an Vaterhänden,
Schützet uns in Kampf und Streit;
Seine Gnade ist's, die täglich
Kraft und Stärke uns verleiht.*

Chor.

*Wenn wir uns von Ihm abwenden,
Wird es finster um uns her;
Unser Gang ist nicht mehr sicher
Und das Herz von Freuden leer.*

Chor.

Morgenrot

*Morgenrot, leuchtest mir zum frühen Tod?
Bald wird die Trompete blasen,
Dann muss ich mein Leben lassen,
Ich und mancher Kamerad.*

One informant said she could still see her father with his large mustache just quivering away as he put great feeling into this song.

My mother told me that her brother sang this song as he, a very young man, lay dying from tuberculosis contracted during a very cold and bitter winter that he had spent on the prairie caring for his cattle.

Songs give us an insight into the philosophy of a people. The theme of the foregoing songs is the Christian way of life, and it exhibits a pietist influence. According to them, this world is a tumultuous place; look inward, keep to yourself, and realize that you are never alone; Jesus is your friend, and only heaven is your home.

There were also folk songs which were not church songs. These slowly died out as the elder pioneers died because there was no written music for them. The religious songs remained popular until today because they were contained in various church hymnal and song books. As mentioned previously, confirmation classes because they were held in German, did much to preserve the language; particularly in America, where schools were conducted in English. The confirmation classes also preserved the music of these old hymns and songs. Since Martin Luther had adapted folk tunes and folk songs for his church music, it was natural that these songs were singable and had a lasting appeal. The old church songs are still very popular even today and are sung at every possible opportunity. They especially loved singing four part harmony.

The following is an example of one of the hymns which was frequently sung with men (tenor and bass), and women (soprano and alto), alternating, holding the end of the phrase, and echoing each other's parts. This song was special and was often sung at the German Baptist wedding ceremonies, although it was sung at other weddings and celebrations as well, and when friends gathered.

Ach mein Jesus Du bist wert
(Oral Tradition)

Ach mein Jesus Du bist wert
dass man Dich im Staube ehrt
dass man Dich beständig lobt und ehrt;
niemand ist so gut wie Du
meine Seele jauchzt Dir zu
meine Seele jauchzt Dir ewig zu.

Women: *Von der Erde* . . . . .
    Men: *Von der Erde* . . . . .
Women: *reiss mich los* . . . . .
    Men: *reiss mich los* . . . . .
Women: *mach meinen* . . . . .
    Men: *mach meinen* . . . . .
Women: *Glauben gross* . . . . .
    Men: *Glauben gross* . . . . .
Women: *gibet mir* . . . . .
    Men: *gibet mir* . . . . .
Women: *einen treuen Sinne* . . . . .
    Men: *einen treuen Sinne* . . . . .
Women: *nimm mich ganz* . . . . .
    Men: *nimm mich ganz* . . . .
Women: *mein Jesus hin* . . . . .
    Men: *mein Jesus hin* . . . . .
All together: *mein Jesus hin.*

The following folk song was remembered by Eva Iszler, sung by her in 1986, and recorded for this collection when she was already 96 years old.

Keine Rose ohne Dornen
(Oral Tradition by Eva Iszler)

Keine Rose ohne Dornen
keine Liebe ohne Treue
nur für dich bin ich geboren
dein Geliebtes will ich sein.

Wenn ich einsam auf der Strasse stehe
schauen mich die Leute an,
meine Äugelein sind voll Tränen
dass ich fast nicht sehen kann.
meine Äugelein sind voll Tränen
dass ich fast nicht sehen kann.

Wenn ich einst noch sterben sollte
und der Tod die Liebe bricht,
so pflanzt mir auf meinem Grabe
eine Rose Vergessmeinnicht.
so pflanzt mir auf meinem Grabe
eine Rose Vergessmeinnicht.

Not all of the songs of the Central Dakota Germans are filled with melancholy and desire for heavenly or earthly love. Many are also filled with humor and show what fun and joy singing together can be. The following song contains other songs within it. The song was sung and as each person's name was called they sang an individual song of their choice, and the round went on. These were especially popular at weddings, but were used on other occasions also.

Dreimal drei ist neune
(Oral Tradition by Emma Fischer)

Dreimal drei ist neune
du weisst ja was ich meine,
zwanzig ist ja zweimal zehn
lass das Liedchen weiter gehen.

Emma sing uns ein Lied, sing uns ein Lied.

(Whoever was called upon would sing a song and the response of the group would be one of two possibilities, they approved or they didn't think it was good, all in good humor, of course).

*Hast schlecht gemacht, hast schlecht gemacht
in deinen jungen Tagen,
darum wirst heute Abend ausgelacht
in deinen alten Tagen.*

*Dreimal drei ist neune
du weisst ja was ich meine,
zwanzig ist ja zweimal zehn
lass das Liedchen weiter gehen.*

Johann sing uns ein Lied, sing uns ein Lied.

(Now we have the another possible answer to the song he sang.)

*Wärst nicht aufgestiege
wärst nicht herunterfalle
hättest meine Schwester geheiratet
wärst mein Schwager geworde.*

*Hast gut gemacht
hast gut gemacht in deinen jungen Tagen,
darum wirst heute Abend nicht ausgelacht
in deinen alten Tagen.*

*Dreimal drei ist neune
du weisst ja was ich meine,
zwanzig ist ja zweimal zehn
lass das Liedchen weiter gehen.
Susanna sing uns ein Lied, sing uns ein Lied.*

(The round continues until everyone has sung their song.)

A song which had different verses and possibilities for people to fill in with their own rhymes is the old German standby, **Ach du lieber Augustin.**

*Ach du lieber Augustin
  das weib ist verloffe
  der mann ist versoffe
  ach du lieber Augustin
  alles ist hin!*

And finally an old favorite of everyone:

Du, Du liegst mir im Herzen
(Oral Tradition)

Du, du, liegst mir im Herzen
Du, du, liegst mir im Sinn
Du, du, machst mir viel Schmerzen
weisst nicht wie gut ich dir bin,
ja, ja, ja, ja, weisst nicht wie gut ich dir bin.

So, so, wie ich dich liebe
so, so, liebe auch mich
die, die zärtlichsten Triebe
fühle ich einzig für dich
ja, ja, ja, ja, fühle ich einzig für dich.

Doch, doch, darf ich dir trauen
dir, dir, mit leichtem Sinn
Du, du kannst auf mich bauen
bis uns die Liebe vereint
ja, ja, ja, ja, bis uns die Liebe vereint.

The songs of the American pioneers most popular with the Central Dakota young people and sung by them, were the following. The young Germans sang them joyfully for it made them a part of their new American heritage.

Sweet Adeline
My Wild Irish Rose
Sweet Violets
Pretty Little Girl
I Want a Girl Just Like the Girl
Springtime in the Rockies
Have You Ever Been Lonely
Birmingham Jail
Nobody's Darling But Mine
Blue Bonnet
She'll Be Coming Round the Mountain
The Red River Valley

5.7 Kiche und Hof: Culinary art and the sustenance of daily life. A simple evening meal was eaten on the day fresh bread was baked when the garden was yielding spring onions and radishes.

Fresh sweet cream
Freshly baked bread
Freshly made butter
Fresh onions and radishes from the spring garden
Dip the thick pieces of baked bread into a dish of heavy sweet cream and eat along with the young onions and radishes.

This was a special and favorite evening meal. Add the evening prayer and it conveys a whole way of life. Although the food of the Dakota Germans was often as simple as this evening repast, their housewives gained a well-deserved fame for their exceptional cooking and baking skills.

The women who left Germany and moved to the Black Sea Colonies of Russia took their old family recipes and traditional methods of preparing food with them. During the years in Russia some new foods, and different dishes were incorporated in the traditional fare. Such favorite dishes as *halupsy* and *borscht* were undoubtedly adaptations of recipes learned in Russia, since they are typical of Eastern European cooking. It is interesting that many of the words incorporated into the language of the Germans during their stay in Russia were related to food (3.3.1).

In America, foods were discovered on the seemingly barren prairies and incorporated into the diet. Horseradish grew wild and is still found that way, and used. Indian garlic, which resembled clover with its white flower, had a thin root which could be peeled and eaten. Indian potatoes and Indian onions were found growing wild. The berry from the "choke cherry" tree, which grows wild, but may have been planted by the Indians, makes a uniquely delicious jelly. It has the taste of French *cassis*, black currants.

A favorite delicacy was the sunflower seed which came to be known as the 'Russian peanut' among the other pioneers. The ripe sunflower was dried in the sun until the seeds could be brushed from the plant and stored. Corn that could be used for popcorn was planted in the fields with regular corn. Children had to help harvest the corn, and looking for the corn that could be used for popcorn amidst the rest of the corn, made the job fun since there would be a future treat.

The major part of cookery consisted of German dishes dating from the eighteenth century and earlier, from South or Southwest Germany.

The cookstove was the center of activity in the pioneer home. Water for all uses was heated in a reservoir behind the stove and a tea kettle was always on. When not working in the field, the farm wife busied herself with preparing and preserving food. Jellies were made from rhubarb, gooseberries, choke cherries, sand cherries, and wild plums.

Green tomatoes were made into a pickle relish. Not only cucumbers, but wax beans, beets, and watermelons were pickled. Small watermelons were placed whole in large crocks and were a wonderful appetizer before winter dinners.

Geese were butchered in the fall, and the fat was rendered and used instead of butter. Bread was baked twice weekly, and even today many housewives customarily spend a day a week baking, making bread for the family needs as well as sweets, including American cookies and cakes. Wednesday was the traditional baking day.

Breakfast usually consisted of homemade rolls, soft boiled eggs, and coffee. The hot meal at noon, the most important meal of the day whenever the whole family gathered, always included potatoes and other traditional foods. Formerly, a drink made from fresh cold well water, soda, and vinegar, was taken before the big noon meal when the family came in from heavy field work such as heathering the grain. Tea was served with the meal. The evening meal often consisted of bread, sausage, homemade cottage cheese, fresh garden vegetables or homemade pickles, hard boiled eggs, boiled potatoes or potato salad.

In the evening when company came, smoked sausage would be served with fresh homemade bread, pickled watermelon, and tea or wine. Many of the pioneers made their own wine when they were able to buy grapes. In addition, most families also brewed their own beer.

Sunday noon after church is still the traditional time to eat a good homemade soup like the rich vegetable soup *borscht*, or chicken noodle soup, or a *riebbele* soup, made with 'bits of dough'. It was said that *Riebbele* soup may be served at any time of day or evening, and this is still stated in the Swabian cookbooks of today. Popular *riebbele suppe* results when dough bits are added to chicken soup broth. E*inlauf suppe* is the name of a dish in which egg and flour batter are added to chicken soup. *Halupsy*, boiled cabbage leaves filled with chopped ham, onions, and rice was a favorite Sunday dish for company, because it can be prepared the day before.

Dough is used in many recipes. There is *blagende*, a filled turnover, usually made with fresh pumpkin filling; *schlitz kiechla* are deep-fried squares of dough; and *strudel* is the long, thinly rolled dough cooked on top of potatoes in a dutch oven. When making the pumpkin *blagende* the seeds of the pumpkin are saved and baked and eaten just as one eats sunflower seeds. *Stirum* is the name for a dish in which egg, milk and flour batter is fried in fat and stirred until the small marble-sized bits of dough are done. *Käse knepfla* are dough squares filled with cottage cheese, first boiled and then fried, while *knepfla* are pieces of dough cut into small pieces with scissors and boiled. When *knepfla* are added to spareribs and sauerkraut the dish is considered a complete meal. *Nudeln*, home-made noodles, are used for various dishes. It can be a meal when cooked raisins are added. *Schupfnudel* are dumplings made of dough, cooked similarly to *strudel*.

Potatoes are also used in a variety of dishes by the creative Dakota German. *Stamfetz* are simply mashed potatoes, and *malotz* are mashed potatoes mixed with flour, crumbled, then fried in fat. Hot potato salad, *kartoffel salat* is a very popular dish. Traditional recipes handed down in the family were used for special occasions such as church holidays, but also simply for the family meals.

Most Dakota German housewives still cook the way their mothers did. They still follow their age old traditions and feel comfortable with them. Why would they want to change? The cooking is good and nutritious and visitors are always delighted with the wonderful foods served them.

All the best foods that the Dakota German household could offer were provided at harvest time for the thrashers, neighbors who would get together and go from farm to farm until everybody's grain was in. The steam tractor driver had to start at 4:00 a.m., and harvesting began at 5:00 a.m. Lunch, served at mid-morning, would be taken to the field. Homemade bread and butter, boiled eggs, goose fat for the bread, bacon and sausages, liverwurst, and *kuchen* were prepared for this meal. The large meal was at noon. Small pigs had been butchered in preparation and the meat hung in the well to keep cool. The meat was fried and stewed with onions. `Pigs in the blanket', *halupsy*, baked rice, and baked or fried potato slices made a hearty meal. The men drank tea, milk or sour milk, a variety of *kuchen* were offered and fresh watermelons from the garden were served.

Another luncheon was taken to the field at 4:00 p.m., usually foods similar to those prepared in the morning. Wine, made from rhubarb, plums, or grapes was offered for the mid-morning and mid-afternoon meals.

Supper at 8:30 p.m., was served in the summer kitchen. This was a separate building near the main farmhouse. There were actually two rooms, a very large kitchen and an eating area. All the cooking and eating was done there, from the beginning of the good weather in the spring until the end of harvest in the fall. A wash stand with lots of towels, soap and water stood at the entrance so all who entered to eat had the opportunity of cleaning up first. Chicken, stewed or fried with onions, potatoes, home-made sausage, baked dessert and coffee had been prepared. After caring for the horses, the men would be asleep in the hayloft by 10:00 p.m. in order to be ready for the morning's work.

Everyone in the family helped to get the grain in. The younger children would drive the wagons that brought the grain from the fields, and two men would shovel it into the storage shed. Nobody worked harder than the farm wife and daughters, who cooked and served all the meals, stayed up during the night to bake bread and dessert *kuchen* for the next day, and often helped shovel the wheat from the wagons into the sheds. Neighboring women helped each other during harvest time, preparing, as the wheat was harvested, the rich and satisfying foods that were a part of the long tradition of the harvest.

The following text describes cooking and kitchen practices in the time before there were modern supermarkets and the abundance that is available today:

> There were not a lot of meat dishes as such. They just didn't have a lot of meat to eat, and what they ate was mostly pork. They had to raise their own chickens with eggs and clucks (brood hens) which didn't give them a lot of chickens. They needed them for eggs to eat, too. So really only the old chickens were eaten and they were used to make a rich noodle soup for special occasions. This soup was also made and given to a friend who was sick or a woman who had just given birth as it was very healthy and gave them strength. They also did not have herds of cattle. They only had one cow, or perhaps two, and this was a much prized possession which produced milk and cream plus all the other dairy products for the family to eat, and income for buying other staples when they took the products to town and sold them. In the spring and fall they went to town by horse and buggy, a long trip, once a month, and sold their cream and eggs. They bought their staples like flour and sugar, coffee, tea, syrup, and spices like salt, pepper, bay leaf, cinnamon, cloves, whole allspice. The syrup was put on homemade bread and taken to school for school lunch. For the men of the family the important purchase was tobacco. The only other income was the grain they harvested in the fall.
>
> The pork they ate was smoked and hung or cured in some other way. They only ate fresh meat when they butchered. Wild goose, duck, pheasant, prairie chickens, and partridges were fall favorites in all the kitchens. These were abundant until the 1960s, and although they are still hunted for the family dinner, it has become a treat rather than a family staple. I remember the huge platters of different wild birds placed in the middle of the table and you could eat your favorites. The wild goose and duck were usually preserved and canned, while the pheasants and smaller birds were eaten fresh. We still can wild goose and wild duck whenever we can get them. A special treat for the children in late August was corn, field corn, picked and fried in *glut* `embers, hot coals' in the cookstove and then eaten for dessert or a snack.

Many foods were stored in the wheat in the fall. Watermelons, pumpkins, sausage made after butchering, smoked hams, all were placed in the wheat to be kept fresh. When it got too cold the watermelons and pumpkins were taken into the house, but the meat stayed there all winter or until used. Onions from the garden were braided and hung in the house for decoration, as was garlic. The onion and garlic *flocken* `braids' were used as needed. Every garden had flowers planted in it along with the vegetables. *Strohblume* `zinnias', little violas, and marigolds were among the favorites. Seeds from everything grown in the garden were saved and replanted each year, for nothing could survive the harsh winter.

It is important to record what we can of our history and traditions, and one of the most important is the handing down of family foodlore. The foodlore of the Central Dakota Germans is recorded in Appendix I for foodways are part of what folklorists call the "vital traditions" of a group. I transcribed the recipes of the old pioneer mothers who no longer have a steady hand and who are not always able to write it all down in modern English.

Each recipe in the foodlore has a major ingredient that never varies: the Dakota German ethos. This ethos encompasses hard work, ingenuity, frugality, simplicity, temperance, a love of nature and of family, and a delight in life's simple pleasures.

The Dakota German Foodlore in Appendix I records the pioneer experience and even makes it possible for you to reexperience it in your own kitchen. What is recorded is not just a series of individual recipes or items, but it presents the entire set of recipes that constitute the Dakota German food traditions.

The recipes collected and recorded in Appendix I were a two-year team effort together with Emma Fischer, a well-known traditional cook, and Rebecca Schroeder, a well-known folklorist and editor.

Chapter 6: Conclusions

6.0 Introduction. A configuration of several traits can be said to characterize the Central Dakota Germans and contributed to the formation of their linguistic and cultural identity. In reviewing the data collected through oral interviews beginning in 1961, and through the recorded dialectal interviews beginning in 1984, I have come to identify the following factors as most characteristic of their language and cultural experience: (1) agrarian society (6.1), (2) common Lutheran religion (6.2), (3) geographical isolation (6.3), (4) previous petrifaction of their language and culture during the Russian period (6.4), and (5) homogeneous language and cultural traditions (6.5).

6.1 Agrarian society. Central Dakota Germans were an agrarian society. Agricultural people tend to see life as a whole, a cyclical whole; the rhythm of the seasons combined with the rhythms of their religion and its liturgical calendar. They were not involved in cultural trends. Their life had its form. They were very family oriented. The family, as a unit, working together, was the way farming had been carried out over the centuries. The "family farm" expressed a whole world and basic concept of life. In reply to questions during interviews, invariably their answers were phrased: *als wir geackert haben* `when we were plowing' or *damals beim grossen sturm* `that time when we had the big storm'. The family finds it difficult to survive as a small unit unless it has a very stable environment. But the family can survive and survive well if it is surrounded by the "greater family" and everyone works together. When informants were asked why they moved to a certain town or county, invariably the answer was that the husband's family had moved there. Women followed their men, and men followed the migrations of the other male members of their family and of their close family friends.

When the Central Dakota German speaks of 'the family', he means a large number of people many of whom may barely know each other, but 'the tribe' stays together. The German concept of *Gross-Familie* 'the larger family' is expressed by the Dakota German as *die freindschaft* 'a relationship of relatives and friends' rather than by the Standard High German *die Verwandtschaft* 'relatives'. The agrarian society of 'relatives and friends' survived and stayed intact because it did not need to go outside for assistance.

6.2 Common Lutheran religion. Another factor which served to keep the Central Dakota German community intact was their common Lutheran religion. Even though the group underwent drastic cultural changes in moving from Germany to Russia and from Russia to the Dakotas, its religion did not change. The language of that religion, Lutheranism, was German. Thus, language and religion supported each other. Their Lutheranism did not need to change and adapt, and, as a consequence, their language did not need to change and adapt. They mutually supported each other in their old forms.

Although there were small German Reformed, Evangelical, and Baptist churches, the Luther translation of the Bible into the German language, the German folksongs which he brought into the church, and his writings, influenced German speaking people in all the Protestant religions.

In America where instruction in the schools was not conducted in German, the Confirmation classes of the Lutheran church carried the language. Instruction in German was given to all young people, and they could not be Confirmed until they read, wrote, and mastered the catechetical material in German.

Moreover, it seems that keeping some church services in German even after the church began holding other church services in English also continued to perform a unifying function.

The need for having a German-speaking minister amounted to the need for someone from the Central Dakotas who had gone on to college and yet retained his family's traditions and language in order that he might be able to come back and minister to these people. If he did not know their language, he could not communicate with them; if he did not understand their traditions he would have difficulty understanding them. Thus, the Central Dakota German community still remained an insular group.

The change from German Confirmation classes to English Confirmation classes occurred in the late 1930s and 1940s. The final change in the type of support provided by their Lutheranism for the maintenance of the German language occurred in the 1980s when the

Lutheran Church shifted to monolingual English services.

6.3 Geographical isolation. The extreme geographical isolation of the area in which the Central Dakota Germans settled also contributed towards keeping their language and culture intact. One can draw a line through the middle of the state of North Dakota, from Jamestown on the James River in the east to Bismarck on the Missouri River in the West, and safely say that to the south of this line lived Germans who had migrated to the United States from the Black Sea Area of Russia and from Bessarabia. North of that line the population was predominantly Scandinavian, with Germans from Russia as the second largest ethnic group.

The straight east-west line I have described, not only divides North Dakota into two practically equal parts and connects major cities of the state but is, even today, the site of the major east-west continental highway and the site of the east-west continental railways through the state. The ethnic division is reiterated by a transportation division, with very few north-south connections.

A similar east-west line, U.S. Route 12, from Aberdeen in the east and extending west across the state to the Missouri River, bisects South Dakota, the state immediately adjacent to North Dakota. It was north of this South Dakota midline and south of the North Dakota midline that the German immigrants from Russia described in this study settled. Hence the name chosen, the Central Dakota Germans.

In this large area, in the middle of the two states of North and South Dakota, there were no major rivers and no major roads, and even today roads in that area are relatively few. In earlier days, there were practically none. The roads that did exist were gravel roads, and there were no paved roads until the 1960s. It was and still is an isolated area; few passed through it unless they were going to a town inside the area. Until very recently this Central Dakota area has remained almost as isolated an area as it was in the days of the early Dakota Territory when only the Fort Yates Trail cut through it, and no one tarried there. It was this isolation combined with their being surrounded by fellow Germans from Russia, in both North and South Dakota as well as in the whole Great Plains area, which contributed so strongly to keeping the language and culture of the Central Dakota Germans intact.

6.4 Previous petrifaction of their language and culture during the Russian period. Another important reason for their staying so culturally and linguistically intact was the years they spent living as German colonists in Russia. There, in both geographical and cultural isolation, they existed as a tightly knit ethnic minority. This was a common phenomenon in the Russian Empire. Their language and culture had little input from Germany and had minimal input from their Russian neighbors. In these unusual circumstances their language and culture were formed, and they became psychologically, socially, and culturally independent, hardened to surrounding linguistic and cultural influences.

When they made their second migration, from Russia to the United States, they came with this linguistic and cultural petrifaction. This greatly helped them move into a new country and stay intact as a cultural group, although they pioneered with other Americans and large numbers of Scandinavian immigrants in North Dakota and South Dakota, with whom they shared experiences and a common devotion to land and country. But as before in Russia, they looked within their own group to find the psychological, social, economic, physical, and cultural resources which would enable them to survive in a harsh and difficult environment. They had survived by their group cohesiveness in Russia; they followed the familiar lessons of their own immediate past, and survived the same way in the Dakotas.

6.5 Homogeneous language and cultural traditions. The sociolinguistic settings for the Central Dakota German dialect were the home, the family, the peer groups, and the church. In Russia, German had been the only language used in their schools until late in the nineteenth century when the Russian language had to be added to the Black Sea Colony schools.

The Central Dakota German dialect speakers became accustomed to bilingualism for Russian was the language of official communication, used in government and in commerce. This use of Russian was always paralleled by the vigorous employment of German in all the other aspects of life. When the Central Dakota German dialect was transferred to an English language environment rather than a Russian environment, the speakers of the dialect were prepared for this new linguistic and cultural shift. English replaced Russian as the language of public life, but the Central Dakota German dialect, accustomed to surviving such a bilingual setting, remained intact.

In the Dakota Territory the Central Dakota German dialect continued to function precisely as it had in the past. Although English replaced Russian as the language of instruction in the schools, and the language of government and commerce, the Central Dakota German dialect continued in the home, in the church, and in their daily life. The language and the people of this closely knit group had for so many generations survived and supported one another.

As a consequence, the shift of the bilingual Central Dakota Germans to monolingualism in English took longer because of their long-term experience with bilingualism. As Staczek (*NWAV-XVI* 1988a) points out, many of the other immigrants who came to America were monolingual in their native language. They were only bilinguals in the period of transition from their mother tongue to the English language, whereas the Central Dakota Germans had been true bilinguals for a long time, first German-Russian then German-English. This certainly helped to sustain the Central Dakota German dialect.

According to Nida (*GURT* 1988:243-249), acceptability of a language is the most important factor in its maintenance. Acceptability reflects cultural factors; for language is a code and one needs to know the code to be a member of the group. The Central Dakota German dialect had proven itself to be a viable language, and therefore had continued to be the language of the people in the group, even though they had been taught Standard High German in the schools and in the church. This language code remained unchanged for several generations, as I have pointed out. Familiarity with the code marked the individual as a member of the group, this warm and closely knit group, that for 200 years had survived because of their group identity which supplied to each the support needed and thus inculcated the need of looking inward to the group, as the source for cultural traditions, personal identity, and individual support.

Being a people with their own cultural traditions did not mean they were not innovative people. Their villages in Russia and Bessarabia not only had schools for higher education, but orphanages, institutes for teaching the deaf, and group funds for maintaining the social fabric of their communities. They manufactured goods and were renowned throughout the Russian Empire for their craftsmen as well as for their farms and vineyards.

It is also interesting to note that a people so tradition-bound, so conservative in their thinking, and so tenacious of their language and other cultural traditions, were great liberals when it came to moving across continents in search of either religious or personal freedom. They grasped the opportunity for self determination, for freedom from the Napoleonic or Russian military draft, from wars, and from rulers. It was their love of their own cultural traditions which gave them this inner courage and decisiveness.

6.6 Conclusion. According to my judgement, the five strands, which I have just described blended together to characterize and define the Central Dakota Germans, their history, language, and culture.

We have viewed the Central Dakota Germans through both written history and oral history. We placed them geographically and historically through a study of their dialect. Their religious practices and views, their folk culture and folk expression, each yields yet further historical perspective. Finally, their foodlore provides a last intimate insight into the culture and history of a people.

It is difficult to conclude this descriptive volume without expressing a value judgment and personal tribute to these staunch German pioneers from Russia. They were and are a kind and gentle people. They live the biblical norm to "Love thy neighbor as thyself". Never militaristic, they left their homes both in Germany and in Russia to avoid war and oppression. They brought their strong value system and firm religious beliefs to this country. Here they found a home, and even today tears fill their eyes when the American flag is presented. They gained much, but they also contributed much. They suffered great hardships to preserve their values and ideals. Now many of their norms and ideals are embodied in what we consider our pioneer traditions and cultural heritage. Their insistence upon freedom of religion and freedom of expression, and upon harmonious relations with other people, brought a moral standard and strength to our society. They pioneered twice and their experience surely strengthened and supported other American pioneers. They were a model for others not only in Russia, but here as well. Their responsibility to the community and to family was one of the basic principles allowing settlement in the vast sea of grass so inhospitable to man. They held together, they helped each other, no sacrifice was too great. They were willing to work hard and contributed their values and the continuity of their cultural ideals to the moral values of our young country. Those ideals have served our nation well.

Today, when we think of the American pioneers and the settlement of the American West, we must also recall those brave German settlers who came from Russia, pioneered, and established themselves on the great American Plain, creating a unique chapter in the story of our American history.

Appendix 1: Central Dakota German Foodlore

SOUPS

Chicken noodle soup. Bring 2 quarts water to boil and add 1 stewing or soup chicken which has been cut up. You can use half a chicken if it is a very large chicken. Boil for about 1 hour, then remove the chicken and strain the broth. Put the chicken and the strained broth back into the kettle and add the following:
1 teaspoon salt—more salt can be added later to taste
4 whole allspice
1 clove
1/2 bay leaf
1 small onion
1 piece of celery (optional)
Also add 1 quart of boiling water.

Now cook the soup for 1 1/2 more hours at a low boil. Remove the meat after the cooking time has ended and strain the broth again. Bring just the strained broth to a full boil and add approximately 2 cups noodles. Boil no longer than 10 minutes or until the noodles are soft. Add chopped fresh parsley on top of the soup just as it finishes boiling. Remove from heat, sprinkle with cinnamon, and serve.

The chicken can be served as it is or fried for a few minutes with onions and served. Fry the boiled chicken lightly on each side in cooking oil. Add 1 small chopped onion. It should take the same amount of time to fry the chicken and onion—10 minutes—as it does to boil the noodles.

Beef noodle soup. Beef noodle soup is cooked the same way, using the same spices as chicken noodle soup. Use 1-1/2 to 2 pounds of beef soup meat or beef short-ribs. The meat can also be fried after cooking if desired. It is more commonly served boiled with a mustard. The mustard is made by adding vinegar to dry mustard (see mustard recipe).

Homemade noodles. Make a dough that is not too soft.
2 cups flour (more if needed)
3 eggs
a few drops of water

It has to be worked well. Divide into 3 small balls and let set for about 15 minutes, covered with a clean dish towel so they won't become dry. Roll each ball out until it is very, very thin (thinner than pie crust). Let the 3 rolled out sheets dry for 20 minutes, lying on a cotton dishtowel and not touching. (The length of drying time depends on the temperature. Warm dry air dries faster and cool or damp air slower.) Turn the 3 sheets every so often until they are dry enough so the dough bends but does not break. Over drying will cause the dough sheets to crack. Cut while still damp.

Cut the dough sheets into quarters. Put 2 quarters together and roll them into a tight roll. Place it on a cutting board and cut the noodles thinly. Just slice thinly along the whole length of the roll. Separate and shake the noodles so they separate, and place them on the dish towel to dry. They must be completely dry before storing. Finish cutting the rest of the noodles. This batch of noodles is enough for 2 soups. If desired, the batch can be stretched to use for 3 soups.

The noodles can be placed in plastic bags and stored dry in the cupboard for one to two weeks or frozen for up to 2 months. They do not need to be thawed before cooking.

Borscht. Place 2 pounds beef soup meat (including bones) in a soup kettle with 2 quarts hot water. Boil for about 1 hour. Be careful so it does not cook over. Skim the top of the water after it starts to boil and the scum of the meat rises. After one hour take the meat out and strain the broth. Put the meat and the broth back into the kettle and add a quart of water which has been boiled. Add to the soup:

2 cups shredded cabbage
1 small diced beet
4 medium size carrots sliced thinly
1 tablespoon salt
Cook for 1/2 hour and add: (taste for salt)
1 medium size onion diced
1 stalk celery diced
2 medium size potatoes diced
4 whole allspice
1 clove
1/2 large bay leaf or 1 small bay leaf
8 fresh green beans (cut up)
1/4 clove of garlic—a very tiny piece (If you grow garlic in your garden, just add 1 small garlic top cut up instead of a clove. This would not be added here but below with the parsley.)
Cook for 1 more hour at a low boil. After the hour add:
1 sprig parsley diced
1 small sprig fresh dill—not too much, and remove before serving
6 whole tomatoes peeled or home canned tomatoes.
Salt to taste
Cook the soup for 10 minutes and serve.

The meat is served either as it is after being taken from the soup or it can be fried for 10 minutes in a bit of oil. Dry mustard mixed with vinegar is served with the meat (see recipe below).

To make a complete pioneer meal, the soup and meat were accompanied by a few potatoes which were boiled with their jackets on, peeled, and then fried briefly.

In the summer when gardens are in bloom you can use chopped beet tops instead of beets, chopped onion tops instead of onions, and chopped garlic tops instead of garlic. For further variations you can make the soup with chicken instead of beef. A favorite was a combination of beef and chicken parts.

Mustard.
2 teaspoons dry mustard
2 teaspoon sugar
1/2 teaspoon flour
2 teaspoons vinegar
Mix and serve. It is especially good with beef used to make soup broth. It peps it up and makes a flavorful addition.

Einlauf soup. Another good soup variation which uses the chicken or beef broth made with the chicken or beef noodle recipes is *einlauf* soup.
Make a batter using:
1/3 cup flour
2 eggs
a bit of water
Bring the broth to a boil and pour this batter into it. Stir to separate the dough into pieces. Cook 5 to 10 minutes and serve.

Riebbele soup.

Riebbele riebbele in der frih
Riebbele riebbele in der zeit
Riebbele riebbele in alle ewigkeit.

This popular verse said `riebbele* soup could be served early in the day, any other time, and even into all of eternity'. *Riebbele* soup is a wonderful way to make a quick special soup, if you have prepared and saved beef or chicken broth.
The following are two versions of how to make *riebbele* soup.

(1) Make the same soup broth with beef or chicken as described in the noodle soup receipe. Instead of adding noodles, you add *riebbele*.
3/4 cup flour—more if needed
1 egg
Crumble the dough made with flour and egg into tiny bits. Bring the broth to a boil and add these tiny bits of dough and boil them for 5 minutes—not more. Serve.

(2) The more old-fashioned *riebbele* soup, which was a simple and quick but a hearty pioneer meal, was made with milk.
1 quart milk
1/2 teaspoon salt—or to taste

Bring the milk and salt to boil and add the *riebbele*. Cook 5 minutes or less, remove from the stove and top with cinnamon. Serve.

One could use this same milk soup and add the thin homemade noodles. This soup was also popular but more difficult to make. The noodles needed to be cooked almost 10 minutes, which is long enough to give the milk a chance to burn. One could precook the noodles for 8 minutes, put them in the milk soup, and bring them to a quick boil again.

The quick cooking *riebbele* were more practical. They were also easier to make than homemade noodles.

Bean soup. Soak about 1 pound white beans (Great Northern) in cold water the evening before you prepare the soup.

The following day, remove the beans and place them in a quart of boiling water. Boil for 10 minutes and drain.

You will have to purchase either the butt end of a smoked ham, a smoked picnic ham, or 3 to 4 smoked ham hocks. Cut the ham into large pieces about the size of the ham hocks. Cook the meat in boiling water for 10 minutes also. Remove and drain.

Put the beans, ham or ham hocks or a combination of both, and 2 quarts water into a clean soup kettle. Bring to a boil. Turn the heat down to a low boil and cook for 1 1/2 hours. Then add:

3 whole allspice
1 small bay leaf
1 medium onion cut up
1 clove garlic cut up
1 or 2 small potatoes
Salt to taste

Two cups of boiling water, or more, can be added here, if needed, or if a less thick soup is preferred.

Cook for 1 more hour. Remove the meat from the soup and place on a platter for serving. Mash the soup which includes the beans, potatoes, onions, and garlic. Remove the bay leaf and allspice if possible. Now add the roux (see recipe below) to the soup, being very careful as it splatters. Stir the roux into the soup and you will notice the soup thickening. Serve. There is no bean soup comparable to this great soup.

Roux. To make the roux, heat about 1/4 cup shortening in a small pan and add 1 tablespoon or so of flour. You must stir continuously until it turns light brown. This goes very quickly.

A side dish is used for the meat. Most people will, of course, cut up the meat and add it to their soup. Vinegar is also served, which can be added to the bean soup but only in small drops. It adds flavor.

The bean soup and ham are considered a whole meal.

Knepfla soup. Put 2 quarts water in a soup kettle and bring to a boil. Add pork bones with meat to the soup. They should weigh 1 to 1-1/2 pounds and are not smoked. The pioneers used the bones left from butchering and they were either used fresh, right at the time of butchering, or they were stored by placing them on top of the hams in the crock. They would not keep very long. (See the section on meat preservation for further information.) Today cooks tend to use chicken or slices of ham.

Boil the water with the bones for 1 hour and then strain. Put the strained broth and the bones back into the kettle and add 1 quart boiling water plus the following ingredients.
1/2 clove garlic
1 small to medium size onion
1/2 bay leaf
2 whole allspice
1 tablespoon salt—more can be added to taste.

Cook another hour. Take the meat out and strain the broth. Bring it to a boil and add the *knepfla*. The *knepfla* used are the same as described in the *knepfla* recipe. Boil the dough *knepfla* for about 5 minutes. They should come to a boil, be stirred, and come to a boil again at least 3 times during these 5 minutes. Do not overboil or it will become doughy.

Serve the meat plain or fried along with horseradish and mixed mustard. It needs only a little frying after being taken out of the broth. (See the recipes for homemade horseradish and for mustard.)

Another version of this recipe is basically a potato soup. The broth and the spices are the same. After the first hour and while adding the onion and spices, also add 3 or 4 medium size potatoes cut in large diced pieces. You can add *knepfla* or just eat it as a hearty potato soup.

Potato soup.
1 tablespoon grated carrot
1 tablespoon scraped onion (finely chopped or diced)
2 tablespoons butter
Cook the carrots and onion in the butter until lightly browned. Blend in:
2 tablespoons flour
Stir this mixture into:
2 cups heated milk
and add to this 1 cup cooked potatoes which have been rubbed through a potato ricer. Add:
1 teaspoon salt
1 teaspoon pepper
1 teaspoon celery salt
Cook the soup in a double boiler for 20 minutes—stirring occasionally.

BREAD AND MAIN DISHES MADE WITH DOUGH

Everlasting yeast. The pioneers made this with dry cubes of yeast. In the evening they cooked 2 medium size potatoes (diced) in 1 quart of water for half an hour or until very soft. The potatoes were mashed in the same cooking liquid. To this liquid in which the potatoes were mashed were added 2 tablespoons of sugar and 1 tablespoon of salt. This mixture was left in the kettle in which the potatoes had been cooked, was covered and left in a warm place. Before going to bed the 2 dry yeast cubes were added, after which another quart of warm water could be added. The kettle was wrapped in a warm blanket and set next to the cook stove. It had to be kept warm.

In the morning 1 pint was taken out, put in a sealed jar and placed in the cellar. Dough was made with the rest of the yeast.

The reserved pint of yeast was then used the next time, along with the potato mixture replacing the yeast cubes. Thus the steps of adding yeast cubes and water were also eliminated. From the new mixture another pint was saved for the next time. The pint had to be used within a week or it would get too old and would not rise. One pint plus the potato mixture was enough to make 4 loaves of bread.

When the cook ran out of the everlasting yeast, instead of starting a new batch she would borrow a pint from a neighbor. For the more the yeast was used and renewed, the better it was.

It is no longer possible to make the original everlasting yeast today because the dry yeast cubes used then are no longer available.

Homemade bread dough. Baking a good bread was the most important thing for a wife to be able to do. Here is an old receipe, which used everlasting yeast, but can also be made with a modern yeast.

With simple yeast: To 1/2 cup lukewarm water add 1 package of yeast (Red Star) and 1/2 teaspoon of sugar. Let rise for about 5 minutes. The cup will fill up.

To make the bread dough, mix the following ingredients.
2 tablespoons sugar
1 tablespoon salt
2 tablespoons oil
1-1/2 cups very warm water

Add the yeast and mix again. Add 1 cup of flour at a time until you have a soft dough. When the dough is finished and is smooth and elastic, add about 1 tablespoon oil to the bottom of the bowl underneath the dough. Knead the dough into it. Cover the bowl with wax paper and a dish towel and set in a warm place, letting the dough rise for 3/4 hour. Then knead it well, cover and let it rise again for 1/2 to 3/4 hour. (If you plan to use the dough for strudels or dumplings, it is ready at this point.) For bread let the dough rise again for about 1/2 hour. Knead the dough again and divide into 3 loaves. Rub 3 bread loaf pans with a bit of oil and place a loaf in each pan, letting the dough rise in the pan for 1 hour or less.

Bake at 350 to 375 degrees for 35 to 40 minutes or until the top is nice and brown. Remove from the oven and let cool.

Instead of making 3 loaves of bread you can use one of the loaves to make biscuits. Add a bit of oil to each biscuit pan before putting the dough in, let the dough rise for about an hour, and bake the same way.

This dough for making bread is the same dough used to make *strudel, schupfnudel,* and *kiechla*. It is enough for 8 people.

Strudel and Schupfnudel. *Schupfnudel* 'dumplings' are made from the same dough that is used for bread. Cut walnut size pieces off the bread dough before it has been kneaded the second time. Roll the small piece of dough into an oblong shape, lay it on a dish towel and let it rise for about half an hour. Cooking instructions are given in the *strudel* recipe. You can make a whole dumpling dinner using half of the dough from the bread dough recipe or you can make just a few dumplings and add them to the *strudel* recipe.

Strudel. *Strudel* are made from the same dough that is used to make bread. For this recipe use 1/2 of the bread dough made with the bread dough recipe. The rest of the dough can be used to make *kiechla* or one loaf of bread.

Use the bread dough after it has been kneaded the second time and before it rises again. Cut the dough into 3 small patties that you can work gently into 3 balls the size of an orange. Let the balls lie for 10 minutes and then roll them out, but not thinly. Let rest another 15 minutes. Rub about 1 teaspoon of oil on each of the 3 rolled out pieces of dough. Pick the dough up, one piece at a time, and hold over your hands which are shaped into a fist. Stretch the dough by working it with your fists until it is very thin. Lay it down again and roll each piece of dough in from each side. You are rolling two sides of the dough to the middle. Cut through the middle, and you now have two long rolls of dough. Cut each of these two lengths of dough into about 4 *strudels* which will measure about 3 to 4 inches in length. When you have done this with all of your 3 balls of dough, you will have about 2 dozen *strudels*, enough for 4 persons. Lay the *strudels* on a piece of cloth and cover for about 20 minutes.

While you are making the *strudels* or *schupfnudel* 'dumplings' you must also start cooking the potatoes needed for this recipe. Have 4 medium sized potatoes diced. Put 1/4 cup cooking oil and 1 medium diced onion in a Dutch oven and fry until the onions are yellow. Place potatoes in the bottom of the pan evenly and add only enough water to cover the potatoes. Add 1 teaspoon salt. Your cooking pan or Dutch oven must have an air-tight cover so no air can move in or out of it. Cover and cook for 1/2 hour. At the end of the 1/2 hour there should still be enough water in the pan so that potatoes are half covered with water. If too much water has cooked away, add a bit, and bring to a boil.

Place the *strudels* plus the dumplings, if you wish to add a few, on top of the potatoes. If you are just making dumplings, the recipe remains the same. Sprinkle pepper on top of the *strudel* and the dumplings. Cover the pot tightly so steam cannot escape. Wrap a wet cloth around the cover as this will help to seal it. Once the cover is on you cannot open it until the cooking is finished.

The *strudels* should cook for 25 to 30 minutes. Start them on high to get them boiling and then change the temperature to medium for 1/2 hour. Listen carefully for a frying noise; they should fry for the last 10 minutes. When you hear the frying sound coming from the kettle, your dinner is ready.

Place the *strudels* and/or *schupfnudel* `dumplings' on a platter. Now you must carefully scrape the potatoes from the bottom of the pan. They will be very crisp on the bottom and moist on the top. The dinner is eaten with stewed beef and fresh cucumber salad (see recipes).

This delicious dinner is a special dish of the Germans living in the Dakotas. It was everyone's favorite.

Left-overs. Cut up the left-over *strudels* or dumplings and, with about 3 tablespoons of cooking oil, fry them along with the left-over potatoes in a pan. Fry only a short time. If desired, add, at the end, 2 beaten eggs. Stir, serve. Delicious.

Beginning cooks may want to learn to make the *schupfnudlen* `dumplings', first and try the more difficult *strudel* after they have gained experience working with the dough. Learning the timing and proper cooking are a matter of experience.

Schlitz Kiechla. Beat 2 eggs well; then add 1/2 cup sugar and beat well again. Add 3/4 cup of cream, 1/4 teaspoon vanilla (optional) and 2 teaspoons baking powder sifted with 1 1/2 cups flour. Add enough flour to make a soft dough.

Roll the dough to 1/4 inch thickness and cut it into squares. Cut 3 slits diagonally in the center of each dough square. Two corners of the square are then pulled through each of the outside 2 slits. This was a special dish served on *Fasenacht* `Shrove Tuesday', and the design may have some symbolism.

Fry in deep fat until brown.

Serve the *schlitz kiechla* with cooked prunes. Add a good hot potato salad and it is a complete meal.

Cooked prunes. Boil 1 small package or less of dried prunes in about 2 cups water with 1/2 cup sugar and 1/4 teaspoon cinnamon until they are soft. There will be about 1/2 cup prune juice left at the end of the cooking time if the proportions and cooking are right.

The *kiechla* are dunked in the juice or eaten plain with the cooked prunes as an accompaniment.

Kiechla. Make small balls of dough from the bread dough which can be either fresh or frozen and thawed. Let the balls of dough rest for about 10 minutes. Stretch the balls into what looks like a large pancake. It will be thinner in the middle and thicker on the outside. Heat 1/2 cup oil to smoking. Stretch the dough a second time and put into the hot fat. Fry on both sides until browned. Be careful and work quickly as they burn easily. Serve with syrup or jelly. Delicious.

Fleisch Kiechla. These are pockets of dough filled with a meat mixture. Make the dough using the following ingredients:
3 cups flour
1 tablespoon sugar
1 teaspoon salt
2 eggs
1/4 cup sour cream
1/2 cup milk.

Be careful to make the dough so it is not sticky. Roll it out as thinly as possible (1/8 inch) on a floured board. With a sharp knife cut 6 inch squares. These dough squares are then filled with a meat mixture. The ingredients are:
3/4 lb. ground beef
1/4 lb. ground pork
1 teaspoon salt
1/2 teaspoon pepper
1 egg
1 medium onion finely chopped

Mix well and add 1/4 cup water (or more if needed) to make the meat mixture soft and pliable.

Put 1 small ball of the meat mixture on each dough square. Fold the dough over the top of the meat and pinch down the edges to seal the pocket. Fry the *fleisch kiechla* in deep fat at 375 degrees, turning constantly. They are done in about 10 minutes, or when they turn golden brown.

Käse Knepfla. *Käse knepfla* are not a typical German dish. It a special dish of the Dakota Germans from the Black Sea colonies of Russia and could be an adaptation of a famous Ukrainian dish called *varenyky*.

Use the following ingredients to make a stiff dough:
2 cups flour
1/2 teaspoon salt
4 egg whites
a few drops of water

Work the dough well. Add more flour if needed. Make 4 loaves and let the dough rest for 10 minutes. Roll the dough out thinly. When all 4 loaves have been rolled out, cut the sheets. Each rolled out sheet of dough should be cut twice lengthwise and twice cross-wise, thus yielding 9 separate pieces of dough. With 4 sheets you should have 36 separate pieces of dough. The rolled out sheets of dough should be turned over before cutting. Thus the damp side of the dough is on top. Divide the cheese filling (see below) equally on each small piece of dough and then press one end of the dough over the top, making a triangle of dough with the cheese filling inside. The dough will stick since the damp side is on the top. Use your fingernails lightly if you need more pressure to seal the dough tightly so that none of the cheese filling can escape during cooking. You now have 36 small cheese-filled dough triangles ready for cooking.

Cheese filling.
2 cups dry cottage cheese (see recipe for making cottage cheese)
1/4 teaspoon flour
1 teaspoon salt
1/2 teaspoon sugar
2 teaspoons diced onions
1-1/2 teaspoons diced fresh parsley
1/2 teaspoon diced fresh chives (optional)
a dash of cinnamon (optional)
4 egg yolks left over from making the dough

Mix well. Add more egg yolk if needed so that the cottage cheese is moist. Put a heaping teaspoon of cheese mixture on each piece of dough.

Bring 3 quarts water with 1 tablespoon salt to a boil. Gently put the *käse knepfla* into the water. Bring the water to a boil again so that the *käse knepfla* rise to the top, and stir so the water subsides. Then bring the water to a boil a second time, so that the *käse knepfla* again rise to the top. Stir gently so that the water subsides. Now repeat this procedure for a third time, letting the water boil and the *käse knepfla* rise to the top. Stir gently until the water subsides. It is very important to work carefully so that the *käse knepfla* do not break apart.

Drain the *käse knepfla* carefully, saving the water they were boiled in. This part of the cooking process takes approximately 10 minutes.

Heat 1/2 cup oil in a frying pan. When hot, add the drained *käse knepfla* and fry them quickly. Turn only once while frying. The frying should only last 5 minutes, including both sides. Serve while hot.

This becomes a complete and delicious dinner eaten with stewed beef or chicken and either fresh garden leaf lettuce salad with cream or cucumbers in cream, if lettuce is out of season (see recipes).

Some people like to use the water left from boiling the *käse knepfla* as a soup. The soup is put in individual soup dishes and the fried cheese-filled dough triangles, are added by each individual as desired. This soup is only meant as a small appetizer and not as the main dish.

Leftovers. Fry the leftover *käse knepfla* in a little cooking oil and add beaten eggs to the top. Stir and serve.

Making cottage cheese. Take 1 gallon of fresh cow's milk. Strain through a cloth to remove any hair or particles. Strain directly into a large kettle and cool. Set in the refrigerator for 24 hours. Then carefully skim the cream off the top and let the milk stand in the kitchen in a warm place until it becomes thick and sour, and water appears on the top. This will take 2 to 3 days, depending on the temperature. The heavy thick cream can be used for many recipes or eaten plain. It is, of course, not pasteurized and must be kept in a cool place.

Place the kettle of milk on low heat and heat for about 1 hour. Carefully stir from the bottom to the top so as to bring the bottom milk to the top. Check the temperature of the milk by placing your hand into it. When it becomes hot, but not uncomfortable to your hand, it must be finished. Start checking with your hand after the first half hour to be sure the milk is not becoming too hot too soon. It should first be hot after one hour; that test, plus the fact that the water will be on top when it is finished, will tell you that it has finished heating.

Pour into a colander and let the cottage cheese set and drain for 3 to 4 hours. This makes a delicious cottage cheese. If you have made more than you can use, it can be frozen.

You can eat the cottage cheese as it is, or you can cook with it. (See the *käse knepfla* recipe, and the *kuchen* recipe.)

The following is a favorite recipe for the fresh cottage cheese; it is served with homemade sausage and boiled potatoes.

Approximately 2 cups cottage cheese
1 teaspoon of sugar
1/8 teaspoon of cinnamon
1/2 teaspoon of salt
1/2 cup of heavy sweet cream
a bit of diced onion (optional)

Mix the cheese and ingredients together and top with lightly sprinkled fresh black pepper.

Spätzle. Combine the following ingredients:
1-1/2 cups flour
2 eggs
1 teaspoon salt
enough water or milk to make a stiff dough

Mix and knead the dough until smooth. Divide into 4 or more oblong rolls which are then rolled slightly to about 1/4 inch or so in thickness. Cut the dough into bits with a scissors. Cut onto a dry dish towel so they lie separately and do not stick together. Bring 2 quarts water to a boil, adding 1 tablespoon salt. Put the *spätzle* in the water and bring them to a boil. Stir and bring to second boil, stir and again bring to a third boil. This takes about 5 minutes. Drain. Put melted butter on the *spätzle* and serve.

Noodles and raisins. This was the favorite dish for meatless religious holidays. It was usually served on Good Friday.

Wash 1 cup raisins. Place the raisins in a sauce pan adding 2 cups water and 2 tablespoons sugar and some cinnamon. Simmer until the raisins are soft and there is only 1/4 cup water left in the saucepan.

Bring 3 quarts water with 1 tablespoon salt to a boil. Cook noodles until soft. Drain. Heat about 4 tablespoons oil in a pan and add 1/2 cup of uncooked noodles. Brown them and pour them over the noodles that were boiled and drained.

Serve the noodles and the warm raisins in their juice.

Homemade noodles are used by the Dakota German housewife, but any narrow or medium egg noodles may be used.

Pumpkin Blagende. The ingredients for making the dough are:
2 cups flour sifted together with 2 teaspoons baking powder
1/4 cup sugar
1 teaspoon salt
2 eggs
1/2 cup sweet cream (or more)

Make a soft dough. Add a bit more cream if necessary. Divide into two and roll out, but not too thinly. Cut the two rolled out sheets of dough into fourths. You will now be able to make 8 *blagende*.

Another, newer and more popular version of *blagende* dough consists of:
2 cups of flour sifted
1 teaspoon salt
1/2 cup Crisco (or more)

Mix until crumbly. Then add 3 to 4 tablespoons water to make a pie-crust type dough. Divide into three parts. Roll out each thinly; cut each into four. You will now have 12 squares of *blagende* dough.

Put 1 tablespoon of pumpkin mixture on each fourth of dough. Fold one side of the dough over the top and seal the edges. Gently use your fingernails if necessary. Place the 8 *blagende* on a greased cookie sheet and bake at 400 degrees until they are light brown. This will take about 15-20 minutes. Cool for a few minutes and serve. Homemade sausage or ham are served with the *blagende*.

Pumpkin filling. Cut up 1 small to medium size pumpkin. This is done by cutting the pumpkin in half and then into slices. Take the outer shell off and clean the pumpkin of seeds etc. from the inner part of the slice. Make small diced squares. Put 1/2 cup cooking oil and 1 small finely diced onion in a pan. Brown the onion lightly; add the pumpkin. Fry on low heat with a cover on top. Stir occasionally. Cook for one hour or more until the pumpkin is soft and any liquid has cooked away. When the pumpkin softens, add the following ingredients. They are measured for about 2 quarts of diced pumpkin. They should cook with the pumpkin for a half hour.
1 teaspoon salt
1/4 teaspoon black pepper
1/4 teaspoon cinnamon

2 teaspoons sugar
More sugar can be added; this makes the *blagende* sweet.

Apple Blagende. Make the same dough as for the pumpkin *blagende*. Pumpkin and apple *blagende* are usually made at the same time. The apple *blagende* is more like a dessert.

Roll out the dough and cut into pieces. Dice 2 apples. Put some of the diced apple on each piece of dough. Top the apples with 1/4 teasooon flour and 1 teaspoon sugar, and sprinkle with cinnamon.

Put a heaping tablespoon of apple filling on each piece of dough. Fold the dough over and seal the filling inside.

Place the apple *blagende* on a greased cookie sheet and bake for 10 or 15 minutes at 400 degrees until lightly brown. Cool slightly and serve.

Ham-potato Blagende. Make the same dough as for the pumpkin *blagende*. Roll out the dough and cut into quarters.

Mix diced potatoes, diced ham, diced onion, salt and pepper. Use whatever proportions you wish. Place the filling on the dough, fold over the top and seal carefully.

Bake in a 300 degree oven until browned. Brush top of dough with cream after removing from oven. Serve.

Knepfla. *Knepfla* are a very popular Dakota German dish. They are similar to German *spätzle* but are made without egg. *Knepfla* can be an accompaniment to many different dishes but are especially good and popular with sauerkraut.

Make a dough with the following ingredients:
2 cups flour
1/2 teaspoon baking powder
1 teaspoon salt
a bit of water, enough to make a stiff dough

Work the dough well. Make about 6 balls of dough. Roll out each ball lightly, leaving it 1/4 inch or more thick. Cut into small pieces of dough with a scissors. They should be about the size of a thumbnail.

Cut the dough onto a dry dish towel so the pieces will not stick together. Bring about 3 quarts water to a boil; add 1 tablespoon salt. Add the *knepfla* and bring the water to a boil so the *knepfla* rise to the top; stir, then let the water come to a second boil, bringing the *knepfla* to the top again. Stir, and let the water come to a boil a third time with the *knepfla* rising to the top. This should all take about 5 minutes. Drain the *knepfla* and set aside, keeping them warm.

Heat 1/4 cup or less of oil. When hot, fry about 2 slices of bread (quartered), in the hot fat. Pour the hot fat and the fried bread over the *knepfla* and serve hot.

A variation on Knepfla. Boil 2 medium size potatoes (peeled and cut-up) in 3 quarts water with 1 tablespoon salt for 1 hour.

Add the *knepfla* and bring them to a boil three times as described previously, letting the *knepfla* rise to the top three times. Strain.

Heat 1/4 cup cooking oil in a pan, add the *knepfla* and fry them quickly, turning them over to fry on each side. Serve.

If desired, add 2 or 3 beaten eggs to the fried *knepfla*, stirring them in quickly.

Fried *knepfla* were served with stewed meat and gravy, and home canned beets.

OTHER MAIN DISHES

Cooking a sauerkraut dinner. Drain the water out of the sauerkraut (1 pound) and put it into a large roaster with a cover. Add a medium onion cut up and 3 cups of water. The meat to be used can vary. You can buy smoked meat like ham hocks, smoked ham or a small picnic ham, a chunk of unsliced bacon, plain or smoked spareribs. Any of these, except for the unsmoked spareribs, are then boiled in water for 10 minutes. Remove and place on the sauerkraut. You can use plain spareribs or any other poorer cut of pork. Cut these into serving pieces and fry lightly to brown on both sides. Place on top of the sauerkraut. Using different kinds of meat makes a real taste treat, but one kind is sufficient and was more apt to be the case years ago.

Cover the roaster. Place in the oven and bake at moderate heat for at least 3 hours. You can stir once or twice and add some water if it seems dry. If it is dry you should also turn back the oven heat. Depending on your sauerkraut, you may also need to add salt. The pioneers cooked this dish on top of the cook stove.

Sauerkraut dinner is served with mashed potatoes or *knepfla* (see *knepfla* recipe).

Sauerkraut is especially good warmed over and enough was usually made to last for a second meal. It was ideal for meals which had to be prepared the day before a Sunday or holiday when people were not supposed to work in the kitchen. The leftover sauerkraut should be reheated in a slow oven.

Sauerkraut in the crock. You need a cabbage shredder and a crock.

Shred the cabbage into a large bowl which fits under the cabbage shredder. To about 2 gallons of cabbage add 1/4 cup salt and a dash of cayenne pepper (no more than 1/8 teaspoonful). Mix well by hand and place in the crock. Press down with anything heavy enough to mash the sauerkraut, so that water rises to the top and stays. Keep adding cabbage and pressing it down so liquid covers the top. When you feel you have enough, place a heavy object equal in weight to a gallon of water on top to hold the cabbage down. Ideal for this purpose is a round piece of wood that fits the crock size and is held in place by a rock. (Remember that cabbage will take on the flavor of the object used if it is metal etc.) Let the crock sit in a cool place, not cold, not warm, for 3 days. At this point you can put the cabbage in quart jars. Seal the lids and keep the jars in your cellar or in the refrigerator. (The latter is the more modern way of storing the sauerkraut as not many people have good cellars anymore. The jars could run over a bit at first.) If you want to leave the sauerkraut in the crock, as the pioneers did, then set it in a cold cellar now and leave it for a week or two before using. It will keep all winter.

The German pioneers had special size crocks for each different item they preserved in this way. Each crock had its own wooden cover cut to fit into it and its own rock to hold the cover down. They were always used for the same thing each year. At the end of winter the crocks, the wooden covers and the rocks were carefully washed and readied for the fall, when they would be refilled.

Halupsy. *Holubtsi* was the Russian word for this popular Eastern European dish which has many versions. It consists of a meat and rice mixture rolled in cabbage leaves. The following is a basic *halupsy* recipe using ground beef as the meat. The pioneers did not have ground beef in their *halupsy*. They used smoked sausage taken out of the casings. Today these homemade sausages are a special treat, and the ground beef has replaced them as the meat ingredient.

Here is a modern recipe, but using the same older methods.

Use a medium size light-weight head of cabbage with loose leaves and not a heavy tight-leafed head. This makes it easy to separate all the leaves. Separate the cabbage leaves and boil them in 1-3/4 cups water with 1/4 cup white vinegar for at least 10 minutes or until the leaves change color.

Wash 1/2 cup rice once in cold water; then wash it twice in hot water. Cook the rice with 1 cup water and 1/8 teaspoon salt until the water is gone. This takes about 15 minutes and is done with the rice uncovered. The rice will be soft and moist.

Mix the moist rice with 1 pound ground beef, 1 medium onion diced, 1 teaspoon salt, pepper, dash of garlic salt, and 2 tablespoons tomato soup. Save the rest of the can of tomato soup for later. Put a small amount of this mixture in each cabbage leaf and roll the leaf around it. No need to tie it as it will stick together.

Place the cabbage rolls in a casserole with 1/2 cup bacon fat or cooking oil. Put in 1/4 bay leaf and cover. Place the casserole in a 350 degree oven and bake for 1/2 hour. Turn the oven back to 325 degrees for 1 more hour of baking. Now taste and add salt if needed. Add the rest of the can of tomato soup spreading it across the top of the cabbage. Bake one-half hour at 300 degrees.

These *halupsy* are delicious as reheated leftovers.

If you like green peppers, you can use the same mixture of meat and rice and spices as for the *halupsy*. Cut the tops from the green peppers and remove all the seeds. Fill with meat mixture and put in a covered casserole with a little bacon fat or cook along side the *halupsy*. Add tomato soup or tomato sauce one-half hour before serving.

Medium sized potatoes can also be baked in the same oven. Put them in for the last 1 1/2 hours of baking. This is the complete meal.

Old fashioned Halupsy. Use a medium size light-weight head of cabbage with loose leaves. Separate all the leaves and boil the leaves in 1-3/4 cups water and 1/4 cup white vinegar until they change color (approximately 10 minutes).

Wash 1/2 cup rice once in cold water; then wash it twice in hot water. Cook the rice uncovered with 1 cup water and 1/8 teaspoon salt until the water is gone. The rice will be moist. This takes about 15 minutes.

Dice pieces of fresh ham. Also dice pieces of slab bacon. You can use the meat in whatever proportion you prefer. Mix about 2 cups of ham and bacon with 1 medium onion diced, 1/2 cup cooked rice, 1 teaspoon salt, pepper. Place a small amount of the mixture in a cabbage leaf and roll the leaf around it. Place the cabbage rolls in a casserole with 1/4 cup bacon fat. Add 1/4 bay leaf and cover. Bake it beginning at 350 degrees for 1/2 hour and then at 325 to 300 degrees for 2 more hours. You do not need a lot of bacon grease in the casserole because the ham and bacon produce grease as they cook.

Serve with potatoes, either boiled or baked.

Lazy Halupsy. *Faule halupsy* `Lazy *halupsy*' were a lot easier to make than the regular *halupsy*. This was eaten as a one-dish meal.

Put 1/3 cup grease in the bottom of a roasting pan. Put in 2 cups sauerkraut which must be fresh from the barrel. The sauerkraut should cover the bottom of the pan.

Wash 1/2 cup rice once in cold water; then wash it twice in hot water. Cook the rice uncovered with 1 cup water and 1/8 teaspoon salt until the water is gone This takes about 10-15 minutes. The rice will be moist.

Spread this rice over the top of the sauerkraut.

Dice two cups of ham. You can include bacon, if you wish. Put the ham on top of the rice.

Spread two cups of sauerkraut on top of the ham. Dice 1 medium onion and place that on top of the sauerkraut.

Bake covered at 350 degrees for 1 hour and then at 300 degrees for another hour.

The pioneers put the Lazy *halupsy* into a casserole and cooked it slowly for 2-1/2 to 3 hours on top of the cookstove.

Stewed meat. This was the common method of meat preparation used by the pioneer women.

Cut up the desired amount of meat. The pieces should be stew meat size. Put 1/2 cup cooking oil into a kettle and fry the meat until it is browned on all sides. Add 2 medium onions chopped, 1 teaspoon salt and 1/2 teaspoon pepper to about 2 pounds of meat. Fry until the onions are browned. Add 1 cup water, cover, and cook at reduced heat for about 2 hours. More water can be added if needed.

Beef prepared this way is still very popular and is often served with the *strudel* and *schupfnudel* and with the *käse knepfla*.

Roast chicken. Rinse the chicken in cold water to freshen it and then dry it. Stuff it with the dressing described in the dressing recipe. Put cooking oil in a roasting pan with a cover. Place the chicken in the roaster and roast at 400 degrees for half an hour. Salt and pepper the chicken and add an onion. Turn the temperature to 350 degrees and roast for an hour.

At this point you can add quartered potatoes and carrots. Whether you add them or not, the chicken is then cooked for another hour at 300 degrees. The chicken, dressing, carrots, and potatoes are a complete meal. Salt and pepper the vegetables when adding them to the roaster.

Fried chicken with gravy. Dip pieces of chicken in flour with salt and pepper. Heat cooking oil and brown the chicken pieces. Add a little onion and a little water. Cover and cook for 1 hour, or more.

This makes very good chicken with gravy. Pour off any fat in the pan. Add water saved from cooking potatoes for mashed potatoes. Bring to a boil scraping the bits into the gravy. Mix either 2 teaspoons flour with 1/4 cup water or 2 teaspoons corn starch with 1/4 cup water. Stir while pouring into the gravy to thicken it. Serve.

Mashed potatoes are served with this chicken. Save the salted potato water to make the gravy.

Roast goose. This is a delicious meal which serves a large group of people because goose is very rich and filling. Goose was a popular Christmas dish.

Rub the goose with oil, put in a covered roasting pan breast-side up, and roast at 400 degrees for 1 hour. Remove most of the excess fat in the pan and save it for further use. If the goose is to be stuffed, it is done at this time (see Dressing recipe). Before stuffing, empty the goose cavity of any liquid.

Return the goose to the oven, breast-side down, with salt and pepper on both sides. Turn the temperature down to 350 degrees, and roast for 1 hour. Salt and pepper the goose again, and turn it back to breast-side up.

Roast for 2 hours at 300 degrees. The total cooking time is 4 hours. During the last 2 hours add 1/4 cup red wine and 1 medium size cut-up onion. Baste frequently, adding salt occasionaly. Save all goose fat to use in cooking.

Dressing. Grind or simply cut up 3 medium onions, 1 stalk of celery, the goose liver and heart. Brown in cooking oil. Break a half loaf of bread into small pieces and sprinkle with salt. Add the onions, celery, liver, and heart plus 2 eggs. Mix. Add milk to make the dressing moist.

Chicken and duck are stuffed with dressing before they begin to cook. Goose should be roasted for a time before stuffing. Goose is stuffed after the first hour or the dressing becomes a bit greasy.

Turkey. Turkey was roasted the same way as goose. Turkey, being a dry meat, needs a lot more basting.

Roast duck. Roast duck was a very popular dish. Most farmers raised their own ducks and chickens, just as they had done in Russia. Since roast goose was a treat because geese were difficult and expensive to raise, ducks were cooked more frequently and were more common.

Rinse the duck in cold water to freshen it; then dry it. Stuff with dressing. If you choose to cook the duck without dressing, simply put salt, an onion, and 2 slices of bread in the cavity. Discard after cooking.

Place the duck in a covered roasting pan breast-side up. Pour 1/8th cup cooking oil over the duck. Cover and roast at 400 degrees for 1/2 hour. (If the duck was frozen, remove any liquid which may have cooked out of it at this point.) Salt and pepper the duck on both sides, place it breast-side down, cover, and roast for 1 hour at 350 degrees. Remove any fat or liquid except for about 1 cup. Salt and pepper on both sides again, and turn the duck breast-side up. Add 1 cut-up medium size onion to the roasting pan, and pour 1/4 cup of wine over the duck. Cover and roast 1-1/2 more hours at 300 degrees. Baste the duck several times during this last 1-1/2 hour period. Total cooking time is 3 hours.

Good gravy. Making a good gravy is easy. Pour off all of the fat left in the cooking or roasting pan. Add two cups water, or less, saved from the water used to boil potatoes for mashed potatoes or any other peeled potato. Stir the water in the pan, loosening all the bits from the sides and bottom. Bring to a boil and add a thickener very slowly. Stir well and remove from the heat before the gravy becomes too thick.

To make a thickener mix 2 teaspoons flour with 1/4 cup water or 2 teaspoons corn starch with 1/4 cup water.

Frying game birds. Wild duck, prairie chicken, partridge, and pheasant were cooked in the following simple way by the pioneers. They did not do oven-roasting. For a more modern preparation, see the recipe for Wild duck.

Cut the bird into pieces and dip the pieces into flour with salt and pepper. Fry in a generous amount of oil, browning the meat slowly on all sides. Add 1 medium onion chopped and about 1/2 cup water, bringing the water to a boil. Add salt and pepper to taste. Cover and cook on low to medium heat for 3 hours or until tender. Add more water after the first hour, if needed.

Wild duck. This is a recipe developed for oven-roasting wild duck.

The pioneers only fried and/or braised meat.

Clean the duck, removing any buckshot. Rub the cavity and outside of the duck with lemon juice and salt. Put inside the cavity of each duck 2 slices of bread, 1/4 of an apple, and 1 small whole onion. Salt and pepper the bird and place it in a covered roasting pan. If possible, use fat saved from roasting a goose or domestic duck and pour it over the wild duck, breast-side up. If this fat is not available, then use olive oil or cooking oil. Wild duck is very dry.

Roast covered at 400 degrees for an hour. If you plan to put dressing inside the duck, remove the bread, apple, and onion after the first hour and replace it with the dressing. Salt and pepper the bird again. Roast at 325 degrees for another hour. Salt and pepper the bird. Add 1/2 cup red wine and 1 small onion. Roast at 300 degrees for another hour or until done. Be sure to baste frequently during the last hour. Be careful or it will over-cook.

Wild ducks were not hung, they were used fresh or were cleaned when fresh, and are frozen for later use.

VEGETABLES AND SIDE DISHES

Fried potatoes. Peel and slice potatoes thinly. Dice a small onion and fry it in oil until brown. Add potatoes, salt and pepper, and fry turning occasionlly. Fry for 30 minutes and serve. If you don't like crisp potatoes, you can cover them for the last 10 minutes.

Baked potato slices. Peel and slice thinly 4 to 5 medium potatoes. Put the potatoes into a flat baking dish. Add salt and pepper, 2 tablespoons butter, 1/4 to 1/2 cup cream, and a small onion diced. Cover with foil and bake in a 400-degree oven for 1/2 hour. Uncover and bake for another 1/2 hour at 350 degrees or until tender. Serve.

Another old version of baked potatoes is to dice 3 or 4 medium potatoes, add 1/2 cup butter, salt and peper, and then bake uncovered in a baking dish for 1 hour at 375 degrees or less. Serve.

Hot potato salad. Boil about 10 potatoes with their jackets on. Peel and slice them. Fry lots of onions (at least 2 medium sized onions) in a little lard. Add 2 cups water and 1/4 cup vinegar plus 2 teaspoons sugar and 1 teaspoon salt. Bring this to a boil and boil for 5 minutes. Add the sliced potatoes to the mixture and simmer slowly for about 1/2 hour. Serve hot.

Cold potato salad. Boil desired amount of potatoes with jackets on. (You can also use left-overs from the day before.) Peel and slice. Sprinkle with salt and a diced small onion.

In a separate glass mix 1/2 cup mayonnaise, 1/2 teaspoon prepared mustard and 3/4 cup cream. Add this to the potato slices and toss. Dice

2 hard-boiled eggs, and mix them in too. Slice 2 hard-boiled eggs and decorate the top of the potato salad. Salt and pepper the top of the eggs. Serve cold with cold sausage.

Potatoes were served in endless variations, the most popular being mashed potatoes and potatoes boiled in water, with the jackets on, or peeled. Plenty of salt was usually added to the water.

Malotz. A wonderful old-fashioned dish which uses left-over mashed potatoes is still popular.

Mix mashed potatoes with a little salt and enough flour to make tiny crumbles of dough-like particles. It takes about 1 cup of mashed potatoes to 1/4 cup flour and 1/4 teaspoon salt.

Heat 1/4 cup oil and add the *malotz* so it is spread out and covers the bottom of the pan. Cover and fry until the bottom of the *malotz* is browned—about 2 to 3 minutes. Uncover and stir constantly so all the crumbs are fried and browned. Serve.

This is usually served at the evening meal with cold sausage. A real treat for the children.

Milk rice. Rice cooked in milk was a whole noon lunch.

Bring to a boil 1 quart milk with 1/2 teaspoon salt added. Then add 1/2 cup rice which has been washed once in cold water and then twice in hot water, and 2 tablespoons sugar (depending on sweetness desired, you can add more or less sugar). Cook until thick. This takes 15 to 20 minutes. If desired, you can add 1/2 cup of thoroughly rinsed raisins at the same time you add the sugar. Add a touch of cinnamon to the finished rice and serve.

Baked rice. Use 1/2 cup white rice. Wash once in cold water and then twice with hot water.

Cook the rice in about 1 cup water with 1/4 teaspoon salt until all the water is gone. It is cooked uncovered and takes about 20 minutes. Cook the rice only until the water is gone and not until it is dry.

Add to the cooked rice:
1 egg—not beaten
4 teaspoons sugar
1/2 cup raisins—wash first with hot water
1/2 cup sweet cream

Put the mixture in a casserole. Sprinkle the top with cinnamon. Bake the rice at 400 degrees for 1 hour. It should be covered for the first 3/4 hour and uncovered for the last 15 minutes.

Fried green peppers. Cut up whole green bell peppers into slices. Heat 1/4 cup oil and fry the green peppers. After 10 minutes, add 1 large (or more) diced onion, salt and pepper. Fry 15 minutes more and serve.

A delicious variation is to add 2 or 3 eggs on top of the peppers and onion and mix them in frying until the eggs are done.

This was a treat eaten with homemade fresh bread and fresh radishes from the garden. It was considered a whole meal.

Fried carrots. Clean the carrots and slice them thinly. Dice a small onion and fry in oil or butter or both. Add the carrots; salt and pepper them. Turn occasionally, frying the carrots slowly for about 30 minutes.

Cucumber salad. Slice 3 or 4 medium size cucumbers. Add 1 small diced onion and salt. Let set for about 2 hours; squeeze all the liquid out of the cucumbers. Be sure to have put enough salt on the cucumbers.

Place the cucumbers which have been squeezed along with the onion in a bowl. Add 1/2 cup water to the bowl and then 1 tablespoon of white vinegar. Add 1 cup of sweet cream and stir.

This cucumber salad is more like a cold soup. It is very delicious in summer and is often served with Käse Knepfla, Strudel, or stewed meat. Ice cubes can be put in the cucumber salad to make it even more refreshing.

Lettuce salad. A similar salad is also made with the fresh green garden lettuce which grows in the form of small leaves. Wash the leaves in cold water and drain. Cut up about 1/4 cup fresh garden chives. Add the chopped chives and 1/2 to 1 teaspoon salt to the lettuce. Add 1/4 cup water and then 1 tablespoon white vinegar. Add the 1 cup of sweet cream and stir.

Horseradish. Clean the horseradish root with a potato peeler or a sharp knife. All of the brown must come off. Only the white part of the horseradish plant is used.

Grind the white horseradish with a fine grind, then mix it with white distilled vinegar so that all of the horseradish is moist. Put in small jars and close tightly. Store in the refrigerator.

Horseradish is very popular and is eaten with beef or pork. It was always popular eaten with homemade sausages. The plant grows wild on the Dakota prairies.

A simple recipe for making jelly. Wash the fruit thoroughly. Put it in a large kettle, adding enough water to cover the fruit, but not more than that. Cook at least 1 or 2 hours, depending on the fruit. Boil slowly until the fruit is soft and pops open. It is then ready to be put in a strainer. Mash the fruit into the strainer so all the juice runs thru into a bowl and all the pits and skins stay in the strainer. They are then discarded. (They can also be put into cheesecloth and hung to drain a bit more juice.)

Measure the amount of juice you have and use 2 cups juice to 1 cup sugar. Bring the juice and sugar to a boil, watching it so that it does not run over. Turn the heat back to a low boil and cook 1 or 2 hours. Timing depends on the fruit and how long it takes until the liquid stiffens. You can check on the progress by putting a little bit in a dish. If the consistency is at the point that you prefer, the jelly is finished. You can also taste it to see if it has the desired sweetness.

For sour fruit you simply use 1 cup juice to 1 cup sugar. Checking for consistency is very simple. You stop cooking the jelly when it is at the thickness that you like. We prefer it only slightly stiff.

When your jelly is finished cooking you put it into small jars and cover them with a normal cover. No special sealing is necessary. Store the jelly jars in the refrigerator. But if you prefer to keep your jelly for a longer time, e.g. for a year, you must add paraffin wax to the top of the jelly. The directions are on the paraffin wax box. If you have added paraffin wax, you can store the jars in the cellar.

In pioneer days jelly was made from choke cherries, wild cherries, goose berries, rhubarb, green tomatoes, wild plums, and sometimes from wild grapes. In the early years, wild grapes were grown along the Missouri River by the Indians. The family would purchase grapes for making wine, and some jelly.

This recipe is so simple and is very rewarding. It can be used for berries, grapes, or cherries.

Homemade butter. Put heavy sweet cream in a container with a cover or in a jar with a cover. You cannot use the thin pasteurized store cream, it must be farm cream. Shake the container back and forth until the cream turns into butter. The old women used to sit and do this while talking to a friend.

Remove the butter and save the buttermilk for drinking or baking. Place the butter in cold water, rinse off quickly and place in a covered dish and store in a cool place. Today we can refrigerate it. When served, it still has the cold drops of water clinging to it.

This method does not produce a lot of butter; the butter did not keep very well and therefore had to be made quite frequently.

Fill the container only 1/3 to 1/2 full so there is plenty of room for the cream to move back and forth and become butter. Salt can be added to the butter after it has been made.

DESSERTS

Kuchen. Make the dough with:
2 cups milk
1/2 cup butter
1 teaspoon salt
1/2 cup sugar

Put milk in saucepan on low heat and melt the butter in the warm milk. Do not scald. When the butter is melted, add the salt and sugar. Cool to lukewarm. While it is cooling, make the yeast.

2 packages dry yeast

1/4 cup warm water
1/2 teaspoon sugar

Mix the yeast, water, and sugar and let them set for about 5 minutes. Add the yeast to the milk mixture.

3 eggs
3 cups or more of flour

Beat 3 eggs well and then add the milk and yeast mixture. Gradually add the 3 cups of flour (or more if necessary) to make a soft dough. Cover and let it set until it doubles in size—about 1/2 to 3/4 hour. Knead down and let it rise again until double. This should take about 1/2 hour or more.

Divide into 8 loaves. Oil 8 pie plates well with cooking oil. Roll each loaf out to a thick dough and put into a pie plate so it covers the bottom but not the sides. Cover the pie plates with a dish towel and let them rise for 15 to 25 minutes.

Now you are ready to add a fruit or cottage cheese filling which will be topped by a wonderful cream custard.

Kuchen dough. There are many variations of the *kuchen* dough. The following is one well-known old-fashioned version.

Cook 1 small to medium size potato for half an hour in 1-1/2 cups water. Pour the water off and save it. Mash the potato through a strainer. Save the part that is strained and throw out the rest.

Mix the following ingredients together and let set for 5 minutes:

1 package dry yeast
1/4 cup warm water
1/2 teaspoon sugar

Have the following ingredients ready:

3 eggs
1 cup sugar
1 cup milk
1/2 cup lard (or cooking oil, crisco, butter)
1/2 teaspoon salt
1 cup potato water (hot)

Beat the eggs well and add the sugar, salt, milk, and lard. Now add the strained potato and the hot potato water to make a warm batter. Add the yeast mixture.

3 cups flour

Add at least 3 cups flour to your batter. It may be necessary to add another whole cup of flour, until you can make a nice soft dough.

Cover with a cloth and let the dough rise for 1/2 to 3/4 hour until it doubles in size. Knead down and let it rise again until double. This takes about 1/2 to 1 hour. Divide into 9 loaves.

Let the loaves rest while you put oil in 9 pie plates. Roll the loaves out thickly and place in the bottom of the pie plate—do not cover the sides. Cover the plates with a cloth and let rise for another 20 minutes. Now you are ready to add the filling and cream custard.

Kuchen filling. In the summer, use fresh fruit such as peaches, apricots, purple plums, apples, cherries, and even rhubarb which is so plentiful in Dakota.

In the winter, use dried fruit such as prunes or apricots. Cook the dried fruit in 1-1/2 cups water with 1/4 cup sugar and 1/4 teaspoon cinnamon until the fruit is soft.

Homemade cottage cheese also makes a delicious *kuchen* (see recipe for making cottage cheese.)

To use cottage cheese as *kuchen* filling:

Mix 2 teaspoons sugar with 1 cup cottage cheese; then mix into it 1/2 cup of the cream custard (see below). Put on top of the *kuchen* dough, and top it with a teaspoon sugar and a sprinkling of cinnamon.

Fruit filling. The fruit is placed in one layer on the *kuchen* dough and 1 teaspoon sugar is put on the fruit. Put 1/2 cup cream custard on each Kuchen on top of the fruit. Top with another teaspoon of sugar and a sprinkle of cinnamon. For sour fruit, add more sugar. Rhubarb *kuchen* needs lots of sugar.

Cream custard.
1 quart heavy sweet cream
1/2 teaspoon salt
5 eggs
1/2 cup sugar
2 tablespoons flour

Heat the cream with the salt to a boil. Beat the eggs and add the sugar and flour, beating well with a spoon. Add to the boiling cream and cook until thick. Cool.

Bake at 375 degrees for 20 to 30 minutes until brown. This is the same for the different doughs or fillings.

Seven-Day sweet dough. The ingredients are:
3 cups hot water
1 cup shortening
1 tablespoon salt
3/4 cup sugar
2 dry yeast
3 eggs
1/2 teaspoon vanilla
9 cups flour

Soak the yeast in 1/2 cup warm water with a little sugar added. Pour 2-1/2 cups hot water over the shortening until it is melted. Add the sugar and let it stand until it is lukewarm. Then add the beaten eggs. Add the yeast mixture and the vanilla. Now add the flour, and make the dough. Let is rise once and work it down. When it rises again, make *kuchen* rolls. Roll out for *kuchen* and put into greased pie pans. Follow previous recipe for filling and baking.

This is a large amount of dough and need not be used all at once. It can be stored in the refrigerator up to 7 days. But it must be kneaded down once each day. The dough can also be used for rolls, buns, etc.

(Eva Iszler, age 96, has been making this recipe since she was 11 years old.)

Doughnuts. The ingredients are:
4 eggs
1 cup sugar
1 cup milk
1/2 teaspoon vanilla
4 teaspoons baking powder sifted with 2 cups flour

Beat the eggs, add sugar, then add milk and vanilla. Mix well and add the flour and baking powder sifted together. Add more flour, if needed, to make a soft dough. Divide into 3 loaves.

Roll out 1 loaf at a time on a floured board. Dip a glass in flour and cut out doughnuts. Use a sewing thimble dipped in flour to cut out the holes. Deep fry at 375 degrees until brown. Roll in regular sugar while hot and serve.

Apple fritters. The ingredients are:
1-1/2 cups flour
1/4 teaspoon salt
2 teaspoons baking powder
1 egg
2 tablespoons sugar
2/3 cup milk
1 large apple diced

Sift together the flour, salt, and baking powder. Beat the egg, adding 2 tablespoons sugar and the milk. Add the flour, then the apple.

Heat a deep-fryer to 375-400 degrees. Drop the batter by the teaspoon full into the hot fat. Fry about 2-3 minutes, turning once until they are brown on both sides. Serve hot.

Sweet pancakes. The ingredients are:
2 eggs
2 teaspoons sugar
1/4 teaspoon salt
1/2 cup milk
1 cup flour
2 teaspoons baking powder

Beat the eggs and add the sugar, salt, and milk. Sift the flour and baking powder together and add to the batter.

Heat oil in a pan until smoking and fry the pancakes.

Stirum. The ingredients are:

3 eggs
1 cup milk
salt to taste
1 teaspoon baking powder
Use enough flour to make a pancake batter.

Mix into a batter. Fry, stirring until the batter is fried and in small marble-size pieces. You must stir and crumble constantly. When browned, serve. This is good with a sweet jelly.

Marble cake. The ingredients are:
1 egg beaten
1 cup sugar
1 cup cream
2 cups flour sifted with
2 teaspoons baking powder and 2 tablespoons cocoa
1 teaspoon vanilla

Beat the egg, adding the sugar and then the cream. Sift the flour, baking powder and cocoa together. Add the vanilla. Place in a greased loaf pan and bake at 350 degrees for about 25 to 30 minutes. Test with a toothpick to see if it is dry and finished.

Corn meal cake. The ingredients are:
1-1/2 cups milk
1 cup corn meal
1 egg beaten
2 tablespoons sugar
1/4 teaspoon salt
1 cup flour
1 teaspoon baking powder
1/4 cup sweet cream

Boil 1-1/2 cups milk and pour onto 1 cup corn meal and let set. Beat 1 egg and add 2 tablespoons sugar. Sift the salt, flour, and baking powder, and add. Now add the corn meal and milk. Add the sweet cream.

Bake in a greased oblong cake pan for 30 minutes at 350 degrees.

Corn meal was also used at breakfast. Bring 1 cup milk and 1/4 teaspoon salt to boil and add 2 tablespoons corn meal. Cook until thick and serve.

Pie crust. The ingredients are:
1 1/2 cups flour sifted
1 teaspoon salt
1/2 cup shortening

Mix until crumbly. Add 4 tablespoons water and make a firm dough. Let the dough rest for 1/2 hour in a cold place. This makes it easier to roll out. This should make 2 nine-inch diameter pie crusts.

For recipes calling for prebaked pie crust, bake at 425 degrees for about 10-12 minutes or until light brown.

Rhubarb pie. The rhubarb plant grew profusely in Dakota. No garden was without it. It was called *garte pie* `garden pie' and was used to make jelly, wine, pie, and *kuchen*. Children loved to eat it plain with lots of sugar, and mothers had to be careful they did not eat all the best stalks. The plant keeps growing and gets bigger year by year.

Put a tablespoon of flour on a pie crust. Fill the pie crust until even with the top, with diced rhubarb. Put at least 1 cup of sugar plus 2 tablespoons flour on the rhubarb. Place a top crust on the pie and cut slits. Bake at 400 degrees for the first 15 minutes and 350 degrees for about 30 more minutes or until brown.

There are of course, newer versions of the popular rhubarb pie. One of the favorites: Mix 2 tablespoons flour, 1 cup sugar (more if desired), 2 egg yolks, 1/2 cup cream, 4 cups diced rhubarb, and cook until thick, about 15-20 minutes. Pour into a baked pie crust and cover with meringue (see recipe). Bake at 325 degrees for 8-10 minutes or until the meringue browns.

Apple pie. Apple pie was made the same way, except that you only use 3/4 cup sugar and you add 1/2 teaspoon cinammon.

Chocolate pie. A delicious chocolate dessert still very popular. The ingredients are:
1-1/2 cups sugar
1/4 cup cornstarch
1/2 cup cocoa
2 cups milk
1 teaspoon vanilla
2 egg yolks
a pinch of salt

Mix together and cook slowly until mixture is thick, about 15-20 minutes. Pour into a baked pie shell and top with meringue (see recipe). Bake at 325 degrees for 8-10 minutes or until the meringue browns.

Lemon pie. Beat 4 egg yolks with 1/2 cup sugar adding the rind and juice of 1 lemon. Cook the mixture in a double boiler until it thickens, stirring constantly, about 15-20 minutes. Let cool. Make a double meringue recipe (see recipe below), and stir 1/2 of the meringue into the mixture. Pour the mixture into a baked pie crust, and put the other half of the meringue on the top of the pie. Bake in a 325 degree oven for 8-10 minutes or until the meringue browns.

Banana pie. This recipe is for two pies. Slice 3 bananas and place in two baked pie crusts. Mix 1-1/2 cups sugar, 1 cup sifted flour, and 1/2 cup cold milk. Then bring 1-1/2 cups milk with a pinch of salt added, to a boil. Add the mixture of cold milk, sugar, and flour to the boiling milk and cook for about 5 minutes or until thick. Beat 3 egg yolks well and then beat them into the mixture. Pour into the two pie crusts on top of the bananas. Top with meringue (see recipe), and bake at 325 degrees for 8-10 minutes or until the meringue browns.

Meringue. Beat the white of 2 eggs with 1/8 teaspoon cream of tarter added, until stiff. Then add 6 teaspoons of sugar and 1/2 teaspoon vanilla and beat a little while longer. This is enough for one pie. When meringue is put on top of a pie, bake in a 325 degree oven for about 8-10 minutes or until the meringue browns.

Molasses cookies. The ingredients for this very old pioneer recipe are:
1 cup lard
1 cup sugar
1 cup milk
1 cup molasses
1 teaspoon soda
1 teaspoon baking powder
1 tablespoon white vinegar
1/4 teaspoon cinnamon (optional)
2 cups flour (add more, if needed, to make a soft dough)

Mix the vinegar and soda into 1/4 cup of the molasses. This bubbles and is added to the batter just before the flour.

Cream the sugar with the lard, add the milk and molasses. Sift the flour with the baking powder. Add the molasses mixed with vinegar and soda. Add the flour—enough to make a soft dough.

Roll the batter out and cut with a cookie cutter. Grease a cookie sheet. Bake at 375 degrees for about 10-15 minutes until brown.

Ammonia cookies. This is a very old and very unusual recipe. It is not very popular now, but is given as a matter of interest in presenting all the old receipes.
Ingredients:
1-1/2 cups sugar
2 cups cream (sweet or sour)
1/2 teaspoon salt
1 teaspoon flavoring (lemon or vanilla)
2 eggs beaten
1 tablespoon melted butter
1 round tablespoon baking ammonia
3-1/2 cups flour or enough to make a soft dough

Combine all the ingredients and make a soft dough. Chill it overnight. Roll it out to be about 1/2 inch thick. Cut it with large cookie cutters. Bake on a greased cookie sheet at 400 degrees for 7 to 8 minutes. When cooled, frost with powder sugar icing. To make this icing, just add a bit of cream to powder sugar.

One mother remembers this to be a very old recipe. She says, `I can still remember when grandma used to buy ammonia for cookies. That stuff was so strong that nobody wanted to work with it. But they were the best cookies. I don't know if you can still buy baking ammonia; but, if you can, I'm sure the old general store in Lehr still has it.'

(Do not confuse baking ammonia with cleaning ammonia.)

Oatmeal cookies. The ingredients are:
1/2 cup lard
1-1/2 cups sugar
1 cup cooked raisins (saving the raisin juice)
2 cups flour
1 teaspoon cinammon
1 teaspoon soda
1 teaspoon salt
2 cups oatmeal
1/2 cup crushed walnuts

Cream together the lard, sugar, and 5 tablespoons of raisin juice. Add the raisins. Sift the 2 cups flour with the cinammon, soda, and salt, and add to the mixture. Add the oatmeal and crushed walnuts. Make small balls from the batter and drop by the teaspoonful on a greased cookie sheet. Bake in a 350 degree oven for about 10 minutes or until done.

Pfeffernuesse. The ingredients are:
2 cups sugar
1/2 cup shortening
1-1/2 cups honey
3 eggs
3/4 cup strong black coffee
7 cups flour or enough to make a soft dough
To 4 of the 7 cups of flour add the following and sift:
1 teaspoon baking powder
1-1/2 teaspoons baking soda
1/2 teaspoon cloves
1/2 teaspoon cinnamon
1/2 teaspoon allspice
1 teaspoon Star anise

Bring the sugar, shortening and honey to a boil. Cool. Add 3 eggs well beaten and 3/4 cup strong black coffee. Sift the 4 cups of flour with the spices and add. Use the last 3 cups of flour only as needed to make a soft dough.

Bake at 375 degrees on a greased cookie sheet. When cool, dampen with 1/2 cup milk. Put 1 cup powder sugar in a bag and shake the dampened cookies until coated.

Chocolate pudding. The ingredients are:
1 cup milk

1-1/2 tablespoons cocoa
1-1/2 tablespoons flour
2 tablespoons sugar

Put all of the ingredients in a sauce pan and cook over medium heat, stirring constantly. Cook for about 20 minutes or until stiff with a pudding consistency.

Homemade ice cream. Beat 5 eggs well with an egg beater. Add 1/4 to 1/2 cup sugar and beat again with a spoon. Add 1 teaspoon of vanilla (also 1/2 teaspoon of mapeline if you prefer more flavor). Add 4 cups of heavy cream. Stir well.

Pour into ice cream container and finish making this delicious ice cream with your old-fashioned ice cream maker.

This ice cream is so simple to make and it is the best.

Hot chocolate topping.
1 cup sugar
1/2 cup cocoa
1 tablespoon butter
1/2 cup milk

Cook on low heat for 2 minutes and serve hot over ice cream.

MAKING WINE AND BEER

Making wine according to pioneer Clara Erlenbusch. One had to have a grape chopper. It was made like a rolling pin with nails all around it. It also had a handle on it so it could be turned like a food chopper. You put that on the barrel and you ground the grapes into the barrel. After this was done, enough water was added just to cover the grapes. You then had to let the mixture set about 5 to 6 days until it started to get foam on top. It had to be stirred once every day. The grapes settled to the bottom and the juice got clear. At this point they took about two gallons of that juice and put sugar into it. How much sugar I don't know but I would say at least one gallon. Bring that to a good boil, then cool it off. If added hot, the wine would get sour. Then the juice and sugar mixture were put back into the grape juice. Next they strained it all into a wine barrel and let it set again. A hose had to be put into the barrels or they would burst. The wine was checked and when the wine looked clear in a glass, it was done.

If a family did not have a grape chopper, they put the grapes in a wash tub and trampled the grapes with their feet. This was lots of fun.

I think we used 2 boxes of grapes to a 30 gallon barrel. The grapes were purchased right from the train. Wild grapes were grown along the Missouri River by the Indians and could be purchased from them.

Home brewed beer. Every Dakota German cellar had its own stock

of homemade beer. Everyone had their own special recipe. Given below is Emily Lippert's recipe which is a basic recipe for making your own beer. The ingredients are:
7 gallons water
7 cups sugar
1 yeast cake
1 can of malt (35 oz.) (extra premier)

Soak the yeast cake in 1/2 cup warm water while mixing the other ingredients. Add the yeast to the ingredients and mix. Pour into a 10 gallon crock. After this point do not mix the ingredients again. Tie a large white dishtowel around the top of the crock, covering it well, and let the crock set in a warm place for 3 days. During this time, beginning with the first day after you've mixed it, you must take the foam and scum off the top of the mixture each day. After three days the liquid should be clear and ready to be bottled.

Put the beer into individual beer bottles; close and seal with a bottle capper.

Years ago people used a hose to get the beer from the crock into the bottles. The hose was put into the crock and the beer started flowing when someone drew on the hose with their mouth. The beer bottles must set in a warm place for two days or they will burst. On the third day, place the bottles in the cellar, or in a cool place. They will be ready to drink in a few days.

Many people throw a handful of raisins into the bottom of the crock when they mix the ingredients. They say it makes the beer stronger.

Even with great care, eventually one or two of the beer bottles will burst. Not to worry; it makes the cellar smell good and gives one a feeling of well being.

PICKLING FRUIT AND VEGETABLES

Pickled whole watermelons. This recipe is for a 30 gallon crock. The watermelons used are whole small round watermelons. Serve the watermelon, cut-up, as an appetizer before the meal. It is delicious.

Put in the bottom of a 30 gallon crock:
Horseradish leaves to cover bottom
Beet leaves to cover them
Dill plant stalks and flowers to cover them

Add the watermelons. They can only be small round whole watermelons. Fill the crock half way and add more dill plus:
2 garlic cloves
4 red pepper pods
1/4 teaspoon Cayenne (can be more)
1 medium onion, cut up
2 green tomatoes
2 teaspoons of whole pickling spices

2 small bell peppers

Add more watermelon, filling the crock. On the top add these following ingredients in the order in which they are listed.

1 medium onion, cut up
4 garlic cloves
2 teaspoons pickling spices
4 red pepper pods (chillies—small, hot, whole red peppers)
1/4 teaspoon Cayenne (can be more)
2 green tomatoes
2 small whole bell peppers
dill stalks and flowers to cover
beet leaves to cover
horseradish leaves to cover

Put a board, cut to fit the top of the crock, on top of the watermelons. If you do not have one, then simply place boards across the top. Place a rock on top of the boards. This must be done before adding the water in order to keep the watermelons in place.

Mix 1 pail of water with 1 heaping cup of canning salt. Mix well and pour into the crock until it is full.

Now they put paraffin wax on top since cellars are usually not cold enough. The paraffin wax seals and protects the watermelon from mould. Let the pickled watermelon set for 4 to 5 weeks in a cool place in your cellar. The longer they set, the more sour they get.

Pickled cucumbers. Buy small pickling cucumbers or grow them in your garden. If the cucumbers seem wilted, put them in cold water for an hour to freshen them.

Mix 1 quart water with 1 heaping tablespoon salt. Mix and let it set. This is enough for 2 quarts of pickles.

Place two dill stalks with flowers in the bottom of a mason jar. Fill your jar with cucumbers, using all sizes of cucumber. Now add the following optional vegetables:

1 small piece of celery
1 small carrot
a piece of green pepper (these vegetables are also good to eat when pickled)

Listed are the ingredients that must be added:

1/4 teaspoon or less of pickling spice
1 chili red pepper, broken in half (another chili red pepper can be added if you prefer very hot pickles)
1 small onion
2 small or 1 large clove garlic, cut in half

Add 2 dill stalks with to the top of the cucumbers and spices.

Pour in the water and salt mixture, filling to the top of the jar. Put on the lids and seal by turning them shut tightly. Shake the jar gently or just turn upside down for a second at least 3 times in the next hour so that the spices and water will mix well.

Keep the jars in the kitchen until the cucumbers change color—at least 2 days. Refrigerate for 2 or more days and serve. If you like your pickles very sour, then they have to set longer. If you open the jar and find them not sour enough, simply reclose the jar and put them into the refrigerator for a few more days.

If you want the pickles to be done quickly, put the jar outside in the sun for a day, and then put them back into the house for 2 days. They are ready to eat. Store in the refrigerator.

The same basic pickle recipe just given can be used for preserving pickles in a crock.

When pickling a larger amount not meant to be eaten until later on in the winter, you only leave the jars in your kitchen for 24 hours and then refrigerate.

Another method for pickling cucumbers which are going to be kept for a longer period of time is to heat the salt water before adding it to the jar. Leave the jars in the kitchen only until the next morning and then refrigerate. Do not set these outside. Pickled cucumbers turn color when they are sour.

All of these recipes are for pickles which have to be kept in the refrigerator until eaten. They can also be kept in a cold root cellar if you have one. Recipes for permanent pickles which do not get refrigerated and can be kept for several years follow.

Most housewives make several different kinds of pickles. The different methods give you pickles to eat at various times and offer a variety of flavors.

Permanent pickles. These pickles are called permanent pickles because they can be kept for a couple of years. They have a sweet sour taste. Put the cucumbers, dill and spices into the pickling jars as described in the basic recipe. Bring the following ingredients to a boil and pour over the cucumbers, filling the jars to the top.

2 cups water
1/4 cup white vinegar
2 tablespoons sugar
2 teaspoons salt

Seal the jars and place them on a rack in a canner with a cover. The jars should be standing in hot water and be steamed (not boiled) on low heat for 1/2 hour or until they change color. Remove. Cool and keep cool.

They can be stored in your cellar or refrigerated.

Aunt Mary's old-fashioned pickles. Put cucumbers, dill, and spices in jars as described in the basic recipe. Cook the following ingredients together, bringing them to a hard boil.

1 quart water
1/2 cup vinegar

2-1/2 tablespoons sugar
1-1/2 tablespoons salt
1/4 teaspoon alum

Cool the mixture and pour over the cucumbers, filling to the top of the jar. Set the jars in water on a rack in a canner with a cover. Cover and steam on low heat until the cucumbers change color. Do not boil. The steaming should take about 25 minutes. Remove the jars and let them cool.

Store the jars in your cellar or refrigerator.

Pickled beans. Use garden fresh yellow wax beans. Wash and pinch off the ends. Place in a pot and add hot water to cover, no salt. Bring to a boil and cook for 1/2 hour or until the beans are soft. Drain the beans and cool them.

Place dill stalks and flowers in the bottom of a quart jar. Fill the jar to half with the beans. Add these spices:

1 whole red pepper pod broken in half (chillies)
1/2 clove garlic
a bit of pickling spice (optional)

Fill the rest of the jar with beans. Add more dill weed to the top.

To 1 quart water add 1 heaping tablespoon plain salt. Mix well and fill the jars to the top. This amount of water will fill 2 quart jars. Seal the jars and let them set in your kitchen for 2 to 3 days. Shake them, or gently turn them upside down, at least twice the first day. When sour, store them in the refrigerator.

Pickled beets. Garden beets freshly dug are washed and cleaned. Place them in a kettle, adding enough water to cover. Boil for 1-1/2 hours. Check by piercing with a fork; they should be soft but firm. Take the beets out of the water and save the liquid. Cool the beets, then peel them.

Take 2 cups of the liquid left from boiling the beets, add 1 cup sugar and 1 cup vinegar and a touch of cayenne pepper. This proportion can be doubled if you do not have enough for the amount of beets cooked. Boil this mixture for 10 minutes and add the beets.

Small beets can be left whole while larger ones have to be halved or quartered. Bring the beets to a boil, remove. Place the beets in pint jars and cover to the rim with the liquid. Seal. Beets were a vegetable staple in winter and were especially good with the dough dishes.

MAKING SAUSAGE AND PRESERVING MEAT AND FOWL

Meat preservation. Meat preservation as well as preserving other foods was the big problem for the pioneer families. Fall was the best time of year. It was the time of harvest and of butchering. It was the only time of plenty, and thought and effort had to be given to preserving food for the entire year.

The meat that was preserved for the whole winter, to be eaten in the spring and summer as well as in the winter, was kept dry in a barrel with salt. It was frozen solid and kept well all winter. The salt was put in the bottom of the barrel so that it was solid white on the bottom. As each ham and bacon slab was added, salt was added too. At the top of the barrel were all the bones left from butchering which still had meat on them and were to be used for soups and stewing. They were added last along with a lot of salt since they had to be eaten soon. They could not be kept very long. The pioneers did not have loin chops or roasts. The meat was cut up and processed or it would not keep.

To keep meat over the summer, holes were dug in the earth of the cellar floor. Large crocks were placed into the holes with only the top showing and not covered with dirt. This way the crocks would keep cool but one could still get the food easily. They had special crocks for each kind of meat or vegetable and they were not used for any other purpose.

A cellar was a small room dug out of the earth which was under the house, or it could be separate, outside. If it was outside, it had a door and stairs leading down to the cellar. It stayed cold even in the summer. It was deep and had no air circulation.

Piglets (80 to 100 pounds) were butchered in the spring and summer. The pieces of the pig were put in containers and were hung down in the well above the water level. It was cold enough to preserve the meat for about 2 weeks. They butchered one about every 3 weeks, and it was all eaten as fresh meat. It was not used for sausages, hams, or bacon. These were made from the large pigs butchered in the fall for use in the winter and spring. The fresh piglets are still a treat today.

Homemade Bratwurst. This is the best sausage in the world. One of the reasons for this is that only the lean meat of the pig is used. This sausage is not made with scraps and fat. Many people still make their own sausage. It can also be purchased in some Dakota butcher shops; villages are known for their own version of *wurst* 'sausage'.

Use all the lean meat of a pig, including just the fat that is on the meat. Do not use pieces of pure fat. All the lean meat was used except for the meat on the bones. These were saved to use in making soup, or sauerkraut, or for stewing.

Cut the meat into pieces which can be ground and then grind finely. Place the meat in a large tub. Add:

1/2 cup garlic water (see recipe for garlic water)
1/4 cup salt
1 teaspoon black pepper

Mix well. Fry a small patty to taste and add more salt or pepper if needed.

Clean the intestines of the hog, washing well with very warm water inside and out until very clean. Lay the intestines in warm water until you are ready to fill them. They will become stiff if you don't. Cut them to 20-inch to 24-inch lengths. Tie one end with string and stuff with the sausage mixture, using a sausage machine. Tie the other end. Twist the sausage in the middle; hold one half and turn the other half. Then hang at that point on a stick until the next morning. The next morning the sausages are put into the smokehouse and smoked for 2 to 3 hours, depending on how well smoked you prefer the sausage.

The pioneers kept the sausage in their granaries. The sausage was hung for a day until it was frozen. It was then stuck into the grain which helped keep it frozen and safe all winter. The pioneers butchered in November, always when it was very cold. This helped them preserve their meat. In later years they began canning this sausage.

To prepare the sausage to eat, place one sausage in a pan with a cup of water and cover. Cook for 1/2 hour slowly and turn once midway through. The sausage should be frying towards the end of the half hour. It is served with small new potatoes boiled with their jackets on (depending on the season) and with fresh cottage cheese. The juice and fat that cooks out of the sausage is eaten on the potatoes or on bread.

Garlic water. Garlic water is a special preparation for use in making sausages. Peel and cut up one entire bulb of garlic. Soak in 2 cups water mixed with 1/4 teaspoon salt. This should be done the night before it will be needed to make sausage. Put the cut up garlic and the water and salt in a glass jar and cover. Let set.

In the morning mash the garlic in the water and then strain the mixture, saving only the juice. This is the garlic juice that is added to the sausage.

Headcheese and Leberwurst. Bring two pails of water to a boil in an oblong boiler used just for making sausages when butchering.

Cut the head of the hog into 4 pieces after removing the ears and eyes and snout. Wash carefully until very clean, then place in the boiling water. Put the ears and tongue in the water too. Put the pork belly and the rinds from the pork fat on the back of the pig into the boiler. Then put the kidneys and heart into the boiler.

Cook all of this in plain boiling water for two hours or until soft. Near the end of the cooking time add the liver, which only needs 15 to 20 minutes of cooking. The liver is finished if, when pierced with a fork, no blood appears. Remove the liver first and then drain the rest of the meat. Save the water. The liver must not be too dry.

Now the meat is divided for making two different sausages, the headcheese and the *leberwurst*. One variation made in the meats just cooked was that some people sometimes added a little lean pork meat.

The pioneers had a large oblong kettle called a *schlachtkessel*, approximately 36 inches long, 18 inches wide, 18 inches in height, with a cover, which they used for making recipes like this or for canning. It also served another purpose, it was used to heat water for washing.

Headcheese. The top half of the pig head is used to make the headcheese, plus the pork bellies, and half the pork fat rinds. If you add lean pork, it is also put in the headcheese. Peel the ears and tongue and use them for the headcheese. The pig's head is not peeled.

Cut the meats into very small pieces. If you want to, you can take a shortcut and grind the meat coarsely. Put the meat in a large bowl and add 1/4 cup garlic water (see garlic water recipe), 2 heaping tablespoons salt (or more, if desired), 1 teaspoon black pepper. Mix well.

This sausage is put into the pig's stomach. The stomach must first be turned inside out and washed very well in salt water. It is then scraped and washed again in salt water, cleaning both sides very carefully. Be careful not to tear the stomach. Lay it in salt water for up to an hour, then rinse in clear water. Stuff the sausage into the inside of the pig's stomach. Be sure to tie one end of the stomach with string before stuffing. Then, when finished, tie the other end too. Tie very tightly.

If preferred, you can also put the headcheese into the large intestines. You will need the sausage machine for this. Use the same method as for Bratwurst to stuff the casings.

Bring the original 2 pails of water almost to a boil, but do not boil. Place the stuffed stomach into the hot water and cook very hot, but not boiling, for about 2 hours. Add cold water if it starts to boil. Remove and place in an oblong pan and press it with something flat and heavy. Be very careful not to burst it. It will press to a flat sausage of 2 to 3 inches in thickness.

Leave the sausage this way until the next morning. Then clean the juices and fat that have escaped from the headcheese. Dry off the headcheese and hang in a smokehouse for about 8 hours. Store in a cold place.

The headcheese is served in slices and eaten cold with bread.

Leberwurst. Use the bottom of the cooked pig head and remove all outer skin. (The pig head was quartered and the top two pieces were used for the headcheese.) Cut the meat into large pieces for grinding. Also cut up the liver, the kidneys, and the heart. All of these meats must be ground together. Alternate different meats so all is well mixed.

Place the meat in a large bowl and add 1/4 cup garlic water (see garlic water recipe), 2 heaping tablespoons of salt (or more, if desired), 1 teaspoon black pepper. Mix well.

Clean the intestines of the hog and wash well with very warm water inside and outside until very clean. Lay the intestines in warm water until you are ready to fill them. They will become stiff if you don't. Cut them to about 12-inch lengths. Tie one end with string and fill them with the liver sausage. Use a sausage stuffing machine. Tie the other end.

Place in the original 2 pails of water, in very hot water but not boiling. Cook very hot, just below the boiling point, for 1/2 hour. Stick a needle into the sausage and if the liquid is clear, then it is done. Cook longer if needed.

Remove from the hot water and dip briefly into cold water. Hang the sausages up. They can be eaten as soon as the fat stiffens, usually the very next day.

If the *leberwurst* was meant to be kept for a long period of time, the dipping into cold water was omitted. The *leberwurst* was taken out of the hot water and put directly into a special two-gallon crock. The liquid or fat which drains out of the liver sausage surrounds it in the crock and this helps to keep it fresh. The crock was stored in a cold place.

Ham. After butchering, keep the hams in a cold place, but not freezing, for 24 hours.

Mix about 2 cups coarse salt with a pail of water. Put an egg in the water and when it rises, there is enough salt in the water. Stand the hams on end in a deep crock. Pour the water into the crock until it covers the tops of the hams. Leave the hams in the crock in a very cold place, not freezing, for 3 weeks. Take the hams out of the crock and wash off the salt with warm water.

Hang them in a smokehouse and smoke for at least 8 to 10 hours. Store them by hanging them in a very cold place with a good air circulation. Cut meat from the ham as needed, or cook a whole ham. Dakota is cold and dry in winter so it was easy to store the ham. In a warmer climate they have to be refrigerated.

The ham can be eaten as is, fried, boiled, or baked. A favorite old recipe follows.

Make a pastry crust using flour, water, and a bit of lard to make the simple dough. Roll out the dough and place on top of the ham. Bake the ham for 3 hours, or until tender, in a low oven, about 325 degrees.

Speck `Bacon'. The sides of the ham along with the rind and sometimes the ribs were cut off when butchering and used for bacon. Treat the bacon the same way as the ham was treated. If possible, put the bacon in the same crock with the ham. It fills up the small empty spaces. If it does not fit, then place in a separate crock with the same brine.

The bacon is left in the crock for only 3 to 4 days. It is then smoked for 6 hours. Hang in a cold place to store.

It was eaten uncooked with bread or cooked with sauerkraut.

Jellied pigs feet. To cook, cover the pigs feet or hocks with about twice as much water as you have meat. Add 1 teaspoon salt and 1/4 teaspoon pepper, a clove of garlic, a small onion, and a bay leaf. Bring to a boil and simmer 1 hour, or until tender. Taste the cooking liquid and add more salt if needed. After cooking, remove all the bones. Let the mixture set and chill. Slice to serve.

Bastram `Beef jerky'. Make a brine using the following proportions:
1 gallon water
1/4 teaspoon black pepper
3/4 cup salt
garlic water made the following way: Soak 2 cloves garlic which have been chopped in 1/2 cup water overnight. Mash and strain. The strained liquid is used for the brine.

Place the beef jerky which has been cut in strips in a crock. The whole round steak was saved when butchering beef and this was cut into strips. The crock can only be used for beef. Pour enough brine over the meat to cover. Cover with a board and a rock to hold the board. Leave the crock in a cold place that has good air circulation for 3 days. Remove it and smoke for 4 to 6 hours, depending on how much smoking you prefer. It was then hung up and eaten as desired.

Beef jerky was called *bastram* by the Dakota Germans from Russia. The word comes either from the Roumanian *pastrama* or the Turkish word *Bastyrma*.

Canning game birds. Wild birds such as geese, ducks, and pheasants can be canned. This may seem unusual, but it was the best way to preserve them. They are delicious eaten this way.

Cut the bird into pieces removing any buckshot you may find. Dip the pieces into flour. Fry in a generous amount of cooking oil, browning the meat slowly on each side. Put the pieces of bird into quart jars, filling them three-quarters. Put 1 teaspoon salt, a touch of black pepper, and a very small onion in each quart jar. Using the proportion of 1/2 cup water for a quart jar, add water to the pan in which the bird pieces were fried, scraping all the bits ogether. Bring to a boil and divide, putting half a cup into each jar.

Seal the jars and place them in a canner, setting them on the rack. Fill the canner with water until it reaches the rim of the jars. Keep the water level at the rim of the jars by adding boiling water to the canner every time the level recedes. The canner has to be kept covered. Boil for 3 hours. Start timing when the water starts to cook. At the end of the 3 hours, turn off the heat and let set for 15 minutes. Take the jars out of the water and let set for 15 minutes. Check to see if the jars are sealing—the cover will invert. When sealing is completed, turn the jars upside down, and let them set until they are cold. Then store in a cold place like a cellar or refrigerator. The jars do not have to be turned upside down after sealing. All that this does is cause the juice cooked out of the birds to rise to the top of the jar, where it becomes jellied.

To serve the canned birds, simply empty the entire contents of the jar into a pan and add a bit of chopped onion. Cook the birds in their own juices. They need to be cooked only until most of the juice has cooked away. The jellied part can also be eaten as it is. This dish was served with fried potatoes or rice, pickled beans or watermelon.

Goose drumsticks and breast. Goose drumsticks or breasts were placed in a crock. Again, it had to be a special crock used just for this recipe. The drumsticks and breasts were covered with the same brine as was made for the beef jerky. Pour on enough brine to cover the goose parts, then place the wood cover and rock on top. Let it set in a cold place that has good air circulation for 3 days. Remove and smoke about 4 hours. Eat as desired. It would keep for a long time.

Goose spread. When butchering geese, the loose fat is taken out of the inside of the goose and rendered. The fat, which has a white color, is cut up and placed in a heavy kettle and cooked about 1/2 hour. A piece of bread or onion is put into the kettle after the first 1/2 hour. When the bread or onion turns brown, the fat is done. Put the goose fat into a small crock (discard the bread or onion). Let the goose fat set and firm. It is a wonderful spread which was put on bread instead of butter and was a great breakfast favorite.

Appendix 2: Manifesto of Catherine the Great

July 22, 1763

VON GOTTES GNADEN

Wir Catharina die Zweite, Kaiserin und Selbstherrscherin aller Russen zu Moskau, Kiew, Wladimir, Nowgorod, Zarin zu Astrachan, Zarin zu Sibirien, Frau zu Plescau und Grossfürstin zu Smolensko, Fürstin zu Esthland und Livland, Carelien, Twer, Jugorien, Permien, Wjatka und Bolgarien und mehr anderen; Frau und Grossfürstin zu Nowgorod des Niedrigen Landes von Tschernigow, Resan, Rostow, Jaroslaw, Belooserien, Udorien, Obdorien, Condinien, und der ganzen Nord-Seite Gebieterin und Frau des Jurischen Landes, der Cartalinischen und Grusinischen Zaren und Cabardinischen Landes, der Tscherkessischen und Gorischen Fürstin und mehr andern Erb-Frau und Beherrscherin.

Da Uns der weite Umpfang der Länder Unseres Reiches zur Genüge bekannt, so nehmen Wir unter anderem wahr, dass keine geringe Zahl solcher Gegenden noch unbebaut liege, die mit vorteilhafter Bequemlichkeit zur Bevölkerung und Bewohnung des menschlichen Geschlechtes nutzbarlichst könnte angewendet werden, von welchem die meisten Ländereyen in ihrem Schoose einen unerschöplichen Reichtum an allerley kostbaren Erzen und Metallen verborgen halten; und weil selbiger mit Holzungen, Flüssen, Seen und zur Handlung gelegenen Meerung gnugsam versehen, so sind sie auch ungemein bequem zur Beförderung und Vermehrung vierlerley Manufacturen, Fabriken und zu verschiedenen Anlagen. Dieses gab Uns Unlass zur Erteilung des Manifestes, so zum Nutzen aller Unserer getreuen Unterthanen den 4. Dezember des abgewichenen 1762 Jahres publiciert wurde. Jedoch, da Wir in selbigen Ausländern, die Verlangen tragen würden, sich in Unserem Reich häuslich niederzulasse, Unser Belieben nur summarisch angekündiget; so befehlen Wir zur besseren Erörterung desselben folgende Verordnung, welche Wir hiermit feierlichst zum Grunde legen, und in Erfüllung zu setzen gebieten.

1. Verstatten Wir allen Ausländern in Unser Reich zu kommen, um sich in allen Gouvernements, wo es einem jeden gefällig, häuslich niederzulassen.

2. Dergleichen Fremde können sich nach ihrer Ankunft nich nur in Unsere Residenz bey der zu solchem Ende für die Ausländer besonders errichteten Tütel-Canzeley, sondern auch in den anderweitigen Gränz-

Städten Unseres Reiches nach eines jeden Bequemlichkeit bey denen Gouverneurs, der wo dergleichen nich vorhanden, bey den vornehmsten Stadts-Befehlhabern zu melden.

3. Da unter denen sich in Russland niederzulassen Verlangen tragenden Ausländern sich auch solche finden würden, die nich Vermögen genug zu Bestreitung der efforderlichen Reisekosten besitzen: so können sich dergleichen bey Unseren Ministern und an auswärtigen Höfen melden, welche sich nicht nur auf Unsere Kosten ohne Anstand nach Russland schicken, sondern auch mit Reisegeld versehen sollen.

4. Sobald dergleichen Ausländer in Unserer Residenz angelangt und sich bei der Tütel-Canzely oder in einer Gränz-Stadt gemeldet haben werden; so sollen dieselben gehalten sein, ihren wahren Entschuluss zu eröffnen, worinn nehmlich ihr eigentliches Verlangen bestehe, und ob sie sich die Kaufmannschaft oder unter Zünfte einschreiben lassen und Bürger werden wollen, und zwar nahmentlich, in welcher Stadt; oder ob sie Verlangen tragen, auf freyem und nutzbarem Grunde und Boden in ganzen Kolonien und Landflecken zum Ackerbau oder zu allerley nützlichen Gewerben sich niederlassen; da sodann alle dergleichen Leute nach ihrem eigenen Wunsche und Verlangen ihre Bestimmung unverweilt erhalten werden; gleich denn aus beifolgenden Register zu ersehen ist, wo und an welchen Gegenden Unseres Reiches nahmentlich freye und zur häuslichen Niederlassung bequeme Ländereyen vorhanden sind; wiewohl sich ausser der in bemeldetem Register aufgegebenen noch ungleich mehrere weitläufige Gegenden und allerley Ländereyen finden, allwo Wir gleichergestalt verstatten sich häuslich niederzulassen, wo es sich ein jeder am nützlichsten selbst wählen wird.

5. Gleich bei der Ankunft eines jeden Ausländers in Unser Reich, der sich häuslich niederzulassen gedenket und zu solchem Ende in der für die Ausländer errichteten Tütel-Canzley oder aber in anderen Gränz-Städten Unseres Reiches meldet, hat ein solcher, wie oben im 4ten vorgeschrieben stehet, vor allen Dingen seinen eigentlichen Entschluss zu eröffnen, und sodann nach eines jeden Religions-Ritu den Eid der Unterthänigkeit und Treue zu leisten.

6. Damit aber die Ausländer, welche sich in Unserem Reiche niederzulassen wünschen, gewahr werden mögen, wie weit sich Unser Wohlwollen zu ihrem Vorteile und Nutzen erstrecke, so ist dieser Unser Wille:

(1) Gestatten Wir allen in Unser Reich ankommenden Ausländern unverhindert die freye Religions-Übung nach ihren Kirchen-Satzungen und Gebräuchen; denen aber, welche nich in Städten, sondern auf unbewohnten Ländereyen sich besonders in Colonien

oder Landflecken nieder zu lassen gesonnen sind, erteilen Wir die Freyheit Kirchen und Glocken-Thürme zu bauen und die dabey nöthige Anzahl Priester und Kirchendiener zu unterhalten, nur einzig den Kosterbau ausgenommen. Jedoch wird hierbey jedermann gewarnt keinen in Russland wohnhaften christlichen Glaubensgenossen, unter gar keinem Vorwande zur Annehmung oder Beypflichtung seines Glaubens und seiner Gemeinde zu bereden oder zu verleiten, falls er sich nicht der Furcht der Strafe nach aller Strenge Unserer Gesetze auszusetzen gesonnen ist. Hiervon sind allerley an Unserem Reiche angrenzende dem Mahometanischen Glauben zugethane Nationen ausgeschlossen; als welche Wir nicht nur auf eine anständige Art zur christlichen Religion zuneigen, sondern auch sich selbige unterhänig zu machen, einem jeden erlauben und gestatten.

(2) Soll keiner unter solchen zur häuslichen Niederlassung nach Russland gekommenen Ausländern an unsere Cassa die geringsten Abgaben zu entrichten, und weder gewöhnliche oder ausserordentliche Dienste zu leisten gezwungen, noch Einquartierung zu tragen verbunden, sondern mit einem Worte, es soll ein jeder von aller Steuer und Auflangen folgendermassen frey sein: diejenigen nehmlich, welche in vielen Familien und ganzen Colonien eine bisher noch unbekannte Gegend besetzen, geniessen dreyssig Frey-Jahre; die sich aber in Städten niederlassen und sich entweder in Zünften oder unter der Kaufmannschaft einschreiben wollen, auf ihre Rechnung in Unserer Residenz Sankt-Petersburg oder in benachbarten Städten in Livland, Estland, Ingermanland, Carelien und Finland, wie nicht weniger in der ResidenzStadt Moscau nehmen, haben fünf Frey-Jahre zu geniessen. Wonächst ein jeder, der nicht nur auf einige kurze Zeit, sondern zur würklichen häuslichen Niederlassung, nach Russland kommt, noch überdem ein halbes Jahr hindurch frey Quartier haben soll.

(3) Allen zur häuslichen Niederlassung nach Russland gekommenen Ausländern, die entweder zum Kornbau und anderer Hand-Arbeit, oder aber Manufacturen, Fabriken und Anlagen zu errichten geneigt sind, wird alle hülfliche Hand und Vorsorge dargeboten und nicht allein hinlänglich und nach eines jeden, erforderlichen Vorschub gereichet werden, je nachdem es die Notwendigkeit und der künftige Nutzen von solchen zu errichtenden Fabriken und Anlagen erheischet, besonders aber von solchen, die bis jetzo in Russland noch nicht errichtet gewesen.

(4) Zum Häuser-Bau, zu Anschaffung verschiedener Gattung im Hauswesen benöthigten Viehes, und zu allerley wie beym Ackerbau, also auch bey Handwerken, erforderlichen Instrumenten, Zubehör und Materalien, soll einem jeden aus Unserer Cassa das nöthige Geld ohne alle Zinsen vorgeschossen, sondern lediglich das Kapital, und

zwar nicht eher als nach Verfliessung von zehn Jahren, in drey zu gleichen Theilen gerechnet, zurück gezahlt werden.

(5) Wir überlassen denen sich etablirten ganzen Colonien oder Landflecken die innere Verfassung der Jurisdiction ihrem eigenen Gutdünken, solchergestalt, dass die von Uns verordneten obrigkeitlichen Personen an ihren inneren Einrichtungen gar keinen Antheil nehmen werden, im übrigen aber sind solche Colonisten verpflichtet sich Unserem Civil-Rechte zu unterwerfen. Falls sie aber selbst Verlangen trügeneine besondere Person zu ihrem Vormunde oder Besorger ihrer Sicherheit und Vertheidigung von uns zu erhalten bis sie sich mit den benachbarten Einwohnern dereinst bekannt machen, er mit einer Salvegarde von Soldaten, die gute Mannszucht halten, versehen sey, so soll Ihnen auch hierinnen gewillfahret werden.

(6) Einem jeden Ausländer, der sich in Russland häuslich niederlassen will gestatten Wir die völlige zollfreye Einfuhr sienes Vermögens, es bestehe dasselbe worinn es wolle, jedoch mit dem Vorbehalte, dass solches Vermögen in seinem eigenen Gebrauche und Bedürfnis, nicht aber zum Verkaufe bestimmt sey. Wer aber ausser seiner eigener Nothdurft noch einige Waaren zum Verkauf mitbrächte, dem gestatten Wir freyen Zoll für jede Familie vor drey Hundert Rubel am Werte der Waaren, nur in solchem Falle, wenn sie wenigstens zehen Jahre in Russland bleibet: widrigenfalls wird bey ihrer Zurück-Reise der Zoll sowol für die eingekommene als ausgehende Waaren abgefordert werden.

(7) Solche in Russland sich niedergelassene Ausländer sollen während der ganzen Zeit ihres Hierseins, ausser dem gewöhnlichen Land-Dienste, wider Willen weder in Militär noch Civil-Dienst genommen werden; ja auch zur Leistung dieses Land-Dienst soll keines eher als nach Verfliessung obengesetzter Freyjahre verbunden seyen: wer aber freywillig geneigt ist, unter die Soldaten in Militär-Dienst zu treten, dem wird man ausser dem gewöhnlichen Solde bey seiner Envollirung beym Regiment Dreyssig Rubel Douceur-Geld reichen.

(8) Solbald sich Ausländer in der für sie errichteten Tütel-Canzeley oder sonst in Unsern Gränz-Städten gemeldet und ihren Entschluss eröffnet haben, in das innerste des Reiches zu reisen, und sich daselbst häuslich niederzulassen, so bald werden selbige auch Kostgeld, nebst freyer Schiesse an den Ort ihrer Bestimmung bekommen.

(9) Wer von solchen in Russland sich etablirten Ausländern dergleichen Fabriken, Manufacturen oder Anlagen errichtet, und

Waaren daselbst verfertigt, welche bis dato in Russland noch nicht gewesen, dem gestatten Wir, dieselben Zehen Jahre hindurch, ohne Erlegung irgend einigen inländischen See oder Gränze-Zolles frey zu verkaufen, und aus Unserm Reiche zu verschicken.

(10) Ausländische Capitalisten, welche auf ihre eigenen Kosten in Russland Fabriken, Manufacturen und Anlagen errichten, erlauben Wir hiemit zu solchen ihren Manufacturen, Fabriken und Anlagen erforderliche leibeigene Leute und Bauern zu erkaufen. Wir gestatten auch

(11) allen in Unserm Reiche sich in Colonien oder Landflecken niedergelassenen Ausländern, nach ihrem eigenen Gutdünken Markt-Tage und Jahrmärkte anzustellen, ohne an Unsere Cassa die geringsten Abgaben oder Zoll zu erlegen.

7. Aller obengenannten Vorteile und Einrichtung haben sich nicht nur diejenigen zu erfreuen, die in Unser Reich gekommen sind, sich häuslichnieder zu lassen, sondern auch ihre hinterlassene Kinder und Nachkommenschaft, wenn sie auch gleich in Russland geboren, solchergestalt, dass ihre Freyjahre von dem Tage der Ankunft ihrer Vorfahren in Russland zu berechnen sind.

8. Nach Verfliessung obangesetzter Freyjahre sind alle in Russland sich niedergelassene Ausländer verpflichtet, die gewöhnlichen und mit gar keiner Beschwerlichkeit verknüpften Abgiften zu entrichten, und gleich Unsern andern Unterthanen, Landes-Dienste zu leisten.

9. Endlich und zuletzt, wer von diesen sich niedergelassenen und Unsrer Bothmässigkeit sich unterworfenen Ausländern Sinnes würde sich aus Unserm Reiche zu begeben, dem geben Wir zwar jederzeit dazu die Freyheit, jedoch mit dieser Erleuterung, dass selbige verpflichtet seyn sollen von ihrem ganzen in Unserm Reiche wohlerworbenen Vermögen einen Theil an Unsere Cassa Zu entrichten; diejenigen nehmlich, die von Einem bis Fünf Jahre hier gewohnet, erlegen den Fünften, die von fünf bis zehen Jahren aber, und weiter, sich in Unsern Landen aufgehalten, erlegen den zehenden Pfennig; nachher is jedem erlaubt ungehindert zu reisen, wohin es ihm gefällt.

10. Wenn übrigens einige zur häuslichen Niederlassung nach Russland Verlangen tragende Ausländer aus einem oder anderen besonderen Bewegungsgründen, ausser obigen noch andere Conditiones und Privilegien zu gewinnen wünschen würde; solche haben sich deshalb an Unsere für die Ausländer errichteten Tütel-Canzley, welche uns alles umständlich vortragen wird, schriftlich oder persönlich zu wenden: worauf Wir alsdann nach Befinden der Umstände nicht entstehen werden, um so viel mehr geneigte Allerhöchste Resolution zu ertheilen,

als sich solches ein jeder von Unserer Gerechtigkeitsliebe zuversichtlich versprechen kann.
   Gegeben zu Peterhof, im Jahre 1763 den 22ten Juli,
   im Zweyten Jahre Unsrer Regierung.
      Das Original haben Ihre Kayserliche Majestät
      Allerhöchst eigenhändig folgendergestalt unterschrieben:
         Gedruckt beym Senate den 25. Juli 1763.
      (*Manifesto* as found in Stumpp 1922:4-9)

BY THE GRACE OF GOD

We, Catherine the Second, Empress and sole ruler of all Russians at Moscow, Kiev, Vladimir, Novgorod, Empress of Astrakhan, Empress of Siberia, Dame of Plescau and Grand Duchess of Smolensk, Duchess of Estonia and Latvia (Livland), Karelia, Tver, Jugoria, Perm, Vyakta and Bulgaria, and many others; Dame and Grand Duchess of Novgorod of the Lowlands of Chernigov, Ryazan, Rostov, Yaroslavl, Belorussia, Udoria, Obdoria, Condinia and Sovereign of all the Northly Territories and Dame of the Jurian states, the Cartalinian and Georgian kingdoms and the Cabardinian states, Duchess of the Cherkessians and Gorians and hereditary Ruler and Sovereign of many more.

Since We are quite aware of the vast expanse of territories comprising our empire, We note that not a small number of these areas lie uncultivated, which could be made useful, with utmost ease, to the human race, from which most of these areas hide an inexhaustible wealth of mineral resources; whereby these areas are amply provided with woods, streams, lakes, and useable open waters, they are also extremely convenient for the transport and growth of various products, enterprises, and different installations. This prompted Us to the delivery of this manifest, which was published for the benefit of all Our faithful subjects on December 4 of the past year of 1762. However, since We have announced Our will only summarily in such foreign places that would harbor the desire to establish domicile in Our empire, in order to better explain it, We proclaim the following decree, which We herewith formally establish, and command its adherence.

   1. All foreigners who come to Our empire are permitted to establish their domicile wherever they wish.

   2. After their arrival, such foreigners can come not only to Our resident capital, seat of the royal court, to the Immigration Chancellery which was specially established for this purpose, but also to the Governors of the border cities of our kingdom, according to their preference, or, if there is no Governor, to the highest city administrator.

3. Since there will be people who do not possess enough capital to pay for the necessary transportation costs among these foreigners wishing to settle in Russia, they can report to Our Ministers or Our Embassies abroad and not only be sent to Russia at Our cost, but also even be provided with travel money.

4. As soon as such foreigners have arrived in our sovereign capital and reported to the Immigration Chancellery or after they report to a border city, they are requested to disclose their true intentions, that is to say, what their real desires are, whether they wish to register with the Merchant's Association or with one of the Guilds; whether they wish to become citizens, and if so, of which city, and if they wish to establish themselves in agriculture or other useful professions, on free and useable soil in whole colonies and villages, so that all such people will immediately receive their destination, according to their own wishes and desires; as it is evident from the enclosed register where and in which areas of Our empire such free territories, appropriate for domestic settlement, are located; furthermore, there exist other vast regions and rural areas besides those in the register, where We also permit domestic settlements, and where each person chooses the place best suited for him.

5. Immediately upon arrival in Our empire, each foreigner who intends to establish a domicile and reports for this purpose to the Immigration Chancellery, which has been established for foreigners, or reports to a border city of Our empire, the foreigner has to disclose first of all his real intention, as instructed in paragraph 4 above, and then swear the oath of fealty and loyalty according to his own religious ritual.

6. So that the foreigners, who wish to establish themselves in Our empire, realize the extent of Our benevolence for their advantage and good fortune, this is Our will—:

(1) We permit all foreigners arriving in Our empire the unencumbered free exercise of their religion according to their church's regulations and customs; to those, however, who wish to establish themselves not in cities, but in uninhabited rural areas in colonies or villages, We grant the freedom to build churches and bell towers and to maintain the necessary number of priests and sextons, except for the building of monasteries. However, everybody be warned not to persuade or tempt any Christian living in Russia, under any pretext, to join or accept his or his community's faith, inasmuch as he is not eager to expose himself to the fear of the punishment according to the full severity of Our law. An exception are several nations bordering Our empire which belong to the Moslem faith, for which We permit not only decent persuasion to the Christian religion but

grant everyone permission to make them their subjects.

(2) No foreigner who came to Russia for such domestic settlement is obligated to pay the smallest tax to our coffers, nor perform ordinary or extraordinary services, nor pay rent, but, in other words, everyone shall be free from taxes or obligations as follows: those, who, with their families and whole colonies, settle in an area that was unknown until now enjoy 30 years free; those who settle in cities and wish to register either with the Guilds or Merchant's Associations, and settle on their own account in Our royal capital of St. Petersburg or in the neighboring cities in Latvia (Livland), Estonia, Ingermanland, Karelia, and Finland, or in the capital city of Moscow, will enjoy 5 free years. Furthermore, everyone who comes to Russia not only for a short period, but for real domestic settlement, can receive a free place to live for one-half year.

(3) All foreigners coming to Russia for domestic settlement, who tend either to growing grain or other manual work, or who intend to do manufacturing, build factories or other installations, will be offered a helping hand and provisions, sufficient and according to each person's needs, and according to the necessity and future use of such factories and installations, especially those, which had not been built in Russia before.

(4) Everyone will be lent from our coffers the necessary money, interest-free, for construction of housing, acquisition of various species of animals necessary for the settlement, and for various equipment necessary for farming, and for all that is necessary for the trades, such as instruments, accessories and material. Only the capital will have to be paid back, in three equal parts, not earlier than after the passing of 10 years.

(5) We leave the inner jurisdiction up to the judgment of the established colonies or villages, such that Our Governors will not take part in those inner arrangements; for the rest, however, such colonists are subject to Our civil laws. Should they, however, have the desire for Us to designate a special person as their speaker or caretaker of their safety and defense, until they have acquainted themselves with their neighbors, and be provided with a guard of soldiers, which keep good order, they will also be accomodated in this matter.

(6) We give permission to each foreigner, who wants to establish domicile in Russia, to import his assets completely duty-free, no matter what they are, under the condition that such assets are for his own use and need and not for resale. To those however, who bring other goods, besides those for their own needs, We grant them

permission to import duty-free, goods of 300 rubles in value for each family, but only if they remain in Russia for ten years, otherwise, they will have to pay duty on such goods when they leave Russia, for bringing the goods in and for taking them out.

(7) Such foreigners, settled in Russia, shall not be taken into the military or civilian service against their will during the whole time of their stay, except for harvest duty, and even for the latter, nobody is obligated to perform this service before passing of the above mentioned free years: those however, who want to volunteer to join the soldiers in the military service will receive 30 rubles enlistment bonus when they register with the regiment, besides their regular salary.

(8) As soon as the foreigners have reported to the Immigration Chancellery which was specially established for them, or to one of Our border cities, and have disclosed their intention to travel to the interior of the empire and settle there, they will be provided with money for food, and free passage to their destination.

(9) Those foreigners settled in Russia, who build factories, manufacturing, or other installations, and produce goods there, which have not been produced in Russia before, We grant permission to sell these goods for the same ten years without paying any in country or border customs taxes, and they may export from our empire.

(10) We permit foreign capitalists, who construct factories, manufacturing and other installations in Russia, at their own cost, to buy necessary slaves and farmers. We permit furthermore

(11) all foreigners settled in Our empire in colonies or villages, to arrange market days and yearly fairs according to their best judgment, without having to pay any duties or customs to our coffers.

7. All above mentioned advantages and provisions apply not only to those who came to Our empire to establish their domicile, but also their children and descendants, if they are born in Russia, then their free years will start to count from the day of arrival of their ancestors in Russia.

8. After passing of the above mentioned free years, all foreigners who settled in Russia, will have to pay the very easy and reasonable duties, and will have to serve the country, just like our other subjects.

9. Last and finally, if such established foreigners who subjected themselves to our authority would become of a mind to leave Our empire, they will be free to do so, however under the provision that they are obliged to pay to our coffers a part of the capital they earned in Our

empire; namely those who have lived here between one and five years will have to pay one fifth, those however, who stayed for five to ten years or more in Our countries, will pay every tenth penny; thereafter everyone may travel where he wishes.

10. Furthermore, if some foreigners wishing to establish domicile in Russia, for one reason or another, wish to be granted other conditions and privileges besides those mentioned above, they will have to contact Our Immigration Chancellery, which was established for the foreigners, where they will explain everything in detail, personally or in writing, upon which We will evaluate the circumstances and express Our all-highest well intentioned resolution, as anybody may expect with confidence from Our love of justice.

Declared at Peterhof, in the year 1763 on the 22nd of July, in the second year of Our reign.

The original has been signed personally by her All-Highest Imperial Majesty: Printed by the Senate on July 25, 1763.

(English translation of the *Manifesto* by Inge Renard, February, 1990.)

Appendix 3: An Act to secure Homesteads to actual Settlers on the Public Domain

May 20, 1862. (12 Stat. 392).

Be it enacted by the Senate and House of Representatives of the United States of America in Congress assembled, That any person who is the head of a family, or who has arrived at the age of twenty-one years, and is a citizen of the United States, or who shall have filed his declaration of intention to become such, as required by the naturalization laws of the United States, and who has never borne arms against the United States Government or given aid and comfort to its enemies, shall, from and after the first January, eighteen hundred and sixty-three, be entitled to enter one quarter section or a less quantity of unappropriated public lands, upon which said person may have filed a preemption claim, or which may, at the time the application is made, be subject to preemption at one dollar and twenty-five cents, or less, per acre; or eighty acres or less of such unappropriated lands, at two dollars and fifty cents per acre, to be located in a body, in conformity to the legal subdivisions of the public lands, and after the same shall have been surveyed: Provided, That any person owning and residing on land may, under the provisions of this act, enter other land lying contiguous to his or her said land, which shall not, with the land so already owned and occupied, exceed in the aggregate one hundred and sixty acres.

Sec. 2. And it be further enacted, That the person applying for the benefit of this act shall, upon application to the register of the land office in which he or she is about to make such entry, make affidavit before the said register or receiver that he or she is the head of a family, or is twenty-one years or more of age, or shall have performed service in the army or navy of the United States, and that he has never borne arms against the Government of the United States or given aid and comfort to its enemies, and that such application is made for his or her exclusive use and benefit, and that said entry is made for the purpose of actual settlement and cultivation, and not either directly or indirectly for the use or benefit of any person or persons whomsoever; and upon filing the said affidavit with the register or receiver, and on payment of ten dollars, he or she shall thereupon be permitted to enter the quantity of land specified: Provided, however, That no certificate shall be given or patent issued therefor until the expiration of five years from the date of such entry; and if, at the expiration of such time, or at any time within two years thereafter, the person making such entry; or, if he be dead, his widow; or in case of her death, his heirs or devisee; or in case of a widow making such entry, her heirs or devisee, in case of her death; shall prove by two credible witnesses that he, she, or they have resided upon or cultivated the same for the term of five years immediately succeeding the time of filing the affidavit aforesaid, and shall make affidavit that no part of said land has been alienated, and that he has borne true allegiance to the Government of the United States; then, in such case, he, she, or they, if at that time a citizen of the United States, shall be entitled to a patent, as in other cases provided for by law: And provided, further, That in case of the death of both father and mother, leaving an infant child, or children, under twnety-one years of age, the right and fee shall enure to the benefit of said infant child or children; and the executor, administrator, or guardian may, at any time within two years after the death of the surviving parent, and in accordance with the laws of the State in which such children for the time being have their domicil, sell said land for the benefit of said infants, but for no other purpose; and the purchaser shall acquire the absolute title by the purchase, and be entitled to a patent from the United States, on payment of the office fees and sum of money herein specified.

Sec. 3. And be it further enacted, That the register of the land office shall note all such applications on the tract books and plats of his office, and keep a register of all such entries, and make return thereof to the General Land Office, together with the proof upon which they have been founded.

Sec. 4. And be it further enacted, That no lands acquired under the provisions of this act shall in any event become liable to the satisfaction of any debt or debts contracted prior to the issuing of the patent therefor.

Sec. 5. And be it further enacted, That if, at any time after the filing of the affidavit, as required in the second section of this act, and before the expiration of the five years aforesaid, it shall be proven, after due notice to the settler, to the satisfaction of the register of the land office, that the person having filed such affidavit shall have actually changed his or her residence, or abandoned the said land for more than six months at any time, then and in that event the land so entered shall revert to the government.

Sec. 6. And be it further enacted, That no individual shall be permitted to acquire title to more than one quarter section under the provisions of this act; and that the Commissioner of the General Land Office is hereby required to prepare and issue such rules and regulations, consistent with this act, as shall be necessary and proper to carry its provisions into effect; and that the registers and receivers of the several land offices shall be entitled to receive the same compensation for any lands entered under the provisions of this act that they are now entitled to receive when the same quantity of land is entered with money, one half to be paid by the person making the application at the time of so doing, and the other half on the issue of the certificate by the person to whom it may be issued; but this shall not be construed to enlarge the maximum of compensation now prescribed by law for any register or receiver: Provided, That nothing contained in this act shall be so construed as to impair or interfere in any manner whatever with existing preemption rights: And provided, further, That all persons who may have filed their applications for a preemption right prior to the passage of this act, shall be entitled to all privileges of this act: Provided, further, That no person who has served, or may hereafter serve, for a period of not less than fourteen days in the army or navy of the United States, either regular or volunteer, under the laws thereof, during the existence of an actual war, domestic or foreign, shall be deprived of the benefits of this act on account of not having attained the age of twenty-one years.

Sec. 7. And be it further enacted, That the fifth section of the act entitled "An act in addition to an act more effectually to provide for the punishment of certain crimes against the United States, and for other purposes," approved the third of March, in the year eighteen hundred and fifty-seven, shall extend to all oaths, affirmations, and affidavits, required or authorized by this act.

Sec. 8. And be it further enacted, That nothing in this act shall be so construed as to prevent any person who has availed him or herself of the benefits of the first section of this act, from paying the minimum price, or the price to which the same may have graduated, for the quantity of land so entered at any time before the expiration of the five years, and obtaining a patent therefor from the government, as in other cases provided by law, on making proof of settlement and cultivation as provided by existing laws granting preemption rights.

APPROVED, May 20, 1862.

[Author's note. This law was amended several times and the final summary paragraph appearing in the United States Code is as follows:]

Every person who is the head of a family, or who has arrived at the age of twenty-one years, and is a citizen of the United States, or who has filed his declaration of intention to become such, as required by the naturalization laws, shall be entitled to enter one quarter-section or a lesser quantity of unappropriated public lands, to be located in a body in conformity to the legal subdivisions of the public lands; but no person who is the proprietor of more than one hundred and sixty acres of land in any State or Territory, shall acquire any right under the homestead law. And every person owning and residing on land may, under the provisions of this section, enter other land lying contiguous to his land, which shall not, with the land so already owned and occupied, exceed in the aggregate one hundred and sixty acres.

Appendix 4: An Act to encourage the Growth of Timber on western Prairies

March 3, 1873. (17 Stat. 605).

Be it enacted by the Senate and House of Representatives of the United States of America in Congress assembled, That any person who shall plant, protect, and keep in a healthy, growing condition for ten years forty acres of timber, the trees thereon not being more than twelve feet apart each way on any quarter-section of any of the public lands of the United States shall be entitled to a patent for the whole of said quarter-section at the expiration of said ten years, on making proof of such fact by not less than two credible witnesses; Provided, That only one quarter in any section shall be thus granted.

Section 2. That the person applying for the benefit of this act shall, upon application to the register of the land-office in which he or she is about to make such entry, make affidavit before said register or receiver that said entry is made for the cultivation of timber, and upon filing said affidavit shall thereupon be permitted to enter the quantity of land specified: Provided however, That no certificate shall be given or patent issue therefor until the expiration of at least ten years from the date of such entry; and if at the expiration of such time, or at any time within three years thereafter, the person making such entry, or if he or she be dead, his or her heirs or legal representatives, shall prove by two credible witnesses that he, she, or they have planted, and for not less than ten years have cultivated and protected such quantity and character of timber as aforesaid, they shall receive the patent for such quarter-section of land.

Section 3. That if at any time after the filing of said affidavit, and prior to the issuing of the patent for said land, it shall be proven after due notice to the party making such entry and claiming to cultivate such timber, to the satisfaction of the register of the land-office that such person has abandoned or failed to cultivate, protect and keep in good condition such timber, then, and in that event, said land shall revert to the United States.

Section 4. That each and every person who, under the provisions of an act entitled "An act to secure homesteads to actual settlers on the public domain" approved May twentieth, eighteen hundred and sixty-two, or any amendment thereto, having a homestead on said public domain, who, at the end of the third year of his or her residence thereon, shall have had under cultivation, for two years, one acre of timber, the trees thereon not being more than twelve feet apart each way, and in a good, thrifty condition, for each and every sixteen acres of said homestead, shall upon due proof of said fact by two credible witnesses receive his or her patent for said homestead.

Section 5. That no land acquired under provisions of this act shall, in any event, become liable to the satisfaction of any debt or debts contracted prior to the issuing of patent therefor.

Section 6. That the commissioner of the general land-office is hereby required to prepare and issue such rules and regulations, consistent with this act, as shall be necessary and proper to carry its provisions into effect; and that the registers and the receivers of the several land-offices shall be entitled to receive the same compensation for any lands entered under the provisions of this that they are now entitled to receive when the same quantity of land is entered with money.

Section 7. That the fifth section of the act entitled ``An act in addition to an act to punish crimes against the United States, and for other purposes" approved March third, eighteen hundred and fifty-seven, shall extend to all oaths, affirmations, and affidavits required or authorized by this act.

APPROVED, March 3, 1873.

[Author's Note: This law was amended March 13, 1874 and June 14, 1878. It was repealed March 3, 1891.]

Appendix 5: Treaty of Nonaggression between Germany and the Union of Soviet Socialist Republics with Additional Secret Protocol

(Sontag and Beddie 1948:76-78).

The Government of the German Reich and the Government of Union of Soviet Socialist Republics, desirous of strengthening the cause of peace between Germany and the U.S.S.R., and proceeding from the fundamental provisions of the Neutrality Agreement concluded in April 1926 between Germany and the U.S.S.R., have reached the following Agreement:

ARTICLE I. Both High Contracting Parties obligate themselves to desist from any act of violence, any aggressive action, and any attack on each other, either individually or jointly with other powers.

ARTICLE II. Should one of the High Contracting Parties become the object of belligerent action by a third power, the other High Contracting Party shall in no manner lend its support to this third power.

ARTICLE III. The Governments of the two High Contracting Parties shall in the future maintain continual contact with one another for the purpose of consultation in order to exchange information on problems affecting their common interests.

ARTICLE IV. Neither of the two High Contracting Parties shall participate in any grouping of powers whatsoever that is directly or indirectly aimed at the other Party.

ARTICLE V. Should disputes or conflicts arise between the High Contracting Parties over problems of one kind or another, both Parties shall settle these disputes or conflicts exclusively through friendly exchange of opinion or, if necessary, through the establishment of arbitration commissions.

ARTICLE VI. The present Treaty is concluded for a period of ten years, with the proviso that, in so far as one of the High Contracting Parties does not denounce it one year prior to the expiration of this period, the validity of this Treaty shall automatically be extended for another five years.

ARTICLE VII. The present Treaty shall be ratified within the shortest possible time. The ratifications shall be exchanged in Berlin. The Agreement shall enter into force as soon as it is signed.

Done in duplicate in the German and Russian languages.
Moscow, August 23, 1939.
For the Government of the German Reich: v. Ribbentrop.
With full power of the Government of U.S.S.R.: V. Molotov.

Secret Additional Protocol

On the occasion of the signature of the Nonaggression Pact between the German Reich and Union of Soviet Socialist Republics the undersigned plenipotentiaries of each of the two Parties, discussed in strictly confidential conversations the question of the boundary of their respective spheres of influence in Eastern Europe. These conversations led to the following conclusions:

1. In the event of a territorial and political rearrangement in the areas belonging to the Baltic states (Finland, Estonia, Latvia, Lithuania), the northern boundary of Lithuania shall represent the boundary of the spheres of influence of Germany and U.S.S.R. In this connection the interest of Lithuania in the Vilna area is recognized by each Party.

2. In the event of a territorial and political rearrangement of the areas belonging to the Polish state, the spheres of influence of Germany and U.S.S.R. shall be bounded approximately by the line of the rivers Narew, Vistula, and San.

The question of whether the interests of both Parties make desirable the maintenance of an independent Polish state and how such a state should be bounded can be definitely determined only in the course of further political developments.

In any event both Governments will resolve this question by means of a friendly agreement.

3. With regard to Southeastern Europe, attention is called by the Soviet side to its interest in Bessarabia. The German side declares its complete political disinterestedness in these areas.

(**Note.** The German text of this article of the Protocol is as follows: 'Hinsichtlich des Südostens Europas wird von sowjetischer Seite das Interesse an Bessarabien betont. Von deutscher Seite wird das völlige politische Desinteressement an diesen Gebieten erklärt.')

4. This Protocol shall be treated by both Parties as strictly secret.

Moscow, August 23, 1939.
For the Government of the German Reich: v. Ribbentrop
Plenipotentiary of the Government of the U.S.S.R.: V. Molotov

Appendix 6: Map showing the site of the Central Dakota German community in the United States

Appendix 7: Map showing the site of the Central Dakota German community in Russia

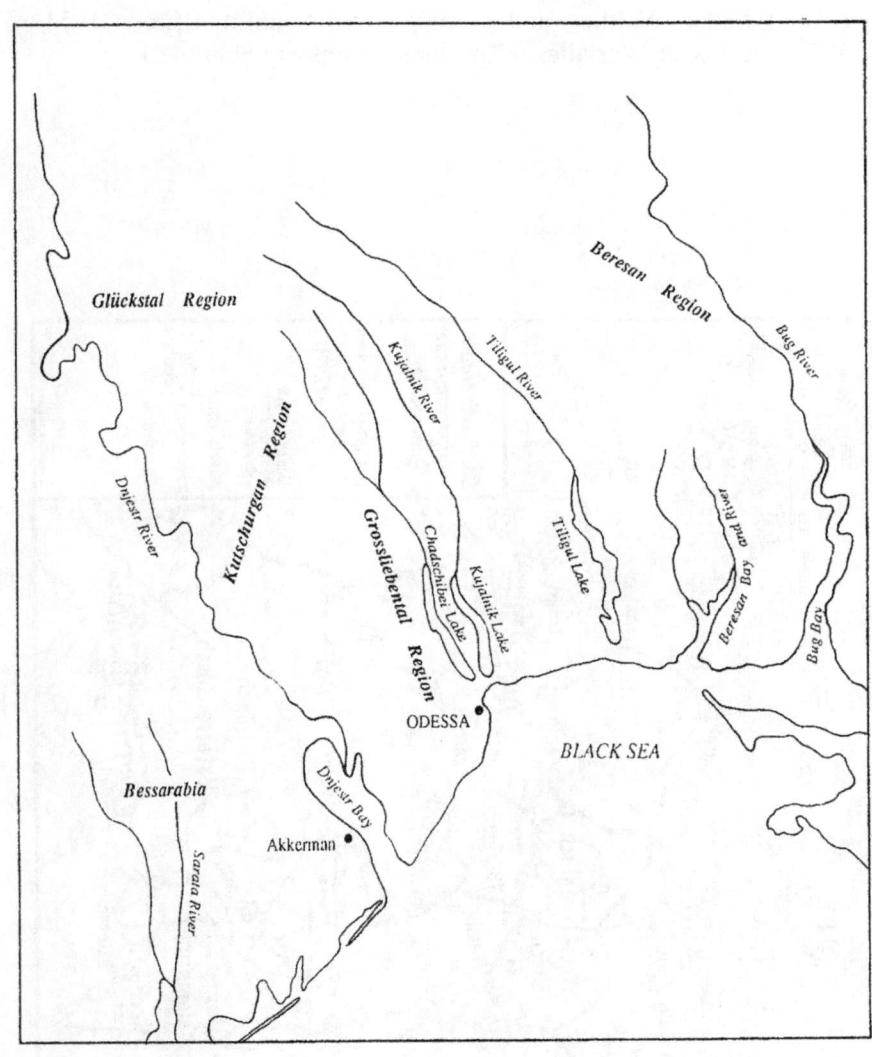

Appendix 8: Map showing the original site of the Central Dakota German dialect of Schwäbisch
(from Mitzka, Walther, and Ludwig Erich Schmitt, Efitors. 1951-1972. Deutcsher Wortatlas. 22 Volumes, Geissen: Schmitz.).

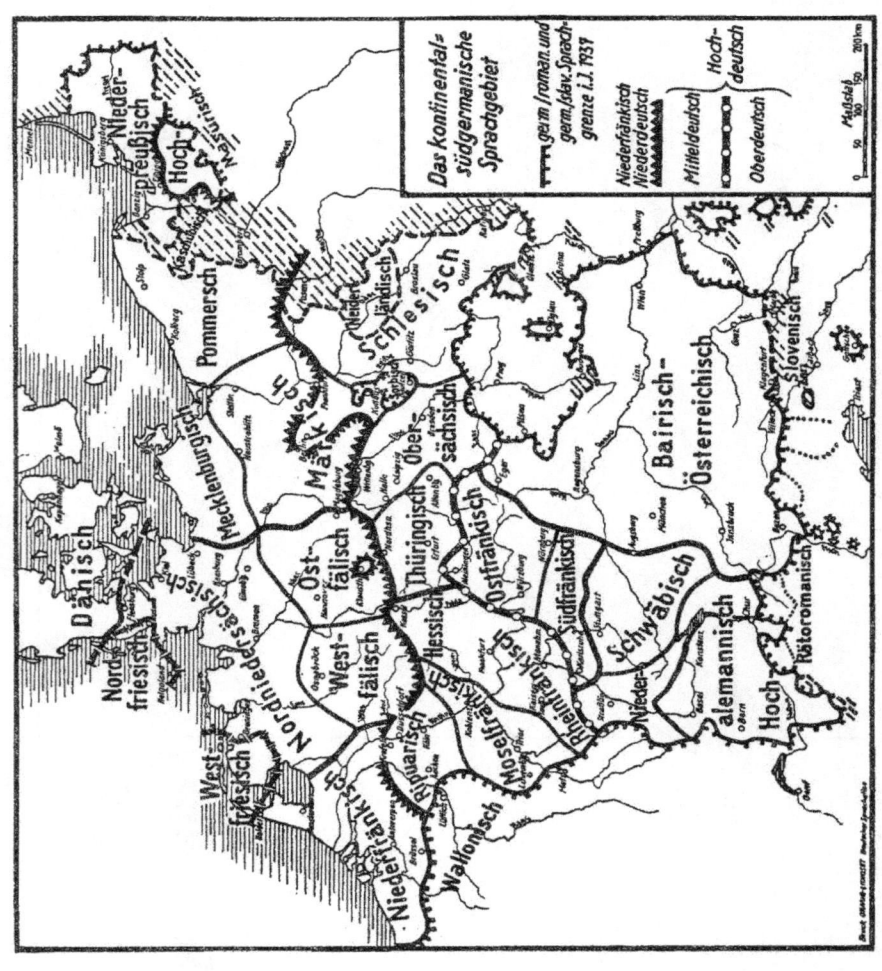

Appendix 9: Map showing the four districts of the Kingdom of Württemberg and their small counties or townships around 1818

(from Württembergisches Landesmuseum. 1987. Baden and Württemberg im Zeitalter Napoleons. Three volumes. Stuttgart-Bad Cannstatt: Cantz'sche Druckerei)

Appendix 10: Description of the recorded orpus (1984-1987) and list of the informants cited in Chapter 3

The following are the informants who were recorded on cassette tape-recorder during the period beginning in 1984 and ending in November 1987 in order to constitute the corpus upon which the description of the Central Dakota German (CDGer.) dialect in Chapter 3 was based.

The recordings were made by Emma Fischer, a native speaker of the Central Dakota German dialect. She was instructed on how to go about her task by Dr. Kurt Rein, Professor of Linguistics at the University of Munich, Germany, who is well known for his work on dialects and geographic word maps. Indeed, the first recording was an elicitation session with Emma and Christoph Fischer made by Dr. Rein. He expressed himself as being surprised to find the dialect so "intact" and undiluted by foreign influences.

Throughout the period in which the recordings were made I was in constant telephone and personal contact with Emma Fischer and supplied her with lists in both Standard High German and in English for use in the field. I prepared a list of informants whom I thought she might contact to obtain accurate results.

In addition to recording the 40 Wenker sentences, she followed each recording of the Wenker sentences with a recording of the 200-item Mitzka word list. At the conclusion of each recording session, she elicited free conversation in the Central Dakota German dialect of which she is a native speaker, and in which she participated.

Although the men of the community were not eager to participate in the actual taping because they seemed to feel that it was the task of the women to respond to inquiries about language, they were present at the meetings, did enjoy the sessions, and would interject if they felt that something was stated incorrectly or inaccurately. They were happy and pleased to supply anecdotes or other recollections if those present needed assistance because of flagging memories.

The list of informants for Chapter 3 is given in alphabetical order with the married name, maiden name, and the age of each informant at the time the recording was made. All the informants were residents of McIntosh County, North Dakota, and McPherson County, South Dakota, the central counties of the dialect area.

Lydia Bader nee Iszler, age 87

Leontina Bender nee Bertsch, age 75
Mary Bendewald nee Strobel, age 82
Leo Bendewald, age 60
Curtis Bendewald, age 29
Emma Bertsch nee Heinrich, age 81
Christoph Dockter, age 75
Louise Dockter nee Weisenberger, age 64
Frieda Ehley nee Babitzke, age 78
Rose Eslinger nee Nitschke, age 80
John Fischer, age 87
Martha Fischer nee Weisser, age 72
Ernest Goehring, age 64
Violet Goehring nee Fischer, age 62
Bertha Hoffmann nee Maier, age 82
Eva Iszler nee Dockter, age 96
Ida Kramer nee Burrer, age 79
Emma Maas nee Schauer, age 77
Anna Maier nee Hoffmann, age 79
Rose Nitschke nee Bendewald, age 82
Rose Retzer nee Maas, age 82
Martha Reuther nee Bendewald, age 80
Emma Reuther nee Bendewald, age 82
Emma Roeszler nee Klipfel, age 81
Rose Schauer nee Wolf, age 83
Matilda Strobel nee Bendewald, age 80
Hilda Vossler nee Deile, age 80

We were able to record three generations of Central Dakota German speakers, Mary Bendewald nee Strobel, her son Leo Bendewald, and her grandson Curtis Bendewald. Often people in the list have the same name but are not closely related; for instance, Matilda Strobel nee Bendewald versus the sisters Emma and Martha Reuther nee Bendewald. The same names keep reoccurring.

The informants listed here are distinct from those who provided the personal interviews which I conducted, from my first interview with Christian Fischer in 1961 to my last interview by means of written correspondence with Helen Frisch, the daughter of Eva Iszler in 1984. At that time Eva Iszler was 96 years of age and no longer able to continue her work as a *brauchere* because of her loss of strength due to her advanced age. She was thus willing to assist me with her vast store of knowledge about *brauche* since my grandmother Friederike had helped her, and because my mother was also a *brauchere*. In fact, Eva believed that I too had inherited from my grandmother and mother the right to have the knowledge.

References and selected bibliography

Abbot, John S.C. 1882. The empire of Russia. New York: Dodd, Mead.
Aberle, George P. 1964. From the Steppes to the Prairies. Bismarck, N.Dak.: Bismarck Tribune Co.
Alatis, James E. and John J. Staczek, Editors. 1985. Perspectives on bilingualism and bilingual education. Washington, D.C.: Georgetown University Press.
Älteste deutsche Dichtung. In der Übertragung von Karl Wolfskehl. 1959. Hamburg: Claassen.
Anaya, Rudolfo A. 1986. Bless me, Ultima. Berkeley: Tonatiuh-Quinto Sol International. (Premio Quinto Sol annual literary award 1971).
Arends, Shirley Fischer. 1966. The Dakota Germans. Unpublished Master's thesis. Kent State University.
Atach, F. 1904. Die deutschen Kolonien in Südrussland. Riga. Auburger, Leopold, Heinz Kloss, and Heinz Rupp, Editors. 1979. Deutsch als Muttersprache in den Vereinigten Staaten. Im Auftrag des Instituts für deutsche Sprache, Mannheim. Wiesbaden: Steiner.
Basler, Theodor. 1911. Das Deutschtum in Russland. Munich: Lehmann.
Baudler, Rev. Theodore R. 1963. Introduction. 75th Jubilee of Ashley, North Dakota. Fargo, N.Dak.: Richtmans. 6-11.
Benware, Wilbur A. 1986. Phonetics and Phonology of Modern German. Washington, D.C.: Georgetown University Press.
Besch, Werner. 1973. Frühneuhochdeutsch. Lexikon der germanistischen Linguistik. Tübingen: Niemeyer. 421-430.
Bettelheim, Bruno. 1977. The uses of enchantment. New York: Vintage Books, Random House.
Bienemann, Friedrich. 1890. Geschichte der evangelisch-lutherischen Gemeinde zu Odessa. Odessa.
Bienemann, Friedrich. 1893. Werden und Wachsen einer deutschen-Kolonie in Südrussland. Geschichte der evangelisch-lutherischen Gemeinde zu Odessa. Odessa
Blackall, Eric A. 1978. The emergence of German as a literary language 1700-1775. Ithaca and London: Cornell University Press.
Bloomfield, Leonard. 1933. Language. New York: Holt, Reinhart, and Winston.
Bohmann, Alfred. 1980. Die Deutschen in der Sowjetunion. Europa Ethnica. Vol. 4. 185-191.
Bond, Anatole. 1978. Deutsche Siedlung am Schwarzen Meer. Lustdorf bei Odessa: DDG.
Bragdon & McCutchen. 1973. History of a free people. New York: Macmillan.

Breneman, Mary Worthy. 1956. The land they possessed. New York: Macmillan.
Breul, Karl. 1939. Cassell's new German and English dictionary. Revised and enlarged by J. Heron Lepper and Rudolf Kottenhahn. New York: Funk and Wagnalls.
Browne, Rt. Rev. G.F.. 1930. The Venerable Bede. London: Society for Promoting Christian Knowledge. New York: Macmillan.
Corominas, Juan. 1954. Diccionario critico etimológico de la Lengua Castellana. Four Volumes. Bern: Francke.
Cunz, Dieter. 1948. The Maryland Germans. Princeton, N.J.: Princeton University Press.
Der kleine Katechismus Dr. Martin Luthers. 1914. Mit kurzer Erklärung in Frage und Antwort von J. M. Reu, Professor am Seminar Wartburg. Chicago: Wartburg.
Dictionary of spoken Russian. 1958. New York: Dover Publications.
Die Bibel, oder die ganze heilige Schrift Alten und Neuen Testaments. Nach der deutschen Übersetzung Dr. Martin Luthers. No date. St. Louis, Mo: Concordia Publishing House.
Die Edda. 1933. Translated into German by Felix Genzmer. Jena: Diederich.
Dill, Marshall Jr. 1961. Germany, a modern history. Ann Arbor: University of Michigan Press.
Dossey, M.D., Larry. 1982. Space, time, and medicine. Boston, London: New Science Library, Shambhala.
Duden, Gottfried. 1829. Bericht über eine Reise nach den westlichen Staaten Nordamerika's. Bonn, Elberfeld: Lucas.
Essex Pharmacological Atlas of Dermatology. 1978. USA: Shering Corporation.
Evangelische Kirche und Auswanderung. 1932. Berlin, Munich: Verband für Evang. Auswandererfürsorge.
Evang.-Lutherisches Gesangbuch für Kirche, Schule und Haus. No date [in use since 1908]. Milwaukee: Verlag der Evang.-Lutherischen Synode von Wisconsin u.a. Staaten. Northwestern Publishing House.
Evangeliums-Lieder. 1897. Ausgewählt und herausgegeben von Walter Rauschenbusch und Ira Sankey. Chicago: Biglow & Main.
Fasold, Ralph. 1984. The sociolinguistics of society. Oxford: Blackwell.
Faust, Albert B. 1909. The German element in the United States. Boston, New York: Houghton Mifflin.
Fiess, Dietrich. 1975. Siedlungsmundart-Heimatmundart: Studien zur Entwicklung der Mundart von Sarata in Bessarabien aus ihren verschiedenen Herkunftsmundarten. Idiomatica, Vol. 4. Tübingen: Niemeyer.
Flenley, Ralph. 1959. Modern German history. London: Dent & Sons.
Florinsky, Michael T. 1964. Russia: a short history. New York: Macmillan.

Forschungsbericht Südwestdeutscher Sprachatlas mit Beiträgen von Eugen Gabriel, et al. 1983. Studien zur Dialektologie in Südwestdeutschland, Vol. 1. Marburg: Elwert.
Friedenthal, Richard. 1963. Goethe, his life and times. Cleveland, New York: Macmillan.
Gesangbuch, für die evangelisch-lutherische Kirche in Bayern. 1855. Wer Gott vertraut hat wohlgebaut. Nürnberg: Verlag Sebald.
Gesangbuch, für die protestantische Gesamt-Gemeinde des Königreichs Bayern. 1823. Sulzbach: Im Verlag der allgemeinen Protestantischen Pfarr-Wittwen-Kasse. In Commission der Seidel'schen Buchhandlung.
Gesangbuch, vollständiges Gesang-Buch in einer Sammlung alter und neuer Geistreichen Lieder. 1753. Glückstadt: Königl. allergnädigsten Befehl zum allgemeinen Gebrauch in den Kirchen und Gemeinden des Herzogthums Schleswig und mit Königl. Allerhöchsten Privilegio herausgegeben.
Giesinger, Adam. 1974. From Catherine to Khrushchev: The story of Russia's Germans. Battleford, Saskatchewan, Canada: Marian Press.
Gilbert, Glenn G. Editor. 1971. The German language in America. A symposium. Austin, London: University of Texas Press.
Glinz, Hans. 1962. Sprache und Welt. Duden-Beiträge. Bibliographisches Institut. Mannheim: Dudenverlag. 8-29.
Grabert, Willy, Arno Mulot and Helmuth Nürnberger. 1983. Geschichte der deutschen Literatur. Munich: Bayerischer Schulbuch-Verlag.
Grimm, Jacob. 1835. Deutsche Mythologie. Göttingen: Dieterich.
Growth of timber on western prairies. US Statutes at Large: 17 Stat. 605.
Hachmann, Rolf. 1971. The ancient civilization of the Germanic peoples. London: Barrie & Jenkins.
Hartmann, J. 1900. Württemberg im Jahr 1800. Stuttgart.
Haugen, Einar. 1969. The Norwegian language in America. Bloomington: Indiana University Press.
Haugen, Einar. 1987. Blessings of Babel. Berlin: de Gruyter.
Heitman, Sidney. 1980. The Soviet Germans in the USSR today. A report prepared for the Office of External Research of the U.S. Department of State. Washington, D.C.
Henne, Pastor. 1932. Auswanderer und Seelsorge. In: Evangelische Kirche und Auswanderung. Berlin. Herausgegeben von dem Verband für Evangelische Auswandererfürsorge. Munich: Kaiser.
Hockett, Charles F. 1958. A course in modern linguistics. New York: Macmillan.
Hoffmann, P. 1905. Die deutschen Kolonien in Transkaukasien. Berlin.
Homestead Act. US Statutes at Large: 12 Stat. 392.
Hutterer, Claus Jürgen. 1982. Sprachinselforschung als Prüfstand für dialektologische Arbeitsprinzipien. Dialektologie. Werner Besch et al., editors. Berlin, New York: de Gruyter. 178-189.
Hymes, Dell. 1974. Foundations in sociolinguistics: An ethnographic

approach. Philadelphia: University of Pennsylvania Press.
Joachim, Rev. S. 1939. Toward an understanding of the Russia Germans. In: Concordia College Occasional Papers, No. 1. August 1939. Moorhead, Minn.: Concordia College Publications.
Kahane, Henry and Renée. 1984. The Krater and the Grail: Hermetic sources of the Parzival. In collaboration with Angelina Pietrangeli. Urbana, Chicago: University of Illinois Press.
Kallbrunner, Franz Wilhelm und Josef. 1932. Vergleichquellen zur deutschen Siedlungsgeschichte in Südosteuropa. Munich: Im Auftrage der Deutschen Akademie und des Gesamtvereins der deutschen Geschichts- und Altertumsvereine bearbeitet. 1. Lieferung Akten ab 1750.
Keller, Albert. 1979. Sprachphilosophie. Munich: Freiburg.
Keller, Konrad. 1905. Die deutschen Kolonien in Südrussland. Prischib, Odessa: von Stadelmeier.
Kern, Albert. 1976. Heimatbuch der Bessarabiendeutschen. Hilfskomitee der evangelisch-lutherischen Kirche aus Bessarabien e.V. Hannover und der Landsmannschaft der Bessarabiendeutschen e.V. Stuttgart. Hannover: Selbstverlag des Hilfskomitees der evangelischen-lutherischen Kirche aus Bessarabien.
Klaus, Alex. 1887. Unsere Kolonien. Studien und Materialien zur Geschichte und Statistik der ausländischen Kolonisation in Russland. Translated by J. Töws. Odessa: Verlag der Odesser Zeitung.
Kloss, Heinz. 1975. Atlas der im 19. und frühen 20. Jahrhundert entstandenen deutschen Siedlungen in USA. Marburg: Elwert.
Kluge Friedrich. 1960. Etymologisches Wörterbuch der deutschen Sprache. Bearbeitet von Walther Mitzka. Berlin: de Gruyter.
König, Werner. 1978. dtv-Atlas zur deutschen Sprache. Tafeln und Texte. Munich: Deutscher Taschenbuch Verlag.
Lamar, Howard Roberts. 1956. Dakota Territory 1861-1889. A study of frontier politics. New Haven: Yale University Press.
Leibbrandt, Georg. 1926. Die deutschen Kolonien in Cherson und Bessarabien. Berichte der Gemeindeämter über Entstehung und Entwicklung der lutherischen Kolonien in der ersten Hälfte des 19. Jahrhunderts. Stuttgart: Ausland und Heimat Verlag.
Leibbrandt, Georg. 1928. Die Auswanderung aus Schwaben nach Russland 1816-1823. Ein schwäbisches Zeit- und Charakterbild. Schriften des Deutschen Ausland-Institutes, Kulturhistorische Series A, Vol. 21. Stuttgart.
Lewin, Percy E. 1916. German road to the east. London: Heinemann.
Liederschatz. 1914. Eine Sammlung alter, kernhafter Lieder. Gesammelt und herausgegeben von Pastor M. Nuss. 2nd edition. Cassel: J. G. Oncken.
Life Magazine. August 2, 1937. Vol. 3, No. 5. 15-24.
Lipperheide, Franz Freiherr. 1935. Spruchwörterbuch. Third Edition. Leipzig: Dörner.

Löffler, Heinrich. 1980. Probleme der Dialektologie. Darmstadt: Wissenschaftliche Buchgesellschaft.
Luebke, Frederick C. 1969. Immigrants and politics, The Germans of Nebraska 1880-1900. Lincoln: University of Nebraska Press.
Malinowsky, Joseph. 1927. Die deutschen katholischen Kolonien am Schwarzen Meere. Berichte der Gemeindeämter über Entstehung und Entwicklung dieser Kolonien in der ersten Hälfte des 19. Jahrhunderts. Stuttgart: Ausland und Heimat Verlag.
Meidinger, John W. and Ed Rau. 1938. Ashley's Golden Jubilee. History of Ashley and McIntosh County. Winona, Minn.: Leicht Press.
Meyer-Lübke, Wilhelm. 1935. Romanisches etymologisches Wörterbuch. Heidelberg: Winters.
Miller, Max. 1936. Ursachen und Ziele der schwäbischen Auswanderung. Württemberg Vierteljahrshefte für Landesgeschichte. 1936, No. 42. Stuttgart. 184-218.
Miller, Michael M. 1987. Annotated bibliography of the Germans from Russia. Heritage Collection. Fargo: Institute for Regional Studies, North Dakota State University.
Milton, John R. 1977. South Dakota, a bicentennial history. New York: Norton.
Mitzka, Walther, and Ludwig Erich Schmitt, Editors. 1951-1972. Deutscher Wortatlas. 22 Volumes. Giessen: Schmitz.
Moltmann, Günter, Ed. 1982. Germans to America: 300 years of immigration 1683-1983. Stuttgart: Institute for Foreign Cultural Relations in cooperation with InterNationes, Bonn-Bad Godesberg.
Moulton, William G. 1962. The sounds of English and German. Chicago: University of Chicago Press.
Müllenhoff, Karl. 1900. Die Germania des Tacitus. Deutsche Altertumskunde. Volume Four. Berlin: Weidmann.
Murphy, G. Ronald, S.J. 1988. The Heliand. Address by the Andrew W. Mellon Distinguished Lecturer in Languages and Linguistics. Georgetown University, Washington, D.C.
Murphy, G. Ronald, S.J. 1989. The Saxon Savior. The Germanic transformation of the Gospel in the Ninth-Century Heliand. New York: Oxford Univeristy Press.
Mutschall, Wilhelm. 1934. Geschichte der Gemeinde Tarutino von 1814 bis 1934. Tarutino: Deutsche Zeitung Bessarabiens.
National Geographic Magazine. North Dakota. Tough times on the Prairie. March 1987. Vol. 171, No. 3. 320-347.
Neue Glaubensharfe. 1916. Gesangbuch der deutschen Baptisten-Gemeinden. Cleveland: Verlag des Publikations-Vereins der deutschen Baptisten.
Nichols, Patricia. 1987. Language policy and change. Gender and ethnic issues. In Georgetown University Roundtable on Languages and Linguistics. Washington, D.C.: Georgetown University Press. 175-186.

Nida, Eugene A. and Charles R. Taber. 1982. The theory and practice of translation. Leiden: Brill.
Nida, Eugene A. 1987. Intelligibility and acceptability in communication. In Georgetown University Roundtable on Languages and Linguistics. Washington, D.C.: Georgetown University Press. 242-249.
Obernberger, Alfred. 1964. Die Mundart der siebenbürgischen Landler. Deutsche Dialektgeographie 67. Marburg: Elwert.
Obernberger, Alfred. 1980. The dialect of the Hutterites in Canada. Occasional Papers of the Society for German-American Studies. No. 8. Morgantown: West Virginia University. 124-130.
Poplack, Shana. 1987. Language status and language accommodation along a linguistic border. In Georgetown University Roundtable on Languages and Linguistics. Washington, D.C.: Georgetown University Press. 90-118..
Ranke, Kurt. et al. 1977-1984. Enzyklopädie des Märchens. Handwörterbuch zur historschen und vergleichenden Erzählforschung. Four Volumes. Berlin: de Gruyter.
Ranke, Kurt. 1961-1962. Professor at University of Goettingen Germany, lectures on magische Heilkunde.
Reese, M. Lisle. 1952. South Dakota. The American Guide Series. Compiled by the Federal Wrtiers' Project of the Works Progress Administration. Second edition. New York: Hastings House.
Rein, Kurt. 1977. Religiöse Minderheiten als Sprachgemeinschaftsmodelle. Wiesbaden: Steiner.
Reinhardt, Kurt. 1961. Germany 2000 years. New York: Ungar.
Sallet, Richard. 1931. Russlanddeutsche Siedlungen in den Vereinigten Staaten von Amerika. German-American Historical Review. Jahrbuch der Deutsch-Amerikanischen Historischen Gesellschaft von Illinois. Chicago: University of Chicago Press. Vol XXXI. 5-126.
Samarin, William J. 1967. Field linguistics. New York: Holt, Reinhart, and Winston.
Sapir, Edward. 1956. The emergence of the concept of personality in a study of cultures. Culture, language, and personality. Selected essays edited by David G. Mandelbaum. Berkeley: University of California Press. 194-207.
Schach, Paul, Editor. 1980. Languages in conflict: Linguistic acculturation on the Great Plains. Lincoln: University of Nebraska.
Schach, Paul. 1983. Phonetic change in German dialects on the Great Plains. Yearbook of German-American Studies. Vol. 18. 157-171.
Schach, Paul. 1984. Observations on Palatine and Hessian dialects on the Great Plains. Dialectology, Linguistics, Literature. Festschrift for Carroll E. Reed.   Göppingen: Kümmerle. 232-248.
Schaeder, H. 1934. Die dritte Koalition und die Heilige Allianz. Königsberg-Berlin.

Schell, Herbert S. 1961. History of South Dakota. Lincoln: University of Nebraska Press.

Schiller, F. P. 1927. Literatur zur Geschichte und Volkskunde der deutschen Kolonien in der Sowietunion für die Jahre 1764-1926. Pokrowsk.

Schirmunski, Viktor. 1928. Die deutschen Kolonien in der Ukraine. Geschichte, Mundarten, Volkslied, Volkskunde. Moscow-Charkow: Zentral-Völker-Verlag.

Schirmunski, Viktor. 1962. Deutsche Mundartkunde. Berlin: Akademie Verlag.

Schrenk, M. Fr. 1869. Geschichte der deutschen Kolonien in Transkaukasien. Zum Gedächtnis des fünfzigjährigen Bestehens derselben. Tiflis.

Schwob, Anton. 1971. Wege und Forschungen des Sprachausgleichs in neuzeitlichen ost-und sudostdeutschen Sprachinseln. Buchreihe des Sudostdeutschen Historischen Kommission 25. Munich, Oldenbourg.

Sontag, Raymond James and James Stuart Beddie, eds. 1948. Nazi-Soviet Relations 1939-1941: Documents from the archives of the German Foreign Office. Washington, D.C.: Department of State.

South Dakota. 1938. A South Dakota guide compiled by The Federal Writers' Project of the Works Progress Administration. American Guide Series. State of South Dakota.

Stach, Jakob. 1904. Die deutschen Kolonien in Südrussland. Prischib: Schaad.

Staczek, John J. 1988a. Crossgenerational case studies in linguistic heritage, language contact, and linguistic choices. In: John Baugh, et al, eds. NWAV-XVI. Austin, Texas: University of Texas. Manuscript in press.

Staczek, John J. 1988b. Particular treasures: On being and becoming a speaker of English. In: Georgetown University Round Table on Languages and Linguistics 1987. Washington, D.C.: Georgetown University Press. 283-299.

Stallybrass, James Steven. 1883. Teutonic mythology by Jacob Grimm. Translated from the fourth edition with notes and appendix. Four Volumes. London: Bell & Sons.

Stapel, Wilhelm. 1984. Parzival. Translation of Wolfram von Eschenbach's Parzival into Standard High German prose. Munich, Vienna: Langen Müller.

Stumpp, Karl. 1922. Die deutschen Kolonien im Schwarzmeergebiet. Schriften des Deutschen Ausland-Instituts. Series A. Vol. 7. Stuttgart: Ausland und Heimat Verlags-Aktiengesellschaft.

Stumpp, Karl. 1954. Heimatbuch der Deutschen aus Russland Kalender. Heimatbuch der Ostumsiedler. Stuttgart: Herausgegeben von der Landsmannschaft der Deutschen aus Russland.

Stumpp, Karl. 1956. Odessa und die deutschen Kolonisten. Heimatbuch der Deutschen aus Russland. Stuttgart: Herausgegeben von der

Landsmannschaft der Deutschen aus Russland.
Stumpp, Karl. 1958. Das Schrifttum über das Deutschtum in Russland, Eine Bibliographie. Stuttgart: Herausgegeben von der Landsmannschaft der Deutschen aus Russland.
Stumpp, Karl. 1966. Die Russlanddeutschen. Freilassing: Pannonia Verlag.
The New Oxford Annotated Bible with the Apochrypha (Revised Standard Version). 1977. London: Oxford University Press.
Tacitus. See Muellenhoff, Karl. 1900.
Trübners deutsches Wörterbuch. 1939-1957. Im Auftrag der Artbeitsgemeinschaft für deutsche Wortforschung herausgegeben von Alfred Götze und Walther Mitzka. Berlin: de Gruyter.
Verdoodt, A. 1973. Les Problèmes des Groupes Linguistiques en Belgique. Centre de Recherches Sociologiques. Université Catholique de Louvain. Personal Interview, Louvain, 1984.
Walsh, Warren B. 1958. Russia and the Soviet Union. Ann Arbor, Michigan: The University of Michigan Press.
Warren, Lieut. G. K. 1856. Explorations in the Dacota Country in the year 1855. Washington, D. C.: Senate Printer, 34th Congress.
Wartburg, Walther von. 1928-. Französisches etymologisches Wörterbuch. Bonn: Klopp. (Schroeder. 1922 first 5 Volumes.)
Weinberg, Gerhard L. 1954. Germany and the Soviet Union: 1939-1941. London: E.J. Brill.
Wenker, Georg. See Wrede.
Wiesinger, Peter. 1983. Deutsche Dialektgebiete ausserhalb des deutschen Sprachgebiets: Mittel-, Südost- und Osteuropa. Dialektologie. Werner Besch, et al. editors. Berlin, New York: de Gruyter. 900-927.
White, Randall. 1986. Dark caves, bright visions: Life in ice age Europe. New York, London: The American Museum of Natural History in Association with W. W. Norton & Co.
Wilkins, Robert P. and Wyonona Huchette Wilkins. 1977. North Dakota. American Association for State and Local History Nashville. New York: Norton.
Wishek, Nina Farley. Reissued 1978. Along the trails of yesterday: A story of McIntosh County. Ashley: The Ashley Tribune.
Wohlwill, A. 1875. Weltbürgertum und Vaterlandsliebe der Schwaben 1789-1815. Hamburg.
WPA Records at the State Capitol in Bismarck, North Dakota. [There are approximately 16,000 interviews taken during the 1930s.]
WPA Federal Writers Project. 1950. North Dakota. Oxford: Oxford University Press.
Wrede, Ferdinand. 1926-1956. Deutscher Sprachatlas auf Grund des von Georg Wenker begründeten Sprachatlas des Deutschen Reichs herausgegeben von Ferdinand Wrede, Bernhard Martin und Walther Mitzka. Marburg: Elwert.

Württembergisches Landesmuseum. 1987. Baden und Württemberg im Zeitalter Napoleons. Three volumes. Stuttgart-Bad Cannstatt: Cantz'sche Druckerei.

About the Author

Shirley Fischer Arends Ph.D. is a North Dakota girl who grew up in a German speaking home and did not learn English until she went to school. The home was an active center as her grandmother could not walk or leave the house. As a child she listened to all the older pioneers visiting and talking, and heard the stories they told about life in Russia and on the western prairies as homesteaders.

In the fall of 1983, she received a full Fellowship for her Graduate School studies at Georgetown University. It was the last step in her goal of research and writing about the Dakota Germans, her original thesis for her Master of Arts degree (1966). Arends graduated with a Ph.D. in German Studies and Linguistics from Georgetown University in 1988. Her Ph.D. Dissertation was awarded a unanimous "With Distinction" honor by the Doctoral Panel. Arends' book, based on her Dissertation, was published by Georgetown University Press in 1989.

Dr. Arends gave the Central Dakota German Dialect its first written form. She then transcribed the dialect phonemically to show how it is spoken. She compared the dialect to Standard High German, and translated all German into English. Arends worked to present a picture of the dialect and the culture it supported.

Dr. Arends studied at the University of Goettingen, Germany. Following this, she lived and worked in Bonn, Frankfurt, Vienna, Geneva, Copenhagen, Munich, and Berlin over a twenty year period.

www.ingramcontent.com/pod-product-compliance
Lightning Source LLC
Chambersburg PA
CBHW022102150426
43195CB00008B/235